The Ultimate PHRASAL VERB Book

Carl W. Hart

All inquiries should be addressed to:
Barron's Educational Series, Inc.
250 Wireless Boulevard
Hauppauge, New York 11788
http://www.barronseduc.com

Library of Congress Catalog Card No.: 99-37007

International Standard Book No.: 0-7641-1028-4

Library of Congress Cataloging-in-Publication Data

Hart, Carl W.
    The ultimate phrasal verb book / Carl W. Hart.
             p.   cm.
       ISBN 0-7641-1028-4
       1. English language — Verb phrase Problems, exercises, etc.
2. English language Textbooks for foreign speakers. I. Title.
PE1319.H35   1999
428.2'4 — dc21   99-37007
                                                                      CIP

PRINTED IN UNITED STATES OF AMERICA
9 8 7 6 5 4 3 2 1

Contents

TABLE OF CONTENTS

TO THE TEACHER

The inspiration for *The Ultimate Phrasal Verb Book* came about when a student asked me for a textbook to help her learn the meanings of common phrasal verbs. I had nothing to offer. The only textbook focusing on common verbs that I could give her contains not one phrasal verb — it teaches *arise* but not *get up*, *awake* but not *wake up*, *seek* but not *look for*.

Phrasal verbs are verbs, not idiomatic curiosities. There is no logic to classifying *take over* with *take the bull by the horns*. Phrasal verbs are an essential part of spoken and written English at all levels, and no student who hopes to master the language can afford to overlook them.

Although this textbook is intended primarily for high-intermediate to advanced students, ambitious students at lower levels will benefit from it as well. Only some *FOCUS* sections may prove to be a little beyond them; otherwise, there is nothing to prevent any student from studying the definitions and examples and attempting the exercises.

A vocabulary textbook should provide mechanics as well as meaning. Students want to know more than what a word means — they want to know how to use it correctly.

The importance of mechanics is the reason for the emphasis on the prepositions required when some phrasal verbs are used transitively and for the inclusion of reviews of points of grammar not specific to phrasal verbs. Prepositions are the glue that holds English together, but many students falter when using newly learned verbs because they do not know that a preposition is also required, or if they do, which one. This aspect of English is not given the attention it deserves because it is difficult to teach — there are no rules that govern when a preposition, or which preposition, is required, and no teacher likes to say "You just have to remember."

The hope of the latter feature, the discussion of points of grammar not specific to phrasal verbs, is that combining practice with phrasal verbs and practice with a variety of grammatical structures will increase not only the student's confidence in the knowledge of phrasal verbs but also his or her willingness and ability to use them in a wider range of situations.

There is inevitably a degree of oversimplification. That phrasal verb particles are sometimes prepositions and sometimes adverbs is mentioned only once. No purpose is served by differentiating between them, and the overlap between the two is confusing to the student. Phrasal verbs are not identified as transitive or intransitive because this is dictated by logic. Less common meanings of some phrasal verbs have not been included. Adverb placement is presented and illustrated in simplified form without discussion of the different types of adverbs — doing so would have gone beyond the scope of this textbook.

And no differentiation is made between recognized adjectives derived from past participles and past participles with adjectival meaning. The adjectival use of past participles (both phrasal and nonphrasal) is an extremely important aspect of spoken English — something every student of English should be familiar with — yet the dividing line between true adjectives derived from past participles and passive sentences employing past participles with adjectival meanings is ill-defined and problematic. Native speakers of English regularly use past participles in superficially passive sentences with purely adjectival meaning. Whether the past participles are verbs or actually adjectives is of no concern to the native speaker and is entirely irrelevant to the student of English. Rather than distract the student with an unnecessary element of confusion, both are referred to as participle adjectives throughout this textbook.

The exercises in this textbook are intended to reinforce meaning and mechanics. A cloze exercise always comes first, followed by exercises focusing on sentence structure and the *FOCUS* discussion. Last are exercises that ask the student to answer questions or write original sentences.

There is a good deal of review built into this textbook. Every section contains two or more exercises requiring the student to refer back to a previous section in order to review a phrasal verb, participle adjective, or noun. When a phrasal verb has two or more meanings, it is intentional that no help is provided to the student in determining which meaning applies; students have to review them all and figure it out for themselves.

I have tried in this textbook to imitate the form and content of everyday English. If occasionally the register and subject matter of some examples and exercises seem not quite right for formal discourse, that is deliberate. Students need to learn formal English, of course, but since most people speak informally most of the time, students need to gain familiarity with the syntax, usage, and content of the informal English they read and hear every day at work, at school, at home, and on television.

TO THE STUDENT

Phrasal verbs are combinations of ordinary verbs like *put, take, come,* and *go* and particles like *in, out, on,* and *off.* They are a very important part of everyday English. Every student of English needs a basic understanding of the most common phrasal verbs and also of common nouns and adjectives made from phrasal verbs.

Most phrasal verbs are *not* informal, slang, or improper for educated speech or formal writing. Exactly the opposite is true — most phrasal verbs are acceptable at all levels of spoken or written English. In fact, for many of the phrasal verbs in this textbook, there is no alternative to the phrasal verb — there is no other way to say it.

However, a few phrasal verbs in this textbook are identified as informal, and it is better not to use them in serious, formal speech or writing. But these informal phrasal verbs are important because they are very common in everyday informal speech and writing.

Some phrasal verbs are very easy to understand. For example, it is not difficult to understand *sit down* or *come in* because their meanings are obvious. But many phrasal verbs are very *idiomatic*. Idiomatic means that there is no way to know what the verb and particle mean together by knowing what the verb and particle mean separately. For example, every beginning-level student learns what the words *call*, *run*, *off*, and *out* mean, but that does not help the student to know that *call off* means *cancel* or that *run out* means *use all of something*.

Each section of this textbook starts with a *FOCUS*, an explanation of something important about phrasal verbs. Then eight phrasal verbs and an explanation of each important meaning of each one are presented along with one or more example sentences for each meaning. Following that are several exercises to help you understand and remember what the phrasal verbs mean and how to use them in a sentence. And like real conversation, questions asked with I or we are answered with *you*, and questions asked with *you* are answered with *I* or *we*.

And because there is a lot to learn in this textbook, there is a lot of review to help you learn it. Every phrasal verb is reviewed at least twice later in the book. The more idiomatic phrasal verbs are reviewed more often, and the more important meanings of phrasal verbs with several meanings are reviewed more often.

Terms, Abbreviations, and Symbols Used in this Textbook

verb	*Verb* refers to the verb part of a phrasal verb. In other words, the phrasal verb minus the particle. In the phrasal verb *pull over*, *pull* is the verb and *over* is the particle.
particle	The adverbs and prepositions in phrasal verbs are both called *particles* in this book. Many particles are adverbs <u>and</u> prepositions, and it can be very difficult and confusing to figure out if a particle in a particular phrasal verb is one or the other. Fortunately, this is almost never important to the student, so it is a lot easier to simply call them both particles.
p.v.	phrasal verb
n.	a noun made from a phrasal verb
part.adj.	participle adjective — a past participle of a phrasal verb used as an adjective
put on it	When words or sentences have a line through them, it means that they are incorrect.
...	Three dots between the verb and the particle mean that the object of the phrasal verb can be placed between the verb and the particle.

1. FOCUS ON: separable and nonseparable phrasal verbs

Phrasal verbs are either *separable* or *nonseparable*. Unfortunately, there is no rule that will help you to look at a phrasal verb and always know whether it is separable or nonseparable.

Separable phrasal verbs

Separable phrasal verbs can be separated by their object. When the object is a noun, it is usually entirely optional whether the object is placed between the verb and the particle or placed after the particle. Both sentences below are correct:

> I ***took*** <u>my shoes</u> **off**.
> I ***took off*** <u>my shoes</u>.

However, when a pronoun is used instead of a noun, the pronoun <u>must</u> be placed between the verb and the particle:

> I ***took*** <u>them</u> **off**.
> ~~I **took off** <u>them</u>.~~

But in one type of sentence, separable phrasal verbs must be separated — when the phrasal verb has two objects:

> She ***put*** <u>a blanket</u> **on**.
> She ***put on*** <u>a blanket</u>.

> She ***put*** <u>a blanket</u> **on** <u>the bed</u>.
> ~~She **put on** a blanket the bed.~~

Nonseparable phrasal verbs

Nonseparable phrasal verbs cannot be separated by their object:

> He ***ran into*** a tree.
> ~~He **ran** a tree **into**.~~

Throughout this book, phrasal verbs that can be separated have three dots (...) between the verb and the particle.

Infinitive

	present tense	-ing form	past tense	past participle
come from				
	come from & comes from	coming from	came from	come from

1. come from *p.v.* When you **come from** a place, you were born there or lived there previously. When you **come from** a family or a social situation, your past experience helps to explain your present attitudes and behavior.

> *Mike **comes from** Alaska, so he's used to cold weather.*
> *Jane had a difficult childhood. She **came from** a broken home.*

1

2. come from *p.v.* When something **comes from** a source, that is where it originated.

> The word "admiral" **comes from** an Arabic word.
> The mechanic heard a strange sound **coming from** the engine.

Infinitive

	present tense	-ing form	past tense	past participle
figure out				
	figure out & figures out	figuring out	figured out	figured out

1. figure ... out *p.v.* *[the object can be a noun or a noun clause]* When you **figure out** something, such as the answer to a question, the solution to a problem, or why a person is a certain way or acts a certain way, you think about and succeed in understanding it.

> Joe's so hostile all the time. I can't **figure** him **out**.
> I looked everywhere for my keys, but I couldn't **figure out** where I put them.

give back				
	give back & gives back	giving back	gave back	given back

1. give ... back (to) *p.v.* When you return something to someone, you **give** it **back**.

> Can I use your pen? I'll **give** it **back** after the test.
> Timmy, **give** that toy **back** to your sister right now!

look for				
	look for & looks for	looking for	looked for	looked for

1. look for *p.v.* When you **look for** things or people, you try to find them.

> I **looked for** you at the party, but I didn't see you.
> Excuse me, can you help me? I'm **looking for** 303 Main St.

put on				
	put on & puts on	putting on	put on	put on

1. put ... on *p.v.* When you place something on or apply something to your body, you **put** it **on**.

> I **put on** my new dress before going to the party.
> Erik forgot to **put** suntan lotion **on**, and now he's as red as a lobster.

2. put ... on *p.v.* When you place something on or apply something to another surface, you **put** it **on**.

> I **put** the book **on** the table.
> Jerry **put** too much fertilizer **on** his lawn, and now he has to cut it twice a week.

3. put ... on *p.v.* When you attach or affix something to another thing, you **put** it **on**.

> The Wilsons **put** a new roof **on** their house last year.
> I told the tailor to **put** red buttons **on** the dress he's making for me.

4. put ... on *p.v.* When you **put on** weight, you gain weight.

*Did you see Mike? He's **put on** so much weight that I didn't recognize him.*
*I need to go on a diet. I've been **putting on** a lot of weight lately.*

5. put . . . on *p.v.* When you organize or perform something for other people's entertainment, such as a play or a concert, you **put it on.**

*The club **put on** a show to raise money for the party.*
*That opera hasn't been **put on** in more than 200 years.*

6. put . . . on *p.v. [informal]* When you **put** people **on,** you kid or tease them.

*You won the lottery? You're **putting** me **on**!*
*Don't **put** me **on** — tell me the truth.*

put-on *n.* Something done with the intention of fooling or deceiving people is a **put-on.**

*He didn't really win the lottery. It was all a big **put-on** to impress his girlfriend.*

Infinitive

	present tense	-ing form	past tense	past participle
run into	run into & runs into	running into	ran into	run into

1. run into *p.v.* When you are driving and hit another vehicle or something near the road, such as a tree or a telephone pole, you **run into** it.

*Ali was driving too fast, and he **ran into** a telephone pole.*
*I was **run into** by a drunk driver.*

2. run into *p.v.* When you meet people unexpectedly or unintentionally, you **run into** them. **Bump into** is the same as **run into.**

*We **ran into** Karen and her new boyfriend at the supermarket yesterday.*
*I owe Frank $300, so I hope I don't **run into** him.*

3. run into *p.v.* When you unexpectedly encounter difficulties or problems, you **run into** them.

*I thought it would be easy to fix my car, but I've been **running into** problems.*
*Janice **ran into** one problem after another at work today.*

4. run into *p.v.* When the total of something grows to a large amount or number, it **runs into** that amount or number.

*If you fixed everything on that old car that needs fixing, it would **run into** thousands of dollars.*
*The number of starving people in the country **ran into** millions.*

show up	show up & shows up	showing up	showed up	shown up

1. show up *p.v.* When you appear somewhere, you **show up. Turn up** is similar to show up.

*I was supposed to meet my sister for lunch, but she hasn't **shown up** yet.*
*Over a hundred people **showed up** for the news conference.*

2. show up *p.v.* When something appears or becomes visible, it **shows up**.

*It's hard to photograph polar bears because they don't **show up** well against the snow.*
*The spots won't **show up** until the last stages of the disease.*

Infinitive			
present tense	-ing form	past tense	past participle
take off			
take off & takes off	taking off	took off	taken off

1. take ... off *p.v.* When you remove something from your body, you **take** it **off.**

*I was so tired when I got home that I **took** my clothes **off** and went straight to bed.*
***Take off** your shoes. You're getting mud on the carpet.*

2. take ... off *p.v.* When you remove something from a surface, you **take** it **off.**

*I **took** the book **off** the table.*
*You need to **take** the old wax **off** the floor before you wax it again.*

3. take ... off *p.v.* When you remove something from something it is attached or affixed to, you **take** it **off.**

*Alfonso always **takes** the skin **off** chicken before he cooks it.*
*After Jane **took** the flat tire **off** her bicycle, she put on the new one.*

4. take ... off *p.v.* When you **take** time **off** from work or study, you do something different, instead of working or studying.

*I can't work tomorrow. I have to **take** the day **off** for some tests at the hospital.*
*Our company always lets us **take** the week between Christmas and New Year's Day **off**.*

5. take off *p.v.* When an airplane leaves the ground and flies up into the air, it **takes off**.

*Our plane **took off** an hour late because of the snow.*
*Put on your seat belt; we're **taking off** now.*

takeoff *n.* **Takeoff** is when an airplane leaves the ground and flies up into the air.

*The **takeoff** was delayed because of the snow.*

6. take off *p.v.* When a business or other organized activity becomes very successful, it **takes off**.

*The new restaurant's business is **taking off** because it got a good review in the news-paper.*
*If this business **takes off**, we could make a lot of money.*

7. take off *p.v.* [informal] When you leave suddenly or quickly, you **take off**.

*After he found out the FBI was looking for him, he **took off** in a hurry.*
*This party's boring — let's **take off**.*

8. take . . . off *p.v.* When you reduce the price of something that is for sale by a certain amount, you **take** that amount **off** the price.

*The sign in the store window said, "Every Monday **take** 10 percent **off** all marked prices."*
*The car dealer **took** $2,000 **off** the list price.*

EXERCISE 1a — **Complete the sentences with phrasal verbs from this section. Be sure the phrasal verbs are in the correct tense.**

Example: Sergeant Jones is very strict with his children. He_____comes_____ _____from_____ a military family.

1. After the police arrived, we _____ _____ quickly.

2. Sales of air conditioners really _____ _____ when the temperature got over 100 degrees last summer.

3. Megan _____ a lot of weight _____ when she was pregnant.

4. I'm going to install a new program tonight, and I hope I don't _____ _____ any problems.

5. The invisible ink _____ _____ only under ultraviolet light.

6. I was expecting 100 people at the party, but only around 50 _____ _____.

7. Jane was lucky; she _____ _____ a good family.

8. Be sure you _____ a coat of primer _____ before you paint the fender.

9. My cousin is so weird that even his mother can't _____ him _____.

10. I don't feel well; I think I'll _____ tomorrow _____ and stay home.

11. We were scared to death when we heard voices _____ _____ the attic.

12. My son always forgets to _____ _____ his coat before he goes outside.

13. I was surprised when our plane _____ _____ on time.

14. We _____ _____ our dog all night, but we couldn't find him.

15. Paul finally _____ _____ my CDs after I asked him for them about a million times.

16. I'm not going to the party because I don't want to _____ _____ Janice.

1

17. The real estate agent said that our asking price was too high and that we should

_____ at least $10,000 _____ it if we want to sell our house.

18. _____ _____ those muddy shoes before you come inside.

19. Sending my son to Stanford and my daughter to Yale is going to _____

_____ some serious money.

20. _____ the ornaments _____ the Christmas tree isn't as much fun as putting

them on.

21. You can't be serious — you're _____ me _____!

22. Don't forget to _____ a stamp _____ that letter before you mail it.

23. A special performance of *The Nutcracker* was _____ _____ at the

children's hospital.

24. The maid _____ the dirty sheets _____ the bed.

25. Be careful! You almost _____ _____ that truck back there.

EXERCISE 1b — **Write three sentences using the objects in parentheses.
Be sure to put the objects in the right place.**

Example: I can't *figure out*. (the answer, it)

I can't figure out the answer.

I can't figure the answer out.

I can't figure it out.

1. I finally *figured out*. (the instructions, them)

_____

_____

_____

2. *Give back* when you are finished. (my tools, them)

_____

_____

_____

3. She *put on*. (her slippers, them)

_____

_____

_____

4. I *took off*. (my shoes, them)

_____

_____

_____

5. The hurricane *took off*. (the roof, it)

_____

_____

_____

EXERCISE 1c — **Write answers to the questions using phrasal verbs and nouns from this section. Be sure the phrasal verbs are in the correct tense.**

Example: I can't understand where my wallet is. What can't I do?

You can't figure out where your wallet is.

1. A lot of guests didn't come to the wedding. What didn't a lot of guests do?

2. Raul thought about the math problem, and he knows the answer now. What did Raul do?

3. The jet is leaving the ground and flying into the air. What is the jet doing?

4. In Question 3, what would you call what the airplane did?

5. Omar speaks Arabic because he was born in Egypt. Why does Omar speak Arabic?

6. We left Bob's house quickly. What did we do?

7. I met Uncle John at the baseball game today. What did I do today?

8. The source of the smoke was a window on the tenth floor. What did the smoke do?

9. You almost hit a tree while you were driving your car. What did you almost do?

10. Mr. Taylor attached his name to his mailbox. What did Mr. Taylor do?

11. I have to remove the flat tire from my car. What do I have to do?

12. We didn't have any problems cooking the turkey. What did we do?

13. I'm removing the dirty dishes from the table. What am I doing?

14. Sales of the company's new product were very successful. What did sales of the company's new product do?

15. Linda is trying to find her golf ball. What is Linda doing?

16. Susie's blue eyes aren't visible in this photo. What don't Susie's eyes do in this photo?

17. Jim always forgets to place salt and pepper on the table. What does Jim always do?

18. Bill didn't go to work last Friday. What didn't Bill do?

19. Sally returned Frank's camera. What did Sally do?

---

2. FOCUS ON: **phrasal verbs and *do*, *does*, and *did***

Like ordinary verbs, phrasal verbs form negatives and questions with *do*, *does*, and *did*.

Present tense questions

In the present tense, questions are formed with *do* (except when the subject is *he*, *she*, *it*, or the name of one person or thing):

> Why <u>do</u> I always **fall for** losers?
> <u>Do</u> you sometimes **doze off** in class?
> <u>Do</u> we ever **give in** to pressure?
> How <u>do</u> these bottle tops **come off**?

When the subject is *he*, *she*, *it*, or the name of one person or thing, *does* is used. Remember that the *-s* form of the verb is not used in questions:

> <u>Does</u> this welding torch **throw** sparks **up** into the air?

Present tense negatives

In the present tense, negatives are formed with *do not* or *don't* (except when the subject is *he*, *she*, *it*, or the name of one person or thing):

*I used to **doze off** while driving, but I <u>don't</u> anymore.*

*I think he has the flu because you <u>don't</u> usually **throw up** when you
    have a cold.*

*We <u>don't</u> usually **fall for** crazy stories like that.*

*If his dogs <u>do</u> <u>not</u> **stay off** our lawn, I'm going to call the dogcatcher.*

When the subject is *he, she, it*, or the name of one person or thing, *does not* or
doesn't is used. Remember that the *-s* form of the verb is not used in negatives:

*If Mark <u>doesn't</u> **pull through**, five children will be without a father.*

Past tense questions

In the past tense, questions are formed with *did*. Remember to use the
infinitive form of the verb:

*I'm so embarrassed. Why <u>did</u> I **fall for** his lies?*

*<u>Did</u> the patient **pull through**?*

*How many times <u>did</u> he **throw up**?*

*<u>Did</u> we **give in** to their demands?*

*<u>Did</u> they **hear about** the explorer who was eaten by piranhas?*

Past tense negatives

In the past tense, negatives are formed with *did not* or *didn't*. Remember to use
the infinitive form of the verb:

*I was really sick, but I <u>didn't</u> **throw up**.*

*You <u>didn't</u> **fall for** that nonsense, I hope.*

*He pulled and pulled, but the bowling ball <u>did</u> <u>not</u> **come off**.*

*We <u>didn't</u> **hear about** the half-price sale until it was too late.*

*I'm sorry. We tried everything, but she <u>didn't</u> **pull through**.*

Infinitive

	present tense	-ing form	past tense	past participle
come off				
	come off & comes off	coming off	came off	come off

1. come off *p.v.* When something **comes off**, it becomes detached from what it was
attached or fastened to.

*Be careful with this old book. The cover's **coming off**.*

*That paint won't **come off** your hands unless you use turpentine.*

2. come off *p.v.* When an event **comes off**, it is successful.

*The party **came off** well. Everyone had a lot of fun.*

*The attack didn't **come off** the way the general planned it.*

3. come off *p.v.* When you say "**Come off** it" to people, you are saying that you think
something they have said is untrue or foolish.

*It's 2:00 A.M., you come home smelling like beer, and you say you were working late
    at the office? Oh, **come off it**!*

Infinitive

	present tense	-ing form	past tense	past participle
doze off				
	doze off & dozes off	dozing off	dozed off	dozed off

1. doze off *p.v.* When you fall into a light sleep, you **doze off**.

> I went to a movie last night, but it was so boring I **dozed off**.
> If I have a drink at lunch, I'm sure to **doze off** at my desk.

fall for				
	fall for & falls for	falling for	fell for	fallen for

1. fall for *p.v.* When someone successfully tricks or deceives you, you **fall for** the trick or deception or you **fall for** it.

> I feel like an idiot. The salesman promised me it was a real diamond, not glass, and I **fell for** it.
> Your girlfriend told you that guy she was dancing with at the party was her brother? How could you **fall for** a story like that?

2. fall for *p.v.* When you suddenly feel a strong attraction to someone or something, you **fall for** that person or thing.

> Jim met Sam's sister last week, and now he calls her every day. I guess he really **fell for** her in a big way.
> When I saw this house, **I fell** for it immediately, and I made an offer the same day.

give in				
	give in & gives in	giving in	gave in	given in

1. give in (to) *p.v.* When someone pressures or forces you to do something or allow something even though you do not want to, you **give in**.

> My son drove me crazy asking me to buy him a new bicycle, and I finally **gave in**.
> The strike lasted for eight months, but the company never **gave in** to the workers' demands.

hear about				
	hear about & hears about	hearing about	heard about	heard about

1. hear about *p.v.* When you hear and learn information about someone or something, you **hear about** it.

> Have you **heard about** the new Thai restaurant downtown?
> I **heard about** the earthquake on CNN.

pull through				
	pull through & pulls through	pulling through	pulled through	pulled through

1. pull through *p.v.* When you recover from a serious illness or injury, you **pull through**.

> The doctor didn't think his chances were very good, but he **pulled through**.
> Erik is very sick, but he's young and strong, so I'm sure he'll **pull through**.

Infinitive

	present tense	-ing form	past tense	past participle
stay off	stay off & stays off	staying off	stayed off	stayed off

1. stay off *p.v.* When you **stay off** something, you don't walk or sit on it.

> You kids can play in the living room, but **stay off** the Persian rug.
> What can I do to get my cat to **stay off** the kitchen counter?

throw up	throw up & throws up	throwing up	threw up	thrown up

1. throw up *p.v.* When people **throw up**, they vomit.

> Alex was so sick that he **threw up** all over my shoes.
> I feel like I'm going to **throw up**.

2. throw . . . up *p.v.* When something causes small particles of dirt, dust, or a liquid to rise into the air, it **throws** them **up**.

> Be careful with that chain saw — it'll **throw** sawdust **up** in your eyes.
> Don't stand too close to the fire; it's **throwing up** sparks.

EXERCISE 2a — **Complete the sentences with phrasal verbs from this section. Be sure the phrasal verbs are in the correct tense.**

1. Heather calls Tom every day. I have a feeling she's _____ _____ him.

2. I went to the shoe repair guy because the heel _____ _____ my shoe.

3. I _____ _____ ten minutes after the movie started, and I missed the whole thing.

4. The bride drank too much champagne, and she _____ _____ all over the best man.

5. I needed a car to go to the party, so I told my father I needed his car to go to the library to study, and he _____ _____ it.

6. Uncle Fred's really sick. If he _____ _____, it'll be a miracle.

7. I just shampooed the carpet in the living room, so _____ _____ it.

8. The coup _____ _____ without any bloodshed.

9. I don't care if you beg me all night — I'm not _____ _____!

10. I _____ _____ your brother's accident last night. Is he all right?

11. Don't get close to the fire. It's _____ _____ ashes and sparks.

12. Do you really expect me to believe a crazy story like that? _____ _____ it!

EXERCISE 2b — **Change the sentences to questions using *do*, *does*, or *did*.**

Example: Francisco usually *dozes off* after dinner.

Does Francisco usually doze off after dinner?

1. The sick boy *threw up*.

2. Rosa *falls for* every boy she meets.

3. The tops *come off* easily.

4. The dog *stays off* the bed.

5. Erik *heard about* the new job.

EXERCISE 2c — **Change the sentences to negatives using *do not* or *don't*, *does not* or *doesn't*, or *did not* or *didn't*.**

Example: Francisco *dozes off* after dinner.

Francisco doesn't doze off after dinner.

1. I always *give in* to her demands.

2. Mr. and Mrs. Taylor *fell for* the salesman's promises.

3. These machines *throw up* sparks.

4. The patient *pulled through*.

5. The plot *came off* as planned.

EXERCISE 2d — **Write answers to the questions using phrasal verbs from this section. Be sure the phrasal verbs are in the correct tense.**

1. My mother told me not to walk on the kitchen floor. What did my mother tell me?

2. When Dan saw that new motorcycle, he decided he had to buy it no matter how much it cost. How did Dan feel about the motorcycle?

3. The students are so tired that they are starting to sleep in class. What are the students doing?

4. Nicole learns about everything that happens in town. What does Nicole do?

5. The meeting didn't happen the way I planned it. What didn't the meeting do?

6. You had an accident after one of the wheels separated from your car. Why did you have an accident?

7. You can ask a thousand times if you want to, but I'm not agreeing to your demands. What am I not doing to your demands?

8. My cousin made a lot of promises to me, and I believed them. How did I react to her promises?

9. Dr. Wood said Ted's disease is very serious, and she doesn't think there's much hope that he'll recover. What doesn't Dr. Wood think?

10. Timmy is very sick, and he was vomiting all night. What was Timmy doing all night?

EXERCISE 2e, Review — **Complete the sentences with these phrasal verbs from Section 1. Be sure the phrasal verbs are in the correct tense. To check their meanings, review Section 1.**

come from	give back	put on	show up
figure out	look for	run into	take off

1. Look what time it is! We have to be at work in fifteen minutes. We'd better _____ _____ right now.

2. I waited for Joe for three hours, but he never _____ _____.

3. The maid _____ _____ the dirty sheets and washed them.

4. I'm _____ _____ a job closer to home.

5. Potatoes originally _____ _____ South America.

6. That's mine! _____ it _____ right now or I'm telling Mom!

7. They were killed when they _____ _____ a truck.

8. The mechanic can't _____ _____ what the problem is with my car.

3. FOCUS ON: three-word phrasal verbs

Phrasal verbs are not always composed of two words. Three-word phrasal verbs are composed of a verb and two particles: the first particle is normally an adverb, and the second a preposition. Like two-word phrasal verbs, three-word phrasal verbs are either separable or nonseparable:

> I know it's been a long day, but do you **feel up to** playing tennis after dinner?
>
> Jake always **went in for** fishing when he was a kid.
>
> It was nice to meet you, and I **look forward to** seeing you again.
>
> I'm sorry I can't say yes about the motorcycle, but I have to **go along with** your mother's decision.
>
> I've **put up with** these love handles long enough — next week I'm getting liposuction.
>
> Mr. Baker tried to **screw** his ex-wife **out of** her share of the lottery prize.
>
> You **talk down to** me like I'm some kind of idiot.
>
> Karen's nervous about the job interview. She just wants to **get** it **over with** so she can stop worrying about it.

Infinitive

	present tense	-ing form	past tense	past participle
feel up to	feel up to & feels up to	feeling up to	felt up to	feel up to

1. feel up to *p.v.* When you **feel up to** doing something, you have the confidence or energy to do it.

> I'm sorry to cancel, but I just don't **feel up to** going dancing tonight.
>
> The top of the mountain is only 1,000 feet away — do you **feel up to** it?

get over with	get over with & gets over with	getting over with	got over with	gotten over with

1. get ... over with *p.v.* [always separated] When you want to **get** something **over with**, it is because it is something unpleasant that you want to finish so that you can stop worrying about it or dreading it.

> Let's fix both cavities today, doctor; I just want to **get** it **over with**.
>
> I think it's better to **get** the exam **over with** first period than to be nervous about it all day long.

go along with	go along with & goes along with	going along with	went along with	gone along with

1. go along with *p.v.* When you agree with people or agree with what they are saying, you **go along with** them.

> I understand your concern, Linda, but I have to **go along with** Maria on this matter.
>
> What's my opinion? I **go along with** Omar.

2. go along with *p.v.* When you obey a rule or follow a decision, you **go along with** it.

Mrs. Taylor wasn't happy about the committee's decision, but she **went along with** it anyway.

I don't care what the boss says — I'm not **going along with** any changes that will mean longer hours for less money.

Infinitive

	present tense	-ing form	past tense	past participle
go in for	go in for & goes in for	going in for	went in for	gone in for

1. go in for *p.v.* When you **go in for** a certain activity, you like it and do it regularly.

Bryan really **goes in for** any kind of outdoor activity.

When I was a kid I **went in for** football, but I don't watch it much anymore.

look forward to	look forward to & looks forward to	looking forward to	looked forward to	looked forward to

1. look forward to *p.v.* When you **look forward to** something or **look forward to** doing something, you are excited about something in the future because you enjoy it or because it will benefit you in some way.

It's been four years since my brother went overseas. I'm **looking forward to** seeing him again.

I **look forward to** an opportunity to meet with you in person.

put up with	put up with & puts up with	putting up with	put up with	put up with

1. put up with *p.v.* When you **put up with** something you do not like or are not happy about, you accept it and do not try to change it.

Her neighbors have loud parties every night, but she doesn't complain. She just **puts up with** it.

My husband said, "I've **put up with** your brother long enough!"

screw out of	screw out of & screws out of	screwing out of	screwed out of	screwed out of

1. screw ... out of *p.v.* *[informal]* When you get money or something valuable from people in a dishonest way, you **screw** them **out of** it.

That con man **screwed** me **out of** my life savings.

Their sleazy son-in-law **screwed** them **out of** thousands of dollars.

talk down to	talk down to & talks down to	talking down to	talked down to	talked down to

1. talk down to *p.v.* When you **talk down to** people, you use a tone of voice or an attitude that shows you think they are less intelligent, less educated, or from a lower level of society than you.

*I was furious about the way he **talked down to** me!*
*Bob hates Jane because of the way she **talks down to** him.*

EXERCISE 3a — **Complete the sentences with phrasal verbs from this section. Be sure the phrasal verbs are in the correct tense.**

1. Thanks for inviting me, but I don't _____ _____ _____ card games.

2. I couldn't _____ _____ _____ my husband's smoking any longer.

   I told him to choose between cigarettes and me.

3. I'm sorry, but I think your plan is a big mistake, and I can't _____ _____

   _____ it.

4. Even though Mr. Watson is the richest man in town, he never _____ _____

   _____ people.

5. It's been only two weeks since the tragedy. I'm sure they don't _____ _____

   _____ going to the party.

6. If that crook thinks he's going to _____ me _____ _____

   500 bucks, he's crazy!

7. The whole family's going to be here for Thanksgiving, and Mom is really _____

   _____ _____ it.

8. I volunteered to give my speech first just so I could _____ it _____

   _____.

9. Even if you don't like the rules, you have to _____ _____ _____

   them.

EXERCISE 3b — **Write answers to the questions using phrasal verbs from this section. Be sure the phrasal verbs are in the correct tense.**

1. Jerry's brother-in-law talks to him like he's an idiot. How does Jerry's brother-in-law

   talk to Jerry?

2. Nicole can't work tomorrow, and she's nervous about telling her boss. What should Nicole do?

3. They paid $5,000 too much for their house because the salesman lied to them. What did the

   salesman do to them?

4. Sally's going to fly in an airplane for the first time, and she's very excited about it. How does Sally feel about flying in an airplane?

5. The winters in Minneapolis are terrible, but you can't move or change the weather. What do you have to do?

6. Erik just got out of the hospital, and he doesn't feel strong enough to go back to work. Why can't Erik go back to work?

7. I thought the new policy was an excellent idea, and I agreed with it 100 percent. How did I feel about the new policy?

EXERCISE 3c, Review — **Complete the sentences with these phrasal verbs from Section 2. Be sure the phrasal verbs are in the correct tense. To check their meanings, review Section 2.**

come off	fall for	hear about	stay off
doze off	give in	pull through	throw up

1. Miguel told me he didn't steal my TV, but I didn't _____ _____ his lies.

2. Jim is really sick, and he stayed home from school today. He _____ _____ twice last night.

3. After a few weeks, the gold on this cheap jewelry starts to _____ _____.

4. He kept nagging and nagging, and I finally _____ _____.

5. If that cat doesn't learn to _____ _____ the table, it will have to go.

6. After Betty's temperature got up to 105 degrees, we started to think she might not _____ _____.

7. The meeting was so boring that I _____ _____.

8. I _____ _____ a country where people use big stones for money.

4. FOCUS ON: **present and past continuous phrasal verbs**

Like one-word verbs, phrasal verbs can normally be used in the *continuous* tense (also called the *progressive* tense) using the *-ing* form of the verb (also called the present participle) and a form of *be*:

> *The principal told me you'd been **cheating on** the test.*
> *I've been **going after** my master's for nearly five years.*
> *Which dictionary is he **looking up** the words in?*
> *How will she be **paying for** her tuition bill?*
> *The compass needle couldn't be **pointing to** the south.*
> *We would be **planning for** a bigger crowd if the weather weren't so bad.*
> *They should be **wrapping** the meeting **up** in a few minutes.*
> *Thanks for all your help. I'm sorry for **putting** you **to** so much trouble.*

Infinitive

	present tense	-ing form	past tense	past participle
cheat on				
	cheat on & cheats on	cheating on	cheated on	cheated on

1. cheat on *p.v.* When you **cheat on** your sexual partner, you have sex or a romantic relationship with another person.

> *Sarah filed for divorce after she caught George **cheating on** her.*
> *Can you believe it? She was **cheating on** me with my best friend!*

2. cheat on *p.v.* When you do something dishonest so that you can do better on a test, you **cheat on** the test.

> *The teacher caught Ali **cheating on** the exam.*
> *If I didn't **cheat on** the tests, I'd never pass any of my classes.*

go after

go after & goes after	going after	went after	gone after

1. go after *p.v.* When you chase and try to physically stop or to attack people, you **go after** them.

> *A policeman saw him stealing the car and **went after** him.*
> *Captain Morgan was ordered to **go after** the enemy soldiers.*

2. go after *p.v.* When law enforcement officials try to prosecute people through a legal procedure, they **go after** them.

> *Federal prosecutors are now **going after** the top drug dealers.*
> *The senator introduced a bill designed to **go after** deadbeat dads.*

3. go after *p.v.* When a business tries to increase its profits by trying to increase its market share or its number of customers, it **goes after** them.

*The tobacco company denied **going after** the teenage market.*
*The CEO said he wanted to **go after** new customers in China.*

4. go after *p.v.* When you **go after** something, you try to obtain it even though it may be difficult to do.

*Sofia **went after** a degree in accounting.*
*Todd trained for a year before **going after** the record in the 100-yard dash.*

Infinitive

	present tense	-ing form	past tense	past participle
look up				
	look up & looks up	looking up	looked up	looked up

1. look . . . up *p.v.* When you get information from a reference book, such as a word from a dictionary or a telephone number from a telephone book, you **look** the word or number **up**.

*The teacher told the students to **look** the new words **up** in a dictionary.*
*I **looked up** his number, but it's not in the phone book.*

2. look . . . up *p.v.* When you locate and visit people you have not seen for a long time, you **look** them **up**.

*I was in Dallas on business, and I **looked up** Dan Jones, my old college roommate.*
*If you're ever in Kempton, **look** me **up**.*

3. look up *p.v.* When a situation is **looking up** or starting to **look up**, it is improving.

*Business was pretty bad for a while, but things are starting to **look up**.*
*I'm much happier than I was last year. Things are **looking up**.*

pay for				
	pay for & pays for	paying for	paid for	paid for

1. pay . . . for *p.v.* When you give someone money in exchange for something, you **pay for** it or **pay** someone **for** it.

*Can I **pay for** this stuff with a credit card?*
*Alfonso **paid** the waiter **for** his dinner.*

paid for *part.adj.* After you have paid for something, it is **paid for**.

*My car is old, but at least it's **paid for**.*

2. pay for *p.v.* When you are punished for something, you **pay for** what you have done.

*I caught the guy who's spreading these false rumors about me, and he **paid for**
    ruining my reputation.*
*Young people think that drugs are harmless, but they'll **pay for** their foolishness
    someday.*

4

Infinitive

present tense	-ing form	past tense	past participle
plan for			
plan for & plans for	planning for	planned for	planned for

1. plan for *p.v.* When you make preparations for something in the future, you **plan for** it.

The festival was a disaster because they didn't **plan for** such a huge crowd.
It's never to early too start **planning for** retirement.

point to			
point to & points to	pointing to	pointed to	pointed to

1. point to *p.v.* When you indicate people or things with your hand or a finger, you **point to** them. When an arrow or a sign indicates something, it **points to** it.

The waitress couldn't hear me, so I **pointed to** my empty glass and she understood.
The prosecutor asked, "Can you **point to** the man you saw carrying the gun?"

2. point to *p.v.* When a situation or occurrence causes you to consider something else, it **points to** that thing.

These terrible test scores **point to** a need for some major changes in our educational system.
The fact that all the people with food poisoning ate tuna salad sandwiches **pointed to** contaminated mayonnaise as the source of the illness.

put to			
put to & puts to	putting to	put to	put to

1. put . . . to *p.v.* When you confront people with a difficult or thought-provoking question, accusation, or proposition, you **put** it **to** them.

He didn't want to tell me the truth, but I really **put** it **to** him, and he finally told me the whole story.
When Prof. Kline **put** his theory **to** me like that, I realized what he was talking about.

2. put . . . to *p.v.* When you **put** people **to** trouble or put them to an expense, you cause them to do extra work or to spend money.

Thanks for helping me with my flat tire. I'm sorry to **put** you **to** so much trouble.
I know my father would pay my dental bill if I asked him, but I hate to **put** him **to** such an expense.

3. put . . . to *p.v.* When you **put** part of your body or something in your hand **to** something, you touch or press it to something.

The neighbors were arguing again, so we **put** our ears **to** the wall to try to hear what they were saying.
When he **put** a gun **to** my head, I realized he wasn't joking.

Infinitive

present tense	-ing form	past tense	past participle
wrap up			
wrap up & wraps up	wrapping up	wrapped up	wrapped up

1. wrap ... up *p.v.* When you enclose an object in some kind of paper, usually gift wrapping paper or packaging paper, you **wrap** it **up**.

*I have to **wrap** this gift **up** before I go to the party.*
*The movers **wrapped up** the china with newspapers.*

wrapped up *part.adj.* After you enclose an object in some kind of paper, usually gift wrapping paper or packaging paper, it is **wrapped up**.

2. wrap ... up *p.v.* When you conclude an event that has been happening for some time, you wrap it up. **Wind up** is similar to **wrap up**.

*We **wrapped up** the meeting around 4:00 and went home.*
*The salesman blabbered for two hours before I finally told him to **wrap** it **up**.*

EXERCISE 4a — **Complete the sentences with phrasal verbs from this section. Be sure the phrasal verbs are in the correct tense.**

1. It's 12:30. Let's _____ this meeting _____ and go to lunch.

2. There was no way he could deny his guilt after the prosecutor _____ it _____ him.

3. The high crime rate _____ _____ a need for more police officers.

4. You'll _____ _____ what you did to me if it's the last thing I ever do!

5. The principal gave a zero to each of the students who _____ _____ the test.

6. I _____ my ear _____ the wall to try to hear what Sally was saying about me.

7. Mike is _____ the words _____ in the dictionary.

8. The police officers _____ _____ the robbers, but they didn't catch them.

9. Linda told Ned that she would divorce him if he ever _____ _____ her again.

10. Yes, it was quite a surprise — we didn't _____ _____ twins.

11. We saw an arrow _____ _____ the door at the end of the hallway.

12. After she won the silver medal, she _____ _____ the gold.

13. Most insurance companies won't _____ _____ plastic surgery.

14. I returned to my hometown for the first time in forty years and _____ _____ my first girlfriend.

4

15. The guy in the seafood store _____ the fish _____ in old newspapers.

16. The FBI is _____ _____ major drug smugglers.

17. These last six months have been difficult for Sally, but now things are starting to

_____ _____.

18. The company started in California, but now it's _____ _____ customers all

over the country.

19. You _____ me _____ a lot of trouble to help you move your piano, and you

didn't even say thank you.

EXERCISE 4b — **Write sentences using the objects in parentheses. Be sure to put
the objects in the right place.**

1. I was *looking up* in the dictionary. (a word, it)

_____

_____

_____

2. I was in Boston *looking up*. (some old army buddies, them)

_____

_____

_____

3. Dad's upstairs *wrapping up*. (Mom's birthday present, it)

_____

_____

_____

4. The committee is *wrapping up*. (their discussion, it)

_____

_____

_____

EXERCISE 4c — **Write answers to the questions using phrasal verbs and participle adjectives from this section. Be sure the phrasal verbs are in the correct tense.**

1. He showed me where the bathroom was with his finger. What did he do?

2. We're preparing for 300 wedding guests. What are we doing?

3. The situation is getting better. What is the situation doing?

4. The little boy ran away, and his father chased him and tried to catch him. What did the father do?

5. Sofia is going to try to break the record in the high jump. What is Sofia going to try to do?

6. Tom did a lot of work to get his guest bedroom ready for me when I visited him. What did I do to Tom?

7. I'm giving money to the cashier for the book I want to buy. What am I doing?

8. In Question 7, how would you describe the book after I give the money to the cashier?

9. The people in the meeting are concluding the meeting. What are they doing?

10. When Rosa was in New Orleans, she looked for and visited a childhood friend. What did Rosa do to her friend?

11. Jim asked you a really difficult question. What did Jim do to you?

12. Megan is trying to find Erik's telephone number in a telephone book. What is Megan doing?

13. Tom is married, but he slept with another woman. What did Tom do to his wife?

EXERCISE 4d, Review — **Complete the sentences with these phrasal verbs from previous sections. Be sure the phrasal verbs are in the correct tense. To check their meanings, review the section number given after each one.**

come from, 2	figure out, 1	hear about, 2	pull through, 2
fall for, 2	give in, 1	look for, 1	show up, 1

1. I _____ _____ your mother on our first date, and we got married three months later.

2. Carmen's family _____ _____ Michoacan around twenty years ago.

3. Paul was supposed to meet us at 8:00, but he never _____ _____.

4. These instructions don't make any sense at all. I can't _____ them _____.

5. After Aunt Mary's stroke, her chances didn't look good, but she _____ _____.

6. My daughter begged me to let her get her ears pierced, and I finally _____

_____.

7. My father was listening to the radio, and he said he _____ _____ a new car

that runs on water.

8. I spent two hours _____ _____ the remote control before I found it.

5. FOCUS ON: pronunciation of two-word phrasal verbs

Nonseparable phrasal verbs

Intransitive nonseparable phrasal verbs (verbs that do not allow an object) are usually accented on the particle:

> *The barn got hit by lightning, and it **burned DOWN**.*
> *Ned drank so much that he **passed OUT** on the bathroom floor.*

Transitive nonseparable phrasal verbs (verbs that require an object) are usually accented on the verb:

> *Hank's been **CHEATING on** his wife for years.*
> *I told the teacher my dog ate my homework, but she didn't **FALL for** it.*

Separable phrasal verbs

Separable phrasal verbs (which are always transitive) are usually accented on the particle:

> *The British soldiers tried to **burn DOWN** the White House.*
> *The teacher **passed** them **OUT**.*

As the examples above show, a single phrasal verb can belong to more than one category depending on its meaning.

Infinitive			
present tense	-ing form	past tense	past participle
break down			
break down & breaks down	breaking down	broke down	broken down

1. break down *p.v.* When something mechanical **breaks down**, it does not function.

*I was late for work because my car **broke down**.*
*This photocopier is a piece of junk — it **breaks down** every day.*

broken-down *part.adj.* When something is old, in bad condition, or not functioning properly, it is **broken-down**.

*My car is a **broken-down** piece of junk.*

breakdown *n.* A **breakdown** is a situation in which something mechanical has **broken down**.

*After that last **breakdown**, I decided it was time for a new car.*

2. break down *p.v.* When an arrangement, agreement, negotiation, plan, or marriage **breaks down**, one or more persons involved is not cooperating or participating because of a disagreement or problem.

*After he started drinking heavily, their marriage started to **break down**.*
*The peace negotiations **broke down** because neither side was willing to compromise.*

breakdown *n.* A situation in which an arrangement, agreement, negotiation, plan, or marriage has **broken down** is a **breakdown**.

*Neither side would give an inch, and there was a **breakdown** in the negotiations.*

3. break down *p.v.* When you **break down**, you lose self-control and become emotionally or mentally confused.

*When the judge sentenced Jones to life in prison, he **broke down** and begged for mercy.*
*Tom **breaks down** whenever he thinks of the tragedy.*

breakdown *n.* A situation in which someone has **broken down** and is very upset or confused is a **breakdown**.

*Marvin had a complete mental **breakdown** and started to see invisible people.*

4. break down *p.v.* When something decomposes or reduces to its smallest parts or is reduced by someone to its smallest parts, it **breaks down**.

*After the poison **breaks down**, it's quite harmless.*
*Anticoagulant drugs are used to **break down** blood clots.*

5. break . . . down *p.v.* When you reduce a process, situation, problem, plan, or idea to its basic parts to make it easier to understand, you **break** it **down**.

*The professor's plan seemed really complicated, but after he **broke** it **down** for us, we understood it a little better.*
*If you **break** the manufacturing process **down** into steps, it's easier to train new workers.*

6. break . . . down *p.v.* When you use force to go through a door that is locked, you **break** it **down**.

5

*The police **broke** the door **down** and arrested the bank robbers.*
*A door had to be **broken down** to rescue the people trapped by the fire.*

Infinitive

present tense	-ing form	past tense	past participle
burn down			
burn down & burns down	burning down	burned down	burned down

1. burn . . . down *p.v.* When a building or other structure **burns down** or someone **burns** it **down**, it is completely destroyed by fire.

*Though most of Chicago **burned down** in 1871, a few buildings survived.*
*The owner was arrested for deliberately **burning** his factory **down**.*

call in			
call in & calls in	calling in	called in	called in

1. call in *p.v.* When you call your place of employment to say you cannot work that day because you are sick, you **call in** or **call in** sick.

*The manager was angry when her secretary **called in** three days in a row.*
***Calling in** sick too often is a good way to get fired.*

2. call . . . in *p.v.* When you request the help of people or of an organization with more experience, power, or knowledge to help with a problem or difficult project, you **call** them **in**.

*When the local police couldn't handle the riot, the National Guard was **called in**.*
*The local police chief considered **calling** the FBI **in** to help solve the crime.*

find out			
find out & finds out	finding out	found out	found out

1. find . . . out *p.v.* [not usually separated — the object can be a noun, a noun clause, or a complete sentence] When you **find out** information or a fact, you learn or become aware of that information or fact.

*If you don't know when the movie starts, look in the newspaper to **find out**.*
*I met a nice man at the party, but I never **found out** his name.*
*I met a nice man at the party, but I never **found out** what his name was.*
*I was surprised when I **found out** that he can speak fourteen languages.*
*I was surprised when I **found out** he can speak fourteen languages.*
*I tried to get the information, but I couldn't **find** it **out**.*

hand back			
hand back & hands back	handing back	handed back	handed back

1. hand . . . back (to) *p.v.* When you return things to people by holding them in your hand and extending your arm, you **hand** them **back** or **hand** them **back** to them.

*The teacher will **hand** the tests **back** in third period.*
*The guard **handed** my ID card **back** to me.*

Infinitive

	present tense	-ing form	past tense	past participle
look at	look at & looks at	looking at	looked at	looked at

1. look at *p.v.* When you focus your eyes on people or things, you **look at** them.

> I **looked at** her and told her I loved her.
> **Look at** me when I talk to you!

2. look at *p.v.* When you examine something or a situation and decide what to do about it, you **look** at **it**.

> The mechanic **looked at** my car but couldn't find anything wrong with it.
> Your finger might be broken; you should have Dr. Smith **look at** it.

3. look at p.v. When you think a certain way or have an opinion about something, that is the way you **look at** it.

> The way I **look at** it, Congress is to blame for this mess, not the President.
> What should be done about this situation depends on how you **look at** it.

4. look at *p.v.* [informal — *always continuous*] When you say that people are **looking at** an amount of money or a length of time, you mean that this is how much they think something will cost or how long something will take.

> That was a serious injury. You're **looking at** months and months of physical therapy.
> Putting a new roof on this house isn't going to be cheap. You're **looking at** at least $15,000.

pile up	pile up & piles up	piling up	piled up	piled up

1. pile . . . up *p.v.* When things increase in number and start to form a pile, they **pile up**. When people add things to a pile, they **pile** them **up**.

> The snow **piled up** so high that I couldn't open my door.
> In the fall we **pile** the dead leaves **up** in the driveway and burn them.

piled up *part.adj.* When things are in a pile, they are **piled up**.

> A lot of dirty laundry is **piled up** in the basement.

2. pile up *p.v.* When work or something else that must be done increases faster than you can do it, it **piles up**.

> I'm really worried about money. My bills are **piling up** faster than I can pay them.
> My work really **piled up** while I was on vacation.

set up	set up & sets up	setting up	set up	set up

1. set . . . up *p.v.* When you arrange the parts of something so that they are in their proper position and can function, you **set** it **up**.

5

*The kids got a swing set for Christmas, and Dad had to **set** it **up** in the snow.*
*When you're camping, be sure to **set** your tent **up** before it gets dark.*

set up *part.adj.* After the parts of something are in their proper position and function properly, they are **set up**.

*The party is starting in one hour. Are the tables **set up**?*

setup *n.* A collection or arrangement of parts or equipment necessary for a certain procedure or task is a **setup**.

*The nurse prepared **setups** for the hospital emergency room.*

2. set . . . up *p.v.* When you plan and organize an activity or project, you **set** it **up**.

*I **set up** a 4:00 meeting with Jones and his lawyer.*
***Setting up** a meeting of all fifty governors took a lot of planning.*

set up *part.adj.* When an activity or project is planned, arranged, or organized, it is **set up**.

*The arrangements for the wedding were very complicated, but everything is **set up** now.*

setup *n.* How an activity or project is planned or arranged is the **setup**.

*What's the **setup** for the Fourth of July picnic?*

3. set . . . up *p.v.* [informal] When you commit a crime but make it appear that another, innocent person is guilty of the crime, you **set** the innocent person **up**.

*Joe robbed the bank and tried to **set** me **up** by leaving some of the stolen money in my apartment and then telling the police about it.*
*The detective didn't believe me when I told him I was **set up**.*

setup *n.* [informal] An attempt by someone to make it appear that an innocent person is guilty of a crime is a **setup**.

*I told the detective it was a **setup** and that I could prove I had been at the racetrack when the bank was robbed.*

EXERCISE 5a — **Complete the sentences with phrasal verbs from this section. Be sure the phrasal verbs are in the correct tense.**

1. When he heard that his brother had been killed, he _____ _____ and cried.

2. We're expecting company. Can you _____ _____ the card table in the

   dining room?

3. Can you help wash the dishes, please? They're really beginning to _____

   _____.

4. I gave the cashier my credit card, and then she _____ it _____ to me.

5. I don't know the answer, but I'll try to _____ _____.

6. We were very busy at work today. Two people _____ _____ sick.

7. Raul _____ _____ his watch and told me he had to leave.

8. My car is a real piece of junk. It _____ _____ at least once a week.

9. I'm a little confused about your theory. Would you mind _____ it _____ for me?

10. I'll tell the judge that I'm innocent and that Ned Kelly _____ me _____.

11. Hey, any way you _____ _____ it, one thing's for sure — we have to get more crooks off the streets and into the jails.

12. This is the FBI — open the door or we'll _____ it _____!

13. Maybe I can fix your computer. I'll _____ _____ it after dinner.

14. The family doctor has never seen a case of malaria before, so he is _____ _____ a specialist.

15. Some chemical compounds start to _____ _____ after only a few hours.

16. The arsonist tried to _____ _____ several houses in the neighborhood.

17. The secretary is _____ _____ a meeting.

18. The civil war started again after the peace talks _____ _____.

19. Jim buys a newspaper every day, but he never puts it in the garbage when he is finished. Newspapers are slowly _____ _____ in his basement.

20. The mechanic said, "To fix a car after an accident that bad, I'd say you're _____ _____ at least $4,000."

EXERCISE 5b — **Review the explanation at the beginning of this section of how two-word phrasal verbs are pronounced. Then, say each sentence in Exercise 5a aloud and circle the verb or particle that is accented.**

EXERCISE 5c — **Write three sentences using the objects in parentheses. Be sure to put the objects in the right place.**

1. The firefighters *broke down*. (the door, it)

_____

_____

2. They *burned down*. (the old barn, it)

_____

_____

_____

3. He *called in*. (Dr. Shapiro, her)

_____

_____

_____

4. Our teacher *handed back*. (the papers, them)

_____

_____

_____

5. I *set up*. (the ironing board, it)

_____

_____

_____

EXERCISE 5d — **Write answers to the questions using phrasal verbs, participle adjectives, and nouns from this section. Be sure the phrasal verbs are in the correct tense.**

1. Jane arranged a baby shower. What did she do?

2. In Question 1, how would you describe the baby shower after Jane arranged it?

3. I get magazines in the mail faster than I can read them. What are my magazines doing?

4. In Question 3, how would you describe my magazines?

5. Todd returned the pen to Mark. What did Todd do?

6. Uncle Fred's car had a mechanical problem, and it stopped running. What did it do?

7. In Question 6, how would you describe Uncle Fred's car?

8. In Question 6, what did Uncle Fred have?

9. The soldiers destroyed the building with fire. What did the soldiers do?

10. The soldiers destroyed the building with fire. What did the building do?

11. When the detective told Jake he could get the death penalty, he became very nervous and upset. What did Jake do?

12. In Question 11, what did Jake have?

13. The boss was angry because you didn't call to say that you were sick and couldn't work. Why was the boss angry?

14. Judy took her new computer out of the box, connected all the cables, and got it ready to use. What did she do to her computer?

15. In Question 14, after Judy took her new computer out of the box, connected all the cables, and got it ready to use, how would you describe it?

16. The door was locked, but Hank forced it open and got inside. What did Hank do?

17. I learned that Ali's excuse was a big lie. What did I do?

EXERCISE 5e, Review — **Complete the sentences with these phrasal verbs from previous sections. Be sure the phrasal verbs are in the correct tense. To check their meanings, review the section number given after each one.**

come off, 2	go in for, 3	talk down to, 3
feel up to, 3	look forward to, 3	throw up, 2
get over with, 3	put up with, 3	
go along with, 3	stay off, 2	

1. Her husband is a real jerk. How does she _____ _____ _____ him?

2. I wasn't sure if Charles _____ _____ _____ going scuba diving again so soon after the shark attack.

3. I'm telling you for the last time! _____ _____ the grass!

4. Can you help me with this jar? The top won't _____ _____.

5. I've never been to Italy, and I'm really _____ _____ _____ going there.

6. I'm sorry I can't agree with you Dad, but I have to _____ _____

_____ Mom.

7. When I had food poisoning I _____ _____ all night long.

8. You can be sure Paul will take his vacation out west. He really _____ _____

_____ outdoor stuff like camping and mountain climbing.

9. Can you believe the nerve of that guy in the meeting yesterday? He _____

_____ _____ me as if I was the stupidest guy on Earth!

10. I'm tired of arguing about the divorce settlement. I just want to _____ it

_____ _____.

6. FOCUS ON: pronunciation of three-word phrasal verbs

The pronunciation of three-word phrasal verbs is generally quite simple: the second, or middle, particle is accented regardless of whether the phrasal verb is separable or inseparable:

> *I think I've **come UP with** an answer to your problem.*
> *The detective didn't **get** any information **OUT of** him.*

Infinitive

	present tense	-ing form	past tense	past participle
boil down to				
	boil down to & boils down to	boiling down to	boiled down to	boiled down to

1. boil down to *p.v.* When you say that something **boils down to** something else, you are saying that it is the basic cause of a more complicated situation or problem.

> *Most of the crime in this city **boils down to** drugs.*
> *My decision to stay at this awful job **boils down to** one thing — money.*

come down with				
	come down with & comes down with	coming down with	came down with	come down with

1. come down with *p.v.* When you are starting to get sick, you are **coming down with** something or **coming down with** an illness.

> *I don't feel well. Maybe I'm **coming down with** something.*
> *My grandmother said, "If you don't wear an undershirt, you'll **come down with** pneumonia."*

Infinitive

	present tense	-ing form	past tense	past participle
come up with				
	come up with & comes up with	coming up with	came up with	come up with

1. come up with *p.v.* When you think of an idea, plan, or solution, you **come up with** it.

*It took me all night, but I **came up with** the answer.*

*Lydia wants to **come up with** a great idea for the party.*

	present tense	-ing form	past tense	past participle
get around to				
	get around to & gets around to	getting around to	got around to	gotten/got around to

1. get around to *p.v.* When you do something after waiting for some time because you are lazy, inefficient, or do not want to do it, you **get around to** it.

*I didn't **get around to** doing my taxes until April 14.*

*Don't worry about the broken window. I'll **get around to** it one of these days.*

	present tense	-ing form	past tense	past participle
get out of				
	get out of & gets out of	getting out of	got out of	gotten/got out of

1. get out of *p.v.* When you **get out of** something or **get out of** doing something you must do but do not want to do, you find a way to avoid it.

*Sam **got out of** gym class by pretending to be sick.*

*The boss wants me to work a double shift, but I'll **get out of** it.*

*I **got out of** going to church with my parents by pretending to be sick.*

2. get ... out of *p.v.* If an activity gives you pleasure, satisfaction, or some other benefit, you **get** pleasure, satisfaction, or some other benefit **out of** it.

*I sat through that boring class for three months and didn't learn a thing. I didn't **get** anything **out of** it.*

*The judge didn't **get** any pleasure **out of** imposing such a harsh penalty.*

3. get ... out of *p.v.* When you use force, pressure, or deceit to get something, such as information or money, from people, you **get** it **out of** them.

*They tortured him for days, but they couldn't **get** any information **out of** him.*

*It took me a while, but I **got** the whole story **out of** her.*

	present tense	-ing form	past tense	past participle
go back on				
	go back on & goes back on	going back on	went back on	gone back on

1. go back on *p.v.* When you make a promise, but you do not do what you promised to do, you **go back on** your promise.

*I promised to take my son to a baseball game, and I'm not **going back on** my word.*

*The President **went back on** his pledge not to raise taxes.*

Infinitive

	present tense	-ing form	past tense	past participle
go through with				
	go through with & goes through with	going through with	went through with	gone through with

1. go through with *p.v.* When you do something that you have decided to do even though it may be dangerous or unpleasant or others may object, you **go through with** it.

> The spokeswoman said the company would **go through with** its plan to move the company to Mexico.
>
> Despite his family's opposition, Erik **went through with** his decision to quit his job and start his own business.

monkey around with				
monkey around with & monkeys around with	monkeying around with	monkeyed around with	monkeyed around with

1. monkey around with *p.v.* *[informal]* When you adjust or try to repair mechanical devices even though you do not have permission or do not have the skill to do it properly, you **monkey around with** them.

> I **monkeyed around with** my camera, and I think maybe I fixed it.
>
> Frank was **monkeying around with** my printer, and now it doesn't work.

EXERCISE 6a — **Complete the sentences with phrasal verbs from this section. Be sure the phrasal verbs are in the correct tense.**

1. I'm not surprised that Ali stayed home from work today. Yesterday he thought he might be

   _____ _____ _____ a cold.

2. Last year, the company _____ _____ _____ its plan to move from

   downtown to the suburbs.

3. I've thought and thought, but I can't _____ _____ _____ any

   reason why your idea won't work.

4. Fixing the leak in the roof is going to be a big job, but I have to _____ _____

   _____ it before the next rain.

5. Heather didn't want to tell me why she was mad, but I finally _____ the reason

   _____ _____ her.

6. I don't _____ much satisfaction _____ _____ teaching students

   who don't want to be in the class.

7. The explanation for our failure to solve this problem isn't complicated. It really _____

_____ _____ a lack of funding.

8. I think you should take your VCR to a repair shop. If you _____ _____

_____ it, you'll just make it worse.

9. I'm supposed to report for jury duty on Monday, but I don't want to. I've got to think of a

way to _____ _____ _____ it.

10. You lied to me! You promised me you would quit smoking, and now you've _____

_____ _____ your word.

EXERCISE 6b — **Write answers to the questions using phrasal verbs from this section. Be sure the phrasal verbs are in the correct tense.**

1. Tom was very nervous about getting married, but he did it. What did Tom do?

2. We were in Paris for five days, but we never found time to go to the Eiffel Tower. What didn't we do?

3. My father said I had to cut the grass, but I told him I would do it tomorrow. What did I do?

4. Janice really likes teaching because it gives her a lot of satisfaction. Why does Janice like teaching?

5. Ms. Cummings thought of a way to manufacture her company's products more cheaply. What did Ms. Cummings do?

6. There are many reasons why one house sells for a higher price than other houses, but the main reason is the house's location. Why does one house sell for more than another?

7. You feel a little sick now, and you think you'll have a cold tomorrow. What's happening to you today?

8. I don't really know what to do, but I'll try to fix the air conditioner anyway. What will I do to the air conditioner?

9. My wife didn't talk to me all day, but she said nothing was wrong. I asked her again and again what the problem was and she finally told me. What did I do?

10. Raquel promised Alex she would go to the dance with him, but she went with Carlos instead. What did Raquel do?

EXERCISE 6c, Review — **Complete the sentences with these phrasal verbs from previous sections. Be sure the phrasal verbs are in the correct tense. To check their meanings, review the section number given after each one.**

burn down, 5	go after, 4	look up, 4	point to, 4
cheat on, 4	hand back, 5	pile up, 5	put to, 4
find out, 5	look at, 5	plan for, 4	wrap up, 4

1. We've been at this meeting all afternoon. Don't you think we should _____ it _____ and go home?

2. If we send out 75 invitations to the wedding, and everyone we invited brings his or her spouse, we should _____ _____ 150 guests.

3. Lydia _____ her best friend from college _____ when she was in Las Vegas.

4. The students who _____ _____ the test by writing the answers on their hands were expelled from school.

5. This camera isn't working right. I'm going to take it to Jim at the photo shop and ask him to _____ _____ it.

6. Bill won't be happy if he _____ _____ that you scratched his car.

7. My son's thinking about _____ _____ his master's degree.

8. Evidence gathered after the air plane crash _____ _____ engine failure as the cause.

9. I really _____ it _____ her, and she admitted that I was right.

10. We'd better do the laundry soon; it's starting to _____ _____.

11. The police officer _____ my driver's license _____ to me along with a ticket.

12. The detective thinks the owner _____ _____ his restaurant for the insurance money.

EXERCISE 6d — **Review the explanation at the beginning of Section 5 of how two-word phrasal verbs are pronounced. Then, say each sentence in Exercise 6c aloud and circle the verb or particle that is accented.**

7. FOCUS ON: **separable phrasal verbs with long objects**

We have seen that the object of separable verbs can be placed between the verb and the particle or after the particle:

> clear: I **looked up** <u>the word</u>.
> clear: I **looked** <u>the word</u> **up**.

When the object is short — one word or just a few words in length — the meaning is clear either way. However, when the object is several words long, it can be awkward and confusing to place the object between the particles:

> clear: I **looked up** <u>the words that our teacher said were really important and would probably be on the final exam.</u>
> confusing: I **looked** <u>the words that our teacher said were really important and would probably be on the final exam</u> **up**.

It boils down to the following.

> Short objects can be placed between the verb and the particle or after the particle:
>
> *She **put on** <u>her dress</u>.*
> *She **put** <u>her dress</u> **on**.*

pronouns, such as *him*, *her*, and *it* <u>must</u> be placed between the verb and the particle:

> *She **put** <u>it</u> **on**.*

and long objects should be placed after the particle to avoid confusion:

> *She **put on** <u>the new dress with the red, yellow, and blue flowers that she bought last week for 40 percent off</u>.*

Infinitive			
present tense	-ing form	past tense	past participle
cut up			
cut up & cuts up	cutting up	cut up	cut up

1. cut ... up *p.v.* When you use a knife or pair of scissors to cut something so that there are many small pieces, you **cut** it **up**.

> The boy's mother is **cutting** a piece of meat **up** for him.
> I was so angry at her that I **cut** her picture **up** and flushed it down the toilet.

cut up *part.adj.* After something has been **cut up**, it is **cut up**.

> This steak is for Aunt Kathy, but give the **cut-up** one to Uncle Fred — he doesn't have any teeth.

Infinitive

present tense	-ing form	past tense	past participle
hold up & holds up	holding up	held up	held up

hold up

1. hold . . . up *p.v.* When a wall, column, or other structure supports the weight of something above it, such as a ceiling, it **holds** it **up**.

*The workers were killed when they removed a column **holding** the roof **up**.*
*The house was **held up** by jacks while the foundation was repaired.*

2. hold . . . up *p.v.* When you prevent something from happening or cause it to happen late, you **hold** it **up**. When things or people delay you, they **hold** you **up**.

*The band hasn't arrived yet, and they're **holding up** the whole wedding.*
*I'm sorry I'm late. I was **held up** by traffic.*

holdup *n.* Something that prevents something else from happening or causes it to happen late is a **holdup**.

*Why haven't you finished this work yet? What's the **holdup**?*

3. hold . . . up *p.v.* When you use a gun or other weapon to rob a person, bank, or store, you **hold** it **up**. **Stick up** is the same as **hold up**.

*The jewelry store owner was **held up** by three men wearing ski masks.*
*Some idiot tried to **hold** the bank **up** with a squirt gun.*

holdup *n.* When someone uses a gun or other weapon to rob a person, bank, or store, it is a **holdup**. A **stickup** is the same as a **holdup**.

*The robber fired his gun in the air and yelled, "This is a **holdup**."*
*There was a **holdup** at First National Bank this morning.*

4. hold up *p.v.* When an object remains in good condition after heavy use, it **holds up**.

*These cheap shoes won't **hold up** more than six weeks.*
*Some Roman aqueducts have **held up** for 2,000 years.*

5. hold up *p.v.* When a plan, idea, or agreement is still believed in or respected after a period of time, it has **held up**.

*Einstein's theories have **held up** despite occasional challenges.*
*The ceasefire is **holding up** longer than anyone expected.*

let out

let out & lets out	letting out	let out	let out

1. let . . . out *p.v.* When you allow animals or people to leave a place by giving permission or opening a door, you **let** them **out**.

*The guard **lets** the prisoners **out** of their cells every day at 1:00.*
*I opened the door and **let** the dog **out**.*

2. let ... out *p.v.* When you make an item of clothing bigger by changing the seams, you **let** it **out**.

> *After I gained twenty pounds, I had to have all my pants **let out**.*
> *The tailor **let** her old dress **out** so that she could wear it again.*

3. let ... out *p.v.* When you reveal secret or sensitive information, you **let** it **out**.

> *This information is secret. Don't **let** it **out**.*
> *I was furious when my secretary **let out** that I had interviewed for a new position.*

4. let out *p.v.* When you make a sound that shows your emotion or feelings, you **let out** that sound.

> *Heather knew Jim was lying again, and **let out** a sigh.*
> *The lion **let out** a loud roar before he attacked the hunter.*

Infinitive

	present tense	-ing form	past tense	past participle
point out				
	point out & points out	pointing out	pointed out	pointed out

1. point ... out *p.v.* When you bring things or people to someone's attention or indicate the location of things or people with your hand or index finger, you **point** them **out**.

> *As we walked through the museum, the tour guide **pointed** several famous paintings **out**.*
> *General Johnston showed the satellite photo to the reporter and **pointed out** the enemy tanks.*

2. point ... out *p.v.* When you are writing or speaking and you stress or emphasize some important information you think the reader or listener needs to know, you **point out** the information.

> *I **pointed** several flaws **out** in Prof. Childress's theory.*
> *He said that he thought my plan was basically good but that he wanted to **point out** several possible problems.*

run over				
	run over & runs over	running over	ran over	run over

1. run over (to) *p.v.* When you run from where you are to where someone else is, you **run over** or **run over** to that person.

> *I saw a man hitting a child, and I **ran over** and stopped him.*
> *When I saw Melanie, I **ran over** to her and gave her a big hug.*

2. run ... over *p.v.* When you drive over people or things with a car, truck, or other vehicle causing damage, injury, or death, you **run** them **over**.

> *John was **run over** by a bus and killed.*
> *I **ran over** a glass bottle and got a flat tire.*

3. run over *p.v.* When liquid in a container fills the container and goes over the top, it **runs over**.

> *Keep on eye on the bathtub so that it doesn't **run over**.*
> *There's too much water in this pot. It's going to **run over** the side.*

4. run over *p.v.* When you go beyond a limit, you **run over** or **run over** the limit.

> *I hope the 11:00 meeting doesn't **run over**; I'm meeting a client for lunch at 12:00.*
> *The speaker was given fifteen minutes for her speech, but she **ran** over.*

Infinitive

	present tense	-ing form	past tense	past participle
see about				
	see about & sees about	seeing about	saw about	seen about

1. see ... about *p.v.* When you talk to someone to get permission for something or to arrange something, you **see about** it or **see** someone **about** it.

> *Is Luis going to **see about** changing his flight from the fifth to the sixth?*
> *The carpet in my office is filthy. I need to **see** the maintenance guy **about** getting it shampooed.*

2. see about *p.v.* When you are upset about a change or a new policy, and you want to say that you will take some action or talk to someone in authority to prevent or reverse the change or new policy, you say "I'll **see about** that" or "We'll **see about** that."

> *Now they're saying I can't even smoke in my own office. I'll **see about** that!*
> *Those crooks in City Hall want to double my real estate taxes. We'll just **see about** that.*

take apart				
	take apart & takes apart	taking apart	took apart	taken apart

1. take ... apart *p.v.* When you completely separate the parts of something, you **take** it **apart**. **Take apart** is the opposite of **put together**.

> *I had to **take** my bike **apart** when I moved.*
> *The mechanic **took** the engine **apart**.*

take in				
	take in & takes in	taking in	took in	taken in

1. take ... in *p.v.* When you bring a car or other household appliance to a mechanic or repair person, you **take** it **in**.

> *Sally **took** her car **in** to have the oil changed.*
> *The VCR is broken again. I need to **take** it **in**.*

2. take ... in *p.v.* When you **take in** a play, movie, museum, or other attraction, you go to it or see it.

> *We stopped in Charleston and **took in** the sights.*
> *After dinner we **took in** a movie.*

3. take ... in *p.v.* When you allow people to live with you, you **take** them **in.**

> Judy's brother had nowhere to go, so she **took** him **in.**
> The Ortegas offered to **take** their neighbors **in** after the fire.

4. take ... in *p.v.* *[usually passive]* When you are **taken in** by someone, that person successfully tricks or deceives you.

> Stalin was **taken in** by Hitler's assurances.
> They were completely **taken in** by Jake's elaborate hoax.

5. take ... in *p.v.* When you make an item of clothing smaller by changing the seams, you **take** it **in.**

> She likes some of her maternity clothes so much that she's going to **take** them **in** after the baby is born.
> If I lose any more weight, I'll have to have all my pants **taken in.**

EXERCISE 7a — **Complete the sentences with phrasal verbs from this section. Be sure the phrasal verbs are in the correct tense.**

1. When the bullet hit him, he _____ _____ a slight gasp and fell dead.

2. My friends were supposed to be here an hour ago. What is _____ them _____?

3. Will you please drive more carefully! You almost _____ _____ that lady back there.

4. Ann _____ _____ that she was going to go to Las Vegas with her boss, and the whole office was talking about it.

5. Take two pounds of beef, _____ it _____, and put it in a frying pan.

6. The expedition leader spoke to us and _____ _____ the importance of taking plenty of water with us in the desert.

7. Open the gate and _____ the horses _____.

8. I'm embarrassed to admit I was _____ _____ by his lies.

9. After Todd's parents were killed, his Aunt Judy and Uncle Henry _____ him _____.

10. The soldier was _____ his rifle _____ and cleaning it.

11. In Ecuador I rode on a steam locomotive that's still _____ _____ after 80 years.

12. After we saw the Empire State Building, we _____ _____ a Broadway play.

13. These aluminum poles _____ _____ the tent.

14. Nicole is at the computer store _____ _____ getting more memory installed in her computer.

15. I had my old uniform _____ _____ so that I could wear it to the reunion.

16. A robber _____ _____ a liquor store with a shotgun last night.

17. When I got into the tub, the water _____ _____ the side and onto the floor.

18. The health department inspector walked around the restaurant and _____ several rats _____ to the owner.

19. Jim's phone was ringing, so I _____ _____ to his desk and answered it.

20. The suit was too big, but the store's tailor said he could _____ it _____.

21. I heard a weird noise coming from my car's transmission. I think I'd better _____ my car _____.

22. It's an unusual arrangement, but it has _____ _____ for several years.

23. The conference is scheduled to end Tuesday at 5:00, but there's a good chance that it will _____ _____.

24. I was just notified that I'm going to be transferred to Mongolia. We'll _____ _____ that! I'm going to talk to the boss.

25. The robber was shot while trying to _____ _____ an off-duty police officer.

EXERCISE 7b — **Write three sentences using the objects in parentheses.**

1. The cook *cut up*. (the meat, it)

_____

_____

_____

2. The snowstorm *held up*. (air travelers, them)

_____

_____

_____

3. Don't *let out*. (the dog, it)

_____

_____

_____

4. The real estate agent *pointed out*. (the swimming pool, it)

_____

_____

_____

5. The truck *ran over*. (the man, him)

_____

_____

_____

6. I'm going to *take apart*. (the broken doorknob, it)

_____

_____

_____

7. The tailor *took in*. (the pants, them)

_____

_____

_____

EXERCISE 7c — **Write answers to the questions using phrasal verbs and nouns from this section. Be sure the phrasal verbs are in the correct tense.**

1. I don't like this hotel room. I'm going to ask the desk clerk about changing to a different room. What am I going to do?

2. No one believes in the scientist's theories anymore. What haven't the scientist's theories done?

3. Janice is going to make her pants smaller. What is she going to do?

4. Mr. Ortega was tricked by the salesman. What happened to Mr. Ortega?

5. A car drove over you. What happened to you?

6. The jeweler showed me several flaws in the diamond. What did the jeweler do?

7. The game started late because it was raining. What did the rain do?

8. Susie is using scissors to make several small pieces of paper from a larger piece of paper. What is Susie doing?

9. The posts are supporting the porch. What are the posts doing?

10. The woman told the bank teller to give her all the money in the cash register or she would shoot him. What did the woman do?

11. In Question 10, what happened at the bank?

12. I put my broken TV in my car, drove to the repair shop, and carried the TV in. What did I do to my TV?

13. Bill separated all the parts of his typewriter. What did Bill do?

14. There was too much water in the bathtub, and it spilled onto the floor. What did the water do?

15. After my parents died, my grandparents let me live with them. What did my grandparents do?

16. Mr. Young told some people about the secret information. What did Mr. Young do with the secret information?

17. I saw an empty luggage cart at the airport, and I went to it quickly and grabbed it. What did I do?

18. When the thief started to open the woman's door, a scream came from her mouth. What did the woman do?

19. I've been using this lawn mower for twenty-five years, and it still works fine. What has the lawn mower done?

20. The cowboy opened the gate so that the cattle could leave the corral. What did the cowboy do?

21. Dr. Smith went to a museum while he was in Rome. What did Dr. Smith do?

22. The meeting was supposed to end at 2:00, but it hasn't ended yet. What is the meeting doing?

23. I'm making my pants bigger. What am I doing?

EXERCISE 7d, Review — **Complete the sentences with these phrasal verbs from previous sections. Be sure the phrasal verbs are in the correct tense. To check their meanings, review the section number given after each one.**

boil down to, 6	figure out, 1	go through with, 6
come down with, 6	get around to, 6	look forward to, 3
come off, 2	get out of, 6	monkey around with, 6
come up with, 6	go after, 4	put on, 1
doze off, 2	go back on, 6	

1. I thought about what I was going to say to her, but when the time came, I was so nervous I couldn't _____ _____ _____ it.

2. The President's news conference didn't _____ _____ well because it revealed his poor understanding of the situation.

3. I _____ _____ _____ watching Aunt Kathy's vacation videotape by saying I had to study for a test.

4. I don't usually _____ _____ _____ doing my Christmas shopping until December 24.

5. I've been _____ _____ _____ this broken refrigerator all day, but I still don't know what's wrong with it.

6. Mexico City's problems _____ _____ _____ one thing — too many people.

7. Have you seen my pen? I can't _____ _____ what happened to it.

8. If you _____ a coat of paint _____ that old house, it wouldn't look so bad.

9. One police officer helped the mugging victim while her partner _____ _____ the mugger.

10. My son promised that he would stop cutting school, and so far he hasn't _____ _____ _____ that promise.

11. The company _____ _____ _____ a way to decrease labor costs without lowering wages.

12. I have never been to Thailand, and I'm really _____ _____ _____ going there.

13. She was so tired she _____ _____ as soon as she sat down.

14. The show was canceled after the star _____ _____ _____ laryngitis. 45

8. FOCUS ON: present perfect phrasal verbs

The *present perfect* is used to talk about the past and the present at the same time:

> *They have **torn down** the building.* (The building is not there now because they tore it down in the past.)

or to say that something is completed:

> *She has **picked out** some library books.*

The present perfect is formed with *have*, or when the subject is *he, she, it,* or the name of one person or thing, *has*, and the *past participle* of the verb:

> present: *The tree **falls over**.*
> past: *The tree **fell over**.*
> present perfect: *The tree <u>has</u> **fallen over**.*

Remember that *have* can be combined with pronouns as *'ve*:

> *They'<u>ve</u> never **heard of** him.*

and *has* with nouns and pronouns as *'s*:

> *The tree'<u>s</u> **fallen over**.*
> *He'<u>s</u> never **heard of** her.*

Be careful not to confuse the *'s* contraction of *has* and the *'s* contraction of *is*:

> *She'<u>s</u> **picked out** some library books.* (She <u>has</u> ...)
> *She'<u>s</u> **picking out** some library books.* (She <u>is</u> ...)

Infinitive

	present tense	-ing form	past tense	past participle
burn out				
	burn out & burns out	burning out	burned out	burned out

1. burn out *p.v.* When a fire, candle, or other flame stops burning because it has no more fuel, it **burns out**.

> *We need more wood; the fire has **burned out**.*
> *Don't worry; the sun won't **burn out** for another four billion years.*

burned-out *part.adj.* After a fire, candle, or other flame stops burning because it has no more fuel, it is **burned-out**.

> *The **burned-out** rocket landed in the ocean.*

burned-out *part.adj.* When people are extremely tired, either physically or psychologically, because of stress or hard work, they are **burned-out**.

> *Teaching those awful students for so many years has left him **burned-out**.*
> *Taking care of four small children day after day would leave any mother **burned-out**.*

2. burn out *p.v.* When a light bulb stops producing light because it has reached the end of its useful life, it **burns out**.

> *These new bulbs are guaranteed not to **burn out** for ten years.*
> *I can't see what I'm doing because this bulb has **burned out**.*

burned-out *part.adj.* A light bulb that no longer produces light because it has reached the end of its useful life is **burned-out**.

> *I climbed the ladder and unscrewed the **burned-out** bulb.*

3. burn ... out *p.v.* When people are forced to leave their home or some other shelter or hiding place because of fire or fire damage, they are **burned out**.

> *The only way to get the enemy soldiers out of the tunnels was to **burn** them **out**.*
> *Seven families were **burned out** of their homes by the huge fire.*

burned-out *part.adj.* Something that has been damaged or destroyed by fire is **burned-out**.

> *After the war, nothing was left but **burned-out** cars and buildings.*

Infinitive			
present tense	-ing form	past tense	past participle
fall over			
fall over & falls over	falling over	fell over	fallen over

1. fall over *p.v.* When people or things **fall over**, they fall to the ground from an upright position.

> *That tree has been dead for fifty years, but it still hasn't **fallen over**.*
> *I almost **fell over** when I heard the terrible news.*

2. fall over *p.v.* When you **fall over** yourself or (usually) **fall** all **over** yourself, you try so hard to serve someone or to make someone like you that you appear foolish.

> *The supervisor **fell** all **over** himself trying to satisfy the customer.*
> *Mike was **falling** all **over** himself trying to impress Heather.*

fight back			
fight back & fights back	fighting back	fought back	fought back

1. fight back *p.v.* When you **fight back**, you fight, either physically or with words, someone or something that attacked you first.

> *The soldiers **fought back** bravely, but the situation was hopeless.*
> *After being accused of corruption, the senator said she would **fight back** and prove her innocence.*

2. fight back *p.v.* When you **fight back** an emotional response, such as tears or fear, you try very hard to overcome the emotion.

> *The mother **fought back** tears when she saw the little white coffins.*
> *I had to **fight back** the urge to punch him in the nose.*

Infinitive

	present tense	-ing form	past tense	past participle
hear of				
	hear of & hears of	hearing of	heard of	heard of

1. hear of *p.v.* When you learn about something for the first time, you **hear of** it.

> *Do I know Fred Smith? No, I've never **heard of** him.*
> *I told my real estate agent, "If you **hear of** a good deal on a three-bedroom house, please call me right away."*

2. hear of *p.v.* When you learn information about something that makes you angry and you say you will not **hear of** it, you mean that you will not tolerate or allow it.

> *Our daughter wants to fly to Mexico with her boyfriend? I won't **hear of** it!*
> *I told him that his scheme was outrageous and that I wouldn't **hear of** such a thing.*

pick out				
	pick out & picks out	picking out	picked out	picked out

1. pick . . . out *p.v.* When you choose something from a group because you prefer it to the others in the group, you **pick** it **out**.

> *Have you **picked out** a dress to wear to the party yet?*
> *Mike's dog had puppies, and he asked me to **pick** one **out**.*

2. pick . . . out *p.v.* When you are able to find and recognize something in a group, you **pick** it **out**.

> *Even though the class photo was fifty years old, I **picked** my father **out** easily.*
> *The police detective asked me if I could **pick** the mugger **out** from a group of photos.*

ring up				
	ring up & rings up	ringing up	rang up	rung up

1. ring . . . up *p.v.* When you want to buy something in a store, a cashier uses a cash register to **ring up** what you want to buy in order to determine how much money you must pay.

> *Well, I guess I'll take this one. Can you **ring** it **up** please?*
> *I couldn't believe it when the clerk finished **ringing** it all **up** — $946!*

2. ring . . . up *p.v.* (mainly British) When you call people on the telephone, you **ring** them **up**.

> *He **rang up** Nancy and asked her to go to the dance.*
> *If you need a ride, **ring** me **up** when you arrive at the airport.*

tear down				
	tear down & tears down	tearing down	tore down	torn down

1. tear . . . down *p.v.* When you **tear down** a building, you deliberately and completely destroy it.

*They **tore** so many old buildings **down** in my hometown that I barely recognize it.*
*A lot of smaller homes in the suburbs are being **torn down** and replaced with larger ones.*

Infinitive

present tense	-ing form	past tense	past participle
work in			
work in & works in	working in	worked in	worked in

1. work . . . in *p.v.* When you make room, with some difficulty, for something in a schedule or plan, you **work** it **in**.

*We're going to be in Chicago for only a couple of days, but I'll try to **work in** a Cubs game.*

*I told him my schedule was pretty tight, but that I'd try to **work** the meeting **in**.*

EXERCISE 8a — **Complete the sentences with phrasal verbs from this section. Be sure the phrasal verbs are in the correct tense.**

1. The Leaning Tower of Pisa still hasn't _____ _____.

2. Every year I have to replace the Christmas tree lights that have _____ _____.

3. The enemy was so strong that there was no way we could have _____

   _____.

4. I don't have time to talk about it now. I'll _____ you _____ after dinner.

5. Sarah always tries to _____ _____ a little sightseeing on her business trips.

6. My brother is pretty easy to _____ _____ in a crowd — he's almost seven

   feet tall.

7. If you haven't _____ _____ a video yet, you'd better hurry — the store's clos-

   ing in five minutes.

8. The firefighters decided to let the fire in the lumberyard _____ itself _____.

9. That cashier has been yakking with his friends for ten minutes and still hasn't _____

   our stuff _____.

10. A screen door on a submarine? That's the most ridiculous thing I've ever _____

    _____.

11. When I told the waiter I was the owner of the restaurant, he _____ all _____

    himself trying please me.

12. The taco stand moved across the street after it was _____ _____ by the fire.

13. When I found out that one of my employees cheated a customer, I said I wouldn't

_____ _____ such a thing in my store.

14. I had to _____ _____ my fear as I waited for my turn to jump from the plane.

15. They'll have to _____ _____ most of the buildings that were damaged by

the earthquake.

EXERCISE 8b — **Write three sentences using the objects in parentheses. Be sure to put the objects in the right place.**

1. The sheriff *burned out*. (the escaped convicts, them)

_____

_____

_____

2. Bill has *picked out*. (a new car, one)

_____

_____

_____

3. The clerk hasn't *rung up* yet. (these CDs, them)

_____

_____

_____

4. The new owners have *torn down*. (the garage, it)

_____

_____

_____

5. The mayor tried to *work in*. (a tour of the factory, it)

_____

_____

EXERCISE 8c — **Write answers to the questions using phrasal verbs and participle adjectives from this section. Make all the phrasal verbs present perfect.**

1. I asked my father if I could smoke in the house, and he became angry and said he wouldn't allow it. What did my father say about smoking in the house?

2. The forest fire has stopped because there aren't any more trees left to burn. What has the fire done?

3. The cashier has totaled how much we must pay for our groceries. What has the cashier done?

4. They have chosen a hotel for their wedding reception. What have they done?

5. Sally's mother couldn't stop her tears. What couldn't Sally's mother do?

6. One of my car's headlights isn't working anymore. What did the headlight do?

7. In Question 6, how would you describe the headlight?

8. The stack of books was too high, and now the books are on the floor. What did the books do?

9. The coffee shop had to move to a different location because of a fire. What happened to the coffee shop?

10. In Question 9, how would you describe the coffee shop's previous location?

11. After they attacked us, we didn't attack them. What didn't we do?

12. I've made room in my busy day for a game of tennis. What have I done?

13. She hasn't called me on the telephone. What hasn't she done?

14. They've completely destroyed the old factory. What have they done?

15. The sergeant tried extremely hard to show the captain how well he was training the soldiers. What did the sergeant do?

16. I asked Jim if anyone had ever told him about the new seafood restaurant in the mall. What did I ask Jim?

8

EXERCISE 8d, Review — **Complete the sentences with these phrasal verbs from previous sections. Be sure the phrasal verbs are in the correct tense. To check their meanings, review the section number given after each one.**

cut up, 7	go in for, 3	point out, 7	see about, 7
fall for, 2	hold up, 7	pull through, 2	show up, 1
get over with, 3	let out, 7	put up with, 3	take apart, 7
give in, 2	look up, 4	run over, 7	take in, 7

1. My bicycle was really dirty, so I _____ it _____ and cleaned it.

2. It was a very serious injury, and no one expected Raul to _____ _____.

3. I've been waiting for the TV repair guy all day, but he still hasn't _____ _____.

4. I feel just awful. I was driving to work, and I _____ _____ a dog.

5. The detectives weren't _____ _____ by the crook's explanation.

6. The detectives didn't _____ _____ the crook's explanation.

7. Mrs. Taylor's husband doesn't have any teeth, so she has to _____ all his food _____.

8. The freight train _____ _____ traffic for twenty minutes, so we were late for work.

9. In his report yesterday, the head of marketing _____ _____ several ways to increase the company's sales.

10. I _____ the word *Internet* _____ in an old dictionary, but I couldn't find it.

11. Susie's mother told her, "I'm not going to _____ you _____ of this house until you finish your homework."

12. The company finally _____ _____ to demands that it hire more women and minorities.

13. I'm having root canal surgery next week. I'll be glad to _____ it _____.

14. David called the travel agency to _____ _____ getting his ticket changed.

15. Karen loves to ski. In fact, she _____ _____ _____ most

winter sports.

16. Betty told the doctor she couldn't _____ _____ _____ the pain any

longer, and she asked him for morphine.

9. FOCUS ON: **two-word phrasal verbs that require an additional particle when used with an object, 1**

With some two-word verbs you must use a <u>second</u> particle when the verb has an object:

> The criminal **broke out**.
> ~~The criminal **broke out** prison.~~
> The criminal **broke out** <u>of</u> prison.
>
> Tom and Jerry don't **get along**.
> ~~Tom and Jerry don't **get along** each other.~~
> Tom and Jerry don't **get along** <u>with</u> each other.

Sometimes, as with **break out** and **break out** *of*, there is no change in meaning. Sometimes, as with **hang up** and **hang up** *on*, there is a small change in meaning. And sometimes, as with **hook up** and **hook up** *to*, the second particle is necessary not when there is one object but only when there are two:

> I **hooked up** my new CD player.
> ~~I **hooked up** my new CD player my stereo.~~
> I **hooked up** my new CD player <u>to</u> my stereo.

There is no good way to always know which second particle must be used or if and how it will change the meaning of the verb. The best thing to do is to simply memorize each case.

Throughout this book, two-word phrasal verbs that require an additional particle when used with an object are shown with the second particle in parentheses: **break out** (of).

Do not confuse two-word phrasal verbs that require an additional particle when used with an object with three-word phrasal verbs. Three-word phrasal verbs always have three words — there is no two-word version, or if there is a phrasal verb with the same verb and first particle, it has a different meaning and is classified as a different verb. For example, **break out** and **break out** (of) are included in one definition because they have the same meaning, but **put up** and **put up with** have different meanings and are classified separately.

9

Infinitive

	present tense	-ing form	past tense	past participle
break out	break out & breaks out	breaking out	broke out	broken out

1. break out (of) *p.v.* When you escape from a place where you are a prisoner, you **break out** or **break out** of that place.

> *Bubba **broke out** of prison last month.*
> *The police have been looking for him ever since he **broke out**.*

breakout *n.* An escape from prison is a **breakout**.

> *There hasn't been a successful **breakout** from the state prison in more than twenty-five years.*

2. break out *p.v.* When fighting begins suddenly, it **breaks out**.

> *Rioting **broke out** after the general canceled the election.*
> *Millions will be killed if nuclear war **breaks out**.*

catch up	catch up & catches up	catching up	caught up	caught up

1. catch up (with) *p.v.* When you move faster and reach the same level or place as people who had been moving faster or doing better than you were, you **catch up** or **catch up** with them.

> *We left an hour before Luis, but he drove fast and quickly **caught up**.*
> *After missing several weeks of class, Raquel is so far behind that she'll never **catch up**.*
> *Pepsi has **caught up** with Coca-Cola in some markets.*
> *The mugger was running so fast that the angry mob couldn't **catch up** with him.*

caught up *part.adj.* After you have moved faster and reached the same level or place as people who had been moving faster or doing better than you are, you are **caught up**.

> *When I was sick, I missed a lot of schoolwork, but I worked hard and now I'm **caught up**.*

2. catch up (on) *p.v.* When you study or learn something you are interested in but have not had time for, you **catch up** on it.

> *I wonder what the latest gossip is. Let's call Michael so we can **catch up**.*
> *After I returned from vacation, I read the newspaper to **catch up** on the local news.*

caught up *part.adj.* After you have studied or learned something you are interested in but have not had time for, you are **caught up**.

> *Now that I've read the newspapers I missed while I was on vacation, I'm **caught up**.*

Infinitive

present tense	-ing form	past tense	past participle
chicken out			
chicken out & chickens out	chickening out	chickened out	chickened out

   1. chicken out (of) *p.v.* *[informal]* When you do not do something because you are afraid, you **chicken out** or **chicken out** of it.

> *I was going to ask Heather to go to the dance with me, but I **chickened out**.*
> *Miguel's mad at himself because he **chickened out** of asking his boss for a raise yesterday.*

get along			
get along & gets along	getting along	got along	gotten/got along

   1. get along (with) *p.v.* When you **get along** with people, you have peaceful, harmonious relations with them. **Get on** is similar to **get along**.

> *Jim and his cousin aren't good friends, but they **get along**.*
> *I haven't **gotten along** with my neighbors for years.*

   2. get along *p.v.* When you are able to do some sort of work without any serious problems, you **get along**.

> *How are you **getting along** in your new job?*
> *Oh, I'm **getting along** okay, thank you.*

give up			
give up & gives up	giving up	gave up	given up

   1. give up (on) *p.v.* When you stop trying to do something because you think you will never succeed, you **give up** or **give up** on it.

> *Forget it! This is impossible — I **give up**!*
> *I've tried for years to have a nice looking lawn, but I've just **given up** on it.*

   2. give . . . up *p.v.* When you are running from or fighting with the police or enemy soldiers and you surrender, you **give up** or **give** yourself **up**.

> *When the bank robbers realized they were surrounded by police, they **gave up**.*
> *The suspect got tired of hiding from the police, and he **gave** himself **up**.*

   3. give . . . up *p.v.* When you stop doing something you do regularly, such as a sport or a job, you **give** it **up**.

> *My father didn't **give** sky diving **up** until he was eighty-two.*
> *I had to **give up** my second job because I was so exhausted all the time.*

hang up			
hang up & hangs up	hanging up	hung up	hung up

   1. hang up (on) *p.v.* When you stop talking on the telephone and put down the receiver, you **hang up** the telephone. When you are angry and **hang up** the telephone without saying good-bye to someone, you **hang up** on the person you are talking to.

9

*After I finished talking to her, I said good-bye and **hung up**.*
*When he called me a moron, I got so mad I **hung up** on him.*

2. hang ... up *p.v.* When you hang something in a high place so that it cannot touch the ground, you **hang** it **up**.

*When I get home, the first thing I do is **hang** my coat **up**.*
*Timmy never **hangs** anything **up**; he just leaves it on the floor.*

hung up *part.adj.* After you have hung something in a high place so that it cannot touch the ground, it is **hung up**.

*Timmy, why are your clothes on the floor and not **hung up**?*

Infinitive

present tense	-ing form	past tense	past participle
hook up			
hook up & hooks up	hooking up	hooked up	hooked up

1. hook ... up (to) *p.v.* When you connect one electronic device to another, you **hook** it **up** or **hook** it **up** to something.

*I bought a new printer, but I haven't **hooked** it **up** yet.*
*I **hooked** my sound system **up** to my TV, and now the TV is in stereo.*

hooked up *part.adj.* After one electronic device has been connected to another, it is **hooked up**.

*There's a VCR on my TV, but don't try to use it because it's not **hooked up**.*

hookup *n.* A **hookup** is an electrical connection.

*The cable TV **hookup** usually costs $20, but it's free this month.*

2. hook up (with) *p.v. [informal]* When you meet people somewhere, usually after you have done some things separately, you **hook up** or **hook up** with them.

*You do your shopping, I'll go to the post office, and we'll **hook up** around 2:30, okay?*
*I'll **hook up** with you at 12:00 at the corner of State and Madison, and we'll have lunch.*

work up			
work up & works up	working up	worked up	worked up

1. work up (to) *p.v.* When you gradually improve at something difficult that you do regularly, you **work up** to that improvement.

*You can't lift 200 pounds on your first day of weight training. You have to **work up** to it.*
*When I started running, I couldn't go more than a mile, but now I've **worked up** to five miles.*

2. work up *p.v.* When you gradually develop the energy, confidence, courage, and so on, to do something difficult or something you do not want to do, you **work up** the energy, confidence, courage, and so on. When you gradually develop a feeling, you **work up** the feeling.

> It took me a long time to **work up** the nerve to ask my boss for a raise.
> If I **work up** some energy, I'll wash the car.
> I really **worked up** a sweat in the gym today.
> Raking leaves all day sure **works up** an appetite.

worked up *part.adj. [informal]* When you are anxious, worried, or upset about something, you are **worked up** or **worked up** about it.

> Mark has been acting nervous all day. What's he all **worked up** about?
> Relax, we're only a few minutes late. It's nothing to get **worked up** about.

EXERCISE 9a — **Complete the sentences with phrasal verbs from this section. Be sure the phrasal verbs are in the correct tense.**

1. My elbow has gotten so bad that I think I might have to _____ _____ tennis.

2. After several years of tension between the two countries, war _____ _____ in 1972.

3. Maria, how are you _____ _____ at your new job?

4. I am so lazy today. I just can't _____ _____ the energy to finish my school project.

5. The murderer was tired of running from the police, and he _____ himself _____.

6. The other runners were so far ahead that I couldn't _____ _____.

7. Susie, _____ _____ your clothes right now!

8. For a long time I could type only around twenty-five words per minute, but I've slowly _____ _____ to sixty.

9. I'm really behind in my work. If I don't take work home with me, I'll never _____ _____.

10. Lydia is a nice, easygoing person. You won't have any trouble _____ _____ her.

11. I tried and tried to learn to speak Japanese, but I finally _____ _____ .

12. Hello Mark? I'm really angry, and I've got some things to tell you, and don't you dare _____ _____ on me!

13. Dan is so shy. He was supposed to give a speech today at school, but he _____ _____.

14. Okay, here's the plan: You go to the bookstore, I'll get my laundry, and we'll _____ _____ around 11:00.

15. I wonder what's been happening while we were on vacation. I think I'll read the newspaper so I can _____ _____.

16. This is a maximum security prison. No one has ever _____ _____.

17. Bob tried to _____ _____ my new dishwasher, but he didn't do it right, and he flooded the kitchen.

EXERCISE 9b — **Complete the sentences with the correct second particles.**

1. I called my girlfriend to apologize for forgetting her birthday, but she *hung up* _____ me.

2. When I started lifting weights, I could lift only thirty kilograms, but little by little I *worked up* _____ fifty.

3. He's very sick, but the doctors haven't *given up* _____ him yet.

4. Sofia was going to bleach her hair, but she *chickened out* _____ it.

5. Don't invite Carmen to Rosa's birthday party. They don't *get along* _____ each other.

6. The bank robber was carrying 2,000 quarters, so it was easy for the police *catch up* _____ him.

7. No prisoner has ever *broken out* _____ this prison.

8. I need a different cable to *hook* my monitor *up* _____ my computer.

9. You've been gone a long time, and you have to *catch up* _____ a lot of things.

EXERCISE 9c — **Write three sentences using the objects in parentheses. Be sure to put the objects in the right place.**

1. Tonight I'm going to try to *hook up*. (my fax machine, it)

_____

_____

2. After my accident, I had to *give up*. (scuba diving, it)

_____

_____

_____

3. You can *hang up* in the closet. (your coat, it)

_____

_____

_____

EXERCISE 9d — **Write answers to the questions using phrasal verbs, participle adjectives, and nouns from this section. Be sure the phrasal verbs are in the correct tense.**

1. When I went on vacation three weeks ago, my sister and her husband were talking about getting a divorce. Now that I'm back from vacation, I want to know what happened while I was gone. What do I want to do?

2. Lydia has to stop driving because her eyesight is so bad. What does Lydia have to do?

3. Susie was walking with us, but she stopped to look in a store window, and we continued walking. What does Susie need to do now?

4. I spilled wine on your white carpet, and you became angry and upset. How would you describe yourself?

5. Connecting a printer to a computer is easy. What is easy?

6. In Question 5, how would you describe the printer after it is connected to a computer?

7. Several prisoners are going to try to escape from the state prison tonight. What are the prisoners going to try to do tonight?

8. In Question 7, if the prisoners are successful, what would their escape be called?

9. Linda and Nicole don't like each other, and they argue sometimes. What don't Linda and Nicole do?

9

10. We argued with our daughter for months, but we stopped trying to get her to stop smoking. What did we do?

11. Fights start in that bar all the time. What happens in that bar all the time?

12. Paul slowly developed the courage to ask his boss for a raise. What did Paul do?

13. In Question 12, what didn't Paul do?

14. The police told the robber to surrender. What did the police tell the robber?

15. Karen is trying to gradually be able to lift 100 pounds. What is Karen doing?

16. Betty was so angry with her boyfriend that she put the telephone receiver down without saying good-bye. What did Betty do to her boyfriend?

EXERCISE 9e, Review — Complete the sentences with these phrasal verbs from previous sections. Be sure the phrasal verbs are in the correct tense. To check their meanings, review the section number given after each one.

burn out, 8	find out, 5	pick out, 8	ring up, 8
cheat on, 4	hand back, 5	pile up, 5	run into, 1
fall over, 8	hear of, 8	point to, 4	tear down, 8
fight back, 8	look at, 5	put to, 4	work in, 8

1. Who is he? I've never _____ _____ him before, and I don't know anything about him.

2. My mail _____ _____ while I was on vacation.

3. Thanks for all your help. I'm sorry to _____ you _____ so much trouble.

4. That dead tree is rotten. I'm surprised it hasn't _____ _____ yet.

5. I _____ _____ several cars last weekend, but I can't decide which one to buy.

6. Can you help me _____ a tie _____ to wear with this shirt?

7. What a surprise! I _____ _____ my fifth grade teacher at the mall today.

8. Charles _____ _____ a beautiful Mercedes-Benz across the street and said it was his.

9. Okay, class, you've got until the bell rings. When you're finished with your tests, _____ them _____ to me.

10. Everyone in town knows that Jake has been _____ _____ his wife for years.

11. I'm not sure if there will be time to meet with you today, but I'll try to _____ it

    _____.

12. The invasion was so sudden that there was no way to _____ _____.

13. The cashier _____ _____ our stuff and said, "That comes to $142.56."

14. Bob's not in a good mood today. He just _____ _____ that he

    needs surgery.

15. It was fun to visit my hometown, but I was sad to see that my old house was being

    _____ _____.

16. I need to buy a new 100-watt bulb; this one _____ _____ yesterday.

10. FOCUS ON: **phrasal verbs used as nouns, 1**

Many two-word phrasal verbs can be used as nouns. All the verbs in this section have a noun form. Notice that the two-word noun is sometimes written with a hyphen:

> verb: **go ahead**   noun: **go-ahead**

and sometimes as one word:

> verb: **lay off**   noun: **layoff**

Unfortunately, there is no rule that will help you to always know which form to use. Also, not everyone agrees which nouns should be hyphenated and which should be written as one word, so you will occasionally see a noun written both ways.

Infinitive			
present tense	**-ing form**	**past tense**	**past participle**
fall off			
fall off & falls off	**falling off**	**fell off**	**fallen off**

1. fall off *p.v.* When people or things drop to a lower level from a higher place, they **fall off** the place where they were.

> The dish **fell off** the table and broke.
> Be careful you don't **fall off** your bicycle.

2. fall off *p.v.* When the quality, degree, or frequency of something decreases, it **falls off**.

> *Sales of fountain pens **fell off** after the ballpoint pen was invented.*
> *The quality of his work has **fallen off** as he has gotten older.*

falloff *n.* A decrease in the quality, degree, or frequency of something is a **falloff**.

> *The chairman was asked to explain the **falloff** in the company's sales.*
> *Egypt experienced a big **falloff** in tourism after several terrorist incidents.*

Infinitive			
present tense	**-ing form**	**past tense**	**past participle**
fill in			
fill in & fills in	**filling in**	**filled in**	**filled in**

1. fill . . . in *p.v.* When you **fill in** a form, you put information in the correct spaces. **Fill out** is the same as **fill in**.

> *Maria **filled in** the job application and gave it to the secretary.*
> *The teacher gave us the quiz and told us to **fill** the blanks **in** with the correct answers.*

filled in *part.adj.* After you write all the information in the correct spaces of a form, the form is **filled in**.

> *Are those forms blank or **filled in**?*
> *This check isn't any good — the amount isn't **filled in**.*

2. fill . . . in *p.v.* When people want or need more information about a plan, situation, or occurrence and you supply that information, you **fill** them **in**.

> *Something interesting happened while you were gone. I'll **fill you in** later.*
> *I fell asleep during the meeting. Can you **fill** me **in**?*

3. fill in (for) *p.v.* When you temporarily do someone else's job, you **fill in** for that person.

> *The regular bartender is on vacation, so Todd is **filling in**.*
> *She's the star of the show. No one can **fill in** for her.*

fill-in *n.* Someone who temporarily does someone else's job is a **fill-in**.

> *Jerry is Ann's **fill-in** while she's on vacation.*
> *The regular driver is in the hospital, and the **fill-in** doesn't know the route.*

go ahead			
go ahead & goes ahead	**going ahead**	**went ahead**	**gone ahead**

1. go ahead (with) *p.v.* When you take an action you have already considered doing, you **go ahead** with the action.

> *I've decided to **go ahead** with my plan to reorganize the company.*
> *After she learned about Jim's drug problem, Raquel **went ahead** with the marriage anyway.*

2. go ahead *p.v.* When you tell people to **go ahead**, you tell them to do something without any further delay or hesitation. If you are in a position of authority and you tell someone to **go ahead** with an action, you give permission for that action.

> *What are you waiting for?* ***Go ahead.***
> *Yes,* ***go ahead*** *and leave work early. It's no problem.*

go-ahead *n.* When you give people permission to perform an action, you give them the **go-ahead**.

> *We approved his plan and gave him the* ***go-ahead.***
> *The Food and Drug Administration gave the pharmaceutical company the* ***go-ahead***
>   *to test the drug on humans.*

Infinitive

	present tense	-ing form	past tense	past participle
grow up	grow up & grows up	growing up	grew up	grown up

1. grow up *p.v.* When you **grow up**, you gradually change from a child to an adult.

> *I* ***grew up*** *on a small farm in North Dakota.*
> ***Growing up*** *without a father wasn't easy.*

grown-up *part.adj.* *[informal — used primarily by children]* When children behave in a mature way, they are **grown-up**. Something that relates to adults, and not children, is **grown-up**.

> *Susie is only eleven, but she acts very* ***grown-up.***
> *Timmy doesn't like* ***grown-up*** *books because they don't have any pictures.*

grown-up *n.* *[informal — used primarily by children]* A **grown-up** is an adult.

> *There were children and* ***grown-ups*** *at the party.*
> *Only* ***grown-ups*** *are allowed to sit in the front seat of the car.*

2. grow up *p.v.* When you tell people to **grow up**, you are saying that their behavior is childish and immature.

> *You're acting like a baby. Why don't you* ***grow up****!*
> *When he put his fist through the wall, I said, "Oh,* ***grow up****!"*

hand out

hand out & hands out	handing out	handed out	handed out

1. hand ... out *p.v.* When you distribute something to other people, you **hand** it **out**. **Give out** is similar to **hand out**.

> *The teacher* ***handed*** *the tests* ***out*** *to the class.*
> *Emergency loan applications were* ***handed out*** *to the flood victims.*

handout *n.* Something given free to people in need to help them is a **handout**.

Handouts of food and clothing were given to the homeless people.
Even though my father was poor, he was too proud to ask for a handout.

handout *n.* Printed material given to students or other people to provide them with important information.

The teacher prepared a handout for his students.
There are several handouts on a table by the library entrance.

Infinitive

	present tense	-ing form	past tense	past participle
kick back	kick back & kicks back	kicking back	kicked back	kicked back

1. kick back (to) *p.v.* When you **kick back** money or **kick back** money to businesspeople or government officials, you illegally and secretly give them a percentage of the money that they spend with your company as a reward for giving you the business.

The prosecutor said that 5 percent of every contract was kicked back to the head of the purchasing department.
She offered to kick back 10 percent if I'd switch to her company.

kickback *n.* Money you illegally and secretly give to businesspeople or government officials as a reward for giving you business is a **kickback**.

The FBI agent heard the governor asking for a kickback.
The reporter discovered that the loan was really a kickback.

2. kick back *p.v.* [informal] When you **kick back**, you relax.

It's been a tough week. Tonight I'm going to buy a case of beer and kick back.
Let's kick back and watch the football game tonight.

lay off	lay off & lays off	laying off	laid off	laid off

1. lay ... off *p.v.* When a company no longer needs workers because it does not have enough business, it temporarily or permanently **lays off** the workers.

Ford laid off 20,000 workers during the last recession.
My wife had to go back to work after I was laid off from my job.

layoff *n.* Jobs cut by a company because it does not have enough business are **layoffs**.

The company said there wouldn't be any layoffs, despite the decline in profits.

2. lay off *p.v.* [informal] When you **lay off** people, you stop criticizing, teasing, or pressuring them.

You've been bugging me all day. If you don't lay off, you're going to be sorry.
Lay off Nancy — she's having a bad day.

3. lay off *p.v.* When you **lay off** something, such as a food or an activity, you stop consuming the food, or doing the activity.

> *Listen to the way you're coughing. You've got to **lay off** cigarettes.*
> *After Ned had a heart attack, he **laid off** cheese and butter sandwiches.*

Infinitive			
present tense	-ing form	past tense	past participle
screw up			
screw up & screws up	screwing up	screwed up	screwed up

1. screw ... up *p.v. [informal]* When you damage something or do something wrong or badly, you **screw up** or you **screw up** what you are doing.

> *I tried to fix my computer, but I couldn't do it, and I just **screwed** it **up** instead.*
> *Mark sent his wife a letter that he wrote to his girlfriend. He sure **screwed up**.*

screwed up *part.adj.* When people or things are **screwed up**, they are damaged or confused.

> *My back is so **screwed up** I can't even walk.*
> *George was a nice guy, but a little **screwed up** in the head.*

screwup *n.* A problem or confused situation caused by someone's mistake is a **screwup**.

> *Two babies were switched because of a **screwup** in the maternity ward.*
> *There was a **screwup** in the finance department, and the bill was paid twice.*

2. screw ... up *p.v. informal]* When people make a mistake that causes a problem for you, they **screw** you **up**.

> *The travel agent forgot to reconfirm my flight, and it really **screwed** me **up**.*
> *You really **screwed** me **up** when you lost my car keys.*

EXERCISE 10a — **Complete the sentences with phrasal verbs from this section. Be sure the phrasal verbs are in the correct tense.**

1. The teacher asked me to _____ the exams _____.

2. Why don't you let a mechanic fix the car? If you try to do it yourself, you'll just _____

   it _____.

3. Nobody likes the new priest in our church, and attendance has _____ _____.

4. My feet were killing me a couple of weeks ago, so I _____ _____ jogging for

   a while, and now they're fine.

5. It really _____ me _____ when you told my boss what I said about him.

6. The Ortegas won't take a vacation this year because Mr. Ortega has been _____ _____ and they need to save money.

7. When Mother was _____ _____, there wasn't any TV. People went to the movies or read instead.

8. The head of purchasing at my company went to jail because he made all the suppliers _____ _____ $2,000 of every contract.

9. My husband told me my plan to enter medical school was crazy, but I _____ _____ with it anyway.

10. The secretary in the human resources department said, "Here's an application. Take it and _____ it _____."

11. If you want to borrow my car tonight, _____ _____. I'm not going anywhere.

12. The other mountain climbers are nervous about Jim because they think he's going to _____ _____ a cliff.

13. You've been criticizing me for the last three hours! Will you _____ _____!

14. The manager asked his assistant to _____ him _____ about the problems in the warehouse.

15. It's Friday night. Let's buy some beer and _____ _____.

16. I can't work tomorrow. Can you _____ _____ for me?

17. You're acting like a big baby. _____ _____!

EXERCISE 10b — **Complete the sentences with nouns from this section.**

1. At the party, the children ate in the living room, and the _____ ate in the dining room.

2. The boss said, "One more _____ and you're fired."

3. The reporter discovered that the mayor was taking _____ from the construction company.

4. Every year at this time the king gives _____ to the poor.

5. Ned will be my _____ while I'm on my honeymoon.

6. The teacher prepared a _____ to give to the students.

7. The CEO said he regretted the _____ but that there was no other way for the

company to avoid bankruptcy.

8. The team lost every game of the season and suffered a 60 percent _____ in

attendance.

9. The president called General Chambers and gave him the _____ for the attack.

EXERCISE 10c — **Write three sentences using the objects in parentheses. Be sure to put the objects in the right place.**

1. You haven't *filled in*. (all the spaces, them)

_____

_____

_____

2. Is the teacher *handing out*? (the tests, them)

_____

_____

_____

3. The company is going to *lay off*. (my brother, him)

_____

_____

_____

4. I'm sorry I *screwed up*. (your plan, it)

_____

_____

_____

10

EXERCISE 10d — **Write answers to the questions using phrasal verbs, participle adjectives, and nouns from this section. Be sure the phrasal verbs are in the correct tense.**

1. I wasn't sure if my plan would work, and I thought about it for a long time before I finally decided to try it. What did I do with my plan?

2. The secretary gave me an application and told me to put the correct information in the spaces. What did the secretary tell me to do?

3. In Question 2, how would you describe the application after I put the correct information in the spaces?

4. The mechanic is trying to fix my car's transmission, but she's making a lot of mistakes. What is the mechanic doing to my car's transmission?

5. In Question 4, how would you describe the transmission after the mechanic finishes fixing it?

6. You give $3,000 to the mayor every month so that he will give your company city business. What do you do every month?

7. In Question 6, what is the $3,000 that you give to the mayor every month?

8. Business is bad at Nancy's company, and they told her that they don't need her anymore. What happened to Nancy?

9. The hotel clerk forgot to call me in the morning to wake me up, and I was late for a very important meeting. What did the hotel clerk do to me?

10. I was born in Hawaii, and I lived there until I was eighteen. What did I do in Hawaii?

11. Sally's parents told her she can't watch a TV show because it's for adults. What did Sally's parents tell her about the TV show?

12. New home construction will decrease if there is a recession. What will new home construction do if there is a recession?

13. In Question 12, if there is a decrease in new home construction, what would it be called?

14. Timmy was teasing Susie all day until his mother told him to stop. What did Timmy's mother tell him to do?

15. Ali is doing Omar's job while Omar is on vacation. What is Ali doing?

16. Blankets and boxes of food will be given to the people whose homes were destroyed by the tornado. What will be done with the blankets and boxes of food?

17. Sarah had to answer the phone while she was watching a movie. After she returned to the TV room, Sarah's friend Sally told Sarah everything she had missed. What did Sally do for Sarah?

EXERCISE 10e, Review — **Complete the sentences with these nouns from previous sections. To check their meanings, review the section number given after each one.**

breakdown, 5	holdup, 7	put-on, 1	takeoff, 1
breakout, 9	hookup, 9	setup, 5	

1. The pilot said that the _____ would be on time.

2. There was a _____ on the highway, and traffic was barely moving at all.

3. A cable _____ is usually $39.95, but this month it's free.

4. The guards suspected the prisoners were planning a _____.

5. Waiter, we've been waiting for our dinner for an hour. What's the _____?

6. I told my lawyer that it was a _____ and that I was innocent.

7. When the detectives came and arrested Hank, we didn't think it was real — just a big

_____.

EXERCISE 10f, Review — **Complete the sentences with these phrasal verbs from previous sections. Be sure the phrasal verbs are in the correct tense. To check their meanings, review the section number given after each one.**

catch up, 9	get along, 9	hook up, 9	talk down to, 3
chicken out, 9	give up, 9	pick out, 8	work up, 9

1. Don't try to run ten miles at first; you have to _____ _____ to it.

2. After searching for three days without any luck, the rescue team _____

_____ on finding any survivors.

3. The police showed me some pictures to see if I could _____ _____ the guy

who mugged me.

4. You go to the bank, I'll go to the post office, and we'll _____ _____ with each other at the corner in forty-five minutes.

5. I wasn't happy about having Nancy for a partner on the project. I don't _____ _____ with her.

6. Just because you went to college and I didn't, doesn't make it okay for you to _____ _____ _____ me.

7. The teacher said, "Your daughter has missed a lot of school, and she'll need to work hard to _____ _____ to the rest of the class."

8. Maria got scared and _____ _____ of jumping off the high diving board.

---

11. FOCUS ON: **phrasal verbs used in compound nouns**

As we saw in Section 10, many two-word phrasal verbs can be used as nouns. Many of these nouns formed from two-word phrasal verbs can be combined with ordinary nouns to form *compound nouns*:

> noun: ***backup***   compound noun: ***backup*** *disk*
> noun: ***follow-up***   compound noun: ***follow-up*** *call*

Like ordinary compound nouns, the first noun has a function similar to that of an adjective:

> question: *What kind of clothes?*
> answer: *Dirty clothes.*
> > *adjective*
> question: *What kind of clothes?*
> answer: *Workout clothes.*
> > *noun*

The adjective *dirty* and the noun *workout* serve the same function: modifying the noun *clothes*.
    Always accent the first word in a compound noun:

> noun: ***BACKup***   compound noun: ***BACKup*** *disk*
> noun: ***FOLLOW-up***   compound noun: ***FOLLOW-up*** *call*

Infinitive

	present tense	-ing form	past tense	past participle
back up				
	back up & backs up	backing up	backed up	backed up

1. back . . . up *p.v.* When you walk backward, you **back up**. When you drive a vehicle in reverse, you **back up** or **back** the vehicle **up**.

> *The fire was so hot that we had to **back up**.*
> *I put the car in reverse and **backed** it **up**.*

2. back up *p.v.* When you are explaining something, and you repeat something that you already said, you **back up**.

> *You're going too fast. Can you **back up** a little and explain your plan again?*
> *Sorry, I forgot part of the story. Let me **back up** a little.*

3. back . . . up *p.v.* When you make a claim or statement and then show people evidence or give them information proving that the claim or statement is true or correct, you **back** it **up**.

> *No one believed Jim's accusations because he couldn't **back** them **up** with*
>   *any evidence.*
> *The IRS asked me for some receipts to **back up** my deductions.*

4. back . . . up *p.v.* When you support people in a conflict or a confrontation, you **back** them **up**. When you support people by doing some work or a difficult assignment, you **back** them **up**.

> *Linda said she would **back** me **up** if I complained about our supervisor.*
> *The general **backed up** his threats with 400,000 soldiers.*
> *Jerry is the bar's main bartender, and Tanya **backs** him **up** when it gets busy.*

backup *n.* Someone or something that supports or is ready to provide support in a conflict or a confrontation by doing some work or a difficult assignment is a **backup**.

> *When the rioters grew more violent, the police called for **backup**.*
> *The firefighter entered the burning building without a **backup**.*

5. back . . . up *p.v.* When you duplicate important information, such as a computer program or data, so that you will still have it if the original information is lost or damaged, you **back** it **up**.

> *If you're going to install that new software, be sure you **back up** your entire hard*
>   *disk first.*
> *I **back** my work **up** every day before I go home.*

backup *n.* A duplicate of important information, such as a computer program or data, is a **backup.**

> *I keep a **backup** of my important computer files on floppy disks.*
> *The major gave a **backup** copy of the battle plan to his secretary.*

backed up *part.adj.* After you duplicate important information, such as a computer program or data, the original is **backed up**.

> *I accidentally erased your book from your computer. I hope your work was*
> ***backed up****.*

6. back ... up *p.v.* When a piece of equipment or machinery is very important and another is kept available in case the one that is normally used fails, the second piece of equipment or machinery **backs up** the first.

> *The hospital bought a generator to **back up** the unreliable city power supply.*
> *We kept the old computer to **back** the new one **up**.*

backup *n.* When a piece of equipment or machinery is very important and another is kept available in case the one that is normally used fails, the second piece of equipment or machinery is a **backup**.

> *The skydiver checked his main parachute and his **backup** before the flight.*
> *The school had to close when the main power and the **backup** both failed.*

7. back ... up *p.v.* When something **backs up**, it is being prevented from moving, progressing, or flowing normally.

> *An accident **backed up** traffic for three miles.*
> *The assembly line is going to **back up** if Erik doesn't get the parts he needs soon.*

backup *n.* A **backup** is a situation in which something is being prevented from moving, progressing, or flowing normally.

> *I sat in that **backup** for three hours without moving an inch.*
> *The huge number of Christmas cards and packages caused a **backup** at the*
> *post office.*

backed up *part.adj.* When something is being prevented from moving, progressing, or flowing normally, it is **backed up**.

> *Let's take the train downtown. Traffic is always **backed up** at this time of*
> *the morning.*

Infinitive

	present tense	-ing form	past tense	past participle
cut off				
	cut off & cuts off	cutting off	cut off	cut off

1. cut ... off *p.v.* When you completely remove part of something with a knife, saw, or pair of scissors, you **cut** it **off**.

> *He **cut off** a piece of cheese so that I could taste it.*
> *One of the kings of England had his head **cut off**.*

2. cut ... off *p.v.* When you stop the supply or flow of something, such as water, electricity, or money, you **cut** it **off** or you **cut off** the people receiving it.

> *I won't be surprised if my electricity is **cut off** — I haven't paid the bill in three months.*
> *The bartender told the drunk guy that she was **cutting** him **off**.*

cutoff *n.* The time when something, such as water, electricity, or money, is **cut off** is the **cutoff**, **cutoff** point, or **cutoff** date.

> I got a notice saying that if I don't pay my water bill soon, the **cutoff** date
>   will be March 10.
> Ninety is the **cutoff** — students with lower scores on the exam won't be accepted
>   into the advanced program.

3. cut ... off *p.v.* When you abruptly and rudely drive a vehicle in front of other people's vehicles, causing them to suddenly slow down or stop, you **cut** them **off**.

> I had to slam on the brakes when some jerk **cut** me **off** on the way to work.
> The lady in the red car tried to **cut** me **off**, but I wouldn't let her get in front of me.

4. cut ... off *p.v.* When someone is **cut off** while speaking on the telephone, the connection is accidentally broken.

> I was in the middle of an important call when I was **cut off**.
> Getting **cut off** happens all the time when you're on the phone to China.

5. cut ... off *p.v.* When you create a physical or psychological barrier between yourself and other people, you **cut** yourself **off** from them. When you are separated from other people because of a barrier or a great distance, you are **cut off** from them.

> After Dan joined a cult, he completely **cut** himself **off** from his family and friends.
> A flash flood **cut** us **off** from the rest of the expedition.

cut off *part.adj.* When you are separated from other people because of a barrier or a great distance, you are **cutoff**.

> The bridge was destroyed by the earthquake, and now we're **cut off.**

Infinitive

	present tense	-ing form	past tense	past participle
drop off				
	drop off & drops off	dropping off	dropped off	dropped off

1. drop ... off *p.v.* When you take things or people to another place and leave them there, you **drop** them **off**.

> Can you **drop** me **off** at the train station on your way to work?
> Luis **dropped off** his laundry at the cleaners.

drop-off *n.* Something that has been **dropped off** is a **drop-off**. The place where something or someone is **dropped off** is a **drop-off** point, **drop off** window, and so on.

> Luis left his laundry at the **drop-off** window.
> The north side of the train station parking lot is for **drop-offs**.

2. drop off *p.v.* When a business's sales, the occurrence of some event, or the interest some people have in something declines, it **drops off**.

> Attendance at baseball games has been **dropping off** in the last few years.
> After CDs were introduced, sales of records **dropped off** sharply.

drop-off *n.* A decline in a business's sales, in the occurrence of an event, or in **the** interest some people have in something, is a **drop-off.**

> There has been a **drop-off** in traffic deaths thanks to strict drunk driving laws.
> The **drop-off** in car sales was explained by the recession.

3. drop off *p.v.* When the level of the ground declines steeply, it **drops off.**

> Be careful hiking this trail. It **drops off** steeply on the other side of the mountain.
> The island has no beach at all. The land **drops off** straight into the sea.

drop-off *n.* A steep decline in the level of the ground is a **drop-off.**

> The bus driver didn't see the **drop-off**, and the bus plunged into the gorge.
> It was hard to see the **drop-off** because of the dense jungle.

Infinitive

present tense	-ing form	past tense	past participle
follow up			
follow up & follows up	following up	followed up	followed up

1. follow up (on) *p.v.* When you **follow up** on something, you return to something that was important to you previously because you now have more information or more time or because you want to make sure some effort you made previously is correct or effective.

> I saw a beautiful house with a "for sale" sign and I **followed up** on it when I got home.
> The doctor told me I'd need to **follow up** the treatment with physical therapy.

follow-up *n.* A **follow-up**, **follow-up** call, **follow-up** visit, and so on, is a return to something that was important to you previously because you now have more information or more time or because you want to make sure some effort you made previously is correct or effective.

> The customer service manager made a **follow-up** call to make sure I was happy with the repair job.
> The doctor asked me to see him two months after the operation for a **follow-up.**

take out

take out & takes out	taking out	took out	taken out

1. take ... out (of) *p.v.* When you **take** something **out** or **take** it **out** of a container, storage place, or building, you remove it. **Put in/into** is the opposite of **take out.**

> I want to **take** some books **out** of the library tonight.
> Jake **took out** a gun and shouted, "This is a holdup!"
> Nancy **took** $500 **out** of the bank.

takeout *n.* **Takeout** is food that is taken from a restaurant to be eaten at another location. **Carryout** and **carry-out** food are the same as **takeout** and **take-out** food.

> I don't feel like cooking tonight. Let's get **takeout.**
> That **take-out** chicken is good, but it sure is greasy.

2. take ... out (of) *p.v.* When you remove something because you do not want it or because it is damaged, you **take** it **out** or **take** it **out** of something. **Put in/into** is the opposite of **take out**.

> The teacher said my story would be a lot better if I **took** this part **out** of the third paragraph.
> The school will be closed while the asbestos insulation is being **taken out** and replaced.

3. take ... out (of) *p.v.* When you **take** money **out** or **take** money **out** of a bank or a bank account, you withdraw the money. **Put in** is the opposite of **take out**.

> I had to **take** money **out** of my savings account to pay for my medical bills.
> Nicole's at the bank **taking** $1,000 **out**.

4. take ... out *p.v.* When you **take** people **out**, you go with them to do something enjoyable — dinner in a restaurant, a movie, and so on — and pay for it yourself.

> What do you think about **taking** Mom **out** for Mother's Day?
> Jim **took** his girlfriend **out** last Friday.

5. take ... out *p.v.* [informal] When you **take** people **out**, you kill them.

> The snipers will try to **take out** the kidnapper when he opens the door.
> The hit man **took** Vito **out** with a shotgun blast to the head.

Infinitive

	present tense	-ing form	past tense	past participle
try out	try out & tries out	trying out	tried out	tried out

1. try ... out *p.v.* When you **try** something **out**, you try it to see if you want to buy it or to see if you want to start using it regularly.

> I'm not going to spend $2,000 on a bicycle unless I **try** it **out** first.
> You can **try** it **out** for thirty days without any obligation.

tryout *n.* When you give something a **tryout**, you test it to see if you want to buy it or start using it regularly.

> I gave Betty's new diet a **tryout**, but I actually gained weight.
> The airline gave the new plane a thorough **tryout** before making a decision.

2. try ... out *p.v.* When you **try** people **out**, you give them a chance to show that they can perform a job well before hiring them or before giving them more difficult work to do.

> The manager agreed to **try** him **out** for a week.
> I told the supervisor that if she **tried** me **out**, she'd see that I could do the job.

tryout *n.* When you give people a **tryout**, you give them a chance to show that they can perform a job well before giving them more difficult work to do.

> **Tryouts** for the football team will be next Saturday and Sunday.
> If you give Mike a **tryout**, I'm sure you won't be disappointed.

3. try out (for) *p.v.* When you **try out** or **try out** for something, you try to show that you can perform a job well in order to get hired.

> A lot of guys will **try out**, but only a handful will make the team.
> Daniela's mother told her, "**Trying out** for the cheerleading squad isn't as important as doing your homework."

Infinitive

present tense	-ing form	past tense	past participle
wake up			
wake up & wakes up	waking up	woke up	woken up

1. wake ... up *p.v.* When you stop sleeping, you **wake up**. When you cause other people to stop sleeping, you **wake** them **up**.

> Ali is so sleepy in class that the teacher must **wake** him **up** every five minutes.
> I **woke up** at 2:00 A.M. and couldn't get back to sleep.

wake-up *part.adj.* When you are staying at a hotel and you ask the desk clerk to call you at a certain time to **wake** you **up**, you ask for a **wake-up** call.

> I asked the desk clerk to give me a **wake-up** call at 7:30.

2. wake ... up *p.v.* When you learn something that causes you to understand the truth about something or someone, it **wakes** you **up** or **wakes** you **up** to the truth about something or someone.

> I used to smoke, but when my best friend died of lung cancer, it really **woke** me **up**.
> Hey, **wake up**! Nicole is lying to you. Can't you see that?

work out			
work out & works out	working out	worked out	worked out

1. work out *p.v.* When a situation **works out** a certain way, it happens that way. When a situation does not **work out**, it is not satisfactory.

> The switch to the new system **worked out** a lot better than anyone expected.
> She said that living with her in-laws wasn't **working out** very well.

2. work out *p.v.* When a situation **works out**, the end result is successful.

> Yes, I thought your idea was terrible, but I must admit it **worked out**.
> The marriage didn't **work out**, and they were divorced after six months.

3. work out *p.v.* When a calculation or measurement **works out** to be a certain amount, this amount is the result of the calculation or measurement.

> The cost of the booze we need for the reception **works out** to more than $1,500.
> The monthly payment on a 6 percent loan **works out** to $642.

4. work ... out *p.v.* When you **work out** a calculation, measurement, or other problem, you do the work necessary to determine the result of the calculation or measurement or think about how to solve the problem.

*Maria **worked out** how much paint we will need for the living room —
    twenty-five gallons.*
*I've forgotten how to **work out** math problems without a calculator.*
*You need to go to the airport, I need to go to work, and we have only one car. How are
    we going to **work** this **out**?*

5. work out *p.v.* When you **work out** a solution or plan, you decide what to do after
careful consideration, either alone or in discussion with other people.

*The opposing lawyers **worked out** a compromise.*
*I think I've **worked out** a way to buy a new car without borrowing money.*

6. work out *p.v.* When you exercise in order to improve your health or physical
appearance, you **work out**.

*Bob **works out** in the gym for two hours every night.*
*I'm a fat slob. I need to start **working out** again.*

workout *n.* A series of exercises done in order to improve your health or physical
appearance is a **workout**. **Workout** clothes are clothes you wear while exercising.

*I'm really sore from that **workout** last night.*
*The trainer designed a **workout** for each player on the team.*

workout *n.* When you say that you gave a mechanical device or system a **workout**,
you mean that you caused it to perform some lengthy or difficult work.

*Driving to Alaska sure gave this old truck a **workout**.*
*The snack bar got a real **workout** when three buses full of hungry tourists stopped
    at the same time.*

EXERCISE 11a — **Complete the sentences with phrasal verbs from this section.
Be sure the phrasal verbs are in the correct tense.**

1. I almost had an accident on the way to work when another driver_____ me

    _____.

2. With so many delivery truck drivers out sick with the flu, deliveries are starting to

    _____ _____.

3. You should always _____ _____ your important computer files.

4. The art restorers are trying to _____ _____ a way to clean the painting

    without damaging it.

5. I hit a tree while I was _____ my car _____.

6. The butcher has only nine fingers. He _____ the other one _____.

7. Professor Childress has some interesting theories, but can he _____ them _____ with any evidence?

8. After every sale, a good salesperson _____ _____ with a call to make sure the customer is satisfied.

9. I'm going to leave early tomorrow so that I can _____ some film _____ at the photo lab.

10. No one believed I was telling the truth until Charles _____ me _____.

11. I usually _____ _____ around 7:00, but this morning I overslept.

12. Lydia had planned to spend the summer in Italy, but it didn't _____ _____.

13. The sharpshooter was ordered to _____ _____ the enemy leader.

14. The designers put in manual controls to _____ _____ the automatic system.

15. David and Maria _____ _____ how much their wedding is going to cost.

16. The cost of their wedding _____ _____ to $225 per person.

17. Be careful — the north side of the mountain _____ _____ sharply.

18. Hello? Hello? The phone is dead; I guess we were _____ _____.

19. Next weekend we're _____ Mom and Dad _____ for their fiftieth wedding anniversary.

20. The professor's lecture was really confusing, so I asked him to please _____ _____ and explain it again.

21. The bank robbers tried to escape through the back door, but the police went to the back of the bank and _____ them _____.

22. People's fascination with the quintuplets _____ _____ quickly after the sextuplets were born.

23. Bob bought some new skis, and this weekend he's going to _____ them _____.

24. I wasn't very responsible when I was younger, but having children really _____ me _____.

25. Ned used to exercise every day, but he hasn't _____ _____ in months.

26. The baseball manager decided to _____ _____ the new pitcher to see what he could do.

27. I like most of this article you wrote about me, but there's one thing I'd like you to _____ _____.

28. Sam had a lot of big ideas when he was young, but his life sure hasn't _____ _____ the way he expected.

29. The electricity was _____ _____ after a tree fell during the storm and cut some power lines.

30. I _____ my ID card _____ of my pocket and showed it to the guard.

31. Lydia has never _____ a penny _____ of her savings account.

EXERCISE 11b — **Write three sentences using the objects in parentheses. Be sure to put the objects in the right place.**

1. Did you *back up*? (your work, it)

_____

_____

_____

2. They're *cutting off*. (the power, it)

_____

_____

_____

3. I *dropped off* at the airport. (Frank, him)

_____

_____

_____

4. Mom asked me to *take out*. (the garbage, it)

_____

_____

_____

5. Alex *tried out*. (his new bicycle, it)

_____

_____

_____

6. Mike has *woken up*. (Ali, him)

_____

_____

_____

EXERCISE 11c — Write answers to the questions using nouns and compound nouns from this section. There may be more than one way to answer a question.

1. The photographer always keeps two cameras with him. One is his main camera. He'll use the second if there's a problem with the first. What is the second camera?

2. The phone company says my telephone service will stop on July 1 if I don't pay my bill before that date. What is July 1?

3. Dr. Smith is a new doctor. If he's not sure how to treat a patient, he'll call Dr. Wood for help. What is Dr. Wood to Dr. Smith?

4. You used the new exercise equipment to see if you wanted to buy it. What did you do to the exercise equipment?

5. The police arrested Mrs. Taylor's husband because he was beating her. A social worker visited Mrs. Taylor a few days later to talk to her. What did the social worker do?

6. The clothes I wore yesterday while I was exercising got very dirty. What got dirty?

7. We got food from a Chinese restaurant and ate it at home. What kind of food did we eat?

8. Because of construction, traffic on the interstate stopped and there was a long line of cars. What was on the interstate?

9. The number of arrests for burglary is a lot lower this year than last year. What has happened to the number of arrests for burglary?

10. Sally lost something very important on her computer because she didn't make another copy in case there was a problem with the original. Why did Sally have a problem?

11. At the edge of the continental shelf, the sea floor falls several thousand feet. What is at the edge of the continental shelf?

12. I made 7,000 copies on this photocopier. What did I do to the photocopier?

EXERCISE 11d — Write answers to the questions using phrasal verbs and nouns from this section. Be sure the phrasal verbs are in the correct tense.

1. The electric company stopped my electricity because I didn't pay my bill. What did they do to the electricity?

2. I bought some fried chicken, and I took it to my house. What kind of food did I buy?

3. Exercising is good for your health. What is good for your health?

4. The long-distance company offered to let me use their service free for thirty days, and I'm going to try it. What am I going to do to the long-distance company's service?

5. In Question 4, what is the long-distance company letting me do?

6. During the flood, a lot of people couldn't leave their houses because of the water. What did the water do to them?

7. In Question 6, how would you describe these people?

8. You're making an extra copy of your work just in case. What are you doing?

9. In Question 8, what would you call the extra copy of your work that you're making?

10. The newspaper reporter is getting more information about something interesting that someone told her on the phone. What is the reporter doing?

11. My exercise routine is very difficult. What is difficult?

12. The prosecutor proved his accusation with some photographs. What did the prosecutor do with the photographs?

13. Jane wants to show the basketball coach that she would be a good member of the basketball team. What does Jane want to do?

14. I have a second alarm clock in case the first doesn't wake me up. What does my second alarm clock do to my first?

15. In Question 14, what would you call my second alarm clock?

16. Nicole takes her friend to the train station every morning. What does Nicole do to her friend?

17. I have an appointment with my doctor next month so that he can see if my surgery was successful. What would you call my appointment next month?

18. Maria's plan isn't happening the way she expected. What isn't Maria's plan doing?

19. Bill went with Judy to dinner and a movie and he paid for everything. What did Bill do?

20. Two hundred guests at $45 each calculates to $9,000. What does 200 guests at $45 each do?

21. I have never stopped sleeping at 3:30 in the morning before. What have I never done before?

EXERCISE 11e, Review — **Complete the sentences with these phrasal verbs from previous sections. Be sure the phrasal verbs are in the correct tense. To check their meanings, review the section number given after each one.**

come from, 1	give back, 1	hand out, 10	look for, 1
fall off, 10	go ahead, 10	hear about, 2	screw out of, 3
feel up to, 3	go along with, 3	kick back, 10	screw up, 10
fill in, 10	grow up, 10	lay off, 10	stay off, 2

1. If the company doesn't _____ _____ 20 percent of its employees, it's going to go out of business.

2. Blankets and boxes of food were _____ _____ to the flood victims.

3. I _____ _____ in Germany because my father was in the Army there.

4. Kathy didn't close her car window last night, and it rained. She really _____ _____.

5. You _____ _____; I'll catch up with you later.

6. The percentage of people who smoke _____ _____ after smoking was linked with lung cancer and heart disease.

7. What can I do to get my black cat to _____ _____ my white couch?

8. I've been _____ _____ an apartment that allows dogs, but I can't find one.

9. He's _____ _____ New York and will be here in two hours.

THE ULTIMATE PHRASAL VERB BOOK

12

past perfect phrasal verbs

10. I was so stuffed from that huge dinner my mother cooked that I didn't _____ _____ _____ playing tennis afterward.

11. Their lawyer tried to _____ them _____ _____ $120,000.

12. I don't feel like going anywhere tonight. Let's just _____ _____ and take it easy.

13. I'm sorry I can't agree with you, Joe, but I have to _____ _____ _____ Linda on this decision.

14. Here's my flashlight. Make sure you _____ it _____ when you're finished using it.

15. I didn't get 100 on the test because I forgot to _____ _____ one of the blanks.

16. This restaurant is wonderful. I'm surprised I haven't _____ _____ it before.

---

12. FOCUS ON: **past perfect phrasal verbs**

The *past perfect* is used to say that one thing in the past happened before another thing in the past:

> Mike **said** the wedding **had fallen through**.
> past   earlier in the past
> When I **got** to work, Mr. Taylor **had** already **signed in**.
> past   earlier in the past

The *past perfect* is formed with *had* and the *past participle* of the verb:

present: *He **wakes up**.*
past: *He **woke up**.*
past perfect: *He **had woken up**.*

Infinitive

	present tense	-ing form	past tense	past participle
back off				
	back off & backs off	backing off	backed off	backed off

1. back off *p.v.* When you move away from danger or a person you are arguing or fighting with in order to avoid injury or a more serious fight or argument, you **back off**. When you tell people to **back off**, you are warning them that you are becoming angry and that a fight or argument is likely.

*I'm warning you! You'd better **back off**.*
*Tom **backed off** when he saw that Jake had a gun.*

Infinitive

present tense	-ing form	past tense	past participle
come across			
come across & comes across	**coming across**	**came across**	**come across**

1. come across *p.v.* When people cross from one side of a space or distance to where you are, they **come across**.

> *As soon as Nicole saw me, she **came across** the room and gave me a big hug.*
> *By 1910, millions of immigrants had **come across** the ocean to America.*

2. come across *p.v.* When you **come across** people or things, you see or find them without planning or expecting to. **Run across** is similar to **come across**.

> *I asked the antique dealer if she had ever **come across** a Windsor chair.*
> *On the trail, we **came across** some hikers from Australia.*

3. come across *p.v.* When something you say or do **comes across** a certain way, your attitude or feelings are perceived in this way by other people.

> *I was just joking, but I don't think it **came across** that way.*
> *His American humor didn't **come across** well in Britain.*

come up			
come up & comes up	**coming up**	**came up**	**come up**

1. come up (to) *p.v.* When people move toward you to a higher level or position, or from the south to the north, they **come up**. **Come down** is the opposite of **come up**.

> *Why don't you **come up** and see me some time?*
> *My cousin from San Antonio **came up** to Detroit last week.*

2. come up *p.v.* When you move to a higher social or professional position, you **come up**.

> *I saw Dan driving a Mercedes. He's really **coming up** in the world.*
> *The major didn't go to the military academy. He **came up** through the ranks.*

3. come up *p.v.* When a new topic is introduced into a conversation, it **comes up**.

> *I don't agree with Jim about anything, so if politics **comes up**, I just leave the room.*
> *We were discussing possible candidates to manage the new office, and your name*
> *   **came up**.*

4. come up *p.v.* When something unexpected happens that requires further attention, it **comes up**.

> *I'm sorry I can't go to your party; something important has **come up**.*
> *Until this situation **came up**, we were having a nice, relaxing weekend.*

5. come up *p.v.* [always continuous] When something is **coming up**, it will happen soon.

*Mother's Day is **coming up**, so I need to buy my mother a gift soon.*

*The TV announcer told the audience what was **coming up** after the commercial.*

Infinitive

present tense	-ing form	past tense	past participle
fall through			
fall through & falls through	**falling through**	**fell through**	**fallen through**

1. fall through *p.v.* When people or things drop through an opening from one side to the other side, they **fall through**.

*The roofer had **fallen through** a hole in the roof.*

*My Uncle Fred was ice fishing when he **fell through** a hole in the ice and was never seen again.*

2. fall through *p.v.* When a plan, an arrangement, or a business deal does not happen or is canceled because of a problem or because someone does not do what is expected, it **falls through**.

*The family reunion **fell through** after Dad got sick.*

*Our house is back on the market. The deal **fell through** because the buyers couldn't get a loan.*

put up

put up & puts up	putting up	put up	put up

1. put . . . up *p.v.* When you move something to a higher level, you **put** it **up**.

***Put** these knives **up** where the baby can't reach them.*

*He aimed the gun at me and said, "**Put** your hands **up** or I'll shoot."*

2. put . . . up *p.v.* When you attach something, such as a picture or a sign, to a wall, you **put** it **up**.

*The teacher had **put** some posters **up** in her new classroom.*

*Our real estate agent is **putting up** a "for sale" sign.*

3. put . . . up *p.v.* When you build or install something, such as a building, shelf, fence, or wall, you **put** it **up**.

*We need to **put up** a fence to keep the rabbits out of our garden.*

*I talked to a carpenter about **putting up** some shelves in the family room.*

4. put . . . up *p.v.* When you erect or assemble something that is collapsed, folded, or in several pieces, you **put** it **up**.

*The circus **put up** their tent outside of town.*

*The Native Americans stopped by the river and **put up** their teepees.*

5. put up *p.v.* When you contribute money to pay for or help pay for something, you **put up** the money.

*The mayor offered to **put up** half the money necessary to build a new stadium for the team.*

*Mr. Taylor said he would **put up** $3 million toward the cost of a new cancer treatment facility.*

6. put up *p.v.* When you fight, resist, or argue against something, you **put up** a fight or **put up** resistance.

*The union **put up** a fight when the company tried to lay off workers.*
*The Japanese **put up** little resistance when the marines landed.*

7. put ... up *p.v.* When you **put** people **up**, you let them stay with you, usually temporarily, in your house or in a hotel.

*Sam didn't have anywhere else to go after the fire, so I said I would **put** him **up** for a couple of nights.*
*The hotel desk clerk apologized for not being able to **put** us **up**.*

Infinitive

	present tense	-ing form	past tense	past participle
screw on				
	screw on & screws on	screwing on	screwed on	screwed on

1. screw ... on *p.v.* When you **screw on** the top of a circular container, you turn it so that it becomes tight and keeps the contents of the container inside.

*I hadn't **screwed** the top of the gas can **on** tight enough, and all the gas leaked out.*
*If you don't **screw** the top of the bottle **on**, the soda pop will go flat.*

screwed on *part.adj.* After you turn the top of a circular container so that it becomes tight and keeps the contents of the container inside, the top is **screwed on**.

2. screw ... on *p.v.* When you attach part of a mechanical device with spiral grooves to another part with spiral grooves, you **screw** it **on**.

*Make sure you **screw** each of the nuts **on** tightly.*
*Put the new ink cartridge in the bottom half of the pen and then **screw on** the top.*

screwed on *part.adj.* After you attach part of a mechanical device with spiral grooves to another part with spiral grooves, the first part is **screwed on**.

*The top of that water bottle isn't **screwed on**, and it might leak all over the place.*

sign in				
	sign in & signs in	signing in	signed in	signed in

1. sign ... in *p.v.* When you **sign in**, you write your name on a list to show that you have arrived at your workplace or at some other place, such as a hotel or a club.

*I'm going to be late. Could you **sign** me **in**?*
*All visitors to the consulate are asked to **sign in**.*

Infinitive

present tense	-ing form	past tense	past participle
sign out			
sign out & signs out	signing out	signed out	signed out

1. sign ... out *p.v.* When you **sign out**, you write your name on a list to show that you have left your workplace or some other place, such as a hotel or club.

Jim isn't here. He **signed out** at 5:06.
Dr. Wood usually forgets to **sign out** when she leaves the clinic.

2. sign ... out *p.v.* When you **sign** something **out**, such as a book or something valuable or important, you write your name on a list to show that you have borrowed the item and are responsible for returning it.

The professor **signed** the book **out** of the rare book room.
Remember to **sign out** your lab equipment before chemistry class.

EXERCISE 12a — **Complete the sentences with phrasal verbs from this section. Be sure the phrasal verbs are in the correct tense.**

1. The information in this file is top secret. You have to _____ it _____ before

   you can remove it from this room.

2. Something _____ _____ at the last minute, and I had to cancel my trip.

3. We'd better _____ _____ the tent before it gets too dark.

4. I was in the library, and I _____ _____ some interesting books.

5. I was sure Janice was still in the building somewhere because she hadn't _____

   _____ yet.

6. The wedding _____ _____ when the groom was arrested for bigamy.

7. My son always _____ _____ a big fight when I try to get him to go to bed.

8. I wasn't in the mood for a fight, so I decided to _____ _____.

9. The search party found that the snowmobiler had _____ _____ a hole in

   the ice and drowned.

10. No one said anything about you last night. Your name didn't _____ _____

    even once.

11. The store owner _____ _____ a "no smoking" sign.

12. To attach the filter to the camera lens, you just _____ it _____.

13. The manager always checked to see who didn't _____ _____ on time.

14. The charity was asked to _____ _____ $2 million toward the purchase of

new medical equipment.

15. Someone had _____ the lid _____ so tightly that I couldn't get it off.

16. My house was destroyed by a tornado. Can you _____ me _____ for a few days?

17. I was upstairs working when my wife _____ _____ to ask me what I wanted

for lunch.

18. The applicant's criticism of his previous employer didn't _____ _____ well

with the interviewer.

19. I bought a plastic Christmas tree that's really easy to _____ _____.

20. Nancy _____ _____ the Golden Gate Bridge every morning to go to work.

21. I didn't go to a fancy Ivy League college. I _____ _____ the hard way.

22. Can you _____ the window shade _____ so that we can get more light in

here, please?

23. Susie's mother told her that Christmas was _____ _____, so she had better

be a good girl.

> EXERCISE 12b — **Write answers to the questions using phrasal verbs and
> participle adjectives from this section. Make all the phrasal verbs past perfect.**

1. Mike told me that Jerry had been angry and was going to hit Bill, but that Jerry had then

   changed his mind and walked away. What had Jerry done?

2. Luis had written his name on a piece of paper to show that he had come to work. What had

   Luis done?

3. The carpenter had dropped suddenly from the second floor to the first floor through a hole in

   the floor. What had the carpenter done?

4. Timmy had argued with his mother because he didn't want to go to bed. What had

   Timmy done?

5. Todd's explanation made a good impression on the jury. What had Todd's explanation done?

6. The rich lady had given the money to build an animal shelter. What had the rich lady done?

7. The host of the TV talk show had said that the dancing bear act was going to take place right after the commercial. What had the host of the TV show said about the dancing bear act?

8. The cook had turned the lid of the jar so that it was tight. What had the cook done?

9. In Question 8, how would you describe the lid of the jar after the cook turned it so that it was tight?

10. The homeless shelter had allowed them to sleep there overnight. What had the homeless shelter done?

11. The president canceled his vacation because a serious problem had suddenly occurred. Why did the president cancel his vacation?

12. We'd had a deal to buy a new house, but we didn't buy it because of a problem. What had happened to our deal?

13. Marsha's name had been mentioned during the meeting. What had Marsha's name done?

14. The Ortegas had built a fence around their swimming pool. What had the Ortegas done?

15. You had found some old newspapers while cleaning the attic. What had you done?

16. Miguel had traveled from Miami to New York. What had Miguel done?

17. The doctor had written her name on a piece of paper to show that she had left the hospital. What had the doctor done?

EXERCISE 12c — **Write eight original sentences using phrasal verbs from this section. Try to make some of them questions, some negative, and some present or past perfect.**

1. _____

2. _____

3. _____

4. _____

5. _____

6. _____

7. _____

8. _____

12

EXERCISE 12d, Review — **Complete the sentences with these phrasal verbs from previous sections. Be sure the phrasal verbs are in the correct tense. To check their meanings, review the section number given after each one.**

back up, 11	follow up, 11	point to, 4	try out, 11
cut off, 11	go after, 4	put to, 4	wake up, 11
drop off, 11	pay for, 4	take out, 11	work out, 11
fall off, 10	plan for, 4	throw up, 2	wrap up, 4

1. I don't care if it takes me the rest of my life, you'll _____ _____ the terrible thing you did!

2. The salesman got a good lead from a friend, and he _____ _____ on it immediately.

3. We need to take the baby to the doctor right now. She's _____ _____ twice in the last hour.

4. Sales have _____ _____ by 13 percent in the last year.

5. That was a very interesting question you _____ _____ Mark at the meeting.

6. Relax, everything's going to _____ _____ okay.

7. Can you follow me in your car so that I can _____ my car _____ at the mechanic?

8. Erik _____ his son _____ and told him it was time for school.

9. I drove into the mountains to _____ my truck's four-wheel drive _____.

10. You should always _____ _____ anything important before you install a new program.

11. The police officer asked the boy where his father was, and the boy _____ _____ the bar across the street.

12. It's getting pretty late. Let's _____ this meeting _____.

13. The guy behind the counter _____ _____ a small piece of cheese so I could taste it.

14. It was a bit of a problem when Jane brought her children with her to my dinner party. I hadn't _____ _____ so many people.

15. The censor told the film director to _____ _____ some of the violent scenes.

16. Jane's going to _____ _____ that new job in the Boston office.

13. FOCUS ON: passive phrasal verbs, 1

The *passive voice* is used when what happened (the verb) is more important than who did it (the subject):

> *The scene of the crime was **closed off** by the police.*

when the subject is obvious:

> *The tests were **handed in**.* (by the students — who else?)

or when the subject is unknown:

> *My dog was **run over**.* (by an unknown person)

The passive is formed with *be* and the past participle of the verb. *Be* can be in any tense and can be continuous:

> *The game <u>has been</u> **called off**.*
> *My name <u>was</u> **left off**.*
> *The tent <u>is being</u> **set up**.*
> *The criminals <u>will be</u> **tracked down**.*

As we saw in the first three examples, saying who performed the action with a *by* phrase is optional, but it is always possible. This is a good way to test a sentence to see if it is in the passive:

> *The game has been **called off** <u>by the referee</u>.*
> *My name was **left off** <u>by Charles</u>.*
> *The tent is being **set up** <u>by the campers</u>.*
> *The criminals will be **tracked down** <u>by the police</u>.*

Infinitive

	present tense	-ing form	past tense	past participle
call off				
	call off & calls off	calling off	called off	called off

1. call ... off *p.v.* When you **call off** an event, such as a party, game, or something else that had been previously planned, you cancel it.

> *The football game was **called off** because of rain.*
> *We can't **call** the party **off** — it's going to start in half an hour.*

close off				
	close off & closes off	closing off	closed off	closed off

1. close ... off *p.v.* When you **close off** an area, you prohibit people from entering it or passing through it by locking the door or blocking the entrance.

> *The police **closed** several streets **off** because of the parade.*
> *The house was so expensive to heat that the owners **closed** several rooms **off**.*

13

closed off *part.adj.* An area that you are prohibited from entering or passing through because the door has been locked or the entrance has been blocked is **closed off**.

> *Three rooms in the museum are **closed off**.*

Infinitive			
present tense	-ing form	past tense	past participle
hand in			
hand in & hands in	handing in	handed in	handed in

1. hand ... in (to) *p.v.* When you complete a test, report, or project and you give it to the person who assigned the work, you **hand** it **in** or **hand** it **in** to that person. **Turn in** is similar to **hand in**.

> *The tests must be **handed in** no later than 11:00.*
> *He finished his investigation and **handed** his report **in** to the committee.*

2. hand ... in *p.v.* When you **hand in** your resignation or letter of resignation, you inform your employer that you are quitting your job.

> *I was so furious that I **handed** my letter of resignation **in** the next day.*
> *The President asked the cabinet members to **hand in** their resignations.*

3. hand ... in (to) *p.v.* When you give something to a person of authority who has demanded it or because you no longer need or want it, you **hand** it **in** or **hand** it **in** to a person of authority. **Turn in** is similar to **hand in**.

> *The guard was ordered to **hand** his gun **in** after he shot the window washer.*
> *The drivers return to the factory at 5:00 and **hand** their keys **in** to the dispatcher before they leave.*

hit on			
hit on & hits on	hitting on	hit on	hit on

1. hit on *p.v.* When you think of an interesting idea or a solution to a problem, you **hit on** it.

> *I think I've **hit on** a way to solve this problem.*
> *After two years of tests, they finally **hit on** the solution.*

2. hit on *p.v.* [informal] When you **hit on** a person of the opposite sex, you approach and aggressively try to interest that person in you romantically or sexually.

> *Lydia had a terrible time at the party. She was **hit on** by every guy there.*
> *Let's go somewhere else — Mark keeps **hitting on** me, and I'm tired of it.*

leave off			
leave off & leaves off	leaving off	left off	left off

1. leave ... off *p.v.* When you do not include people or things on a list, either accidentally or deliberately, you **leave** them **off**.

> *After what happened at the last party, Dan wasn't surprised that he was **left off** the guest list.*
> *Check to make sure you don't **leave** anyone **off** the list.*

2. leave off *p.v.* When you interrupt something that you intend to finish later, you **leave off** at the point where you stop.

> Okay class, we **left off** on page 92 last week, so open your books to page 93.
> Finish your story, Uncle Fred. You **left off** where the giant octopus was about to eat you.

Infinitive

	present tense	-ing form	past tense	past participle
let off	let off & lets off	letting off	let off	let off

1. let ... off *p.v.* When you **let** someone **off** a bus or other form of transportation, you stop it so that person can leave it.

> The driver **let** her **off** at the corner.
> That's my house there. Can you **let** me **off** please?

2. let ... off *p.v.* When you are **let off** by a person in authority, you are not punished or you are given only a light punishment.

> It was Jake's first offense, so the judge **let** him **off** with a warning.
> People were shocked that he had been **let off** so lightly.

3. let ... off *p.v.* When you fire a gun or explode bombs or fireworks, you **let** them **off**. (regional) When you **let off** steam, you express angry feelings or frustration or do something to relieve those feelings.

> The high school was evacuated after someone **let off** a smoke bomb.
> When I was a kid I used to love **letting off** firecrackers on the Fourth of July.
> I'm sorry I was so angry this morning; I was just **letting off** steam.

light up				
	light up & lights up	lighting up	lit up	lit up

1. light ... up *p.v.* When you shine lights on something or attach lights to something, you **light** it **up**.

> Airport runways are **lit up** so that pilots can see them in the dark.
> The police **lit** the house **up** with their spotlights.

lit up *part.adj.* After a light is shined on something or you put lights inside or attach lights to the outside of something, it is **lit up**.

> The signs aren't **lit up**, so it's hard to see them at night.

2. light ... up *p.v.* When you **light up** a cigarette, cigar, or pipe, you use a match or lighter to start it burning.

> Here are the matches — let's **light up**.
> **Lighting** a cigarette **up** next to the gasoline truck was the last thing he ever did.

Infinitive

present tense	-ing form	past tense	past participle
track down			
track down & tracks down	tracking down	tracked down	tracked down

1. track . . . down *p.v.* When you find things or people after looking very hard for them, you **track** them **down**.

*The terrorists were **tracked down** by Interpol.*
*I finally **tracked down** that book I've been looking for.*

EXERCISE 13a — **Complete the sentences with phrasal verbs from this section. Be sure the phrasal verbs are in the correct tense.**

1. The judge _____ her _____ with a warning.

2. It wasn't cold enough, so we _____ _____ the hockey game.

3. As soon as Nancy's boyfriend went to the washroom, the guy at the next table _____ _____ her.

4. Every Christmas my father used to _____ _____ our house with thousands of lights.

5. The police finally _____ the killers _____ and arrested them.

6. The principal caught me as I was _____ _____ a cigarette in the washroom.

7. The room that was damaged by the fire was _____ _____ to the public.

8. I was really angry that I was _____ _____ the list.

9. That's a great idea! You've really _____ _____ something.

10. Three students got a zero because their projects weren't _____ _____ on time.

11. Driver, can you _____ me _____ at the next corner?

12. Dr. Smith resumed his lecture where he had _____ _____ before the lunch break.

13. After Wilson screwed up the finance department, he was asked to _____ _____ his letter of resignation.

14. Even though the enemy soldiers were half a mile away, we _____ _____ a few shots.

15. The crooked police officers were ordered to _____ their badges _____.

EXERCISE 13b — Write three sentences using the objects in parentheses. Be sure to put the objects in the right place.

1. The bride hasn't *called off*. (the wedding, it)

_____

_____

_____

2. Are they *closing off*? (the gallery, it)

_____

_____

_____

3. The accountant *handed in*. (her report, it)

_____

_____

_____

4. Have you *left off*? (Carmen, her)

_____

_____

_____

5. The judge *let off*. (the pickpocket, him)

_____

_____

_____

6. I told him not to *light up*. (the cigarette, it)

_____

_____

_____

7. The EPA *tracked down*. (the polluters, them)

_____

_____

_____

EXERCISE 13c — **Write answers to the questions using phrasal verbs and participle adjectives from this section. Make all the phrasal verbs passive.**

1. He discovered the source of the rumor. What happened to the source of the rumor?

2. The students finished their quizzes and gave them to the teacher. What happened to the quizzes?

3. The judge never sends first-time offenders to jail. What always happens to first-time offenders?

4. A guy started talking to Heather at the dance. What happened to Heather?

5. The list of candidates didn't include your name. What happened to your name?

6. The referee canceled the game. What happened to the game?

7. They are putting ropes around the plaza so that no one can go in. What is happening to the plaza?

8. In Question 7, after they finish putting ropes around the plaza, how would you describe it?

9. The battleship shined lights on the enemy submarine. What happened to the enemy submarine?

10. In Question 9, how would you describe the submarine after the battleship shined lights on it?

EXERCISE 13d, Review — **Complete the sentences with these phrasal verbs from previous sections. To check their meanings, review the section number given after each one.**

burn down, 5	let out, 7	point out, 7	set up, 5
call in, 5	look at, 5	run into, 1	take apart, 7
give back, 1	pile up, 5	run over, 7	take off, 1
hand back, 5	plan for, 4	screw out of, 3	talk down to, 3

1. Most of the city was _____ _____ by the invading soldiers.

2. Teacher, will points be _____ _____ for spelling?

3. Dan is so rude — I have never been _____ _____ _____ like that before.

4. A conference will be _____ _____ between the lawyers for each side.

5. The Taylors were _____ _____ _____ their life savings by their

    stockbroker.

6. The children were happy to be _____ _____ of school early.

7. The entire staff was _____ _____ to the office and given pink slips.

8. Several flaws in the plan were _____ _____.

9. Raquel was almost _____ _____ by a cement truck while she was driving

    to work.

10. There wasn't enough room inside the cabin, so the firewood had to be _____

    _____ outside.

11. The general said the occupied territory would never be _____ _____.

12. The test will be _____ _____ to the students tomorrow.

13. This engine has been _____ _____ three times, but no one can figure out

    what's wrong with it.

14. This is a very important project. Every possible problem must be _____ _____.

15. My neighbor stopped at the side of the road to change a flat tire, and he was _____

    _____ and killed by a drunk driver.

16. Each proposed design for the new flag was _____ _____ and rejected.

14

14. FOCUS ON: **participle adjectives formed from phrasal verbs, 1**

The past participles of many English verbs can also be used as adjectives. You will see that sentences with adjectives formed from past participles are very similar to sentences with verbs in the passive voice: in both cases a form of *be* is used with the past participle. For this reason, it is not always easy to say whether a sentence contains an adjective formed from a past participle or a verb in the passive voice:

>*The door <u>was</u> <u>closed</u>.* (Is this a passive sentence or is *closed* an adjective?)

Sometimes, whether a sentence contains an adjective formed from a past participle or a verb in the passive voice is clear from the sentence structure:

>*The door <u>was</u> <u>closed</u> by the secretary.* (passive)
>*The door <u>was</u> <u>closed</u> when I came home last night.* (adjective)

or the context:

>question: *What happens if the health inspector finds rats in a restaurant?*
>answer: *It's <u>closed</u>.* (passive)
>
>question: *Is the window open?*
>answer: *It's <u>closed</u>.* (adjective)

But in some cases it is not possible to say absolutely whether a sentence contains an adjective formed from a past participle or a verb in the passive voice. Fortunately, it is usually not very important because the meaning is often essentially the same. For that reason, throughout this book true adjectives formed from past participles and past participles functioning as adjectives are both classified as *participle adjectives*.

Much more important than the difference between adjectives formed from past participles and past participles functioning as adjectives is what the words mean.

Some participle adjectives are written with a hyphen (*make-up*), some without a hyphen (*fixed up*), and some as one word (*rundown*). Because not everyone agrees which participle adjectives should be hyphenated, which should not, and which should be written as one word, you will occasionally see the same participle adjective written with or without a hyphen or written as one word. Also, British English hyphenates many participle adjectives that are not normally hyphenated in American English; many of the participle adjectives shown unhyphenated in this book are hyphenated in British English.

Infinitive

	present tense	-ing form	past tense	past participle
butt in				
	butt in & butts in	butting in	butt in	butt in

1. butt in *p.v.* When you enter a conversation, situation, or place (especially a line) aggressively, rudely, and without invitation, you **butt in**.

> *I was trying to talk to Jim at the party, but Bob kept **butting in**.*
> *My father taught me that it's not polite to **butt in** line; you have to go to the back and wait your turn.*

dress up				
	dress up & dresses up	dressing up	dressed up	dressed up

1. dress ... up *p.v.* When you **dress up**, you wear very nice clothes, often for a special occasion. When you **dress** people **up**, you put very nice clothes on them, often for a special occasion.

> *You should always **dress up** for a job interview.*
> *The Taylors **dressed** their children **up** so they could take some pictures.*

dressed up *part.adj.* When you are **dressed up**, you are wearing very nice clothes, often for a special occasion.

> *Where are Tom and Nancy going? They're all **dressed up**.*
> *I felt like an idiot at the party — everyone was really **dressed up** except me.*

2. dress up (like/as) *p.v.* When people wear old-fashioned clothes or costumes, they **dress up**, **dress up** like someone, or **dress up** as someone.

> *Did you see Charles at the Halloween party? He **dressed up** like a cowboy.*
> *At Jane's costume party, everyone has to **dress up** as a clown.*

dry up				
	dry up & dries up	drying up	dried up	dried up

1. dry ... up *p.v.* When something **dries up** or something **dries** it **up**, all the water or other liquid in it goes away.

> *The sun came out and **dried up** all the rain.*
> *The Great Salt Lake is slowly **drying up**.*

dried up *part.adj.* After all water or other liquid in something goes away, it is **dried up**.

> *The cowboys reached the river only to find that it was **dried up**.*
> *These leaves will burn okay now that they're **dried up**.*

2. dry up *p.v.* When the amount or supply of something gets smaller and then disappears completely, it **dries up**.

> *The factory switched to synthetic rubber after the supply of natural rubber **dried up**.*
> *The small grocery store's business **dried up** after a huge supermarket opened across the street.*

Infinitive

	present tense	-ing form	past tense	past participle
fill out				
	fill out & fills out	filling out	filled out	filled out

1. fill ... out *p.v.* When you **fill out** a form, you put information in the correct spaces. **Fill in** is the same as **fill out**.

> The personnel director asked Sofia to **fill out** an application.
> **Fill** the withdrawal slip **out** and give it to the teller.

filled out *part.adj.* After all the information is in the correct spaces of a form, the form is **filled out**.

> Here's my application; it's all **filled out**.
> Are these forms blank or **filled out**?

2. fill ... out *p.v.* When slender people gain weight, they **fill out**.

> Jake was really thin when he got out of prison, but he has really **filled out** since then.
> Nicole started to **fill out** after she started working at the candy shop.

put away				
	put away & puts away	putting away	put away	put away

1. put ... away *p.v.* When you return something to the place where it is usually stored while it is not being used, you **put** it **away**.

> I told you to **put away** your toys before you go outside.
> Todd always dries the dishes, and I **put** them **away**.

put away *part.adj.* If something is in the place where it is usually stored while it is not being used, it is **put away**.

> Where is my tool kit? I looked in the closet, and it's not **put away**.
> The dishes are **put away**. Now let's watch TV.

2. put ... away *p.v.* When people are **put away**, they are sent to prison or a mental institution.

> I hope they **put** that maniac **away** and throw away the key.
> Jake was **put away** for ten years after he was convicted of murder.

3. put ... away *p.v.* [informal] When you consume large quantities of food or drink (especially alcoholic drink), you **put** it **away**.

> Be sure to buy plenty of beer if David is coming to the party. He can really **put** it **away**.
> I don't feel well. I **put away** four hot dogs and a bag of cookies.

stick up				
	stick up & sticks up	sticking up	stuck up	stuck up

1. stick ... up *p.v.* When you use a gun or other weapon to rob people, banks, or stores, you **stick** them **up**. **Hold up** is the same as **stick up**.

*Call the police! They're **sticking up** the bank.*
*If we need some money, we can always **stick up** a liquor store.*

stickup *n.* When someone uses a gun or other weapon to rob a person, bank, or store, there is a **stickup**. A **holdup** is the same as a **stickup**.

*A man wearing a ski mask yelled, "This is a **stickup!**"*
*The detective was asking questions about the **stickup** last night.*

2. stick ... up *p.v.* When you put something, such as a picture, sign, or notice, in a place where people can see it, you **stick** it **up**.

*Sam **stuck** a notice **up** about his lost dog.*
*I'm going to **stick** these "no smoking" signs **up** all over the school.*

3. stick ... up *p.v.* When you push something inside a container or space that is long and narrow, you **stick** it **up**.

*We had to take Susie to the emergency room after she **stuck** a paper clip **up** her nose.*
*Mark **stuck** his hand **up** the chimney to try to find the hidden key.*

4. stick up *p.v.* When something long and narrow is raised above the surface, it **sticks up**.

*Be careful walking around a construction site — there might be a nail **sticking up**.*
*My hair was **sticking up** in the back after I woke up from my nap.*

stuck-up *part.adj.* [informal — although the participle adjective **stuck-up** derives from **stick up**, the verb form is never used in this sense] When you think you are better than other people because you are more beautiful or more intelligent or because you come from a higher level of society, you are **stuck-up**.

*Heather is the most popular girl in the school, but she isn't **stuck-up**.*
*They're so **stuck-up** — they'll never sit at our table.*

Infinitive

	present tense	-ing form	past tense	past participle
use up				
	use up & uses up	using up	used up	used up

1. use ... up *p.v.* When you **use up** something, you use all of it.

*After you **use** something **up**, be sure to write it on the grocery list.*
*I **used up** all the glue; we need to buy more.*

used up *part.adj.* After all of something has been used, it is **used up**.

Do we have another tube of toothpaste in the house? This one's **used up**.

wind up				
	wind up & winds up	winding up	wound up	wound up

1. wind ... up *p.v.* When you turn the handle or key of a mechanical toy, watch, or clock to make it operate, you **wind** it **up**.

*I overslept because I forgot to **wind up** my alarm clock.*
*This toy doesn't use batteries; you have to **wind** it **up**.*

wound up *part.adj.* After someone turns the handle or key of a mechanical toy, watch, or clock, it is **wound up**.

*The toy soldier is **wound up**. Just push the button to make it walk.*
*What is wrong with this watch? It's **wound up**, but it still doesn't work.*

wound up *part.adj.* When you are nervous or tense, you are **wound up**.

*Don't even talk to Joe today. He's really **wound up**.*
*I'm feeling really **wound up** — I need a drink.*

2. wind up *p.v.* When you say that someone or something **winds up** a certain way or **winds up** doing something, you mean that this situation was the result of a series of decisions, actions, or unplanned and unexpected occurrences. **End up** is similar to **wind up**.

*We got totally lost and **wound up** 100 miles from the campground.*
*If you don't start driving more carefully, you're going to **wind up** dead.*

3. wind ... up *p.v.* When you **wind up** an activity or event, you finish it or get ready to finish it. **Wrap up** is similar to **wind up**.

*The detective **wound up** her investigation and made several arrests.*
*We'd better **wind** things **up** here; it's getting late.*

4. wind ... up *p.v.* When you wrap something long, such as an electrical cord, rope, string, or measuring tape, around and around so that it is in a ball or on a spool, you **wind** it **up**.

*That's enough fishing for today. Let's **wind up** our lines and go home.*
*The firefighters **wound up** their fire hoses and went back to the station.*

wound up *part.adj.* When you wrap something long, such as an electrical cord, rope, or measuring tape, around and around so that it is in a ball or on a spool, it is **wound up**.

*This rope is a mess. You should keep it **wound up**.*
*This electrical cord is really **wound up** tight.*

EXERCISE 14a — **Complete the sentences with phrasal verbs from this section. Be sure the phrasal verbs are in the correct tense.**

1. We couldn't decide where to go, so we _____ _____ staying home.

2. Be sure you _____ this form _____ carefully.

3. My son loves to eat. He can _____ _____ an extra large pizza in less

than fifteen minutes.

4. I'll _____ this notice _____ on the wall.

5. We're going out to a nice restaurant tonight, so be sure to _____ _____ .

6. Business at the ski shop always _____ _____ in summer.

7. When you're finished with your Monopoly game, _____ it _____ .

8. Congress is _____ _____ some unfinished business before the summer recess.

9. The firefighter _____ her hand _____ the drain pipe to try to reach the kitten.

10. The meeting's almost over —they're _____ it _____ now.

11. Janice went to the costume party _____ _____ like Marie Antoinette.

12. The desert is so hot that rainwater _____ _____ almost immediately.

13. I don't know what time it is. I forgot to _____ my clock _____ .

14. Be careful when you sail your boat in this shallow water. Sometimes logs _____ _____ from the bottom.

15. Lydia has _____ _____ a little since she had the baby.

16. Aunt Kathy finished knitting the sweater and _____ _____ her knitting needles.

17. Frank and Jesse James _____ _____ a bank in Northfield, Minnesota, in 1876.

18. I hope they catch those crooks and _____ them _____ for a long time.

19. I _____ all my time _____ on the first half of the test and didn't have any time left for the second half.

20. My brother is so rude! Whenever I try to talk to my friend Karen, he _____ _____ and won't let me talk.

EXERCISE 14b — **Complete the sentences with participle adjectives from this section.**

1. I hope it rains soon. Our lawn is really _____ _____ .

2. Why are you _____ _____ ? Are you going to a party?

3. Some of these forms are blank and others are _____ _____ .

4. All the people who live in that neighborhood think they're better than everyone else in town. They're so _____ _____ .

5. I can't use my printer. The toner cartridge is _____ _____, and I need to buy a new one.

6. The clock isn't working because it isn't _____ _____.

7. Timmy, are your toys all over the floor where they were last night, or are they _____

_____?

EXERCISE 14c — **Write three sentences using the objects in parentheses. Be sure to put the objects in the right place.**

1. Janice *dressed up*. (her son, him)

_____

_____

_____

2. The sun quickly *dries up*. (the water, it)

_____

_____

_____

3. *Filling out* isn't necessary. (the entire form, it)

_____

_____

_____

4. Ed *put away* in an hour. (six beers, them)

_____

_____

_____

5. They *stuck up*. (notices, them)

_____

_____

_____

6. I'm *winding up*. (my clock, it)

_____

_____

_____

EXERCISE 14d — **Write answers to the questions using phrasal verbs and participle adjectives from this section. Be sure the phrasal verbs are in the correct tense.**

1. Jake was riding his motorcycle too fast and not being careful. Now he is in the hospital with a broken leg. What happened to Jake?

2. It was hard talking to my mother because my sister kept rudely interrupting our conversation. What did my sister keep doing?

3. A lot of rain fell and made a small lake in the field. Now, after a week, the water is not there anymore. What happened to the water?

4. Alex was playing with his toy trains. Now they are in the box where he keeps them when he is not playing with them. What did Alex do?

5. In Question 4, how would you describe Alex's toys?

6. It rained three hours ago, but now there is no more water in the streets. How would you describe the streets?

7. I turned the key in this grandfather clock, and now it is working. What did I do to the clock?

8. In Question 7, how would you describe the clock?

9. Daniela put on her best clothes for the dance. What did Daniela do?

10. In Question 9, how would you describe Daniela?

11. Luis wrote all the necessary information on the form. What did Luis do?

12. In Question 11, how would you describe the form?

EXERCISE 14e, Review — **Complete the sentences with these participle adjectives from previous sections. To check their meanings, review the section number given after each one.**

backed up, 11	cut off, 11	hooked up, 9	screwed up, 10
broken-down, 5	cut up, 7	hung up, 9	set up, 5
burned-out, 8	filled in, 10	paid for, 4	wake-up, 11
caught up, 9	grown-up, 10	piled up, 5	worked up, 9

1. The clothes are _____ _____ in the closet.

2. I don't owe any money to the bank for my house. It's _____ _____.

3. My VCR is connected to my TV. My VCR is _____ _____.

4. We live far out in the country away from town, our friends, and our families. I don't like

   being so _____ _____.

5. My car's _____, so I have to take the bus to work.

6. All the plans and arrangements for our vacation are ready; everything is _____ ____.

7. All the spaces in this form have the necessary information in them. The form is

   _____ _____.

8. Nancy's four-year-old son was playing with her computer, and now it's all _____ ____.

9. I was sick and missed several homework assignments in school. But I worked hard and finished

   all the homework I missed, and now I'm _____ _____.

10. I'm very nervous and upset about something. I'm_____ _____.

11. These videotapes aren't for children — they're _____ videotapes.

12. Timmy's mother used a knife to cut his meat into many small pieces. Timmy's meat is

    _____ _____.

13. I'm tired all the time, I hate my job, and I need a vacation. I'm _____.

14. My computer crashed last night, but fortunately all my important files are

    _____ _____.

15. The hotel forgot my _____ call, and I missed my plane.

16. The magazines are _____ _____ in a big stack.

15. FOCUS ON: **phrasal verbs and *will* or *be going to***

Both *will* and *be going to* are used to talk about the future in English, but they are not the same.

Predictions: *will* or *be going to*

Use *will* or *be going to* for <u>predictions</u>. When you predict the future, you say what you think will happen:

> *The wind <u>will</u> **blow away** these paper plates.*
> *The wind <u>is going to</u> **blow away** these paper plates.*

Willingness: *will*

Use only *will* for <u>willingness</u>. When you offer to do something that you do not have to do, you are willing to do it:

> *I <u>will</u> **put up** the shelves for you.*

Plans: *be going to*

Use only *be going to* for <u>plans</u>. When you decide to do something in the future, whether it is long and complicated or short and simple, you plan to do it:

> *He <u>is going to</u> **head for** Mexico next week.*

The future with *will* is formed by using *will* plus the infinitive form of the verb:

> statements: *He <u>will</u> **come through** San Francisco.*
> question: *<u>Will</u> he **come through** San Francisco?*
> negative: *He <u>will</u> **not come through** San Francisco.*

These contractions are used with *will*:

I will	=	*I'll*
you will	=	*you'll*
he will	=	*he'll*
she will	=	*she'll*
it will	=	*it'll*
they will	=	*they'll*
will not	=	*won't*

When two contractions are possible, it is more common to contract *will* with *not* rather than with a pronoun:

> common: *He <u>won't</u> **come through** San Francisco.*
> uncommon: *He'<u>ll</u> <u>not</u> **come through** San Francisco.*

The future with *be going to* is formed with a form of *be* plus *going to* plus the infinitive form of the verb:

> statement: *He <u>is going to</u> **head for** Mexico next week.*
> question: *<u>Is</u> he <u>going to</u> **head for** Mexico next week?*
> negative: *He <u>is</u> <u>not going to</u> **head for** Mexico next week.*

These contractions are used with *be going to*:

I am	=	*I'm*
you are	=	*you're*
he is	=	*he's*
she is	=	*she's*
it is	=	*it's*
they are	=	*they're*
are not	=	*aren't*
is not	=	*isn't*

When two contractions are possible, both are equally common:

common: *He's <u>not going to</u> **head for** Mexico next week.*
common: *He <u>isn't going to</u> **head for** Mexico next week.*

In informal spoken English, *going to* is often pronounced *gonna*. It is not necessary to pronounce *going to* in this way, but it is necessary to understand it.

Infinitive			
present tense	**-ing form**	**past tense**	**past participle**
blow away			
blow away & blows away	**blowing away**	**blew away**	**blown away**

1. blow ... away *p.v.* When the wind moves something away from where it was, it **blows** it **away**.

> *Don't leave the newspaper outside. The wind will **blow** it **away**.*
> *The picnic wasn't much fun. It was really windy, and everything kept **blowing away**.*

2. blow ... away *p.v.* [informal] When a person or company has an ability, product, or service that is much better than that of a competing person or company, it **blows away** the competing person or company.

> *Apple's new computer is so fast it's going to **blow away** the competition.*
> *I thought I had a chance to win the race, but Erik just **blew** me **away**.*

3. blow ... away *p.v.* [informal] When something you have seen or heard makes you very shocked, amazed, or emotional, it **blows** you **away**.

> *The first time I saw the Pyramids, they just **blew** me **away**.*
> *I was **blown away** when my mother told me that I was adopted.*

come through			
come through & comes through	**coming through**	**came through**	**come through**

1. come through *p.v.* When you are in a place and people or things **come through** it, they pass from one side to the other side where you are.

> *Betty **came through** the door and sat down at our table.*
> *The soldiers were **coming through** the hole in the wall.*

2. come through *p.v.* When people travel to your town, stay for a while, and then leave, they **come through** or **come through** town.

> *Aunt Sally promised she'd **come through** Milwaukee on her way to Indianapolis.*

3. come through *p.v.* When important information, authorization, or permission that you have been waiting for is received, it **comes through**.

> *We can buy the house — the loan finally **came through**.*
> *The execution was stopped when the call from the governor **came through**.*

4. come through (with) *p.v.* When you promise to do something or produce something and keep your promise, you **come through** or **come through** with what you promised to do or promised to produce.

> *We were all surprised when Bob **came through** with front row tickets just like*
>   *he said he would.*
> *The state legislature promised to provide the financing for a new stadium,*
>   *but they didn't **come through**.*

5. come through *p.v.* When you **come through** a difficult or dangerous experience, you survive it.

> *My Uncle Fred saw lots of action during the war, but he **came through** without*
>   *a scratch.*
> ***Coming through** the earthquake alive was a miracle.*

6. come through *p.v.* When someone's feelings, attitudes, or opinions can be perceived by someone else, they **come through**.

> *The author's hatred of the dictatorship **came through** in the novel.*
> *The professor's enthusiasm for the subject really **comes through** in his lectures.*

Infinitive

	present tense	-ing form	past tense	past participle
dry out	dry out & dries out	drying out	dried out	dried out

1. dry ... out *p.v.* When something **dries out** or something **dries** it **out**, all the water or other liquid in it goes away.

> *Before you put this tent away, be sure you **dry** it **out**.*
> *After the flood, it took weeks for our house to **dry out**.*

dried out *part.adj.* After all the water or other liquid in something goes away, it is **dried out**.

> *My skin always gets **dried out** in the winter.*
> *We shampooed our carpet a week ago, and it's still not **dried out**.*

fix up	fix up & fixes up	fixing up	fixed up	fixed up

1. fix ... up *p.v.* When you **fix up** a place, such as a building, street, or park, you repair and decorate it.

*I am going to **fix** this place **up** and try to sell it.*
*The city decided to **fix up** the park.*

fixed up *part.adj.* After you repair and decorate a place, such as a building, street, or park, it is **fixed up**.

*Now that his house is **fixed up**, it looks pretty nice.*
*When you see how **fixed up** Jim's apartment is now, you'll be surprised.*

fixer-upper *n. [informal]* A **fixer-upper** is a building in poor condition that can be repaired, renovated, or redecorated in order to increase its value.

*The way to make money in real estate is to buy a **fixer-upper** and do as much of the work yourself as you can.*

2. fix . . . up *p.v.* When you **fix** yourself **up**, you style your hair nicely and put on make-up and nice clothes.

If you're going to that fancy restaurant, you'd better fix yourself up.
*Heather is upstairs **fixing** herself **up** for the prom.*

fixed up *part.adj.* After you style your hair nicely and put on make-up and nice clothes, you are **fixed up**.

*Where's Lydia going? She's all **fixed up**.*
*I got all **fixed up**, and my boyfriend took me to a demolition derby.*

3. fix . . . up (with) *p.v.* When you **fix** people **up** with something, you arrange for them to have or to use something that they need or want.

*We told the hotel desk clerk that we wanted their best room, and she **fixed** us **up** with the honeymoon suite.*
*The travel agent **fixed** me **up** with a limo to take me to the resort.*

4. fix . . . up (with) *p.v. [informal]* When you **fix** people **up** or **fix** them **up** with someone, you arrange a date for them with a member of the opposite sex.

*Linda and Tom are perfect for each other. I'm going to **fix** them **up**.*
*I asked Jerry if he'd **fix** me **up** with his sister.*

Infinitive

	present tense	-ing form	past tense	past participle
go with	go with & goes with	going with	went with	gone with

1. go with *p.v.* When one thing is usually or always found with another, they **go with** each other.

*A lot of responsibility **goes with** being a doctor.*
*I never wanted to own an old house because of all the maintenance that **goes with** it.*

2. go with *p.v.* When two things are part of one unit or set or are meant to be with each other, they **go with** each other.

One of the fringe benefits of that job was the car that went with it.
You can't buy the cup without the saucer that goes with it.

3. go with *p.v.* When one item of clothing looks nice with another, they **go with** each other.

She needs to find a blouse that goes with her new skirt.
I like white shirts because they go with everything.

4. go with *p.v.* When you **go with** people, you agree with and support their idea or plan.

Senator Dolittle has no opinions. He just goes with the majority.
We've decided to go with the committee's recommendation.

5. go with *p.v.* When you choose someone or something from a group, you **go with** your choice.

That gray suit was nice, but I think I'm going to go with the black one.
Everyone who applied for the job is highly qualified. I don't know who I'm going to go with.

Infinitive

	present tense	-ing form	past tense	past participle
head back	head back & heads back	heading back	headed back	headed back

1. head back (to) *p.v.* When you **head back** or **head back** to a certain location, you return to a place where you were before. When you are **headed back** or are **heading back** to a certain location, you are returning to a place where you were before.

We'll spend a month in California and then head back to Des Moines.
We got to the beach around 10:00, and we headed back when it started to get dark.

head for	head for & heads for	heading for	headed for	headed for

1. head for *p.v.* When you **head for** a certain location, you move toward it. When you are **headed for** or are **heading for** a certain location, you are planning to go there or you have stopped and will resume going there. **Head toward** is the same as **head for**.

Tomorrow we're going to leave Des Moines and head for California.
I told the guy at the gas station I was headed for Santa Fe.

2. head for *p.v.* When you are **headed for** or are **heading for** a certain situation, condition, or consequence, it is becoming more likely.

If you don't shut your mouth you're headed for trouble.
This is going to be a great vacation — we're heading for a good time!

Infinitive

	present tense	-ing form	past tense	past participle
tell on	tell on & tells on	telling on	told on	told on

1. tell on *p.v.* [*informal — used primarily by children*] When you **tell on** people, you inform someone in authority, such as a parent or teacher, that they have made a mistake or broken a rule.

*I broke a glass. You're not going to **tell on** me, are you?*

*Timmy didn't do his homework, and his sister **told on** him.*

EXERCISE 15a — **Complete the sentences with phrasal verbs from this section. Be sure the phrasal verbs are in the correct tense.**

1. The first time I held my newborn son in my arms it just _____ me _____.

2. I asked Linda if she would _____ me _____ with her friend Nancy.

3. Bob said he could get us backstage after the concert, and he _____ _____ just like he promised.

4. This house is dump now, but after I _____ it _____, it'll look nice.

5. I saw you eating cookies before dinner when Mommy told you not to. I'm going to _____ _____ you.

6. The composer's love for his native land really _____ _____ through in his music.

7. Can you help me? I'm _____ _____ Toronto, but I'm lost.

8. I've never been to the opera before. I think I'd better _____ myself _____.

9. The train _____ _____ town three times a week.

10. If you keep charging stuff like crazy on your credit cards, you're _____ _____ bankruptcy.

11. Do you think these brown pants _____ _____ this blue shirt?

12. All the books damaged in the flood have to be _____ _____.

13. Coke's new sales promotion is going to _____ Pepsi _____.

14. We sat by the phone nervously waiting for the judge's decision to _____ _____.

15. My brother works in a car rental place, and he said he can _____ me _____ with a Mercedes at no extra cost.

16. After looking at pictures of several models, the photographer decided to _____ _____ Nicole.

17. Dr. Wood _____ _____ the door and said hello.

18. All the clothes I left outside to dry were _____ _____ by the storm.

19. My father hated being a salesman because of all the travel that _____ _____ the job.

20. Two of my brothers went to Vietnam, but only one _____ _____ it alive.

21. I asked the clerk in the computer store if the monitor _____ _____ the computer.

22. It's getting late and I'm tired. I think I'm going to _____ _____ to my house

23. His proposal made a lot of sense, so we decided to _____ _____ it.

EXERCISE 15b — **Write answers to the questions using phrasal verbs and participle adjectives from this section. Use *will* or *be going to* with all phrasal verbs.**

1. I asked the restaurant manager for the best table in the house, and he is going to give us a table next to the fireplace. What is the restaurant manager going to do?

2. Linda's father promised to pay for her wedding, and she is sure that he will. What is Linda sure about?

3. Raquel's husband is going to be very surprised when she tells him she won $10 million in the lottery. What is the news going to do to her husband?

4. He'll repair some things in his house and paint it before he puts it on the market. What will he do?

5. In Question 4, how will the house be after he makes some repairs and paints it?

6. Timmy won't tell the teacher that Susie didn't do her homework if she gives him a candy bar. What won't Timmy do?

7. Those mobile homes aren't going to be there after the tornado. What is the tornado going to do?

15

8. If there's an earthquake, no one in this old building will survive. What won't the people do if there's an earthquake?

9. She'll put on her nicest outfit and her best jewelry and get a perm. What will she do?

10. In Question 9, how will she look after she puts on her nicest outfit and her best jewelry and gets a perm?

11. Tomorrow, you're going to leave San Diego and go to Tucson. What are you going to do tomorrow?

12. A month from now, you're going to leave Tucson and return to San Diego. What are you going to do a month from now?

13. Erik said he won't ask his sister if she will go on a date with Mike. What won't Erik do?

14. Lydia is at the paint store to choose a paint color for her house. She hates the color blue. What isn't Lydia going to do?

15. IBM has a new chip that's twice as fast as the competition's fastest chip. What is IBM going to do to the competition?

16. Uncle Fred is going to visit our town, stay for a short time, and then continue on his trip to Florida. What is Uncle Fred going to do?

17. This pond is going to slowly evaporate and disappear. What is the pond going to do?

18. In Question 17, after the pond evaporates, how will it be?

EXERCISE 15c — **Write eight original sentences using phrasal verbs from this section. Try to use *will* and *be going to*.**

1. _____

2. _____

3. _____

4. _____

5. _____

6. _____

7. _____

8. _____

EXERCISE 15d, Review — **Complete the sentences with these phrasal verbs from previous sections. Be sure the phrasal verbs are in the correct tense. To check their meanings, review the section number given after each one.**

back off, 12	come up, 12	leave off, 13	screw on, 12
call off, 13	fall through, 12	let off, 13	sign in, 12
close off, 13	hand in, 13	light up, 13	sign out, 12
come across, 12	hit on, 13	put up, 12	track down, 13

1. Did my ex-husband talk about me at the party? Yes, your name _____

_____ several times.

2. Our vacation plans _____ _____ after Tom broke his leg.

3. I told you not to _____ that cigarette _____ in here.

4. Flying Mom here for the holidays is going to cost $1,000. My brother is going to pay $300, and

I'm going to _____ _____ the rest of the money.

5. So far, the police have been unable to _____ _____ the stolen paintings.

6. The searchlights _____ _____ the night sky, looking for enemy bombers.

7. You can't go in that part of the museum; it's been _____ _____.

8. When you travel, always _____ the tops of your toiletries _____ tightly.

9. We decided to _____ our ski trip _____ because there wasn't enough snow.

10. I was getting really angry, and I told him that I was going to punch him in the nose if he didn't

_____ _____.

11. The teacher told the students to _____ _____ their homework.

12. I didn't agree with that list of the 100 best movies. They _____ some of my favorites

_____.

13. The manager reminded Maria not to forget to _____ _____ when she comes

to work in the morning.

14. Mrs. Nash isn't in the office anymore. She _____ _____ about an hour ago.

15. The judge told Jake that the next time he got in trouble he wouldn't _____ him

_____ with a warning.

16. I was going through some stuff in the attic, and I _____ _____ some

interesting old pictures.

---

16. FOCUS ON: phrasal verbs with gerund objects, 1

Gerunds — verbs in the *-ing* form that function as nouns — can serve as objects of many phrasal verbs.

> It is more common to use gerund objects with nonseparable two- and three-word phrasal verbs:
>
> > She's **counting on** <u>getting</u> that job.
> >
> > *gerund*
> >
> > I don't **feel up to** <u>playing</u> hockey.
> >
> > *gerund*
>
> but gerund objects are sometimes used with separable phrasal verbs:
>
> > I wouldn't **put** <u>robbing</u> a bank **past** him.
> >
> > *gerund*
> >
> > Mr. Taylor wants to **give** <u>smoking</u> **up**.
> >
> > *gerund*

Infinitive

present tense	-ing form	past tense	past participle

believe in

believe in & believes in	believing in	believed in	believed in

1. believe in *p.v.* When you **believe in** something or **believe in** doing something, you have a strong opinion about something that is important to you.

> I **believe in** working hard and saving money.
> Maria doesn't **believe in** sex before marriage.

2. believe in *p.v.* When you **believe in** something, you think it exists.

> Do you **believe in** ghosts?
> Ned is an atheist; he doesn't **believe in** God.

3. believe in *p.v.* When you **believe in** people, you have confidence in them and believe what they say because you think they are honest, correct, or competent.

*I don't care what anyone else says, I still **believe in** you.* *yeterli*

*We want to **believe in** you, but we need some proof that your invention really works.*

Infinitive

present tense	-ing form	past tense	past participle
carry on			
carry on & carries on	carrying on	carried on	carried on

1. carry on *p.v.* When you **carry on**, you continue as before, despite a difficult experience in your life.

*You'll have to **carry on** for the sake of the children.*

*It was difficult for Mrs. Nelson to **carry on** after her husband died.*

2. carry on (with) *p.v.* When you **carry on**, **carry on** with an activity, or **carry on** doing an activity, you continue it or continue doing it.

*The men stopped working when General Chambers entered the room, and he told them to **carry on**.*

*She plans to **carry on** with her career after the baby is born.*

*They knew I was trying to sleep, but they **carried on** talking and singing anyway.*

3. carry ... on *p.v.* When you **carry** something **on** an airplane, you keep it with you in the passenger compartment instead of giving it to an airline agent to put in the baggage compartment.

*This suitcase is pretty big. I hope they'll let me **carry** it **on**.*

*You should **carry** your laptop computer **on**. You don't want to take any chances.*

carry-on *n.* **Carry-on**, **carry-on** luggage, **carry-on** baggage, **carry-on** bags, and so on, are not given to an airline agent to put in the baggage compartment but are kept in the passenger compartment of an airplane.

*I'm staying only one night in New York, so all I'll need is a **carry-on** bag.*

4. carry on (about) *p.v. [informal]* When you **carry on** or **carry on** about something, you are very persistent and vocal about something that upsets you.

*I forgot our anniversary, and she **carried on** all day.*

*I said I was sorry; now will you please stop **carrying on** about it?*

count on

count on & counts on	counting on	counted on	counted on

1. count on *p.v.* When you need something important to happen or a certain condition to exist, you are **counting on** it. When you need someone to do something important, you are **counting on** that person.

ile gitmek

*I'm **counting on** getting a ride to the airport with Betty.*

*Farmers **count on** a lot of rain in the spring.*

2. count on *p.v.* When you rely on someone or something for help or support if you need it, you are **counting on** that thing or that person.

> I'm going to sell this car and buy one that always starts. I need a car I can **count on**.
> The governor said that she's **counting on** our support in the next election.

3. count on *p.v.* When you are certain than something will happen or that a certain condition will exist, you are **counting on** it.

> Marvin makes a fool of himself at every party. You can **count on** it.
> You can **count on** crowds and long lines at Disney World if you go in August.

Infinitive

present tense	-ing form	past tense	past participle
get through			
get through & gets through	getting through	got through	gotten/got through

1. get through (with) *p.v.* When you **get through**, **get through** with an activity, or **get through** doing an activity, you finish it or finish doing it.

> I have so much homework that I might not **get through** with it until midnight.
> After you **get through** washing the dishes, you can start ironing.

2. get through (to) *p.v.* When you **get through** or **get through** to someone, usually on a telephone or radio, you are able to speak to that person.

> Nancy tried calling Jim last night, but she couldn't **get through**.
> It wasn't easy, but I finally **got through** to my brother in Borneo.

3. get through (to) *p.v.* When you **get through** or **get through** to someone, you make that person understand your opinion or point of view.

> Mr. Taylor has tried to make his daughter understand why it's important to work hard in school and get good grades, but he just can't **get through**.
> I've explained it a hundred times! What do I have to do to **get through** to you?

4. get ... through *p.v.* [informal] When you **get** something **through** someone's head, you make that person understand your opinion or point of view. When you **get** something **through** your own head, you understand it.

> I finally **got** it **through** my son's head that I was serious about sending him to military school.
> When are you going to **get** it **through** your head that our marriage is over?

5. get ... through *p.v.* When something **gets** you **through** a difficult experience, it comforts and supports you.

> Julia's faith in God was what **got** her **through** the loss of her husband.
> He was very nervous about giving the speech, so he had a drink to help **get** him **through** the ordeal.

Infinitive

	present tense	-ing form	past tense	past participle
go for				
	go for & goes for	going for	went for	gone for

1. go for *p.v.* *[informal]* When you **go for** something, you like it a lot.

> Erik really **goes for** scuba diving.
> Let's go to a different nightclub. I don't **go for** jazz.

2. go for *p.v.* When you **go for** something, you try to achieve it.

> The gymnast said she was going to **go for** the gold at the next Olympics.
> After she finished her master's, she **went for** a Ph.D.

3. go for *p.v.* *[always continuous]* When you have something **going for** you, you have an advantage that makes it easier for you to do something or get something that you want.

> Sam's not especially good at basketball, but he has one thing **going for** him — he's
>   seven feet tall.
> I have ten years of experience **going for** me, so I think I have a good chance of
>   getting the job.

4. go for *p.v.* When you say that a statement about one person or thing **goes for** another person or thing, you mean that it is also true about the other person or thing. When you say "That **goes for** me," you are agreeing with someone else's opinion.

> Heather said that Tom was a jerk, and I said that that **goes for** Tom's brother Bill, too.
> Betty's really angry about it, and that **goes for** me, too.

hold off				
	hold off & holds off	holding off	held off	held off

1. hold off *p.v.* When you **hold off** or **hold off** doing something, you delay doing it.

> I **held off** selling our house until our youngest child moved out.
> You'd better **hold off** accusing Mike until you're 100 percent sure.

2. hold ... off *p.v.* When you **hold off** an attack, you prevent the attacker from getting close to you or from winning the fight. If you **hold off** a competitor, you prevent the competitor from winning.

> The enemy was so strong that there was no way to **hold** them **off**.
> The champion **held off** the challenger and won the game.

put past

1. put ... past *p.v.* *[used only in the infinitive form and only in negative sentences]* When you want to say that you think someone is capable of doing something wrong, you say that you wouldn't **put** it **past** that person. When you want to warn someone that you think another person is capable of doing something wrong, you say "Don't **put** it **past** (that person)."

*Is he capable of murder? Well, I wouldn't **put** killing someone **past** him.*

*Marvin is evil. There isn't any crime I wouldn't **put past** him.*

*You don't think Hank would steal money from his grandmother? I know him better than you do — don't **put** it **past** him.*

Infinitive

present tense	-ing form	past tense	past participle
think about
think about & thinks about	thinking about	thought about	thought about

1. think about *p.v.* When you **think about** something or **think about** doing something, you consider it before making a decision.

*The salesman tried to get me to sign the contract, but I said I'd **think about** it.*

*I'm **thinking about** quitting my job.*

EXERCISE 16a — Complete the sentences with phrasal verbs from this section. Be sure the phrasal verbs are in the correct tense.

1. This house is too small for our family. We're _____ _____ moving to a bigger one.

2. These skis are pretty big. Do you think they'll let me _____ them _____?

3. This work is very important, and I know you can do it. I'm _____ _____ you.

4. At the next Olympics, Raul's going to _____ _____ a new record in the pole vault.

5. I don't _____ _____ talking about people behind their backs.

6. I tried several times to call Tim in Timbuktu, but I couldn't _____ _____.

7. The roller coaster is very popular. If you go on the weekend, you can _____ _____ waiting in line for three hours.

8. As soon as you _____ _____ washing the car, come inside and eat lunch.

9. I wanted to buy a digital camera, but I _____ _____ buying one until the prices fell.

10. Marvin seems like a nice guy, but he isn't. I wouldn't _____ anything _____ him.

11. David asked me to buy beer when I went to the store, but I forgot, and he _____ _____ about it for an hour.

12. The defenders _____ _____ the attackers as long as they could.

13. Mike really _____ _____ auto racing when he was young.

14. Sally has a good education and a pleasant personality. She has a lot _____

_____ her.

15. How can I _____ _____ after this terrible tragedy?

16. I've explained the rules a thousand times. Why can't you _____ it _____

your head that I'm the boss around here, not you?

17. Everyone else thinks Dr. Hatcher's ideas are crazy, but I _____ _____ him.

18. Uncle John was the only one who knew how to run this business. Now that he's dead, we

won't be able to _____ _____.

19. I didn't used to _____ _____ ghosts, but what I saw last night changed

my mind.

20. I've tried to get her to understand my point of view, but I can't _____ _____

to her.

21. The Republicans are idiots, and that _____ _____ the Democrats, too.

22. Letters from his family helped Jake _____ _____ his prison sentence.

23. I always knew that my brother was the one person I could _____ _____

if I had a problem.

EXERCISE 16b — Write answers to the questions using phrasal verbs and nouns from this section. Be sure the phrasal verbs are in the correct tense.

1. Judy likes taking pictures a lot. How does she feel about taking pictures?

2. Maria didn't finish studying until 11:00 P.M. What didn't Maria do until 11:00 P.M.?

3. The Ortegas took two bags with them to keep in the passenger compartment when they

flew to New York. What did they do to the two bags?

4. In Question 3, what kind of bags did the Ortegas keep with them?

5. Jane is considering spending the summer in Bolivia. What is Jane doing?

6. Bill feels strongly that hunting is wrong. How does Bill feel about hunting?

16

7. Paul couldn't continue his career as a dancer after his accident. What couldn't he do after his accident?

8. We delayed having children until after we had done some traveling. What did we do?

9. You think stealing is something Hank would do. What do you think about Hank?

10. Nancy is going to try to call her sister in Nepal tonight. What is Nancy going to try to do tonight?

11. Hank isn't reliable. You can't be certain he will do what he says he will do. What can't you do to Hank?

12. Dan was very angry, and he yelled and complained for three hours. What did Dan do for three hours?

13. You can't be 100 percent certain that the weather will be nice in Florida in the winter. What can't you do to the winter weather in Florida?

14. Many children are sure that monsters are real. What do many children think about monsters?

EXERCISE 16c — **Write eight original sentences using phrasal verbs from this section. Try to use gerund objects.**

1. _____

2. _____

3. _____

4. _____

5. _____

6. _____

7. _____

8. _____

EXERCISE 16d, Review — **Complete the sentences with these participle adjectives from previous sections. To check their meanings, review the section number given after each one.**

closed off, 13	filled out, 14	put away, 14	used up, 14
dressed up, 14	fixed up, 15	screwed on, 12	wound up, 14
dried up, 14	lit up, 13	stuck-up, 14	wrapped up, 4

1. Charles is so _____ _____. He thinks he's better than everyone else because he comes from a rich family.

2. Now that your house is _____ _____, it's worth a lot more.

3. There isn't any more paper for the copier — it's _____ _____.

4. I washed and dried the dishes, and now they're _____ _____ in the cabinet.

5. Frank's really _____ _____ about his wedding tomorrow.

6. The presents have wrapping paper on them. They're _____ _____.

7. This form has all the information in the correct spaces. It's _____ _____.

8. The floor of the bathroom isn't wet anymore; it's _____ _____.

9. Why is Sarah all _____ _____? Is she going out dancing?

10. Be sure the top of the Coke bottle is _____ _____. If it isn't, the Coke will go flat.

11. You can't go in the east wing of the palace because it's _____ _____.

12. I can see the road easily at night when I'm driving because it's _____ _____.

EXERCISE 16e, Review — **Complete the sentences with these phrasal verbs from previous sections. Be sure the phrasal verbs are in the correct tense. To check their meanings, review the section number given after each one.**

break down, 5	get over with, 3	put up with, 3
break out, 9	give up, 9	see about, 7
butt in, 14	go in for, 3	take in, 7
feel up to, 3	leave off, 13	wind up, 14
get around to, 6	look forward to, 3	work out, 11
get out of, 6	put up, 12	

1. We couldn't decide where to go for dinner last night, so we _____ _____ staying home.

2. Sally loves all outdoor sports, and she especially _____ _____ _____ swimming.

3. I hate cigarettes, and I will not _____ _____ _____ smoking in my house!

4. It's been seven years since Tom saw his sister. He's really _____ _____ _____ seeing her again.

5. My eyesight got so bad that I had to _____ _____ driving.

6. I'm exhausted. I really don't _____ _____ _____ doing any more sightseeing.

7. The heat in my apartment doesn't work. I need to _____ the manager _____ getting it fixed.

8. It's been three hours since I asked you. When are you going to _____ _____ _____ taking out the garbage?

9. I promised Sally I would lend her $1,000, but now I don't want to give it to her. How can I _____ _____ _____ lending her the money?

10. Raking the leaves is a big job, but I have to _____ it _____ _____ before it snows.

11. The teacher continued her lecture where she _____ _____ the previous week.

12. I haven't _____ _____ all the details, but I've decided to quit my job and start my own business.

13. I was late to work because my car _____ _____ on the expressway.

14. My TV was broken, so I _____ it _____ and had it fixed.

15. When you're camping, you should always _____ your tent _____ before it gets dark.

16. Fighting between protesters and government troops _____ _____ after the general canceled the election.

17. The line to buy tickets for the football game was really long, so a lot of people tried to _____ _____.

17. FOCUS ON: **adverbs and phrasal verbs**

Adverbs are words that modify verbs. Many adverbs end with *-ly*, for example, *quickly, slowly, suddenly, foolishly*; but other adverbs, such as *always, sometimes,* and *never*, do not. The placement of adverbs in sentences with phrasal verbs depends on whether the verb is intransitive or transitive, and if transitive, whether it is separable or nonseparable. In general, adverbs are placed like ordinary one-word verbs with the exception of nonseparable phrasal verbs, which also allow for the placement of adverbs between the verb and the particle. All possible placements of adverbs in sentences containing the various types of phrasal verbs are shown with Xs:

Intransitive phrasal verbs

X subject X verb particle X.

> *Immediately* he **came over**.
> He *immediately* **came over**.
> He **came over** *immediately*.

Separable phrasal verbs

X subject X verb particle object X.

X subject X verb object particle X.

> *Angrily* she **ripped up** the paper.
> *Angrily* she **ripped** the paper **up**.
> She *angrily* **ripped up** the paper.
> She *angrily* **ripped** the paper **up**.
> She **ripped up** the paper *angrily*.
> She **ripped** the paper **up** *angrily*.

Nonseparable phrasal verbs

X subject X verb X particle object X.

> *Slowly* we **headed into** town.
> We *slowly* **headed into** town.
> We **headed** *slowly* **into** town.
> We **headed into** town *slowly*.

Three-word phrasal verbs

X subject X verb? particle? object X.

> *Eventually* I **grew out of** the sweater.
> I *eventually* **grew out of** the sweater.
> I **grew out of** the sweater *eventually*.

Placing adverbs within three word phrasal verbs is sometimes possible, but it can be problematic. Sometimes an adverb between the verb and first particle sounds acceptable and other times it does not. Sometimes, an adverb placed between the two particles sounds acceptable, and other times it will not. This is more a matter of style than of what is correct or incorrect, so unless you are sure it sounds okay, it is better not to place adverbs within three-word verbs.

Infinitive			
present tense	-ing form	past tense	past participle
come over			
come over & comes over	coming over	came over	come over

1. come over (to) *p.v.* When people move from one side of a place to the other, where you are, they **come over** or **come over** to where you are.

Come over here and say that again.

When he saw me, he immediately came over to my table and said hello.

2. come over (to) *p.v.* When people come to your house for a visit, they **come over** or **come over** to your house.

Would you like to come over tonight?

Jim comes over to my house every night.

3. come over *p.v.* When people cross a river or cross the ocean from east to west or west to east, they **come over**.

My grandparents came over from Sweden in 1904.

The ferry comes over to this side of the lake every day at 5:30 P.M.

fall apart			
fall apart & falls apart	falling apart	fell apart	fallen apart

1. fall apart *p.v.* When the parts of something become completely separated because it is old or in bad condition, it **falls apart**.

These old shoes are starting to fall apart.

There's no way to fix this thing. It has completely fallen apart.

2. fall apart *p.v.* When a plan, arrangement, system, or agreement fails, it **falls apart**.

After five difficult years, their marriage totally fell apart.

The peace agreement is slowly falling apart.

3. fall apart *p.v.* When people suddenly lose control and start laughing or become very upset or emotional, they **fall apart**.

Sally fell apart when she heard the tragic news.

Tom was so funny at the party last night that I just fell apart laughing.

get back at			
get back at & gets back at	getting back at	got back at	gotten/got back at

1. get back at *p.v.* When you **get back at** people, you do something bad to them because they have done something bad to you.

*John won't forget what you did to him. He'll definitely **get back at** you someday.*

*She wants to **get back at** her ex-husband for the way he treated her.*

Infinitive

	present tense	-ing form	past tense	past participle
go about				
	go about & goes about	going about	went about	gone about

1. go about *p.v.* When you **go about** something or **go about** doing something, you begin or continue to follow all the steps necessary to do it.

*I have no idea how to **go about** opening a restaurant.*

*Everyday he quietly **went about** his business and never caused any problems.*

grow out of				
	grow out of & grows out of	growing out of	grew out of	grown out of

1. grow out of *p.v.* When people become too tall or too big to wear an item of clothing, they **grow out of** the item of clothing.

*I bought Susie's shoes one size too big, but she's quickly **growing out of** them.*

*Do you want these clothes for your daughter? Mine has **grown out of** them.*

2. grow out of *p.v.* When people become too mature for a toy, for an interest, or for a form of behavior, they have **grown out of** it.

*Judy had a big crush on a rock star when she was in high school, but after a while she **grew out of** it.*

*Jim's son is going through a difficult stage, but he'll **grow out of** it in a couple of years.*

head into				
	head into & heads into	heading into	headed into	headed into

1. head into *p.v.* When you **head into** or are **headed into** a place or area, you begin to enter it.

*I almost had an accident as I was **heading into** town.*

*We scared away the bear, and it **headed** slowly **into** the woods.*

*Jim was **headed into** Ashland when his car broke down.*

rip up				
	rip up & rips up	ripping up	ripped up	ripped up

1. rip . . . up *p.v.* When you tear paper or cloth into many pieces, you **rip** it **up**.

*Nancy was furious when she read Tom's letter, and she angrily **ripped** it **up**.*

*Always **rip up** a check before you put it in the wastebasket.*

ripped up *part.adj.* After a piece of paper or cloth has been torn into many small piece, it is **ripped up**.

*After the kids opened their Christmas presents, the floor was covered with **ripped up** paper.*

17

Infinitive			
present tense	**-ing form**	**past tense**	**past participle**
wear down			
wear down & wears down	wearing down	wore down	worn down

1. wear . . . down *p.v.* When something **wears down** or when someone **wears** something **down**, the top or surface gradually disappears because of friction.

*The feet of thousands of visitors a year have **worn down** the marble steps.*
*The mechanic told me that my car's brake pads have **worn down** badly and need to be replaced.*

worn down *part.adj.* After the top or surface of something has gradually disappeared because of friction, it is **worn down**.

*The marble steps are very old and **worn down**.*
*The tread on these tires is dangerously **worn down**.*

2. wear . . . down *p.v.* When people **wear** you **down**, they gradually persuade you, through persistent pressure, to change your mind about a decision.

*He wouldn't tell me the answer, but little by little, I **wore** him **down**.*
*She still will not give us permission, but I think we're **wearing** her **down**.*

EXERCISE 17a — **Complete the sentences with phrasal verbs from this section. Be sure the phrasal verbs are in the correct tense.**

1. I waved to Jim when I saw him across the street, and he _____ _____ and talked to me.

2. This company has been _____ _____ since that idiot was made the manager.

3. Don't leave the newspaper where the dog can get it. He'll totally _____ it _____.

4. We need a lot of things from the supermarket. When are you _____ _____ town?

5. Jake told the boss I was drinking on the job, and I got fired, but I _____ _____ _____ Jake — I told his wife about his girlfriend.

6. During the American Revolution, the French fleet _____ _____ and helped the Americans fight the British.

7. The heels on my boots have _____ _____ badly, and I need to get them replaced.

8. Can you help me get hooked up to the Internet? I have no idea how to _____ _____ it.

9. Don't spend a lot of money on baby clothes — she'll _____ _____ _____ them in a few weeks.

10. I need a new car. This piece of junk is _____ _____.

11. Sally asks her parents for a pony about a hundred times a day. She's trying to _____ them _____.

12. When his wife said she wanted a divorce, he just _____ _____.

13. If you're not busy tonight, would you like to _____ _____ and watch TV?

14. My four-year-old son thinks it's really funny to say bad words. I hope he _____ _____ _____ it.

EXERCISE 17b — **Rewrite these sentences and place the adverb in parentheses in two possible positions.**

1. (frequently) Ms. Taylor *comes over*.

_____

_____

2. (sometimes) These cheap toys *fall apart*.

_____

_____

3. (nervously) He *went about* making the bomb.

_____

_____

4. (eventually) Sally will *grow out of* her childish behavior.

_____

_____

5. (reluctantly) Jim *headed into* the swamp.

_____

_____

6. (suddenly) Pat *ripped up* Mike's letter.

_____

_____

7. (soon) Frank will *get back at* Todd.

_____

_____

8. (gradually) He *wore down* my resistance.

_____

_____

EXERCISE 17c — **Write answers to the questions using phrasal verbs and participle adjectives from this section. Be sure the phrasal verbs are in the correct tense.**

1. The contract was torn into many small pieces. What was done to the contract?

2. In Question 1, how would you describe the contract?

3. Her plan is not working properly, and there's a lot of confusion. What is happening to her plan?

4. My friends visited me last night. What did my friends do last night?

5. Mike doesn't know anything about applying for a mortgage. What doesn't he know?

6. Tomorrow we're going to drive from the country to the city. What are we going to do tomorrow?

7. When Judy was a teenager, she was very shy, but she's not shy anymore. What did she do to her shyness?

8. The old lion's teeth are not as sharp or as long as they used to be. What has happened to them?

9. In Question 8, how would you describe the lion's teeth?

10. I did something bad to my brother, and now he has done something bad to me. What has my brother done to me?

11. The Vikings crossed the ocean before Columbus. What did the Vikings do before Columbus?

12. The teacher walked across the room and looked at your paper. What did the teacher do?

13. Jim became very sad and lost control when he heard that his brother had died. What did Jim do?

14. This sweater will be too small for my daughter soon. What will my daughter do to the sweater soon?

15. The pages are coming out of this old book. What is the book doing?

16. The police are pressuring the suspect to tell the truth. What are the police trying to do to the suspect?

EXERCISE 17d, Review — **Complete the sentences with these phrasal verbs from previous sections. Be sure the phrasal verbs are in the correct tense. To check their meanings, review the section number given after each one.**

boil down to, 6	fight back, 8	hear of, 8
chicken out of, 9	find out, 5	kick back, 10
come down with, 6	get along, 9	monkey around with, 6
come up, 12	go ahead, 10	set up, 5
fall over, 8	go through with, 6	work in, 8

1. I don't know when the train to Boston leaves. I'll ask the ticket agent and _____ _____.

2. I don't like our neighbors, and they don't like me. We don't _____ _____.

3. Julia was nervous about bleaching her hair blond, and she decided not to _____ _____ _____ it.

4. Sarah was nervous about bleaching her hair blond, and she _____ _____ _____ it.

5. The ambassador will try to _____ _____ a meeting between the president and the rebel leader.

6. We have a really busy day planned, but I'd like to _____ _____ a visit to the museum.

7. If someone hits you, you have to _____ _____.

8. I missed a week of work when I _____ _____ _____ German measles.

9. Having a mechanic fix my car will cost a lot of money, so I'll _____ _____ _____ it to see if I can fix it myself.

10. The owner of the construction company was _____ _____ thousands of dollars to the mayor.

11. Are you kidding? That's the most ridiculous thing I've ever _____ _____.

12. The country's economic problems are very complicated. Can you tell me what it _____ _____ _____?

13. I'm sorry I have to cancel our lunch date, but something very important has _____ _____, and I have to return to my office immediately.

14. After the car hit the telephone pole, the pole _____ _____ and crushed the car.

15. I was so angry at my boss that I told him I was going to quit, and he said, "_____ _____, I don't care!"

18. FOCUS ON: **phrasal verbs and *can, could, will,* and *would***

Can, could, will, and *would* are *modal auxiliary verbs,* often called *modals.* Modals are very important in English, but they can be confusing because they are used to say many different things. Here is a basic review of *can, could, will,* and *would* and their most common uses.

Could is used as the past tense of *can*:

> I <u>can't</u> **come over** tonight.
> I <u>couldn't</u> **come over** last night.

Would is used as the past tense of *will* (the future use of *will* has already been discussed in Section 15) to talk about something that was future in the past:

> I didn't buy that nice coat for my son because I knew he <u>would</u> quickly
>   **grow out of** it.

Would is used in place of *will* when repeating someone else's words:

> She said she <u>would</u> **get** next Friday **off**.

Would is used as the past tense of *will* to talk about a repeated past action:

> When I worked as a bank guard, I <u>would</u> **stand around** all day doing nothing.

Normally, *can, could, will,* and *would* have different uses, and it is important to use the correct one; however, in one special case — making requests — they can be used with very little difference in meaning:

> <u>Can</u> you **get off** the couch?
> <u>Could</u> you **get off** the couch?
> <u>Will</u> you **get off** the couch?
> <u>Would</u> you **get off** the couch?

Can and *could* are used, with little difference in meaning, to ask for permission:

> <u>Can</u> I **think about** it before I make a decision?
> <u>Could</u> I **think about** it before I make a decision?

Can, could, will, and *would* are used in *conditional* sentences. Conditional means that a condition, usually stated in an *if clause,* must be satisfied for the *main clause* to be true. When the condition is something that is actually possible, the verb in the *if* clause is normally in the present tense. If the condition in the *if* clause is something that could not actually be true, the past tense form of the verb is used.
   When the condition in the *if* clause is something that is actually possible, *can* is used in the main clause to discuss a <u>real</u> <u>ability</u>:

> If I have a car, I <u>can</u> **come over**.

When the condition in the *if* clause is something that is actually possible, *will* is used in the main clause to discuss a <u>real</u> <u>willingness</u> or <u>intention</u>:

> If I have a car, I <u>will</u> **come over**.

When the condition in the *if* clause is not something that is actually possible, *could* is used in the main clause to discuss an <u>unreal</u> or <u>imaginary</u> <u>ability</u>:

> If I had a car, I <u>could</u> **come over**.

When the condition in the *if* clause is not something that is actually possible, *would* is used in the main clause to discuss an <u>unreal</u> or <u>imaginary</u> <u>willingness</u> or <u>intention</u>:

> If I had a car, I <u>would</u> **come over**.

Either the *if* clause or main clause can occur first in a sentence, with a slight change in punctuation:

> If I had a car, I <u>would</u> **come over**.
> I <u>would</u> **come over** if I had a car.

Infinitive

present tense	-ing form	past tense	past participle
break through			
break through & breaks through	**breaking through**	**broke through**	**broken through**

1. break through *p.v.* When you use force to go through a wall or other barrier, you **break through** it.

> The thieves **broke through** the wall of the jewelry store.
> The attackers couldn't **break through** the thick walls of the fort.

2. break through *p.v.* When you cannot do something because of a problem and you find a way to solve or eliminate the problem, you **break through**.

> After the problem of tissue rejection is **broken through**, organ transplants will become more common.
> It took three days of negotiation, but we finally **broke through** the deadlock.

breakthrough *n.* An important discovery or development that solves or eliminates a problem that is preventing you from doing something is a **breakthrough**.

> Dr. Wood announced an important **breakthrough** in the search for a cure for AIDS.

figure on

figure on & figures on	figuring on	figured on	figured on

1. figure on *p.v.* When you **figure on** something, you expect it or plan for it.

> I didn't **figure on** such cold weather. I wish I'd brought a coat.
> You can **figure on** spending a least hundred bucks if you're going to that restaurant.

Infinitive

	present tense	-ing form	past tense	past participle
get off				
	get off & gets off	getting off	got off	gotten/got off

1. get off *p.v.* When you **get off** a bus, airplane, or train, you leave it.

*The bus stopped and I **got off**.*
*You can't **get off** the train while it's moving.*

2. get off *p.v.* When you are standing, lying, or sitting on something, such as a horse, bicycle, motorcycle, stage, platform, or piece of furniture, and you step down from it onto the ground, you **get off** it.

*You're so lazy. Why don't you **get off** the couch and help me?*
***Get off** your bicycle and come inside.*

3. get off *p.v.* When you are standing within an area of ground, or on something that covers an area of ground, and you move to the side of it and step off of it, you **get off** it.

*The referee told the player to **get off** the field.*
*You're standing on our beach blanket — **get off** it!*

4. get . . . off *p.v.* When you **get** something **off**, you remove it even though it may be difficult.

*I can't **get** this paint **off** my hands.*
*The top of this bottle is on so tight I cannot **get** it **off**.*

5. get . . . off *p.v.* When you **get** a certain period of time **off**, you are allowed by your employer to miss work during this period.

*Pregnant women usually **get** three months **off** with pay.*
*Could I **get** tomorrow morning **off** to go to the doctor?*

6. get off *p.v.* When you **get off**, or **get off** work, you finish that day's work and leave your place of employment.

*Sally said she wouldn't **get off** work until 6:00.*
*I haven't **gotten off** early all week.*

7. get . . . off *p.v.* When you do something wrong but are not punished, or you are punished only lightly for it, you **get off**. Someone who helps you to avoid punishment **gets** you **off**.

*He killed four people, but he **got off** with only three years in jail.*
If his lawyer hadn't been so incompetent, he would have
    ***gotten** him **off** with a lighter sentence.*

8. get off *p.v.* When you stop talking on the telephone, you **get off** the telephone.

***Get off** the phone — I need to use it!*
*It's late, we'd better **get off** the phone.*

Infinitive

present tense	-ing form	past tense	past participle
go beyond			
go beyond & goes beyond	going beyond	went beyond	gone beyond

1. go beyond *p.v.* When people or things are better or worse, or do something in a better or worse way than is normal or expected, they **go beyond** what is normal or expected.

> *Did you say Jackson's new book is good? I think it **goes beyond** good — it's fantastic!*
> *Sam's wife discovered that he wasn't just friends with his secretary; their relationship **went** way **beyond** friendship.*

lift upon			
lift up & lifts up	lifting up	lifted up	lifted up

1. lift ... up *p.v.* When you **lift up** something, you use your hands to raise it above the surface that it was on.

> *That rock is too heavy — I can't **lift** it **up**.*
> ***Lift up** the cover and look in the box.*

line up			
line up & lines up	lining up	lined up	lined up

1. line ... up *p.v.* When people or things form a row, they **line up**. When you arrange people or things so that they form a row, you **line** them **up**.

> *People **lined up** to buy Superbowl tickets.*
> *Timmy is **lining** his toy cars **up**.*

lined up *part.adj.* People or things that form a row are **lined up**.

> *People have been **lined up** outside the box office for three days.*
> *The children are **lined up** for attendance.*

2. line ... up *p.v.* When something **lines up** with something else, or when you **line up** something with something else, it is positioned correctly in relation to something else.

> *If this bolt doesn't **line up** with that hole, the lock won't work.*
> *The holes in part A have to **line up** with the holes in part B before you screw them together.*

3. line ... up *p.v.* When you arrange for someone or something to be available at a future activity or event, you **line** that thing or person **up**.

> *I couldn't **line** a clown **up** for Susie's birthday party.*
> *Who have they **lined up** for the show?*

lined up *part.adj.* Someone or something that you have arranged to be available for a future activity or event is **lined up**.

> *Don't worry about the show; everything is **lined up**.*
> *The singer is **lined up**, but the band isn't.*

lineup *n.* The people or things planned for an event are the **lineup**.

> The network has planned quite a **lineup** of entertainers for the half-time special.
>
> There's always a trapeze act in the circus **lineup**.

Infinitive

	present tense	-ing form	past tense	past participle
stand around				
	stand around & stands around	standing around	stood around	stood around

1. stand around *p.v.* When you **stand around**, you stand in a place wasting time and not doing anything useful.

> I have all this work to do, and you guys just **stand around** watching me.
>
> The manager told them to stop **standing around** and get to work.

tell apart				
	tell apart & tells apart	telling apart	told apart	told apart

1. tell ... apart *p.v.* When it is possible to see how two similar things are different, you can **tell** them **apart**.

> The twins are identical; no one can **tell** them **apart**.
>
> All the puppies look the same, and I have a hard time **telling** them **apart**.

EXERCISE 18a — **Complete the sentences with phrasal verbs from this section. Be sure the phrasal verbs are in the correct tense.**

1. Could you _____ _____ the phone? I want to make an important call.

2. Neither side would give an inch. There was no way to _____ _____ the stalemate.

3. If you put this fake Rolex watch next to a real one, you can _____ them _____ easily.

4. Jim wanted to go to a movie tonight, but I told him I wouldn't _____ _____ work until late.

5. If the holes don't _____ _____, the screws won't go in.

6. There weren't any chairs at the party, so we just _____ _____ talking.

7. I told Frank that his drinking problem isn't just hurting him; it _____ _____ that — it's hurting his family, too.

8. The lawyer was sure he could _____ him _____ with only two years in prison.

9. When I took this job after I finished high school, I never _____ _____ spending thirty-five years here.

10. Mother was the last one to _____ _____ the airplane.

11. Bob _____ _____ everything in his cabinet so that it's easy to find what he's looking for.

12. Lydia told me she would try to _____ three weeks _____ so we can go on vacation.

13. There were police barricades around the palace, but some of the protesters _____ _____.

14. Children, stop jumping on the bed with your dirty shoes. _____ _____ right now!

15. Can you _____ _____ the TV while I put the VCR under it?

16. Some CDs come wrapped in plastic that's almost impossible to _____ _____.

17. I couldn't _____ _____ a magician for the birthday party.

18. _____ _____ the carpet. I just shampooed it.

EXERCISE 18b — **Write answers to the questions using phrasal verbs and participle adjectives from this section. Be sure the phrasal verbs are in the correct tense.**

1. Paul said he would remove his cat from the table. What did Paul say?

2. I can't see any difference between the original and the copy. What can't I do?

3. Erik can't raise the box of books because it's too heavy. What can't Erik do?

4. Bill said he hadn't expected snow in May. What did Bill say?

5. Nancy arranged for a great band to play at the prom next week. What did Nancy do?

6. In Question 5, how would you describe the band?

7. Jerry thought the problem with his car is that it needs a tune-up, but the mechanic said it's worse than that. What did the mechanic say?

8. The soldiers smashed a hole in the wall and entered the city. What did the soldiers do to the wall?

9. Carlos stops working at 5:00 everyday. What does Carlos do at 5:00 everyday?

10. You were arrested for drunken driving, but the judge gave you only a warning. What did you do?

11. The teacher moved all the desks in his classroom so that they were in straight rows. What did the teacher do?

12. In Question 11, how would you describe the desks?

13. She asked me if I would stop talking on the telephone. What did she say?

14. I stood at the bus stop for an hour waiting for the bus. What did I do for an hour?

15. The personnel manager at my new job said I wouldn't have to work on Sundays. What did the personnel manager say?

16. When you put a doorknob on a door, the two sides have to be directly across from each other. How do the two sides have to be?

17. Sam stepped from the train. What did Sam do?

18. Mark's father told him to move from the grass to the sidewalk. What did Mark's father tell Mark?

EXERCISE 18c — **Complete these sentences, using your own words, with phrasal verbs from this section or previous sections.**

1. Last week, he couldn't _____.

2. When I was younger, I could _____.

3. He'll _____.

4. When I _____, I would _____.

5. Could you _____?

6. Would you _____?

7. Can I _____?

8. Could I _____?

EXERCISE 18d, Review — **Complete the sentences with these phrasal verbs from previous sections. Be sure the phrasal verbs are in the correct tense. To check their meanings, review the section number given after each one.**

believe in, 16	go along with, 3	hold off, 16
carry on, 16	go for, 16	put past, 16
come over, 17	go with, 15	tell on, 15
come through, 15	grow out of, 17	think about, 16
count on, 16	head back, 15	
get through, 16	head for, 15	

1. I suggested that we go to Paris, and she really _____ _____ the idea.

2. After I _____ _____ it, I decided not to take the job.

3. I _____ _____ buying a new computer because I thought they would be on sale in January.

4. Do you think this yellow tie _____ _____ this blue shirt?

5. Her uncle promised to pay for her wedding, and he _____ _____.

6. It's very important that you do this work correctly. I'm _____ _____ you.

7. Timmy broke a window, and his sister _____ _____ him.

8. The detective asked me if Jake had robbed the liquor store, and I said I didn't know but that I wouldn't _____ it _____ him.

9. Todd said he would _____ _____ to my house after dinner and help me with my homework.

10. The reason Charles is vice-president of the company is that he _____ _____ _____ the boss on every decision.

11. Tomorrow I'm going to leave Winnipeg and _____ _____ Toronto.

12. I probably won't _____ _____ to Winnipeg for a month or more.

13. I didn't get Sally what she wanted for her birthday, and she _____ _____ about it all day.

14. You have so much work to do. When do you think you'll _____ _____?

15. I bought these pants for my son a month ago, and he's _____ _____

_____ them already.

16. Ned didn't _____ _____ UFOs until he saw one.

19. FOCUS ON: **phrasal verbs and the adverb *right***

The adverb *right* is often used to intensify the meaning of a phrasal verb. Placed before the particle, *right* means *directly, immediately,* or *quickly*. It is not important whether the phrasal verb is intransitive, separable, or nonseparable. What does matter is whether the action of the verb is something that can logically be done directly, immediately, or quickly. For example, it would be illogical to use *right* with *stand around,* or *wear down*:

> She **aimed** <u>right</u> **at** me. (She **aimed** <u>directly</u> **at** me.)
> I'll **bring** it <u>right</u> **over**. (I'll **bring** it **over** <u>immediately</u>.)
> The room **warmed** <u>right</u> **up**. (The room **warmed up** <u>quickly</u>.)

Right can be used when a separable phrasal verb is separated by its object; however, *right* cannot be used when the object follows the particle:

> He **brought** my radio <u>right</u> **back**.
> ~~He **brought** <u>right</u> **back** my radio.~~

Infinitive			
present tense	-ing form	past tense	past participle
aim at			
aim at & aims at	aiming at	aimed at	aimed at

1. aim ... at *p.v.* When you point a weapon at people or things, you **aim** it **at** them.

> The robber **aimed** the gun right **at** my head.
> He was **aiming** the arrow **at** the apple, but he missed.

2. aim at *p.v.* When you **aim at** something you want, you do what is necessary to get it.

> The manager said she was **aiming at** a 14 percent increase in sales next year.
> The new law is **aimed at** reducing crime in the streets.

3. aim ... at *p.v.* When you do something designed to affect one class or type of people, you **aim** it **at** those people.

> Cigarette manufacturers were accused of **aiming** their advertising **at** young people.
> The candidate's speech was **aimed at** female voters.

Infinitive

	present tense	-ing form	past tense	past participle
bring back				
	bring back & brings back	bringing back	brought back	brought back

1. bring . . . back *p.v.* When you take something to another place and then bring it from that place to the place where you were before, you **bring** it **back**.

> *I told Tom to **bring** my pen right **back**.*
> *Sally borrowed my blue sweater and **brought** it **back** yesterday.*

2. bring . . . back *p.v.* When something that was popular or current in the past is introduced again, it is **brought back**.

> *Many schools are **bringing back** uniforms for children.*
> *Every few years designers try to **bring** miniskirts **back**.*

3. bring . . . back *p.v.* When something causes you to recall memories and emotions from the past, it **brings** the memories and emotions **back**.

> *Looking at these old pictures **brought back** wonderful memories.*
> *I had tried to forget that awful incident, but this magazine article has **brought** it all **back**.*

bring over				
	bring over & brings over	bringing over	brought over	brought over

1. bring . . . over *p.v.* When people take something from one place to the place where you are, they **bring** it **over**.

> *I called Frank to ask if I could use his electric drill, and he **brought** it right **over**.*
> *Linda is going to **bring** her wedding pictures **over** tonight.*

cool off				
	cool off & cools off	cooling off	cooled off	cooled off

1. cool off *p.v.* When the temperature of a thing or place becomes lower, it **cools off**.

> *It was really hot yesterday, but it **cooled off** in the evening.*
> *This is too hot — I'll eat it after it **cools off**.*

2. cool . . . off *p.v.* When people or things cause a thing or place to become cooler, they **cool** it **off**.

> *The coffee was really hot, but he put an ice cube in it and it **cooled** right **off**.*
> *This bath is too hot. Put more cold water in it to **cool** it **off**.*

3. cool off *p.v.* When you become less angry or less excited, you **cool off**.

> *He's furious now, but he'll **cool off** by morning.*
> *Their passion for each other has **cooled off**.*

Infinitive

	present tense	-ing form	past tense	past participle
go back	go back & goes back	going back	went back	gone back

1. go back (to) *p.v.* When you return to a place where you were before, you **go back** or **go back** to that place.

> *That restaurant was terrible. We'll never **go back**.*
> *Dorothy left the Emerald City and **went back** to Kansas.*

2. go back (to) *p.v.* When a condition, problem, practice, or custom **goes back** to a certain time, it began at that time.

> *The tradition of saluting in the military **goes back** to the Middle Ages.*
> *His drug problem **goes back** to his college years.*

3. go back (to) *p.v.* When you are discussing the age of something, you **go back** or **go back** to when it was created or started.

> *This table is very valuable. It **goes back** to the 1760s.*
> *The archeologist found ruins that **go back** 5,000 years.*

hand over	hand over & hands over	handing over	handed over	handed over

1. hand . . . over (to) *p.v.* When you give something to people because they demand it, because they require it, or because you are not its rightful owner, you **hand** it **over** or **hand** it **over** to them. **Turn over** is similar to **hand over**.

> *I found some money in the street, and I **handed** it **over** to the police.*
> *That's my calculator — **hand** it right **over**!*

handover *n.* When you transfer ownership or control of something to someone because that person has demanded it or because you are not its rightful owner, a **handover** takes place.

> *The Chinese celebrated Britain's **handover** of Hong Kong.*
> *The President demanded the immediate **handover** of the occupied territory.*

2. hand . . . over *p.v.* When you give someone responsibility for an important project, duty, or problem, you **hand** that project, duty, or problem **over** or **hand** it **over** to someone.

> *Mr. Wilson retired and **handed** control of the company **over** to his son.*
> *The TV news anchor **handed** the show **over** to the reporter at the White House.*

pull over	pull over & pulls over	pulling over	pulled over	pulled over

1. pull . . . over *p.v.* When you are driving and then move your vehicle to the side of the road, reduce your speed, and then stop, you **pull over** or **pull** your vehicle **over**.

> *I **pulled over** to fix a flat tire.*
> *We're lost. Let's **pull** the car **over** and ask someone for directions.*

2. pull . . . over *p.v.* When you are driving and a police officer signals you to move your vehicle to the side of the road, reduce your speed, and stop, the police officer **pulls** you **over** or **pulls** the vehicle **over**.

> *Jim was driving on the wrong side of the road, and he got **pulled over** by the state police.*
>
> *When the police officer saw the driver go through a red light, he **pulled** the car right **over**.*

Infinitive

	present tense	-ing form	past tense	past participle
warm up	warm up & warms up	warming up	warmed up	warmed up

1. warm up *p.v.* When the temperature of a thing or place becomes higher, it **warms up**.

> *It's cold outside. I hope it **warms up** before the picnic.*
>
> *I set the thermostat at eighty degrees, and the house **warmed** right **up**.*

2. warm . . . up *p.v.* When people or things cause a thing or place to become warmer, they **warm** it **up**.

> *The fireplace doesn't really **warm** the house **up** much.*
>
> *That soup is cold. You can **warm** it **up** in the microwave.*

warmed up *part.adj.* After a thing or place has become warmer, it is **warmed up**.

> *Give the baby the bottle with the flowers on it; it's **warmed up**.*

3. warm . . . up *p.v.* When you allow a mechanical device to run for a short time before being used, you **warm** it **up**. When a mechanical device runs for a short time before being used, it **warms up**.

> *You should always **warm** your car **up** for a few minutes before you go anywhere.*
>
> *In the winter I always let my car **warm up** while I eat breakfast.*

warmed up *part.adj.* After a mechanical device has been allowed to **warm up** and is ready to be used, it is **warmed up**.

> *We have to go — is the car **warmed up** yet?*

4. warm up *p.v.* When you do light exercises before playing a sport or exercising with greater effort, you **warm up**. When performers play musical instruments or sing just before a performance in order to be ready, they **warm up**.

> *Before a race most runners **warm up** with stretching exercises.*
>
> *The singer **warmed up** in her dressing room before the concert.*

warm-up *n.* Light exercises done before playing a sport or exercising with greater effort are called a **warm-up**. When a performer plays an instrument or sings just before a performance in order to be ready, this is a **warm-up**.

> *The runners got to the stadium early so they would have time for a **warm-up**.*

warm-up *n.* **Warm-up** clothes are worn during a **warm-up**. **Warm-up** exercises are done before playing a sport or exercising. A **warm-up** game, round, and so on, is played in order to **warm up** for the actual game.

*The baseball players wore their **warm-up** jackets when they weren't on the field.*

EXERCISE 19a — **Complete the sentences with phrasal verbs from this section. Be sure the phrasal verbs are in the correct tense.**

1. The pizza was cold, so I put it in the microwave to _____ it _____.

2. My car was making a strange noise, so I _____ _____ to look at the engine.

3. Can I use your lawn mower? I'll _____ it _____ tomorrow.

4. Jim always puts milk in his coffee to _____ it _____.

5. The roots of the trouble in the Middle East _____ _____ thousands of years.

6. The new police chief said that he thinks that abolishing capital punishment was a mistake and that it should be _____ _____.

7. The judge ordered the thieves to _____ _____ the stolen merchandise immediately.

8. Hearing Uncle John's stories about the old country _____ _____ a lot of memories.

9. With this new antipollution law we're _____ _____ reducing the amount of pollution by 50 percent in ten years.

10. I asked Judy if I could use her video camera, and she said she would _____ it right _____.

11. The mechanic recommended letting the car _____ _____ before driving it.

12. The robber changed his mind when he saw the guard _____ his shotgun right _____ him.

13. The local police chief _____ the investigation _____ to the FBI agents.

14. Your father's angry right now. Talk to him about your miserable report card after he's _____ _____.

15. The changes at the factory are _____ _____ reducing costs and increasing profits.

16. The mystery of the Pyramids _____ _____ nearly 5,000 years.

17. The coach always makes the players _____ _____ before the game.

18. After lunch Jerry _____ right _____ to work.

19

19. This coffee is too hot. I can't drink it until it _____ _____.

20. I was _____ _____ by the sheriff for going eighty miles per hour in a school zone.

21. It's cold now, but it'll _____ _____ by noon.

EXERCISE 19b — Write three sentences using the objects in parentheses. Be sure to put the objects in the right place.

1. Could you *bring back*. (my tool kit, it)

_____

_____

_____

2. I'll *bring over*. (your tool kit, it)

_____

_____

_____

3. The air conditioner quickly *cooled off*. (my apartment, it)

_____

_____

_____

4. Todd *handed over*. (his wallet, it)

_____

_____

_____

5. The sheriff *pulled over*. (the suspects, them)

_____

_____

_____

6. The drivers are *warming up*. (their trucks, them)

_____

EXERCISE 19c — **Write answers to the questions using phrasal verbs from this section. Be sure the phrasal verbs are in the correct tense. Replace the underlined adverbs with *right*. Remember that *right* can be used only when the verb and the particle are separated.**

1. They lit a fire, and the cabin became warm <u>quickly</u>. What did the cabin do?

2. You will return to work <u>immediately</u>. What will you do?

3. After the sun set, the backyard became cooler <u>quickly</u>. What did the backyard do?

4. If I saw the flashing lights of the police car, I would slow my car and stop at the side of the road <u>immediately</u>. What would I do?

5. Sergeant Jones pointed his rifle <u>directly</u> at the enemy soldier. What did Sergeant Jones do?

6. She told me to return her dictionary <u>immediately</u>. What did she say?

7. Linda's father told her to give him his credit card <u>immediately</u>. What did Linda's father tell her to do?

8. I called Lydia and told her I needed medicine for my son, and she took the medicine from her house to my house <u>immediately</u>. What did Lydia do to the medicine?

EXERCISE 19d, Review — **Complete the sentences with these phrasal verbs from previous sections. Be sure the phrasal verbs are in the correct tense. To check their meanings, review the section number given after each one.**

back off, 12	go beyond, 18	stand around, 18
break through, 18	head into, 17	tell apart, 18
come across, 12	hit on, 13	track down, 13
come up with, 6	let off, 13	wind up, 14
fall through, 12	lift up, 18	
figure on, 18	put up, 12	

1. The prisoners _____ _____ the wall of the prison and escaped.

2. It was easy for them to escape because the guards had been _____ _____ smoking cigarettes.

3. The warden wasn't just upset with the guards — the problem _____ _____ that.

4. The guards used dogs to _____ _____ one of the escaped prisoners the next day.

5. The other prisoner _____ _____ some dense forest.

6. The prisoner tried to steal a man's car, but when he saw the man's large dog, he _____ _____.

7. The police had a meeting to try to _____ _____ _____ a way to capture the prisoner.

8. They finally _____ _____ the idea of using a helicopter.

9. The helicopter plan _____ _____ because the weather was so bad.

10. The police thought the prisoner would probably _____ _____ at his family's house.

11. The prisoner has a twin brother, and the police couldn't _____ them _____.

12. That was one problem the police didn't _____ _____.

13. One police officer walked behind the house and _____ _____ some garbage cans.

14. He heard a noise from the garbage can, so he _____ _____ the top and saw the prisoner.

15. The prisoner _____ _____ a fight, but the police were able to capture him.

16. Both prisoners were charged with escaping from prison, but the judge _____ them _____ with a warning.

20. FOCUS ON: **phrasal verbs followed by the *-ing* form**

Some phrasal verbs can be followed by the *-ing* form of verbs:

> He **ended up** <u>staying</u> home.
> She **lies around** <u>doing</u> nothing.

The *-ing* form can be negative:

> He **ended up** <u>not going</u> anywhere.
> She **lies around** <u>not doing</u> anything.

Nouns and pronouns can come between the phrasal verb and the *-ing* form:

> The doctor **went around** <u>the hospital</u> visiting his patients.
> Jim **hangs around** <u>Janice</u> hoping she'll fall in love with him.

Prepositional phrases can come between the phrasal verb and the *-ing* form:

> My luggage **ended up** <u>on the wrong flight</u> going to the wrong city.
> I **started out** <u>at the bottom</u> working in the mailroom.

Other adverbs and adverbial expressions can come between the phrasal verb and the *-ing* form:

> Bill **goes around** <u>constantly</u> looking for bargains.
> She **stayed up** <u>late</u> watching TV.
> I **went around** <u>all day</u> not knowing I had spinach in my teeth.
> He **ended up** <u>here</u> asking for money.

Infinitive				
	present tense	-ing form	past tense	past participle
end up	end up & ends up	ending up	ended up	ended up

1. end up *p.v.* When people **end up** doing something or **end up** a certain way, it is the result of a series of decisions, actions, or unplanned and unexpected occurrences. **End up** is similar to **wind up**.

> A hurricane was approaching Florida, so we **ended up** coming home from our
>   vacation early.
> Judy has never gone skydiving before, so she'll probably **end up** in the hospital
>   with two broken legs.

2. end up *p.v.* When people or things **end up** in a place, this place is where their journey ends even though the outcome may have been unplanned or unexpected.

> How did London Bridge **end up** in Arizona?
> The taxi driver didn't understand me, and we **ended up** in Newark instead
>   of New York.

Infinitive

present tense	-ing form	past tense	past participle
go around			
go around & goes around	going around	gone around	gone around

1. go around *p.v.* When people or things follow a circular path and return to the same place, they **go around**.

> The horse has **gone around** the track three times.
> It took seven days to **go around** the island.

2. go around *p.v.* When people or things follow an indirect or curved path in order to avoid an obstacle or to change direction, they **go around** or **go around** the obstacle.

> Heather **went around** the curve too fast, and she ended up in the ditch.
> There was some broken glass in the street, but I **went around** it.

3. go around *p.v.* When an object spins or turns, it **goes around**.

> The disk drives in computers **go around** very fast.
> The children have to stay on the merry-go-round until it stops **going around**.

4. go around *p.v.* When you **go around** a place, you visit various parts of it.

> The president **went around** the state giving the same speech at every stop.
> The exterminator is **going around** the house looking for rats.

5. go around *p.v.* When you **go around** in a certain condition or **go around** doing something, you go to various places and allow other people see you.

> I was so embarrassed — I **went around** all day with my zipper open.
> Are you going to **go around** all day wearing that stupid hat?

6. go around *p.v.* When you **go around** doing something, you go to various places and deliberately do something that may bother or upset other people.

> The new manager **goes around** telling everyone how to do their jobs.
> Don't **go around** sticking your nose in other people's business.

7. go around *p.v.* When something **goes around**, it spreads to various parts of a larger place.

> A rumor **went around** that the plant was going to close.
> He probably has the flu; it's been **going around**.

8. go around *p.v.* When something is being distributed to a group of people and there is enough for everyone, there is enough to **go around**.

> There wasn't enough food to **go around**, and some of the famine victims got nothing.
> Don't make the pieces of wedding cake too big, otherwise there won't be enough to
>   **go around**.

Infinitive

	present tense	-ing form	past tense	past participle
go off				
	go off & goes off	going off	went off	gone off

1. go off *p.v.* When a gun **goes off**, it fires. When a bomb **goes off**, it explodes. When an alarm or alarm clock **goes off**, it makes a loud noise.

> *The terrorists were killed when the bomb **went off** accidentally.*
> *I was late for work because my alarm clock didn't **go off**.*

2. go off *p.v.* When an electrical device or system **goes off**, it stops operating. **Come on** is the opposite of **go off**.

> *The electricity **went off** at 8:30 last night.*
> *A thermostat makes the air conditioner **go off** if it gets below a certain temperature.*

3. go off (with) *p.v.* When you **go off**, you leave a place or the people you are with and go to a different place. When you **go off** with someone, you leave a place or the people you are with and go to a different place with them.

> *Mark **went off** not realizing he had left his wallet at home.*
> *At the museum Sally **went off** with her friends to see some things we weren't*
> *interested in.*

4. go off *p.v.* When an event or plan **goes off** well, smoothly, without a problem, or without a hitch (a *hitch* is a problem), it happens as planned.

> *The drug bust **went off** without a hitch.*
> *The invasion didn't **go off** the way the general planned it.*

5. go off *p.v.* When a road, trail, path, and so on, **goes off**, it leaves the main road, trail, or path, and goes in a different direction.

> *This trail that **goes off** to the left will take you to the campground.*
> *We didn't know which way to go — one path **went off** to the left, the other*
> *to the right.*

go on				
	go on & goes on	going on	went on	gone on

1. go on *p.v.* When an electrical device or system **goes on**, it begins to operate.

> *A thermostat makes the air conditioner **go on** if it gets above a certain temperature.*
> *The lights **goes on** automatically if someone walks near the door.*

2. go on *p.v.* When something **goes on**, it happens. "What's **going on**?" is a common informal greeting.

> *Tell me what **went on** at the party last night.*
> *If you see anything illegal **going on**, call the police immediately.*

3. go on *p.v.* When people **go on**, they continue doing something. Sometimes, **on** is repeated for emphasis.

20

*I asked her to be quiet, but she **went** right **on** singing.*
*Just **go on** with what you're doing. I'll wait until you're finished.*
*I told him to stop talking, but he **went on** and **on** and **on** and **on**.*

4. go on *p.v.* When an event or activity **goes on**, it continues.

*The party **went on** until dawn.*
*I hate long meetings that **go on** for hours.*

5. go on *p.v.* When you **go on** information, you are able to continue an investigation or other project because you have this information.

*The detective said he needs more to **go on** and asked the public for information.*
*The auto company won't recall 75,000 cars because of one accident. That's just not enough to **go on**.*

6. go on *p.v.* When you **go on** a diet, you start a plan to lose weight.

*I **go on** a diet every January.*
*I have to **go on** a diet; my high school reunion is in two months.*

7. go on *p.v.* When you say "**Go on**" to people, you are encouraging them to do something.

*Yes, caviar is fish eggs, but it's good — **go on**, try it.*
*Oh, **go on** — don't be afraid.*

Infinitive

present tense	-ing form	past tense	past participle
hang around			
hang around & hangs around	hanging around	hung around	hung around

1. hang around *p.v.* [informal] When you **hang around** or **hang around** doing something, you stay in a place without a purpose for being there or because you are waiting for someone or something.

*I had to **hang around** for three hours waiting for the bus.*
*Bob's been **hanging around** the house all day. Doesn't he have anything to do?*

2. hang around *p.v.* [informal] When people stay in a place instead of leaving, they **hang around**.

*What's the hurry? **Hang around** for a while, and when I finish my homework we can watch TV.*
*Do you have to go or can you **hang around** for a while?*

3. hang around *p.v.* [informal] When you **hang around** people, you spend a lot of time with them. When you **hang around** a place, you spend a lot of time there.

*Erik's mother is worried. She doesn't like the guys he's **hanging around** with.*
*Jim and Bill were good friends. They always **hung around** when they were kids.*

Infinitive

	present tense	-ing form	past tense	past participle
lie around				
	lie around & lies around	lying around	lay around	lain around

1. lie around *p.v.* When you **lie around** or **lie around** doing something, you recline and relax and do not do anything important.

*Today is my day off, so don't ask me to do any work. I'm just going to **lie around**.*
*All my sister ever does is **lie around** watching soap operas.*

2. lie around *p.v.* [always continuous] When something is **lying around**, it is disorganized and no one is using it or paying attention to it.

*Jake is a slob. There are empty beer cans and old newspapers **lying around** all over his house.*
*We need to do something about all that junk **lying around** in the backyard.*

start out				
	start out & starts out	starting out	started out	started out

1. start out *p.v.* When you begin something, you **start out**. **Start out** is used to discuss how the end of something was different from its beginning.

*The stock market **started out** in positive territory but closed 200 points lower.*
*Nancy **started out** as a secretary, thinking she might have a future with this company, but she doesn't feel that way anymore.*

stay up				
	stay up & stays up	staying up	stayed up	stayed up

1. stay up *p.v.* When something **stays up**, it remains in a place that is higher than ground level.

*That shelf won't **stay up** if you put all those books on it.*
*The astronauts **stayed up** for 241 days.*

2. stay up *p.v.* When you **stay up**, you go to bed later than you normally do.

*Judy's tired because she **stayed up** until dawn studying for a chemistry test.*
*Don't **stay up** late — tomorrow's a school day.*

EXERCISE 20a — **Complete the sentences with phrasal verbs from this section. Be sure the phrasal verbs are in the correct tense.**

1. This is a dangerous neighborhood — so stay with me and don't _____ _____ by yourself.

2. Yesterday at work Leticia _____ _____ showing everyone her

   engagement ring.

3. Wedding ceremonies in some countries can _____ _____ for days.

4. The bomb will _____ _____ at exactly 6:00.

20

5. Where are you going? Why don't you _____ _____ until Jim comes home and then we can order a pizza.

6. The driver took a wrong turn, and we _____ _____ in the middle of nowhere.

7. On Sundays my husband usually _____ _____ on the couch watching football games.

8. My lazy son _____ _____ the house all day not lifting a finger to help with anything.

9. She's going to _____ _____ at her new job working only part-time, but later she'll switch to full-time.

10. Buy lots of champagne for the party; you want to be sure there's enough to _____ _____.

11. Bill likes to go to bed early — he can't _____ _____ past 8:00 P.M.

12. Rosa wanted to study medicine in college, but she _____ _____ studying law instead.

13. The paleontologist was amazed to find dinosaur eggs just _____ _____ in the desert.

14. I can't believe you _____ _____ town wearing those dirty clothes all day.

15. I'm sorry I missed the party. Did anything exciting _____ _____?

16. I'm nervous about the wedding. I hope it _____ _____ the way we planned it.

17. A rumor is _____ _____ the school about two of the teachers.

18. It's normal for the power to _____ _____ during a thunderstorm.

19. If that poster doesn't _____ _____ with tape, we'll have to use thumb tacks instead.

20. In the morning Dr. Smith usually _____ _____ the hospital visiting his patients.

21. Jim is usually a good boy, but when he _____ _____ with Jake he gets in trouble.

22. He was trying to _____ _____ a slow truck when he had the accident.

23. I _____ _____ a diet two weeks ago, and so far I haven't lost an ounce.

24. In the past no one believed that the earth _____ _____ the sun.

25. If you're leaving, what are you waiting for? _____ _____, leave!

26. How can I make such an important decision with so little information? I need more to _____ _____.

27. I'm surprised that the heat _____ _____ last night — it's only September.

28. Miguel's new race car is really fast. Yesterday he _____ _____ the track in record time.

29. After you cross the bridge, you'll see a gravel road that _____ _____ a lake and heads toward the mountains.

30. I don't want to retire. I'm going to _____ _____ working as long as I can.

EXERCISE 20b — **Write answers to the questions using phrasal verbs from this section. Be sure the phrasal verbs are in the correct tense.**

1. You're going to spend the day on the sofa watching TV. What are you going to do all day?

2. Lydia walked to various places in her new house making decorating plans. What did Lydia do in her new house?

3. The letter was supposed to go to Austria, but it finally arrived in Australia. What happened to the letter?

4. The electricity stops working everyday at 2:00. What does the electricity do?

5. Joe called and asked what was happening. What did Joe ask?

6. Bob goes to every office at work telling awful jokes. What does Bob do at work?

7. Janice didn't go to bed all night. What did Janice do?

8. Dan stays in his house all day. He doesn't go anywhere or do anything. What does Dan do all day?

9. You were late to work because your alarm clock didn't ring this morning. What didn't your alarm clock do this morning?

10. Jerry went to many places wearing a Hawaiian shirt. What did Jerry do?

11. When it gets dark the street lights begin to operate automatically. What do the lights do?

12. I bought only twenty-five hot dogs for the party, but thirty people showed up, so some people didn't get a hot dog. Why didn't some people get a hot dog?

13. There are a lot of potholes in the street, and I have to avoid them while I'm driving. What do I have to do while I'm driving?

14. I couldn't decide between the red car and the blue car, but I finally decided on the red car. What did I finally do?

15. Mr. Watson is the brains of this company. If he left we couldn't continue. What couldn't we do without Mr. Watson?

16. Jane began the project thinking it would take only a few weeks. What did Jane do?

EXERCISE 20c — **Write original sentences using these phrasal verbs from this section and previous sections followed by the *-ing* form. The first number after the verb is the section; the second number is the meaning. It is only that meaning that can be followed by the *-ing* form. Try to make some of the sentences similar to those in the *FOCUS* section.**

break down, 5/3	go on, 20/3	start out, 20/1
come over, 17/1,2,3	hang around, 20/1	stay up, 20/2
end up, 20/1	lie around, 20/1	take off, 1/7
go around, 20/4,5,6	show up, 1/1	wind up, 14/2
go off, 20/3	stand around, 18/11	

1. _____

2. _____

3. _____

4. _____

5. _____

6. _____

7. _____

8. _____

9. _____

10. _____

11. _____

12. _____

13. _____

14. _____

EXERCISE 20d, Review — **Complete the sentences with these phrasal verbs from previous sections. Be sure the phrasal verbs are in the correct tense. To check their meanings, review the section number given after each one.**

aim at, 19	call off, 13	go about, 17	rip up, 17
blow away, 15	cool off, 19	go back, 19	screw out of, 3
break out, 9	dry out, 15	hear of, 8	see about, 7
bring over, 19	give up, 9	pay for, 4	work up, 9

1. My teacher made a mistake when he corrected my test and _____ me _____ _____ ten points.

2. You'd better wear a jacket — it has _____ _____ outside.

3. Her letter made me so mad that I _____ it _____.

4. You don't need to rake the leaves; the wind will _____ them _____.

5. We knew we didn't have any hope of winning the battle, so we _____ _____.

6. You can't run ten miles on the first day of your exercise program. You have to _____ _____ to it.

7. Michael didn't see the red light and hit a gasoline truck. He _____ _____ his mistake with his life.

8. Sam asked me if I knew someone named Francisco, and I said I had never _____ _____ him.

9. My family has been in Massachusetts since the seventeenth century. They _____ _____ on the *Mayflower*.

10. Our trip to Miami was _____ _____ because of the hurricane.

11. I'm going to _____ the dentist _____ getting my teeth whitened.

12. Do you know how to _____ _____ getting a passport?

13. This rug is wet; let's take it outside to _____ _____ in the sun.

14. The new restrictions on cigarette advertising are _____ _____ reducing the level of teenage smoking.

15. They _____ _____ of prison by tunneling under the prison wall.

16. We don't have enough plates for the party, so I called Maria and asked her to _____ some _____ .

---

21. FOCUS ON: **phrasal verbs and *should* and *ought to***

Should and *ought to* have two important meanings in English. One is familiar to most students, but the other is not.

A good idea: *should* and *ought to*

Should and *ought to* can be used to say that doing something is a good idea because it will benefit the person you are speaking about:

> *You <u>should</u> **zip up** your coat.*
> *You <u>ought to</u> **zip up** your coat.*

or because the person you are speaking about is expected, though not required, to do something:

> *You <u>should</u> **bring in** the groceries for your mother.*
> *You <u>ought to</u> **bring in** the groceries for your mother.*

Although *should* and *ought* are modal auxiliary verbs, *ought* <u>must</u> be used with *to*. In other words, *ought* does not equal *should*, *ought <u>to</u>* equals *should*. Never say *should to*.

Very probable: *should* and *ought to*

Both *should* and *ought to* are used to say that something is very probable, very likely, or 90 percent sure to happen — that if everything is normal, as expected, or as planned, a condition will very probably exist or something will very probably happen:

> *The rebel territory <u>should</u> **settle down** once winter comes.*
> *The rebel territory <u>ought to</u> **settle down** once winter comes.*

In the examples above, either *should* or *ought to* can be used — they have the same meaning — however, only *should* is used in questions:

> *Should* Tom **zip up** his jacket?
> ~~*Ought* Tom *to* **zip up** *his jacket?*~~

and only *should not* or *shouldn't* is used in negative sentences:

> Tom *should* *not* **zip up** his jacket.
> ~~*Tom* *ought* *not* *to* **zip up** *his jacket.*~~

Should not (or *shouldn't*) is used to say that something is not probable. It means that something is very improbable, very unlikely, or 90 percent sure not to happen — that if everything is normal, as expected, or as planned, a condition will very probably not exist or something will very probably not happen:

> *I set the thermostat at sixty-five degrees, and I'm sure it won't get below seventy tonight, so the heat* *shouldn't* ***go on***.

Infinitive			
present tense	-ing form	past tense	past participle
look around			
look around & looks around	looking around	looked around	looked around

1. look around *p.v.* When you turn your head to see what is behind you or around you, you **look around**.

> *I heard a sound, and I* ***looked around*** *to see who it was.*
> *Sally* ***looked around*** *the room and didn't recognize anyone.*

2. look around *p.v.* When you **look around** or **look around** a place, you go to various parts of the place in order to see what it is like or what is there.

> *You should* ***look around*** *before you decide whether you want to buy the house.*
> *Linda* ***looked around*** *the bookstore but didn't find anything interesting.*

look over			
look over & looks over	looking over	looked over	looked over

1. look ... over *p.v.* [usually separated] When you **look** something **over**, you look at it or read it carefully and thoroughly.

> *He ought to* ***look*** *the car* ***over*** *before he buys it.*
> *Here's the first chapter of my new book;* ***look*** *it* ***over*** *and tell me what you think.*

pick on			
pick on & picks on	picking on	picked on	picked on

1. pick on *p.v.* When you **pick on** people, you continually tease and criticize them.

> *Susie, you shouldn't* ***pick on*** *your little brother.*
> *The teacher never criticizes anyone else — she* ***picks*** *only* ***on*** *me.*

21

Infinitive

present tense	-ing form	past tense	past participle
settle down			
settle down & settles down	settling down	settled down	settled down

1. settle ... down *p.v.* When you **settle down**, you become less active, nervous, or upset. When you **settle** other people **down**, you do something to make them less active, nervous, or upset. **Calm down** is similar to **settle down**.

> *Why are you so nervous about the test? Just **settle down**; you'll do just fine.*
> *Can't you **settle** the children **down**? All that noise is driving me crazy.*

2. settle ... down *p.v.* When a confused or violent situation becomes less confused or violent, it **settles down**. When you **settle** a confused or violent situation **down**, you make it less confused or violent and more calm. **Calm down** is similar to **settle down**.

> *Rioting and arson continued for three days before the area **settled down**.*
> *The head of the union spoke to the angry strikers to try to **settle** them **down**.*

3. settle down *p.v.* When people **settle down**, they start to live a less active life and perhaps get married, buy a house, and start a family.

> *Mike led a pretty wild life when he was in his early twenties, but he got married when he was 29 and **settled down**.*
> *My son is forty-one. I wish he'd **settle down** and raise a family.*

step on

step on & steps on	stepping on	stepped on	stepped on

1. step on *p.v.* When you **step on** something, you place your foot on it.

> *If the carpenter **steps on** a nail, she'll have to go to the hospital for a tetanus shot.*
> *Sam **stepped on** a cockroach.*

2. step on *p.v. [informal]* When you say "**Step on** it" to someone who is driving a car, you are telling the driver to drive faster.

> *Hank needed to get to the airport in fifteen minutes, so he told the taxi driver to **step on** it.*
> ***Step on** it! We have to be at work in ten minutes.*

take out on

take out on & takes out on	taking out on	took out on	taken out on

1. take ... out on *p.v.* When you **take** something **out on** people, you unfairly criticize or punish them because you are angry about something that has occurred or about something that someone else has done.

> *If you're mad at your boss, you shouldn't **take** it **out** on your wife.*
> *Hey! It's not my fault you got a speeding ticket. Why are you **taking** it **out on** me?*

Infinitive

present tense	-ing form	past tense	past participle
think ahead			
think ahead & thinks ahead	thinking ahead	thought ahead	thought ahead

1. think ahead *p.v.* When you **think ahead**, you plan for a future situation or activity so that you will not have a problem.

> When we're out camping, there won't be any stores around if you forget something, so **think ahead**.
> We **thought ahead** before we drove through the desert; we took forty liters of water.

zip up			
zip up & zips up	zipping up	zipped up	zipped up

1. zip ... up *p.v.* When you **zip up** a coat or other item of clothing, you close it with a zipper.

> It's freezing outside — **zip** your coat **up**.
> I can't **zip** my dress **up**. Can you?

zipped up *part.adj.* After you **zip up** a coat or other item of clothing, it is **zipped up**.

> Look at Timmy out there in the snow without his coat **zipped up**.
> Before you go to the airport, make sure your suitcases are **zipped up**.

EXERCISE 21a — **Complete the sentences with phrasal verbs from this section. Be sure the phrasal verbs are in the correct tense.**

1. It's not your brother's fault you failed the math test. You shouldn't _____ it _____ _____ him.

2. Timmy left some of his toys on the floor. Be careful not to _____ _____ them.

3. There's a guy in my class who's really mean and makes jokes about me. I told the teacher that he's always _____ _____ me.

4. Someone called my name, and I _____ _____ to see who it was.

5. Jane is already thirty-four, but she's not interested in _____ _____ and having children.

6. I've _____ _____ your résumé, and I think you're the right person for this job.

7. Timmy and Susie were running around the house like crazy, so I played their favorite videotape to try to _____ them _____.

8. You should _____ your backpack _____; otherwise all your books are going to fall out.

9. The two countries have a history of border clashes, but things have _____

_____ in the last few years.

10. I've never been in your house before; I'd like to _____ _____ and see how

you've decorated it.

11. You don't want to arrive in Tokyo and realize you forgot something important back in

Vancouver, so _____ _____.

12. We're late — _____ _____ it!

EXERCISE 21b — **Write answers to the questions using phrasal verbs from this section. Be sure the phrasal verbs are in the correct tense.**

1. Dan ought to look at the car very carefully before he decides whether to buy it. What should Dan do?

2. You went to a big bookstore and walked around so that you could see what books they have. What did you do in the bookstore?

3. Our neighbors were arguing all evening, but they stopped arguing and got quieter at around 1:00 A.M. What did our neighbors do around 1:00 A.M.?

4. It's freezing outside, so you ought to close the zipper on your jacket. What should you do to your jacket?

5. In Question 4, how would you describe the jacket after it is closed?

6. At the meeting, the boss asked Betty some difficult questions, and Betty wasn't ready with the answers. What didn't Betty do?

7. Frank unfairly criticizes his son. What does Frank do to his son?

8. Mark had a bad day at work, and when he came home he yelled at his wife. What did Mark do to his wife?

9. When Mike was dancing with Heather, he put his foot on her foot. What did Mike do to Heather's foot?

EXERCISE 21c, Review — **Rewrite the underlined words in the sentences using these phrasal verbs from previous sections and** *should* **or** *ought to*. **Remember that** *ought to* **is not usually used in negative sentences.**

break through, 18	cool off, 19	hold up, 7
burn out, 8	fall off, 10	pull through, 2
come over, 17	get off, 18	warm up, 19
come through, 15	get through, 16	wind up, 14
come up, 12	go for, 16	

Example: If they go to that restaurant, they <u>will</u> <u>very</u> <u>probably</u> <u>expect</u> <u>to</u> <u>pay</u> $200.

If they go to that restaurant, they should figure on paying $200.

or

If they go to that restaurant, they ought to figure on paying $200.

1. Business in this restaurant <u>will</u> <u>very</u> <u>probably</u> <u>decrease</u> in January.

2. They <u>are</u> <u>very</u> <u>probably</u> <u>finishing</u> the investigation.

3. These cheap shoes <u>will</u> <u>very</u> <u>probably</u> <u>not</u> <u>stay</u> <u>in</u> <u>good</u> <u>condition</u> more than three months.

4. Jim flies from Florida to Boston every year in April, and it's April now. Jim <u>will</u> <u>very</u> <u>probably</u> <u>travel</u> to Boston soon.

5. It almost always gets cooler in October, and it's October 1st today, so it <u>will</u> <u>very</u> <u>probably</u> <u>get</u> <u>cooler</u> soon.

6. Raul's disease is not serious, so he <u>will</u> <u>very</u> <u>probably</u> <u>be</u> <u>well</u> <u>again</u>.

7. Francisco almost never works past 5:00, and it's 4:50 now. He <u>will</u> <u>very</u> <u>probably</u> <u>stop</u> <u>working</u> in a few minutes.

8. Lydia likes skiing a lot, so if you suggest that we go skiing next weekend, she <u>will</u> <u>very</u> <u>probably</u> <u>like</u> the idea.

9. The enemy soldiers have been trying to smash a hole in the wall of the fort for two hours, and they <u>will</u> <u>very</u> <u>probably</u> <u>smash</u> <u>a</u> <u>hole</u> in the wall soon.

10. Sally said she would come to my house at 5:30 and it's 5:40 now. She <u>will</u> <u>very</u> <u>probably</u> <u>come</u> <u>to</u> <u>my</u> <u>house</u> soon.

11. This work normally takes four hours to finish, so if you start at 9:00 you <u>will</u> <u>very</u> <u>probably</u> <u>finish</u> around 1:00.

12. The train almost always passes through town at 3:25, and it's 3:20 now, so the train <u>will</u> <u>very</u> <u>probably</u> <u>pass</u> <u>through</u> town in five minutes.

13. I put a lot of wood on the fire, so it <u>very</u> <u>probably</u> <u>will</u> <u>not</u> <u>stop</u> <u>burning</u> before morning.

14. The car heater is on maximum, so it <u>will</u> <u>very</u> <u>probably</u> <u>get</u> <u>warm</u> soon.

EXERCISE 21d, Review — **Complete the sentences with these phrasal verbs from previous sections. Be sure the phrasal verbs are in the correct tense. To check their meanings, review the section number given after each one.**

bring back, 19	go around, 20	hand over, 19	pull over, 19
end up, 20	go back, 19	hang around, 20	ring up, 8
fall apart, 17	go off, 20	lie around, 20	start out, 20
get back at, 17	go on, 20	line up, 18	stay up, 20

1. After Mark's father died, Tom _____ _____ the office collecting money to buy some flowers for the funeral.

2. Who said you could use my camera? _____ it _____ right now!

3. The smoke alarm in our kitchen _____ _____ every time I fry chicken.

4. We've been driving for five hours straight. Let's _____ _____ and rest for a few minutes.

5. Our travel agent is trying to _____ _____ a hot air balloon to take us to the top of Mt. Everest.

6. Last night I _____ _____ late watching *Casablanca* on TV.

7. My old bicycle is in very bad condition. I ought to buy a new one before it completely _____ _____.

8. I'm mad at Sarah for telling my husband what happened at the office party. I'll _____ _____ _____ her someday.

9. I _____ _____ thinking it wouldn't cost more than $300 to fix my car, but I've already spent more than $700.

10. Jimmy didn't used to get in trouble until he started to _____ _____ with Jake.

11. If you don't quit smoking and lose some weight, you're going to _____ _____ dying before you're fifty.

12. Visiting my old high school last week _____ _____ a lot of great memories.

13. Are you going to do anything today or just _____ _____ watching TV?

14. I'm sorry I interrupted your story. Please _____ _____.

15. The cashier _____ _____ my stuff and said, "That comes to $47.21."

16. Alfonso left his credit card at the restaurant, so he had to _____ _____ to get it.

---

22. FOCUS ON: **the particle *up* and the adverbs *right* and *all***

The particle *up* is used in many phrasal verbs, and one of its uses is to say that something has been done thoroughly or completely:

> The building **burned**. (The building was damaged but not destroyed.)
> The building **burned up**. (The building was completely destroyed.)

Right, discussed in Section 19, is often used in phrasal verbs with *up* to indicate that the action of the verb not only happened thoroughly and completely but also quickly:

> They **ate** it **up**. (They ate all the food.)
> They **ate** it *right* **up**. (They ate all the food, and they ate it quickly.)

Remember that *right* can be used in this way only after an object that is separating the verb and particle:

> They **ate** the pizza *right* **up**.
> ~~They **ate** *right* **up** the pizza.~~

Even though *up* indicates that the action of the verb is thorough and complete, *all* is sometimes used for further emphasis with participle adjectives derived from phrasal verbs with *up*:

> My taxes are *all* **paid up**.
> The drain is *all* **plugged up**.

Infinitive

present tense	-ing form	past tense	past participle
burn up			
burn up & burns up	burning up	burned up	burned up

1. burn up *p.v.* When something is completely destroyed by heat or fire, it **burns up**.

> The meteor **burned up** in the atmosphere.
> The rocket's fuel will **burn up** after only forty seconds.

2. burn ... up *p.v.* When people or things destroy something with heat or fire, they **burn** it **up**.

> There's no more coal. We **burned** it all **up**.
> Jet engines **burn up** fuel at a tremendous rate.

burned up *part.adj.* After something is completely destroyed by heat or fire, it is **burned up**.

> There isn't anymore firewood; it's all **burned up**.
> The house is all **burned up**. There's no way it can be saved.

3. burned ... up *p.v.* [informal] When something makes you very angry, it **burns** you **up**.

> It really **burns** me **up** when other people take credit for my work.
> I have to say something to Sally about what she did. It's **burning** me **up**.

burned up *part.adj.* [informal] When you are very angry, you are **burned up**.

> Jim was **burned up** when his boss criticized him during the meeting.
> Relax — it's nothing to get all **burned up** about.

clear up			
clear up & clears up	clearing up	cleared up	cleared up

1. clear up *p.v.* When a problem, misunderstanding, or disease goes away, it **clears up**.

> The misunderstanding **cleared up** right away after we talked about it.
> My rash is **clearing up** by itself. I don't need to go to the doctor.

cleared up *part.adj.* After a problem, misunderstanding, or disease goes away, it is **cleared up**.

> I feel great. My sinus infection is all **cleared up**.
> Everything's okay. It was a big misunderstanding, but it's **cleared up** now.

2. clear ... up *p.v.* When you do something to solve a problem or misunderstanding or do something to cure a disease, you **clear** it **up**.

> Everyone was confused about the new policy, so a memo was issued that **cleared** everything **up**.
> The medicine Dr. Smith gave me **cleared** the infection **up**.

3. clear up *p.v.* When clouds in the sky go away, the weather **clears up**.

> Unless it **clears up**, we'll have to cancel the picnic.
> It was a beautiful day after the sky **cleared up**.

Infinitive

	present tense	-ing form	past tense	past participle
count up	count up & counts up	counting up	counted up	counted up

1. count ... up *p.v.* When you count all of something to see how many of them there are, you **count** them **up**.

> **Count** the money **up** and tell me what the total is.
> **Counting up** the yes and no votes is going to take a long time.

eat up	eat up & eats up	eating up	ate up	eaten up

1. eat ... up *p.v.* When you **eat** food **up**, you eat all of it.

> There's no more pizza; David **ate** it all **up**.
> Don't **eat up** the cake before your father gets a piece.

2. eat ... up *p.v.* When something **eats up** something else, such as money or time, it uses all of it.

> I'm broke. Fixing my car last week **ate up** my entire paycheck.
> I don't want to go shopping with you. It'll **eat up** the whole day.

heat up	heat up & heats up	heating up	heated up	heated up

1. heat ... up *p.v.* When something or someone makes something hotter, they heat it up.

> Waiter, this soup is cold. Would you **heat** it **up** for me?
> Sometimes the sun **heats up** the desert to 120 degrees.

heated up *part.adj.* After something or someone makes something hotter, it is **heated up**.

> Don't give the baby that cold bottle; give her this **heated up** one.
> The spaghetti has been in the microwave for five minutes, so I'm sure it's **heated up**
>   by now.

pay up	pay up & pays up	paying up	paid up	paid up

1. pay up *p.v.* When you **pay up**, you pay all the money you owe to a person, bank, and so on, usually as a result of pressure to pay the money.

> A guy from the collection agency called and told me I'd better **pay up**.
> I wasn't surprised when the insurance company refused to **pay up**.

paid up *part.adj.* After you are **paid up**, you have paid all the money you owe to a person, bank, and so on.

> *I told the bill collector that he had made a mistake. I'm all **paid up**.*
> *Betty's VISA card is **paid up**, so there won't be any finance charge next month.*

plug up

plug up & plugs up	plugging up	plugged up	plugged up

1. plug . . . up *p.v.* When people or things block a narrow passage, such as a pipe, drain, or hole, so that nothing can flow through it, they **plug** it **up**.

> *Don't pour bacon grease in the sink; it'll **plug up** the drain.*
> *I need to **plug up** the hole in the roof where the rain is leaking in.*

plugged up *part.adj.* When a narrow passage, such as a pipe, drain, or hole, is completely blocked so that nothing can flow through it, it is **plugged up**.

> *Call the plumber; the sink's **plugged up**.*
> *My nose is all **plugged up**, and I can't smell anything.*

wipe up

wipe up & wipes up	wiping up	wiped up	wiped up

1. wipe . . . up *p.v.* When you completely remove a liquid from a surface by moving a towel or sponge across it with a sweeping motion, you **wipe** the liquid **up**. (**Wipe up** is similar to **wipe off**; however, you **wipe up** a liquid, but you **wipe off** the surface the liquid is on.)

> *Susie spilled her milk, and her mother told her to **wipe** it all **up**.*
> *You'd better **wipe up** the water on the bathroom floor before someone falls.*

EXERCISE 22a — **Complete the sentences with phrasal verbs from this section. Be sure the phrasal verbs are in the correct tense.**

1. Don't _____ _____ the potato chips. Leave some for me.

2. We have to _____ the hole in this boat _____ fast before it sinks.

3. It _____ me _____ when people smoke in a nonsmoking section.

4. There was a lot of confusion about the new plan, so we asked Tom to _____ it

   _____ for us.

5. The bill collector threatened to repossess my car if I didn't _____ _____.

6. The pain I had in my shoulder _____ right _____ after I tried the new therapy.

7. Okay, let's _____ _____ the points to see who won the game.

8. It was cloudy in the morning, but around 11:00 it _____ right _____.

9. It hasn't rained in months, so this dry forest will really _____ _____

   if there's a fire.

10. Would you get a towel and _____ _____ the coffee you spilled?

11. I'll put your dinner in the refrigerator, and you can _____ it _____ when you

come home.

12. I'm going to _____ _____ all these old papers in the fireplace.

13. I didn't have any insurance, so paying for those hospital bills really _____

_____ all my savings.

EXERCISE 22b — **Write three sentences using the objects in parentheses. Be sure
to put the objects in the right place.**

1. They *burned up*. (the wood, it)

_____

_____

_____

2. He ought to *clear up*. (the misunderstanding, it)

_____

_____

_____

3. Would you *count up*? (the votes, them)

_____

_____

_____

4. Have they *eaten up*? (all the candy, it)

_____

_____

_____

5. I can't *plug up*. (the hole, it)

_____

_____

_____

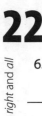

6. *Wipe up* right now! (that water, it)

_____

_____

_____

EXERCISE 22c — **Write answers to the questions using phrasal verbs and participle adjectives from this section. Be sure the phrasal verbs are in the correct tense.**

1. You completely blocked the drain so that water couldn't go through it. What did you do to the drain?

2. In Question 1, how would you describe the drain?

3. I'm putting my coffee in the microwave to make it hotter. What am I doing to my coffee?

4. In Question 3, how would you describe my coffee after I take it out of the microwave?

5. Erik hasn't counted all the money. What hasn't Erik done?

6. You'll pay all your late mortgage payments. What will you do to your mortgage?

7. In Question 6, how will you be regarding your mortgage?

8. The police used fire to destroy all the drugs. What did the police do?

9. In Question 8, how would you describe the drugs now?

10. My disease went away immediately. What did my disease do?

11. Sarah is cleaning up all the orange juice that she spilled on the floor. What is Sarah doing?

12. Carlos always eats all his baby food, and he eats it quickly. What does Carlos do?

EXERCISE 22d, Review — **Complete the sentences with these phrasal verbs from previous sections. Be sure the phrasal verbs are in the correct tense. To check their meanings, review the section number given after each one.**

carry on, 16	go with, 15	look around, 21	step on, 21
count on, 16	hand in, 13	put away, 14	take out on, 21
dress up, 14	head back, 15	sign in, 12	think ahead, 21
dry up, 14	head for, 15	sign out, 12	zip up, 21

1. I'll be there when you need me. You can _____ _____ me.

2. Do you think these shoes _____ _____ my dress?

3. _____ _____ so that you have everything you need when you get there.

4. Linda is here in the office somewhere — she _____ _____ at 8:52.

5. Linda always leaves at 5:00, and it's almost 6:00 now, so I'm sure she has already _____

   _____.

6. That guy is crazy. He ought to be _____ _____.

7. When you finish with the job application, you can _____ it _____ to the secretary.

8. I don't think we should make any changes now. Let's _____ _____ our

   original plan.

9. The party will be casual, so you don't have to _____ _____.

10. Maria told me she would be in the library between 7:00 and 8:00, but I _____

    _____ and couldn't find her.

11. There's some broken glass there — don't _____ _____ it.

12. I hope it rains soon. The lake is starting to _____ _____.

13. _____ _____ your coat — it's fifteen degrees below zero outside.

14. Janice hates her job, and she _____ it _____ _____ her husband.

15. I'm _____ _____ San Diego, and I should get there by late afternoon.

16. I'll stay in San Diego for a week and then _____ _____ to Los Angeles.

23. FOCUS ON: two-word phrasal verbs that require an additional particle when used with an object, 2

As we saw in Section 9, many phrasal verbs that can be used both intransitively and transitively require a second particle when they are used transitively, which makes them three-word phrasal verbs.

Although these phrasal verbs have a three-word version, they remain classified as two-word verbs because the two-word and three-word phrasal verbs have the same meaning — they are variations of the same verb:

> He **filled in**.
> He **filled in** <u>for</u> Mike.

There are, however, three-word phrasal verbs that share the same verb and first particle as another two-word phrasal verb but have an entirely different meaning. These are two different phrasal verbs and are classified separately:

> He **put up** a poster.
> He **put up with** her rudeness.

Infinitive

present tense	-ing form	past tense	past participle
crack down			
crack down & cracks down	cracking down	cracked down	cracked down

1. crack down (on) *p.v.* When you **crack down** or **crack down** on someone or something, you enforce rules and laws more than you enforced them before or you make new, stronger rules and laws.

> The chief of police said he was going to **crack down** on car theft.
> The students have been coming to class later and later everyday. It's time to start **cracking down**.

crackdown *n.* When you enforce rules and laws more than you enforced them before, this is a **crackdown**.

> The FBI is planning a major **crackdown** on organized crime.
> After the **crackdown**, the crime rate plunged.

cut down			
cut down & cuts down	cutting down	cut down	cut down

1. cut ...down *p.v.* When you **cut down** a tree, you use a saw or an axe to cut it and make it fall to the ground.

> You should **cut** that dead tree **down** before it falls on your house.
> The builder was criticized for **cutting down** so many trees when he built the house.

2. cut ...down *p.v.* [*informal — always separated*] When you **cut** people **down** to size, you do or say something to make them feel less important or less powerful.

*I'm tired of that jerk. I'm going to **cut** him **down** to size.*
*Hank thinks he's such a tough guy. Someone ought to **cut** him **down** to size.*

3. cut down (on) *p.v.* When you **cut down** or **cut down** on something that you consume, you use it less. When you **cut down** or **cut down** on something you do, you do it less. **Cut back** is similar to **cut down**.

*If you can't quit smoking, you should at least **cut down**.*
*My doctor said **cutting down** on fat in my diet would lower my cholesterol.*

Infinitive

	present tense	-ing form	past tense	past participle
drop out				
	drop out & drops out	dropping out	dropped out	dropped out

1. drop out (of) *p.v.* When you **drop out** or **drop out** of a school, a training course, or other program, you leave before completing it.

*The program is very difficult, and about 70 percent of the students **drop out**.*
*Linda's father was very disappointed when she **dropped out** of college.*

dropout *n.* A **dropout** is someone who has left school, usually high school or college, before graduating.

*Many successful people are college **dropouts**.*

get away				
	get away & gets away	getting away	got away	gotten/got away

1. get away (from) *p.v.* When you escape from people who are chasing you because they want to hurt you or because you have committed a crime, you **get away** or **get away** from them.

*When he took the knife out of his pocket, I **got away** from him fast.*
*By the time the police arrived, the robbers had already **gotten away**.*

getaway *n.* When you escape from people who want to capture or hurt you, you make a **getaway**.

*The robbers made their **getaway** in a blue Ford.*
*The car used for the **getaway** was found abandoned in the next town.*

2. get away (with) *p.v.* When you do something that is sneaky or wrong and you are not punished or criticized for it because no one knows or cares about it, you **get away** with it.

*Jake has been cheating on his taxes for years, and he always **gets away** with it.*
*He **got away** with killing his ex-wife even though everyone knew he was guilty.*

3. get away (from) *p.v.* When you **get away** from people or places, you leave them even though it may be difficult.

*I'm tired of this town. I need to **get away**.*
*Frank was talking and talking, and I couldn't **get away** from him.*

4. get away *p.v.* When you **get away**, you go on vacation.

*I have a lot of work to do, but I'll try to **get away** for a week or two.*
*We always try to **get away** in January and go skiing.*

Infinitive

	present tense	-ing form	past tense	past participle
hold out	hold out & holds out	holding out	held out	held out

1. hold...out *p.v.* When you **hold out** your hand, you extend it in front of your body so that someone can shake hands with you or put something in your hand. **Hold out** is similar to **put out**.

*Maybe Mr. Young is mad at me. I **held out** my hand, but he didn't shake it.*
*The street was filled with beggars **holding** their hands **out**.*

2. hold out *p.v.* When a supply of something is enough for your needs, the supply **holds out**.

*The beer **held out** until the end of the party, but we didn't have enough wine.*
*This is all the money I have, so it has to **hold out** until I get paid again.*

3. hold out *p.v.* When you **hold out**, you resist an attack, pressure, or temptation or you continue to survive in a dangerous situation.

More than 1,000 enemy soldiers attacked the fort. There were only 98 of us inside,
*   but we **held out** for two weeks.*
I haven't had a cigarette in three days, and I don't know how much longer I
*   can **hold out**.*

holdout *n.* Someone who resists an attack, pressure, or temptation is a **holdout**.

*The enemy soldiers are in control of the country, but there are some **holdouts** hiding*
*   in the mountains.*
*There are still a few **holdouts** who don't have credit cards.*

4. hold out (for) *p.v.* When you **hold out** or **hold out** for something, you refuse to compromise in a negotiation and accept anything less than your original demands.

*The basketball player is **holding out** for a million dollars a game.*
*The union spokesman said the union members would **hold out** until their demands*
*   were met.*

holdout *n.* When you refuse to compromise in a negotiation and accept anything less than your original demands, you are a **holdout**.

*All the players have signed contracts except for two **holdouts**.*

make up				
	make up & makes up	making up	made up	made up

1. make...up *p.v.* When you invent a story to entertain or fool people, you **make** the story **up**. When you invent a lie to deceive people, you **make** the lie **up**.

*My son asked me to **make up** a story about monsters.*
Hank told his boss he was late for work because he had to go to the doctor, but he just
*   **made** that excuse **up**.*

made-up *part.adj.* When a story is invented or fictional, it is **made-up**.

*There's no truth to any of this — it's just a **made-up** story.*

2. make up (of) *p.v. [often passive]* When people or things **make up** a larger thing, they together form that larger thing. When a larger thing is **made up** of people or things, they together form that larger thing.

*Children under fifteen **make up** 50 percent of the population.*
*An airplane is **made up** of thousands of parts.*

3. make . . . up *p.v.* When you **make up** your mind, **make up** your mind about something, or **make up** your mind about doing something, you decide which choice to make or which action to take.

*I like both the blue dress and the red dress. I can't **make up** my mind.*
*My daughter still hasn't **made up** her mind about which college to attend.*
*Marsha **made** her mind **up** about quitting her job and joining the Navy.*

made up *part.adj.* After you **make up** your mind or **make up** your mind to do something, your mind is **made up**.

*Don't waste your time talking to Tom about it — his mind is **made up**.*

4. make . . . up *p.v.* When you have an amount of money that is not enough for a certain requirement and you add more money so that it will be enough, you **make up** the difference between the amount you have and the amount you need.

The cashier was supposed to have $755 at the end of her shift, but she had only $735,
*   so she had to **make** the shortage **up** with her own money.*
*I didn't have enough saved to pay for college, but my Uncle Fred **made up***
*   the difference.*

5. make . . . up *p.v.* When you do something that you were required to do earlier but did not, such as attend a class, take a test, or complete a homework assignment, you **make** it **up**.

*Karen asked the teacher about **making up** the test that she missed.*
*The teacher told her she could **make** it **up** tomorrow after school.*

6. make . . . up *p.v. [the noun and adjectives derived from this verb are much more commonly used than the verb itself]* When you **make** yourself **up**, you put lipstick, eye shadow, and so on, on your face.

*She **made** herself **up** and went to the party.*

make-up *n.* **Make-up** is cosmetics: lipstick, mascara, and so on.

*Heather's father thinks she wears too much **make-up**.*

made-up *part.adj.* After people have put on **make-up**, they are **made-up**.

> *Did you see Lydia? She's really beautiful when she's all **made-up**.*

7. make up (with) *p.v.* When two people **make up** or **make up** with each other, they end an argument and resume friendly relations.

> *Sally and Jim had a big fight, but they **made up** the next day.*
> *Mr. Baker said he won't **make up** with his wife until she apologizes.*

Infinitive

	present tense	-ing form	past tense	past participle
stay out	stay out & stays out	staying out	stayed out	stayed out

1. stay out *p.v.* When you **stay out**, you do not return to your house.

> *Do you let your kids **stay out** past 7:00?*
> *I **stayed out** late last night, and I'm really exhausted.*

2. stay out (of) *p.v.* When you **stay out** of a place, you do not go inside it.

> *Your father's busy cooking dinner, so **stay out** of the kitchen.*
> *You can't come in here. **Stay out**!*

3. stay out (of) *p.v.* When you **stay out** of a situation, such as an argument, fight, battle, or war, you do not get involved in it.

> *This fight doesn't involve you, so **stay out**.*
> *Jake has **stayed out** of trouble since he left prison.*

watch out				
	watch out & watches out	watching out	watched out	watched out

1. watch out (for) *p.v.* When you **watch out** or **watch out** for something, you remain alert for someone or something that is dangerous or important. When you tell people to **watch out** or **watch out** for something, you are warning them of possible danger. **Watch out** is the same as **look out**.

> ***Watch out** when you're crossing a busy street.*
> *Karen said she would meet us here at 12:00, so **watch out** for her.*
> ***Watch out**! There's a snake in the grass.*
> *I dropped a glass in the kitchen, so **watch out** for broken glass.*

EXERCISE 23a — **Complete the sentences with phrasal verbs from this section. Be sure the phrasal verbs are in the correct tense.**

1. Are you telling me the truth, or did you ـــــــــــــــ that ـــــــــــــــ?

2. You're going to a dangerous area. ـــــــــــــــ ـــــــــــــــ for muggers.

3. I have to ـــــــــــــــ ـــــــــــــــ on salt in my diet because of my high blood pressure.

4. We had to ـــــــــــــــ ـــــــــــــــ two trees to make room for the new swimming pool.

5. _____ _____ of the water — someone saw a shark.

6. The soldiers in the fort couldn't _____ _____ against such a huge and

   powerful army.

7. The United States is _____ _____ of people from many different races and cultures.

8. It was too hard to work and go to school at the same time, so Todd had to _____

   _____ of college.

9. Carmen can pay only half of the money she owes me, but Luis promised to _____

   _____ the difference.

10. A group of concerned citizens is demanding that the police _____ _____

    on prostitution in their neighborhood.

11. The bank robbers _____ _____ in a white sedan with Florida license plates.

12. When the President walks past you, _____ your hand _____ and maybe he'll

    shake it.

13. I really need a vacation. I haven't _____ _____ in three years.

14. I told my son that if he can't _____ _____ of trouble, I'm going to send him

    to military school.

15. The airline pilots are _____ _____ for a 15 percent raise, and they will not

    accept anything less.

16. The store's closing in five minutes, so you need to _____ _____ your mind

    about which pair of shoes you want.

17. After fourteen years he thought he had _____ _____ with the murder, but

    he was wrong.

18. All Joe does is complain and criticize. I need to _____ _____ from him.

19. Mike didn't come home until 4:30 in the morning, and his father was furious that he

    _____ _____ so late.

20. He thinks he's so smart. I hope someone _____ him _____ to size someday.

21. Be careful about how much you spend — this money has to _____ _____

    until payday.

22. Bob and Marsha had a big argument, but they _____ _____ with each other, and now everything is okay.

23. The professor warned the students that if they missed the final examination, they could not _____ it _____.

EXERCISE 23b — **Complete the sentences with the correct second particles.**

1. The principal is going to *crack down* _____ smoking in the bathroom.

2. If you want to lose weight, *cut down* _____ cake and cookies.

3. He *dropped out* _____ college before graduation.

4. After Jake robbed the liquor store, he was arrested and sent to jail. He didn't *get away* _____ robbing the liquor store.

5. The French workers are *holding out* _____ a 100 percent raise and a two-day workweek.

6. There are a lot of rattlesnakes around here, so *watch out* _____ them.

7. Timmy's mother told him to *stay out* _____ the cookie jar.

EXERCISE 23c — **Write answers to the questions using phrasal verbs, participle adjectives, and nouns from this section. Be sure the phrasal verbs are in the correct tense.**

1. The union members are on strike, and some will not go back to work unless they get the 10 percent raise they demanded in the beginning. What are the union members doing?

2. Some union members accepted a 7 percent raise and went back to work, but not the union members in Question 1. What would you call the union members in Question 1?

3. Jim and his sister had a big fight, but they apologized to each other, and now everything is okay. What did Jim and his sister do?

4. Jake stopped going to high school before he graduated. What did Jake do?

5. In Question 4, what is Jake?

6. You considered buying either a Toyota or a Nissan, and then you made your decision. What did you do?

7. My elbow is very sore, so my doctor told me to play less tennis. What did my doctor tell me?

8. Most of the Democrats will vote in favor of the new law, but a few are resisting pressure to vote yes. What are the Democrats who don't want to vote yes doing?

9. In Question 8, what are the Democrats who don't want to vote yes?

10. Mr. and Mrs. Ortega went to a party and didn't come home until 3:00 A.M. What did they do?

11. The explorer's supply of food and water has to last for three months. What does the explorer's supply of food and water have to do for three months?

12. Erik invented a funny story for his daughter. What did Erik do?

13. In Question 12, Erik's funny story wasn't true. How would you describe it?

14. Mr. Flores cheats on his taxes, but so far he hasn't been caught. What has Mr. Flores done so far?

15. There are a log of big trucks on the road, so when you drive, you have to be careful. What do you have to do when you drive?

16. The police are going to start working harder to prevent crime. What are the police going to do?

17. In Question 16, what can you call the plan to work harder to prevent crime?

EXERCISE 23d, Review — **Complete the sentences with these phrasal verbs from previous sections. Be sure the phrasal verbs are in the correct tense. To check their meanings, review the section number given after each one.**

aim at, 19	fall apart, 17	stand around, 18
believe in, 16	get through, 16	tell apart, 18
break through, 18	go for, 16	think about, 16
burn up, 22	grow out of, 17	wipe up, 22
come over, 17	hold off, 16	
count up, 22	put past, 16	

1. Do you want these baby clothes? My daughter has _____ _____

   _____ them.

2. It's always a good Idea to _____ _____ installing a new software version

   until they get all the bugs out.

3. Get a paper towel and _____ _____ the grape juice you spilled.

4. I'm not sure what I will do. I have to _____ _____ it.

5. I have a lot of work to do, so I probably won't _____ _____ until 4:00.

6. The twins look exactly like each other. How do you _____ them _____?

7. The walls of this fort are ten feet thick. No one could _____ _____.

8. We finished our card game, and Sean _____ _____ the points.

9. The new law is _____ _____ reducing air pollution.

10. I need to fix this table. It's _____ _____.

11. Raquel suggested moving to the suburbs, and her husband _____ _____ the idea.

12. That guy's a lunatic. There's nothing I wouldn't _____ _____ him.

13. We _____ _____ the old wood in the fireplace.

14. My niece is thirteen years old, but she still _____ _____ Santa Claus.

15. The sign in the store window said they open at 10:00, but we had to _____ _____ until 10:20 before they opened the doors.

16. Would you like to _____ _____ to my house tonight and have dinner?

---

24. FOCUS ON: **phrasal verbs used as nouns, 2**

As we saw in Section 5, two-word phrasal verbs are sometimes accented on the verb and sometimes on the particle. Two-word nouns, however, are always accented on the verb even if it is the particle of the two-word verb that is accented:

> verb: ***SHOW off***   noun: ***SHOW-off***
> verb: ***slow DOWN***   noun: ***SLOWdown***

Infinitive

present tense	-ing form	past tense	past participle
come down			
come down & comes down	coming down	came down	come down

1. come down (to) *p.v.* When someone moves toward you to a lower level position, or from north to south, that person **comes down** or **comes down** to where you are. **Come up** is the opposite of **come down**.

*It's been raining for an hour! It's really **coming down**.*

*My friend from Canada **comes down** to visit us in New Mexico once in a while.*

2. come down *p.v.* When you move to a lower level socially or financially and receive less respect from other people because of this change, you **come down** in life.

> *Hank certainly has **come down** in life — he lost his job, house, and family because of his gambling problem.*
> *Mark used to be so successful, but now he has so many problems. He has really **come down** in life.*

comedown *n.* A **comedown** is a move to a lower level socially or financially that causes you to receive less respect from other people.

> *A few years ago he was the manager of this restaurant, but now he's only a waiter — what a **comedown**.*

3. come down (to) *p.v.* When you lower the price you are asking for something, you **come down** or **come down** to a lower price.

> *I won't buy her car unless she **comes down** to $12,000.*
> *The union won't **come down** a nickel in its salary demands.*

Infinitive	present tense	-ing form	past tense	past participle
let up	let up & lets up	letting up	let up	let up

1. let up (on) *p.v.* When something becomes less strong, less intense, or less severe, it **lets up**.

> *The rain finally **let up** yesterday.*
> *Mike's parents are very strict with him. He's only a boy. They should **let up** on him.*

letup *n.* A **letup** is a reduction in how strong, severe, or intense something is.

> *There was no **letup** in terrorist bombings after the peace treaty was signed.*

print out	print out & prints out	printing out	printed out	printed out

1. print ... out *p.v.* When you make a computer write something on paper, you **print** it **out**.

> *After I finished writing my letter, I **printed** it **out** and signed it.*
> *I can't **print** this **out** — my printer is broken.*

printout *n.* When you make a computer write something on paper, the paper is a **printout**.

> *I put the **printout** of the October sales report on the sales manager's desk.*

shake up	shake up & shakes up	shaking up	shook up	shaken up

1. shake ... up *p.v.* When something upsets, shocks, or frightens you badly, it **shakes** you **up**.

*Seeing all those dead bodies sure **shook** me **up**.*

*I was really **shaken up** when I learned that my uncle had been killed.*

shaken up *part.adj.* When something upsets, shocks, or frightens you badly, you are **shaken up**.

*Leave Frank alone. He just got some bad news, and he's a bit **shaken up** about it.*

2. shake ... up *p.v.* When you mix something by shaking it, you **shake** it **up**.

*You have to **shake up** Italian dressing before you open the bottle.*

*Did you **shake** this can of paint **up**?*

3. shake ... up *p.v.* When you make major changes in an organization or business, you **shake** it **up**.

*The new CEO **shook up** management at my company, and a lot of people lost their jobs or were transferred.*

*People are getting a little lazy around here. It's time to **shake** things **up**.*

shake-up *n.* A major change in an organization or business is a **shake-up**.

*There was a big **shake-up** at my company, and a lot of people lost their jobs or were transferred.*

Infinitive

present tense	-ing form	past tense	past participle
show off			
show off & shows off	**showing off**	**showed off**	**shown off**

1. show ... off *p.v.* When you **show off**, you let people see something you have or something you can do in a very obvious and excessive way.

*Sally's boyfriend gave her a huge diamond engagement ring, and she **showed** it **off** to all her friends.*

*The boy was **showing off** by riding his bicycle with no hands when he fell and hurt himself.*

show-off *n.* Someone who **shows off** is a **show-off**.

*Did you hear Alfonso speaking French at the party so everyone could hear? What a **show-off**!*

slow down			
slow down & slows down	**slowing down**	**slowed down**	**slowed down**

1. slow ... down *p.v.* When something causes people or things to do something more slowly, it **slows** them **down**.

*I was driving pretty fast, but I **slowed down** after I saw the police car.*

*Production at the factory **slowed down** when half the workers got sick.*

slowdown *n.* When people or things do something more slowly, a **slowdown** occurs.

*The snow caused a big **slowdown** on the highway this morning.*

Infinitive

present tense	-ing form	past tense	past participle
stop over			
stop over & stops over	stopping over	stopped over	stopped over

1. stop over *p.v.* When you interrupt a journey (usually an airplane journey) for a short stay somewhere, you **stop over**.

> David **stopped over** in London on his flight from New York to Moscow.
> **Stopping over** in Dubai on the way to Bangkok wasn't any fun — we couldn't even leave the airport.

stopover *n.* When you interrupt a journey for a short stay somewhere, usually an airplane journey, you make a **stopover**.

> I flew from Istanbul to Philadelphia with a four-day **stopover** in Amsterdam.

2. stop over *p.v.* When you visit someone for a short time, you **stop over**.

> Would you like to **stop over** after dinner and see our vacation pictures?
> Can you vacuum the living room, please? The Youngs are **stopping over** tonight, and I want the place to look nice.

trade in			
trade in & trades in	trading in	traded in	traded in

1. trade ... in *p.v.* When you give an old car or other piece of expensive equipment to someone you are buying a new car or piece of equipment from in order to get a lower price, you **trade** the old car or piece of equipment **in**.

> After the twins were born, Raul **traded** his pickup truck **in** for a station wagon.
> We'll get a good price on our new photocopier if we **trade in** our old one.

trade-in *n.* An old car or piece of equipment that you **trade in** for a newer one is a **trade-in**.

> Most of the used cars sold by dealers are **trade-ins**.

EXERCISE 24a — **Complete the sentences with phrasal verbs from this section. Be sure the phrasal verbs are in the correct tense.**

1. You're driving too fast. Please _____ _____.

2. _____ _____ that bottle of salad dressing before you open it.

3. The real estate agent says he thinks the sellers will _____ _____ a little in their

   asking price.

4. My new car cost $24,000, but I _____ my old car _____ for $15,000.

5. Jim is upstairs. Ask him to _____ _____ here for a minute, okay?

6. _____ _____ in London for a few days on your way to India is a good way to get

   over jet lag.

7. I was pretty _____ _____ by the news, but now I'm okay.

8. Luis _____ his new car _____ to his friends yesterday.

9. The bombing continued for four days before it finally _____ _____.

10. Leticia used to be rich, but she lost all her money gambling, and now she can't even pay her

    bills. She's really _____ _____ in life.

11. When you finish writing that story, _____ it _____ and give it to me. I want

    to read it.

12. This company was losing money until the new owners came in and _____ things

    _____.

13. I have to clean the house because Pat and Mike might _____ _____ tonight.

EXERCISE 24b — **Complete the sentences with nouns from this section.**

1. I worked for my company for thirty-one years before I got fired in the big

   _____.

2. I had a four-hour _____ in Los Angeles on my way to Hawaii.

3. Nicole used to have her own company, and now she's driving a taxi. That's quite a

   _____.

4. The wind blew all night without any _____.

5. New car dealers usually have a lot of _____ for sale at low prices.

6. The snow caused a big _____ on the interstate this morning.

7. After the computer finished with the data, I took the _____ upstairs to the

   sales department.

8. He's lost a lot of weight, and now he wears really tight pants everyday. What a

   _____ he is.

EXERCISE 24c — **Write three sentences using the objects in parentheses. Be sure
to put the objects in the right place.**

1. The rain *slowed down*. (traffic, it)

   _____

2. He *printed out*. (his letter, it)

_____

_____

_____

3. The bad news has *shaken up*. (Jim and Nancy, them)

_____

_____

_____

4. I got $5,000 for *trading in*. (my old car, it)

_____

_____

_____

5. Chelsea's parents *showed off*. (her perfect report card, it)

_____

_____

_____

EXERCISE 24d — **Write answers to the questions using phrasal verbs, participle adjectives, and nouns from this section. Be sure the phrasal verbs are in the correct tense.**

1. After the computer finished the calculations, I printed the answers on a piece of paper. What did I do?

2. In Question 1, what would you call the paper with the answers?

3. Todd's friend in Minnesota is going to visit Todd in New Orleans. What is Todd's friend going to do?

4. Ned walks around without a shirt so the girls can see his muscles. What does Ned do?

5. In Question 4, what is Ned?

6. When I buy my new car, I'll give the dealer my old car so that I can get a lower price on the new car. What will I do with my old car?

7. In Question 6, what would you call my old car?

8. The new boss fired a lot of employees, hired new employees, and made a lot of changes. What did the new boss do?

9. In Question 8, what would you call what the new boss did?

10. Sandra used to be married to a prince, but now she's divorced and broke. What has Sandra done?

11. In Question 10, what would you call what happened to Sandra?

12. It rained for two weeks straight before it stopped. What did the rain do?

13. In Question 12, what would you call what the rain did?

14. There was a big accident on the highway yesterday morning, and traffic was awful. What did the accident do to the traffic?

15. In Question 14, what would you call the traffic situation?

16. You flew from Denver to Miami, but you had to spend a few hours in Atlanta on the way. What did you do in Atlanta?

17. In Question 16, what would you call my visit to Atlanta?

18. Mike saw a terrible accident this morning while he was driving, and it upset him a lot. What did the accident do to Mike?

19. In Question 18, how would you describe Mike after he saw the accident?

EXERCISE 24e, Review — **Complete the sentences with these nouns from previous sections. To check their meanings, review the section number given after each one.**

backup, 11	drop-off, 11	follow-up, 11	tryout, 11
crackdown, 23	dropout, 23	lineup, 18	workout, 11

1. The doctor said I was cured, but he wants me to see him in a year for a _____.

2. Drugs are getting to be a big problem in my son's school. I think it's time for a _____.

3. When I was nineteen, I was a _____ with no future, but then I got smart and finished school.

4. After the accident, the human cannonball was dropped from the circus _____.

5. The _____ for the basketball team will be next Saturday at 10:00 A.M.

6. Janice just got back from the gym, and she's really exhausted from her _____.

7. I use the program on the hard disk, but I have a _____ on a floppy.

8. Business at the restaurant used to be good, but there was a big _____ after that case of food poisoning.

EXERCISE 24f, Review — **Complete the sentences with these phrasal verbs from previous sections. Be sure the phrasal verbs are in the correct tense. To check their meanings, review the section number given after each one.**

bring over, 19	go beyond, 18	look around, 21	tell on, 15
cool off, 19	hang up, 9	settle down, 21	watch out, 23
count up, 22	hold out, 23	stay out, 23	wipe up, 22
figure on, 18	lift up, 19	step on, 21	

1. Young man, if you don't _____ _____ of trouble at school, I'm going to send you to military school!

2. These suitcases are so heavy I can barely _____ them _____.

3. A good history book doesn't simply tell you what happened, it _____ _____ that and tells you why.

4. Todd got in trouble with his mother after he broke a window and his sister _____ _____ him.

5. If you're going to that bad neighborhood late at night, please be careful and _____ _____ for muggers.

6. That museum is huge. If you want to see everything, you should _____ _____ spending the entire day there.

7. This coffee's way too hot. Can you get me an ice cube so I can _____ it _____?

8. That company wants to hire me, but I'm _____ _____ for more money.

9. My brother is going to visit tonight, and he's _____ his fiancée _____.

10. I've never been to this store before; I want to _____ _____ and see what they have.

11. My husband was very angry when our thirteen-year-old daughter came home at 4:00 in the

    morning, so I told him to _____ _____ and let me talk to her.

12. We had only twenty minutes to get to the airport, so we told the taxi driver to _____

    _____ it.

13. After the votes were _____ _____, Senator Dolittle was declared the winner.

14. Timmy, get a paper towel and _____ _____ this juice you spilled on the floor.

15. Leticia said good-bye and _____ _____ the telephone.

---

25. FOCUS ON: **phrasal verbs and *have to, have got to,* and *must***

Have to, have got to, and *must* have two important uses in English. One is familiar to most students, the other is not.

But before discussing that, let's pay special attention to *have got to. Have to* and *have got to* mean exactly the same thing. Both are commonly used, and both are acceptable standard English. *Have to* derives from *have,* and *have got to* derives from *have got.* So why the *got* in *have got to*? A good question. *Got* in *have got to* means nothing and serves no purpose whatever. *Have got to* is a unique, idiomatic variation of *have to.* There is no point in trying to understand the grammar of *have got to* because there isn't any. Like other idioms, it must simply be memorized. Though *have to* and *have got to* mean the same thing, their forms are different, especially in questions and negative sentences. In the examples below, the contracted forms are the most common in everyday spoken English:

statement: *You <u>have to</u> **come down**.*   *You <u>have got to</u> **come down**.*
            *You <u>have to</u> **come down**.*   *You'<u>ve got</u> to **come down**.*

question: *<u>Do</u> you <u>have to</u> **come down**?*   *<u>Have</u> you <u>got to</u> **come down**?*

negative: *You <u>do not have</u> to **come down**.*   *You <u>have not got</u> to **come down**.*
          *You <u>don't have</u> to **come down**.*   *You <u>haven't got</u> to **come down**.*

Requirement

Have to, have got to, and *must* are both used to say that something is required, necessary, mandatory — there is no choice in the matter:

*You <u>have</u> <u>to</u> **make up** the test.*
*You'<u>ve</u> <u>got</u> <u>to</u> **make up** the test.*
*You <u>must</u> **make up** the test.*

Although most students learn this use of *must* early in their studies, it is actually the least common way to use *must*. Both *have to* and *have got to* are much more commonly used for this purpose.

Near certainty

The other important use of *have to, have got to,* and *must* is to say that something is 99 percent certain — that based on the facts and based on what we see and know, no other conclusion is possible about something. We are 99 percent certain, and all we need is confirmation to be 100 percent certain:

> *Janice, you have been working for 12 hours without a break. You <u>have</u> <u>to</u> be tired.* (A logical assumption, but until Janice confirms that she is tired, the speaker cannot be 100 percent certain.)
> *I would never take that book out of this room. It'<u>s</u> <u>got</u> <u>to</u> be here somewhere.* (A logical assumption, but until the speaker finds the book, he cannot be 100 percent certain that it is in the room.)
> *That man is from Japan. I've never spoken with him, but he <u>must</u> speak Japanese.* (A logical assumption, but until the speaker hears the man speaking Japanese, he cannot be 100 percent certain.)

When *have to, have got to,* and *must* are used in this way, it is *must* that is more common than the others. *Have to* and *have got to*, when used for this purpose, have greater emphasis and are used for dramatic effect:

> *Mark <u>has</u> <u>to</u> be the biggest idiot in the entire world.*
> *Where is Lydia? She'<u>s</u> <u>got</u> <u>to</u> be here somewhere.*

Infinitive			
present tense	**-ing form**	**past tense**	**past participle**
do with			

1. do with *p.v. [used only in the infinitive form]* When you say that one thing has something to **do with** another, you mean there is a connection between the two.

> *Don't blame me for what happened; I had nothing to **do with** it.*
> *I'm not sure what this part does, but I think it must have something to **do with** the transmission.*

have on			
have on & has on	**having on**	**had on**	**had on**

1. have . . . on *p.v.* When you wear something, such as an item of clothing, perfume, or cosmetics, you **have** it **on**.

> *Sally **had** red pants and a blue shirt **on**.*
> *I didn't **have** a raincoat **on**, and I got all wet.*

25

2. have . . . on *p.v.* When you **have** an electrical device **on**, you are using it.

> *Last summer was so cool that we **had** the air conditioner **on** only two or three times.*
> *What's that sound? Dan must **have** the radio **on**.*

Infinitive

	present tense	-ing form	past tense	past participle
hurry up	hurry up & hurries up	hurrying up	hurried up	hurried up

1. hurry up *p.v.* When you **hurry up**, you do something quickly.

> *Nicole has to **hurry up** if she's going to finish her work before 5:00.*
> *If we don't **hurry up**, we're going to miss the beginning of the movie.*

2. hurry . . . up *p.v.* When you **hurry** something **up**, you do it more quickly. When you **hurry** people **up**, you urge them to do something more quickly. When you say "**Hurry up**," to people, you are telling them to do something more quickly.

> *Everyone was really hungry, so I asked our cook to **hurry** dinner **up**.*
> *There were only five minutes left to finish the test, so the teacher **hurried** the students **up**.*
> ***Hurry up**! I'm not going to wait for you all day.*

knock over	knock over & knocks over	knocking over	knocked over	knocked over

1. knock . . . over *p.v.* When you **knock** people or things **over**, you use force to make them fall to a horizontal position.

> *The force of the explosion **knocked** me **over**.*
> *The children were playing, and they **knocked** the lamp **over**.*

lighten up	lighten up & lightens up	lightening up	lightened up	lightened up

1. lighten up (on) *p.v. [informal]* When you **lighten up** or **lighten up** on people, you become less harsh or less strict in your treatment of them.

> *You're awfully hard on your daughter. Maybe you ought to **lighten up** on her.*
> *You've been criticizing me all day. Will you please **lighten up**?*

2. lighten . . . up *p.v.* When you **lighten up**, you change the subject of conversation from something serious to something more cheerful and pleasant.

> *Enough talk about business. Let's **lighten** things **up** around here.*
> ***Lighten** it **up** — you've been talking about death and taxes all night.*

plan ahead	plan ahead & plans ahead	planning ahead	planned ahead	planned ahead

1. plan ahead *p.v.* When you **plan ahead**, you plan for a future situation or activity so that you will not have a problem then. **Plan ahead** is similar to **think ahead**.

> *Janice is a good manager. She always **plans ahead** in case there's a problem.*

Plan ahead — *you don't want any problems when you're 200 miles from the nearest town.*

Infinitive			
present tense	**-ing form**	**past tense**	**past participle**
settle for			
settle for & settles for	settling for	settled for	settled for

1. settle for *p.v.* When you **settle for** something, you accept it even though it may not be exactly what you want or need.

*The strikers wanted an 8 percent pay increase, but they **settled for** 5 percent.*

*Dr. Smith has very high standards. He won't **settle for** second best.*

think up			
think up & thinks up	thinking up	thought up	thought up

1. think ... up *p.v.* When you **think up** something, such as an idea, solution, or plan, you use your imagination to create it.

*I have to **think up** a way to solve this problem.*

*Maria **thought up** a great way to make some extra money.*

*Stop worrying — I'll **think** something **up**.*

EXERCISE 25a — **Complete the sentences with phrasal verbs from this section. Be sure the phrasal verbs are in the correct tense.**

1. We're going to be late if you don't _____ _____.

2. I told the store manager that I wanted a full refund and that I wouldn't _____ _____ anything else.

3. Mr. Wolfe _____ a white suit _____ last night.

4. Joe's been angry all day. I wish he'd _____ _____.

5. The truck hit the light pole and _____ it _____.

6. You have to talk to someone in the shipping department about your missing order. I have nothing to _____ _____ shipping.

7. If you're going on an important business trip, you should _____ _____ so that you don't forget something you'll need later.

8. Jake is trying to _____ _____ a way to make money without working.

9. Go upstairs and _____ your sister _____. I'm afraid she's going to be late for school.

10. We've been talking politics all night. Let's _____ things _____, okay?

11. I like to _____ the radio _____ when I go to bed.

EXERCISE 25b — **Write answers to the questions using phrasal verbs from this section. Be sure the phrasal verbs are in the correct tense.**

1. Charles wore a red shirt yesterday. What did Charles do?

2. Sean wants a 15 percent raise, and he won't accept less. What won't Sean do?

3. Dr. Wood is thinking about the important meeting she will go to next week so that she will be ready. What is Dr. Wood doing?

4. Jake hit Jerry so hard that Jerry fell to the floor. What did Jake do to Jerry?

5. Ned told Todd to work more quickly. What did Ned tell Todd to do?

6. I got a letter about my income taxes. What was the letter about?

7. Sergeant Jones has been yelling at the soldiers all day. What should Sergeant Jones do?

8. Betty needs a Halloween costume, and she's using her imagination to create one. What is Betty doing?

EXERCISE 25c — **Write eight original sentences using phrasal verbs from this section.**

1. _____
2. _____
3. _____
4. _____
5. _____
6. _____
7. _____
8. _____

EXERCISE 25d, Review — **Complete the sentences with these participle adjectives from previous sections. To check their meanings, review the section number given after each one.**

burned up, 22	lined up, 18	ripped up, 17	zipped up, 21
cleared up, 22	made-up, 23	shaken up, 24	
dried out, 15	paid up, 22	warmed up, 19	
heated up, 22	plugged up, 22	worn down, 17	

1. It's freezing outside — make sure your coat is _____ _____.

2. Don't start driving yet; the car's not _____ _____.

3. We talked about the problem, and now everything is _____ _____.

4. I need lotion; my skin is really _____ _____.

5. Hank is such a liar. Don't believe any of his _____ excuses.

6. After I give Bill ten bucks, I won't owe him another penny. I'll be totally _____ _____.

7. Pat was pretty _____ after the accident.

8. Bill was furious at his ex-wife, and now all his photos of her are _____ _____ and in the garbage.

9. People are _____ _____ for three blocks to buy World Series tickets.

10. Don't drink that coffee — it's not _____ _____.

11. I can't smell or taste anything; my nose is all _____ _____.

12. I was really _____ _____ after he took my calculator without asking me and then lost it.

13. The heels of my old cowboy boots are _____ _____. I need to get them fixed.

EXERCISE 25e, Review — **Complete the sentences with these phrasal verbs from previous sections. Be sure to use the correct tense. To check their meanings, review the lesson number given after each one.**

call in, 5	hand out, 10	screw on, 12	stop over, 24
clear up, 22	hook up, 9	show off, 24	trade in, 24
come down, 24	let up, 24	slow down, 24	warm up, 19
go back, 19	print out, 24	stick up, 14	

1. The car dealer is asking $27,000 for the car I want, but I think he might _____ _____ to $24,000.

2. While you go to the library, I'll go to the grocery store, and we'll _____ _____ at the corner in one hour.

3. Be sure you _____ the top of that mustard jar _____ tightly.

4. Erik checks the time every five minutes so that he can _____ _____ his new Rolex watch.

5. Mike wasn't at work today. He _____ _____ sick.

6. When Bill flies to Los Angeles, he always _____ _____ in Bangkok.

7. The car dealer said he'll give me a good deal if I _____ _____ my old car.

8. We _____ the notices _____ all over town.

9. The memo from the personnel office _____ _____ a lot of confusion about

   the new vacation policy.

10. This weather is terrible. I wonder if this storm is ever going to _____ _____.

11. Turn the heater on, and the room will _____ right _____.

12. Nancy was driving too fast, so I told her to _____ _____.

13. The teacher won't _____ _____ the tests until the students are quiet.

14. After you finish writing your report, _____ it _____ and give it to me.

15. Raul's from Colombia, but he hasn't _____ _____ there for seven years.

---

26. FOCUS ON: **phrasal verbs and the adverb *back***

The adverb *back* is sometimes used with phrasal verbs to mean *again*. The following sentences have the same meaning:

> We **got together** again.
> We **got** <u>back</u> **together**.

Back is always placed directly before the particle. When *back* is used with separable phrasal verbs, the object must separate the verb and particle, and *back* must be placed between the object and the particle:

> I **put** the engine <u>back</u> **together**.
> ~~I **put** <u>back</u> **together** the engine.~~

Do not confuse the adverb *back*, which modifies phrasal verbs, with the particle *back* that is part of some phrasal verbs (and has the same meaning of *again*).

Infinitive

	present tense	-ing form	past tense	past participle
get together				
	get together & gets together	getting together	got together	gotten/got together

1. get together (with) *p.v.* When two people **get together**, they meet and spend time together. When you **get together** with someone, you meet and spend time with that person. When a man and woman resume a relationship after separating, they **get** back **together**.

> *If you're not busy tomorrow night, would you like to **get together**?*
> *We're going to **get together** with Bill and Nancy tomorrow.*
> *Judy and Sam had separated, but now they've **gotten** back **together**.*

get-together *n.* An informal gathering is a **get-together**.

> *I'm having a little **get-together** tonight. Would you like to come?*

2. get . . . together *p.v.* When you **get** things **together**, you collect them so they are in the same place.

> *You should **get** all your tools **together** so you will have them when you need them.*
> *Linda **got** all her tax records **together** to show to her accountant.*

3. get . . . together *p.v. [informal]* When you **get** yourself **together**, or **get** it **together**, you gain control of your emotions after you have become upset or emotional.

> *Bob was very upset before the party, but he **got** it **together** before the guests came.*
> *Hey, **get** yourself **together**! Everyone is watching you.*

Infinitive

	present tense	-ing form	past tense	past participle
go over	go over & goes over	going over	went over	gone over

1. go over (to) *p.v.* When people move from where you are to a place, thing, or person that is farther away from you, they **go over** or **go over** to that place, thing, or person.

> *I'm busy. **Go over** there and stop bothering me.*
> *I was hot, so Maria **went over** to the window and opened it.*

2. go over (to) *p.v.* When you go to someone's house for a visit, you **go over** or **go over** to that person's house.

> *Have you **gone over** to Nicole's house to see her new baby yet?*
> *I **went over** to Erik's for dinner last night.*

3. go over *p.v.* When you carefully read or review important written material, you **go over** it.

> *Here's a magazine article I just finished writing. **Go over** it and tell me what you think.*
> *The actor **went over** his lines before the audition.*

going-over *n.* When you examine or inspect something carefully, you give it a **going-over**.

> *I gave his report a good **going-over** and found a lot of mistakes.*

4. go over *p.v.* When you carefully explain something, usually something that is complicated but important, you **go over** it.

*Before the trial Hank and his lawyer **went over** what Hank was going to say.*

*No one understood the manager's plan after he explained it, so he **went** back **over** it.*

5. go over *p.v.* When an idea, suggestion, or performance is accepted and liked by other people, it **goes over**.

*Senator Dolittle's plan to raise taxes didn't **go over** with the voters.*

*The singer's performance **went over** well with the critics.*

Infinitive

	present tense	-ing form	past tense	past participle
go up	go up & goes up	going up	went up	gone up

1. go up (to) *p.v.* When you move to a higher level or position, or from south to north, you **go up** or **go up** to that place. **Go down** is the opposite of **go up**.

*Suzie came down from her tree house to eat lunch, but she **went** back **up** after she finished.*

*I spend the winters in Mexico, and **go up** to my home in Ohio in the summer.*

2. go up (to) *p.v.* When the cost, rate, quality, quantity, or level of something increases, it **goes up**. **Go down** is the opposite of **go up**.

*The price of gas hasn't **gone up** in two years.*

*In the summer the temperature in Saudi Arabia can **go up** to 125 degrees.*

3. go up (to) *p.v.* When a schedule or plan ends at a certain time or date, the schedule or plan **goes up** to that time or date.

*Do you have the new schedule? This one **goes up** only to the end of April.*

*The teacher gave the students a syllabus that **went up** to the midterm.*

4. go up (to) *p.v.* When something extends to a certain point that is farther north or at a higher elevation, it **goes up to** that point. **Go down** is the opposite of **go up**.

*This trail **went up** to the base camp at the foot of the mountain.*

*Interstate 5 **goes up** to Seattle.*

5. go up (to) *p.v.* When you approach a person, you **go up** to that person.

*There's Sarah. **Go up** and introduce yourself.*

*Janice isn't shy — she **went** right **up** to the president of the company and asked for a raise.*

let in on

	let in on & lets in on	letting in on	let in on	let in on

1. let ... in on *p.v.* When you tell people information that is secret or not widely known, you **let** that person **in on** the information.

*General Chambers **let** me **in on** the top secret information.*

*I'm going to **let** you **in on** something not many people know about me.*

Infinitive

	present tense	-ing form	past tense	past participle
open up				
	open up & opens up	opening up	opened up	opened up

1. open . . . up *p.v.* When you **open** something **up**, you reveal what is inside so that people can see it.

> Sofia **opened** the box **up** and looked inside.
> Mike's going to **open up** his computer to try to find the problem.

2. open . . . up *p.v.* When you **open** a room or building **up**, you unlock or open the doors so that people can enter.

> The office closes at 12:00 for lunch and **opens** back **up** at 1:00.
> The manager was late and didn't **open up** the store until 10:30.

3. open . . . up *p.v.* When a new business starts, it **opens up** or is **opened up** by someone.

> I was driving through town, and I noticed that a new book store has **opened up** on Maple Street.
> Jimmy wants to **open up** a restaurant near the new office building.

put together				
	put together & puts together	putting together	put together	put together

1. put . . . together *p.v.* When you assemble the parts of something, you **put** it **together**. **Put together** is the opposite of **take apart**.

> Sally got a bicycle for her birthday, and her father **put** it **together** after dinner.
> It was easy taking my car's engine apart, but **putting** it back **together** was a lot harder.

2. put . . . together *p.v.* When you organize some ideas, plans, or suggestions in order to show them to someone or discuss them with someone, you **put** them **together**.

> Mr. and Mrs. Flores want to redecorate their house, so they asked an interior designer to **put** some ideas **together**.
> I have an interesting idea for a new business, and I'm **putting together** a proposal.

3. put . . . together *p.v.* When you position people or things so that they are close to each other or touching, you **put** them **together**.

> The teacher told Timmy and Mike to **put** their desks **together** so they could work on their project.
> When you plan your dinner party seating arrangement, **put** Heather and Jimmy **together**.

shut off				
	shut off & shuts off	shutting off	shut off	shut off

1. shut . . . off *p.v.* When you **shut off** an electrical or mechanical device, you cut the power going to it so that it stops operating. **Turn off** and **switch off** are similar to **shut off**.

*Timmy's mother told him to **shut off** the TV and go to bed.*

*I'm freezing. Would you mind **shutting** the air conditioner **off**?*

shut off *part.adj.* After you **shut off** an electrical or mechanical device, it is **shut off**. **Turned off** and **switched off** are similar to **shut off**.

*Well, no wonder it's so cold in here — the heat's **shut off**.*

shutoff *n.* When you **shut off** something, or when something **shuts off**, this action is a **shutoff**. When you **shut off** something, you use the **shutoff** switch, button, valve, and so on.

*The electricity **shutoff** lasted twenty minutes.*

*In case of emergency, turn this **shutoff** valve here.*

start up

start up & starts up	starting up	started up	started up

1. start . . . up *p.v.* When an electrical or mechanical device **starts up** or someone **starts** it **up**, it begins to operate.

*My car's engine died at a red light, and it wouldn't **start up** again.*

*You push this button here to **start** the computer **up**.*

start-up *n.* When you **start up** something, or something **starts up**, this action is a **start-up**. When you **start up** something, you use the **start-up** switch, button, and so on.

*To **start** the computer **up**, push this **start-up** button.*

*If your computer's hard disk crashes, you can use a floppy as the **start-up** disk.*

2. start . . . up *p.v.* When you **start up** a new business or company, you take the steps necessary to begin a new business or company.

*You should have a detailed business plan before **starting** a business **up**.*

*Jane borrowed the money she needed to **start up** her business from her uncle.*

start-up *n.* A **start-up** or **start-up** business or company is a new business or company.

*Most **start-up** businesses aren't successful.*

EXERCISE 26a — **Complete the sentences with phrasal verbs from this section. Be sure the phrasal verbs are in the correct tense.**

1. Your important papers are all over the house. You should _____ them _____

   and keep them in a safe place.

2. It was so cold this morning that it took half an hour to _____ my car _____.

3. This is awfully complicated. Could you _____ _____ it one more time?

4. The police ordered the people in the house to _____ the door _____.

5. The sergeant _____ _____ the hill to look for the enemy soldiers.

6. The account executive was asked to _____ some ideas _____ for a new advertising campaign.

7. I'm trying to sleep. Would you please _____ _____ the lights?

8. Linda saw her favorite movie star, but she was too shy to _____ _____ to him and ask for his autograph.

9. I'll _____ you _____ _____ a little secret.

10. I'm going to _____ _____ to Todd's house to help him with his math homework.

11. This calendar is useless — it _____ _____ only to August.

12. Thank you for your application. I will _____ _____ it carefully and call you in a few days.

13. This jigsaw puzzle has 1,000 pieces. It'll take forever to _____ it _____.

14. If that big discount store _____ _____ outside of town, all these little shops will go out of business.

15. The level of water in the river always falls during the summer but _____ back _____ the next spring.

16. Sam's idea of giving all the workers a 10 percent pay raise didn't _____ _____ well with management.

17. I know you're upset, but you have to _____ yourself _____.

18. On Saturday nights Mike usually _____ _____ with some friends and plays poker.

19. As soon as we arrived at the party, David _____ _____ to the buffet table and grabbed a plate.

20. Without the combination, there's no way to _____ this safe _____.

21. _____ all your Spanish books _____ on the same shelf.

22. This road _____ _____ to the next town, but that's where it ends.

23. I'll need around $25,000 to _____ _____ my new business.

EXERCISE 26b — **Write three sentences using the objects in parentheses. Be sure to put the objects in the right place.**

1. I wish they would *open up* near me. (a branch office, one)

_____

_____

_____

2. Lydia *put together*. (the food processor, it)

_____

_____

_____

3. Do you know how to *shut off*? (the photocopier, it)

_____

_____

_____

4. Push this button to *start up*. (the generator, it)

_____

_____

_____

EXERCISE 26c — **Write answers to the questions using phrasal verbs and nouns from this section. Be sure the phrasal verbs are in the correct tense.**

1. Frank read my report carefully. What did Frank do to my report?

2. In Question 1, what did Frank give my report?

3. Judy walked toward the king, stopped next to him, and gave him the petition. What did Judy do to the king?

4. Mike told me a secret. What did Mike do?

5. Bill and some friends are going to meet and spend some time together. What are Bill and his friends going to do?

6. In Question 5, what is this activity called?

7. My computer begins to operate from the hard disk. What does my computer do from the hard disk?

8. In Question 7, what would you call the hard disk?

9. The mayor's plan to fight crime in the streets was very successful with the voters. What impression did the mayor's plan have on the voters?

10. The heater stops operating automatically when the temperature reaches a certain point. What does the heater do automatically?

11. In Question 10, what is the temperature that makes the heater stop operating called?

12. You quit your job so that you could begin your own company. Why did you quit your job?

13. In Question 12, what would you call your new company?

14. You assembled all the parts of your model airplane. What did you do to your model airplane?

15. This airplane schedule gives flight times until December 31. What does the airplane schedule do?

16. The supermarket unlocks its doors and lets people in at 7:00 A.M. every day. What does the supermarket do at 7:00 A.M. every day?

EXERCISE 26d, Review — **Complete the sentences with these phrasal verbs from previous sections. Be sure the phrasal verbs are in the correct tense. To check their meanings, review the section number given after each one.**

do with, 25	have on, 25	look over, 21	settle for, 25
end up, 20	hurry up, 25	pick on, 21	show off, 24
go off, 20	knock over, 25	plan ahead, 25	take out on, 21
go on, 20	lighten up, 25	put on, 1	think up, 25

1. I'm asking $10,000 for my car, but I'll _____ _____ $8,500.

2. That new manager is really hard on the employees. He ought to _____ _____.

3. At the supermarket, Tom hit the stack of boxes with his shopping cart and _____ them _____.

201

4. We had planned to go to France on our vacation, but we _____ _____ going to Spain instead.

5. Will you _____ _____! If we don't leave soon we're going to be late.

6. Mark hates his job, and he comes home every night and _____ it _____ _____ his family.

7. My doctor got the test results from the lab, and she _____ them _____ very carefully.

8. _____ your coat _____. It's cold outside.

9. Don't wait until the last minute to make your vacation airline reservations. You have to _____ _____.

10. The detective didn't believe that the gun had _____ _____ accidentally.

11. I hated my older brother when I was a kid. He always _____ _____ me.

12. How are we going to get $500 in two days? We need to _____ _____ a good plan.

13. I didn't understand everything the computer shop guy said, but it had something to _____ _____ memory.

14. Jim tries to answer every question the teacher asks. He's always _____ _____.

15. That meeting was so boring. It seemed like it was going to _____ _____ forever.

16. The police officer must be off duty; he doesn't _____ his uniform _____.

---

27. FOCUS ON: phrasal verbs with the particle *off* and the adverb *right*

The particle *off* is used in many phrasal verbs to say that something is separated or removed:

> The cup handle **broke**. (The handle is broken, but it is still attached to the cup.)
>
> The cup handle **broke off**. (The handle is no longer attached to the cup.)

Right, discussed in Section 19, is often used with these phrasal verbs to indicate that the action of the verb happened quickly:

*He **washed** the dirt **off**.* (The dirt was removed.)
*He **washed** the dirt <u>right</u> **off**.* (The dirt was removed quickly.)

Remember that *right* can be used in this way only after an object that separates the verb and the particle:

*He **washed** the dirt right **off**.*
~~He **washed** right **off** the dirt.~~

Infinitive

	present tense	-ing form	past tense	past participle
bite off	bite off & bites off	biting off	bit off	bitten off

1. bite ... off *p.v.* When you **bite off** something, you use your teeth to remove a piece. When you **bite off** more than you can chew, you agree to do something that you do not have the time or the ability to do.

> *The lion **bit off** a huge piece of the zebra's flesh.*
> *You can't finish that huge project by tomorrow. I think you've **bitten off** more than you can chew.*

break off	break off & breaks off	breaking off	broke off	broken off

1. break ... off *p.v.* When something **breaks off** or someone **breaks** something **off**, a part or smaller piece is separated from something larger by force.

> *Jim **broke off** a piece of chocolate and gave it to his girlfriend.*
> *One of the arms **broke off** the statue when it fell off the pedestal.*

broken off *part.adj.* After something **breaks off**, it is **broken off**.

> *The handle of the coffee cup is **broken off**.*

2. break ... off *p.v.* When you **break off** relations or contact with someone, you decide to end relations or contact with that person.

> *The two countries **broke off** relations with each other.*
> *I was so angry at my in-laws that I **broke off** all contact with them.*

dry off	dry off & dries off	drying off	dried off	dried off

1. dry ... off *p.v.* When something **dries off** or you **dry** something **off**, water or other liquids that are on it evaporate.

> *It rained for only a few minutes, so the streets **dried off** quickly.*
> *Leave your wet clothes outside and let the sun **dry** them **off**.*

dried off *part.adj.* After something has **dried off**, it is **dried off**.

> *They can't play baseball because the field isn't **dried off**.*

Infinitive

	present tense	-ing form	past tense	past participle
knock off				
	knock off & knocks off	knocking off	knocked off	knocked off

1. knock ... off *p.v.* When you **knock** something **off**, you either accidentally or deliberately use force to make it fall from a place above the ground to the ground below.

> Susie **knocked** a glass **off** the table and broke it.
> The cat **knocked** the clock **off** the shelf.

2. knock off *p.v.* [informal] When you **knock off**, you finish working.

> I quit working at 5:00 last night, but Sean didn't **knock off** until 8:30.
> You've been working all day. Why don't you **knock off**?

3. knock ... off *p.v.* [informal] When you say "**Knock** it **off**" to people, you want them to stop doing something that is bothering you.

> If you don't **knock** it **off**, you'll be sorry.
> I'm tired of listening to you criticize me. **Knock** it **off**!

4. knock ... off *p.v.* When you **knock** something **off**, you make something quickly and not very carefully.

> The artist **knocked off** a quick sketch and gave it to the waiter.
> Dan prefers writing novels, but he sometimes **knocks off** a magazine article to make a few bucks.

5. knock ... off *p.v.* [informal] When you **knock** people **off**, you kill them.

> Jake was sent to prison for **knocking off** his brother-in-law.
> Mario was the head of a gang of criminals until he was **knocked off** by a rival.

tear off				
	tear off & tears off	tearing off	tore off	torn off

1. tear ... off *p.v.* When you use force to remove a piece of something that is flexible — paper, cloth, and so on — you **tear** it **off**.

> I **tore off** a coupon for frozen pizza at the supermarket.
> Alex always **tears** the tags **off** his shirt collars.

torn off *part.adj.* After something has been **torn off**, it is **torn off**.

> There aren't any more coupons. They're all **torn off**.

wash off				
	wash off & washes off	washing off	washed off	washed off

1. wash ... off *p.v.* When you **wash** something **off** or **wash** the dirt **off** something, you use water and soap to remove dirt or unwanted items from a surface.

> Mike **washed off** his car.
> Mike **washed** the dirt **off** his car.

washed off *part.adj.* After you **wash** something **off** or **wash** the dirt **off** something, it is **washed off**.

> The maid said she had **washed** the grease **off** the wall, but the wall didn't look
> **washed off** to me.

Infinitive

	present tense	-ing form	past tense	past participle
wear off	wear off & wears off	wearing off	wore off	worn off

1. wear off *p.v.* When the surface of something is gradually removed by friction or exposure to the elements so that what is beneath the surface is exposed, the surface **wears off**.

> You could see the wood where the paint had **worn off**.
> The gold **wears off** this cheap jewelry right away.

worn off *part.adj.* After something has worn off, it is **worn off**.

> These ancient temples used to be very colorful, but now all the paint is **worn off**.

2. wear off *p.v.* When the effects of drugs or alcohol gradually go away, they **wear off**.

> The wounded soldier was in great pain after the morphine **wore off**.
> He's going to have a big headache after the vodka **wears off**.

3. wear off *p.v.* When an emotional feeling gradually goes away, it **wears off**.

> After the shock of getting fired **wore off**, I started to get angry.
> When I met Jim I fell in love immediately, but that **wore off** quickly as I got to know
> him better.

wipe off	wipe off & wipes off	wiping off	wiped off	wiped off

1. wipe ... off *p.v.* When you completely remove a liquid from a surface by moving a towel or sponge across it with a sweeping motion, you **wipe** the surface **off**. You can either **wipe off** something that is wet or **wipe off** the liquid. **Wipe up** is similar to **wipe off**; however, you **wipe up** a liquid, but you **wipe off** the surface the liquid is on.

> **Wipe off** your face.
> **Wipe** the food **off** your face.

wiped off *part.adj.* After something has been **wiped off**, it is **wiped off**.

> That table doesn't looked **wiped off** to me. **Wipe** it **off** again.

EXERCISE 27a — **Complete the sentences with phrasal verbs from this section. Be sure the phrasal verbs are in the correct tense.**

1. Raquel _____ a piece of paper _____ and wrote her phone number on it.

2. After I washed the windows, I _____ them _____ with some old newspapers.

3. Jerry has to finish a lot of work before he goes home, so he probably won't _____

_____ until late.

4. It rained last night, so don't play outside until the grass _____ _____.

5. Be careful when you feed horses. They can _____ your finger right _____.

6. The doctor said the sedative would _____ _____ after four or five hours.

7. The shop owner was afraid to _____ the gang graffiti _____ his wall.

8. After Jake _____ _____ Hank, he was charged with murder.

9. During the storm, a tree branch _____ _____ and fell on the roof.

10. You two kids have been arguing all day. _____ it _____ right now!

11. I can't use this old typewriter anymore. The painted letters have _____

_____ the keys.

12. The two sides couldn't agree on a solution, and the negotiations _____

_____.

13. I'll try to _____ _____ a few more pages of my book before I go to bed.

14. It was a long time before the shock of his brother's death _____ _____.

15. Don't put your glass of wine so close to the edge of the table. Someone might _____

it _____.

EXERCISE 27b — Write three sentences using the objects in parentheses. Be sure to put the objects in the right place. Use *right* with questions 2 and 6.

1. Alex has *bitten off*. (the head of the gingerbread man, it)

_____

_____

_____

2. The movers *broke off*. (the cup handle, it)

_____

_____

_____

3. Please *dry off.* (the dishes, them)

_____

_____

_____

4. Don't *knock off.* (the ash tray, it)

_____

_____

_____

5. Can I *tear off*? (these mattress tags, them)

_____

_____

_____

6. The janitor *washed off.* (the blood, it)

_____

_____

_____

7. She didn't *wipe off.* (the milk, it)

_____

_____

_____

EXERCISE 27c — **Write answers to the questions using phrasal verbs and participle adjectives from this section. Try to use *right* with some of the answers. Be sure the phrasal verbs are in the correct tense.**

1. I used water to remove the mud from my car. What did I do to my car?

2. Timmy forcibly removed the propellers of my model airplane. What did Timmy do to my model airplane's propellers?

3. In Question 2, how would you describe the model airplane's propellers?

4. You put your arm in the water, and the shark removed it with its teeth immediately. What did the shark do to your arm?

5. You could see that the ring wasn't solid gold because the brass under the gold was visible. What happened to the gold?

6. In Question 5, how would you describe the gold?

7. I accidentally hit the lamp with my arm, and it fell to the floor. What did I do to the lamp?

8. You used a paper towel to remove the glass cleaner from the mirror. What did you do to the mirror?

9. In Question 8, how would you describe the mirror after you removed the glass cleaner?

10. You have to remove the water from the table before you paint it. What do you have to do to the table before you paint it?

11. In Question 10, how would you describe the table after the water is removed?

12. You removed the gift wrapping paper from the gift. What did you do to the gift wrapping paper?

13. In Question 12, after using force to remove the gift wrapping paper, how would you describe the wrapping paper?

EXERCISE 27d, Review — **Complete the sentences with these phrasal verbs from previous sections. Be sure the phrasal verbs are in the correct tense. To check their meanings, review the section number given after each one.**

clear up, 22	go up, 26	open up, 26	shut off, 26
come down, 24	heat up, 22	pay up, 22	start up, 26
eat up, 22	let in on, 26	plug up, 22	think ahead, 21
go over, 26	let up, 24	put together, 26	trade in, 24

1. If I don't come up with $230 by Friday, they're going to _____ _____ my electricity.

2. The guy from the collection agency demanded that Miguel _____ _____ immediately.

3. It rained for forty days and forty nights before it _____ _____.

4. If you had _____ _____, you would have everything you need now.

5. We had a lot of questions about our school project, but the teacher _____ them _____.

6. Mark said his audition didn't _____ _____ well, and he doesn't think he'll get the part.

7. Soldiers are trained to take their rifles apart and _____ them back _____.

8. I think $15,000 is a little high for that car. If you _____ _____ a little, I might be interested.

9. The police closed the illegal casino, but it _____ right back _____ a few days later.

10. No one at the party ate the carrot sticks, but they _____ the shrimp right _____.

11. I hate using the stove on really hot summer days; it _____ the whole house _____.

12. The minimum wage hasn't _____ _____ in more than three years.

13. The senator _____ her aides _____ _____ her plan to run for the presidency.

14. I doubt if I'll get much if I _____ this old car _____.

15. The engine _____ right _____ when I turned the key.

16. My daughter put one of her stuffed animals in the toilet and _____ it _____.

28. FOCUS ON: passive phrasal verbs, 2

When separable phrasal verbs are in the passive, they cannot be separated by the object of the verb because the object of the active verb is the subject of the passive sentence — there is no object:

active: *Jim **called back** <u>Mike</u>.*
      subject   *object*

passive: *<u>Mike</u> was **called back**.*
          subject

active: *Jim **called** <u>Mike</u> **back**.*
       subject   *object*

Infinitive			
present tense	-ing form	past tense	past participle
beef up			
beef up & beefs up	beefing up	beefed up	beefed up

1. beef . . . up *p.v.* When you **beef up** security or some other arrangement to prevent or deal with a problem, you make this arrangement stronger.

*After the terrorist attack, security was **beefed up** at the embassy.*
*The hospital decided to **beef up** its emergency facilities.*
*The coach is planning to **beef** the defense **up**.*

beefed-up *part.adj.* After security or some other arrangement to prevent or deal with a problem has been made stronger, it is **beefed-up**.

*The ambassador is confident that the **beefed-up** security will prevent any further terrorist attacks.*

break up			
break up & breaks up	breaking up	broke up	broken up

1. break . . . up *p.v.* When you **break up** a fight, you stop the fight.

*Two students were fighting, and the teacher **broke** them **up**.*
*There was no way I could **break up** the fight between the two dogs.*

2. break . . . up *p.v.* When a gathering of people separates, it **breaks up**. When the police tell people who are gathered together in a crowd to separate and leave the area, the police **break** the gathering **up**.

*The meeting should **break up** around 3:00.*
*The police ordered the gang members to **break** it **up**.*
*The demonstration was **broken up** by riot police.*

3. break . . . up (with) *p.v.* When two people end a romantic relationship, they **break up**. When you end a romantic relationship with another person, you **break up** with that person. When other people cause a couple to **break up**, they **break** the couple **up**.

*I was sad to hear that Jim and Nancy had **broken up**.*
*It was Jim's secretary who **broke** them **up**.*

breakup *n.* When two people end a romantic relationship, a **breakup** occurs.

*Nancy is very upset about the **breakup**.*

4. break . . . up *p.v.* When something breaks into smaller pieces, it **breaks up**. When you break something into smaller pieces, you **break** it **up**.

*The meteor **broke up** when it entered Earth's atmosphere.*
*Sally **broke** the cookie **up** before giving it to her baby.*

breakup *n.* When something breaks into smaller pieces, a **breakup** takes place.

*The **breakup** of AT&T created several smaller telephone companies.*

5. break . . . up *p.v.* When something **breaks up** the day or some other period of time, it interrupts that time and makes it less boring.

*The bank guard likes to chat with the tellers once in a while to **break up** the day.*
*My day was **broken up** by a going-away party for one of my coworkers.*

Infinitive

	present tense	-ing form	past tense	past participle
call back				
	call back & calls back	calling back	called backed	called back

1. call . . . back *p.v.* When you **call** someone **back**, you call a person on the telephone who has called you earlier.

*Janice left a message asking me to **call** her **back**.*
*Bob was **called back** by the salesman.*

2. call . . . back *p.v.* When you leave a place or walk away from a person and are then asked to return, you are **called back**.

*I remembered something after she walked away, and I **called** her **back**.*
*Mike handed his letter of resignation to his boss, but he was **called back** after he left the office.*

call up				
	call up & calls up	calling up	called up	called up

1. call . . . up *p.v.* When you **call** people **up**, you call them on the telephone.

*Nicole **called** me **up** and asked me to come to her party.*
*Every evening I'm **called up** by charities asking for money.*

carry out				
	carry out & carries out	carrying out	carried out	carried out

1. carry . . . out *p.v.* When you **carry out** a duty, task, assignment, or order, you do it.

*Sean will **carry** your duties **out** while you're on vacation.*
*The boss was furious because his orders hadn't been **carried out**.*

2. carry . . . out (of) *p.v.* When you **carry** something **out** of a place, you hold it in your hands and take it from that place.

*It took four guys to **carry** the pool table **out**.*
*David was so drunk that we had to **carry** him **out** of the bar.*

carryout *n.* Food that you take from a restaurant and eat in another place is **carry-out** or **carryout** food. **Takeout** and **takeout** food are the same as **carryout** and **carryout** food.

*We usually take **carryout** food when we go to visit Aunt Kathy.*

Infinitive

present tense	-ing form	past tense	past participle
give away			
give away & gives away	giving away	gave away	given away

1. give ... away *p.v.* When you **give** something **away**, you give it to someone without asking for anything in return because you do not want it or because you want to help the person you are giving it to.

*This old furniture isn't worth very much, so I think I'll just **give** it **away**.*
*He made nearly a billion dollars, but after he retired he **gave** most of his money **away**.*

2. give ... away *p.v.* When you **give** a secret **away**, you accidentally reveal that secret.

*I haven't seen that movie yet, so don't **give away** the ending.*
*You can trust me with the secret. I haven't **given** it **away**.*

3. give ... away *p.v.* When you **give** yourself **away**, you accidentally reveal something secret about yourself. When something **gives** you **away**, it accidentally reveals something secret about you.

*Mark tried to keep his affair a secret, but he was **given away** by his credit card bills.*
*Todd claimed he didn't care about Sally anymore, but he **gave** himself **away** when he asked who she had gone to the party with.*

giveaway *n.* A **giveaway** is a statement or action that reveals secret information.

*I knew I was going to be fired from my job when everyone stopped talking to me — that was the **giveaway**.*

mess up			
mess up & messes up	messing up	messed up	messed up

1. mess ... up *p.v. [informal]* When you **mess up** a place, you make it dirty or disorganized.

*Jim made spaghetti sauce, and he really **messed up** the kitchen.*
*You kids can play in the living room, but don't **mess** it **up**.*

messed up *part.adj.* After you **mess up** a place, it is **messed up**.

*It looks like Timmy was the last one in the bathroom — it's really **messed up**.*

2. mess ... up *p.v. [informal]* When you **mess up** a situation, you create problems. When you **mess up** a plan or arrangement, you interfere with it and prevent it from happening as planned. **Mess up** is similar to **screw up**.

*Everything was perfect until you **messed** it **up**.*
*Our honeymoon was **messed up** by the airline strike.*

messed up *part.adj.* When you interfere with a plan or arrangement and prevent it from happening as planned, it is **messed up**. **Messed up** is similar to **screwed up**.

*Bob changed my plan, and now it's totally **messed up**.*

Infinitive

	present tense	-ing form	past tense	past participle
stand up	stand up & stands up	standing up	stood up	stood up

1. stand up *p.v.* When you **stand up**, you change from a sitting position to a standing position. **Get up** is similar to **stand up**.

*Everyone **stands up** when the judge enters the courtroom.*
*When the students are sleepy, the teacher makes them **stand up**.*

2. stand ... up *p.v.* [informal] When you **stand** people **up**, you do not arrive at their house as you have promised or at a social event or meeting where you are expected.

*Heather had a date with Jim last Saturday night, but she was **stood up**.*
*The senator was scheduled to speak at our meeting, but he **stood** us **up**.*

EXERCISE 28a — **Complete the sentences with phrasal verbs from this section.**
Be sure the phrasal verbs are in the correct tense.

1. If you _____ _____ a long airplane flight into two or three shorter flights, it

   isn't as boring.

2. My workroom was clean and neat, but my brother did some work and he _____ it

   _____.

3. It's going to be a surprise party, so don't _____ it _____.

4. The neighborhood council asked the police to _____ _____ their patrols in

   high crime neighborhoods.

5. I haven't talked to Sam in a long time. I think I'll _____ him _____ tonight.

6. The general expects his orders to be _____ _____ immediately.

7. In some countries, students always _____ _____ when they speak in class.

8. The huge iceberg _____ _____ when it drifted into warmer water.

9. Breaking my leg sure _____ my ski trip _____.

10. Janice didn't come to my house last night as she promised. She _____ me _____.

28

11. Timmy and his friend were fighting, and Timmy's mother _____ the fight

_____.

12. These boxes are really heavy. Can you help me _____ them _____ of the house?

13. After the rally ended, the crowd quickly _____ _____ and went home.

14. I'm too busy to talk on the phone now. Can you _____ me _____ later?

15. Bob claimed to have an excellent education, but he was _____ _____ by his

poor grammar.

16. Mark is very upset. His girlfriend just _____ _____ with him.

17. Jim told the Girl Scouts that he didn't want to buy any cookies, but as they walked away he

changed his mind and _____ them _____.

18. Instead of charging for the software program, the company decided to _____ it

_____ free.

EXERCISE 28b — **Write three sentences using the objects in parentheses. Be sure to put the objects in the right place.**

1. The White House *beefed up*. (security, it)

_____

_____

_____

2. The police are *breaking up*. (the protest, it)

_____

_____

_____

3. A trained technician ought to *carry out*. (the experiment, it)

_____

_____

_____

4. The foundation *gave away*. (the money, it)

_____

_____

5. Susie always *messes up*. (the bathroom, it)

_____

_____

_____

6. Todd *stood up*. (Heather, her)

_____

_____

_____

EXERCISE 28c — Write answers to the questions using phrasal verbs and participle adjectives from this section. Make all the phrasal verbs passive.

1. Dr. Wood will do the test of the new drug. What will happen to the test?

2. The statue was smashed by thieves. What happened to the gold statue?

3. The children made the house dirty and disorganized. What happened to the house?

4. In Question 3, how would you describe the house?

5. Mike's friend promised to come to his house, but he didn't. What happened to Mike?

6. Karen called Sarah, but Sarah was at school. Sarah didn't call Karen later. What didn't happen to Karen?

7. A supermarket chain gave the food to charity and didn't receive any money for it. What happened to the food?

8. The palace is making security stronger. What is happening to security at the palace?

9. In Question 8, how would you describe the security now?

10. The personnel manager will call all the candidates for the job. What will happen to all the candidates for the job?

28

EXERCISE 28d, Review — **Complete the sentences with these phrasal verbs from previous sections. Be sure the phrasal verbs are in the correct tense. To check their meanings, review the section number given after each one.**

back up, 11	fix up, 15	rip up, 17	tear down, 8
blow away, 15	hand out, 10	stick up, 14	track down, 13
cut off, 11	hold up, 7	take in, 7	use up, 14
drop off, 11	lay off, 10	take out, 11	wake up, 11

1. The hard disk is _____ _____ by the computer operator every day.

2. The old buildings are being _____ _____ to make room for a new office building.

3. The isn't any paper in the copier. Someone _____ it _____.

4. Last night I was _____ _____ by a loud noise.

5. I can't believe I was naive enough to be _____ _____ by him.

6. The library book I wanted had already been _____ _____.

7. Something amazing happened yesterday. You are going to be _____ _____ when I tell you about it.

8. After the old house had been _____ _____, it looked a lot better.

9. Many employees are really worried that they're going to be _____ _____.

10. I was talking to my brother on the phone when I was suddenly _____ _____.

11. My shirt was _____ _____ when I fell off my bicycle.

12. The entire building is _____ _____ by these four steel beams.

13. The pamphlets will be _____ _____ in train stations and airports.

14. The liquor store was _____ _____ again last night.

15. The film was _____ _____ at the photo lab.

16. The escaped prisoner was easily _____ _____ by the FBI agents.

29. FOCUS ON: **phrasal verbs and *might, may,* and *can***

Possibility: *may* and *might*

Both *may* and *might* are used to express a medium level of possibility. When *may* and *might* are used to express possibility in the present or future, their meaning is the same, but *may* has a slightly more formal sound. *Might* is slightly more common in everyday American English:

> *Nancy <u>might</u> **drop in** tonight.*
> *Nancy <u>may</u> **drop in** tonight.*

The speaker believes that the possibility that Nancy will **drop in** and the possibility that she will not **drop in** are approximately equal.

Requests: *may* and *might*

Both *may* and *might* are used to make requests. *May* has a formal sound, and is less common than *might*. *Can* is the most common in American English:

> most common: <u>Can</u> *I* **drop in** *tonight?*
> formal: <u>May</u> *I* **drop in** *tonight?*
> very rare: <u>Might</u> *I* **drop in** *tonight?*

Permission: *may* and *can*

May and *can* are also used to give permission. In this case, *may* is much more formal and is much less common than *can*. *Might* is not used for this purpose:

> *You <u>can</u> **drop in** after dinner.*
> *You <u>may</u> **drop in** after dinner.*

Infinitive

	present tense	-ing form	past tense	past participle
ask for	ask for & asks for	asking for	asked for	asked for

1. ask . . . for *p.v.* When you **ask for** something, you tell someone that you want it.

> *We **asked** the waiter **for** some more coffee.*
> *My wife might **ask for** more vacation time instead of a raise.*

2. ask for *p.v.* When you say that people are **asking for** something or **asking for** it, you mean that they are doing or saying something that is likely to result in punishment or a negative consequence.

> *I'm warning you — if you keep doing that, you're **asking for** trouble.*
> *You're **asking for** it! Don't say that again.*

Infinitive

present tense	-ing form	past tense	past participle
come apart			
come apart & comes apart	coming apart	came apart	come apart

1. come apart *p.v.* When something **comes apart**, the parts separate because it is old or in bad condition or because the parts were not strongly connected to each other.

> This toy airplane is such a piece of junk that it **came apart** in my hand.
> Be careful with this old book. It's **coming apart**.

drop in			
drop in & drops in	dropping in	dropped in	dropped in

1. drop in (on) *p.v.* When you **drop in** on people, you visit them unexpectedly.

> If you're ever in my neighborhood **drop in**.
> Sally **dropped in** on Marsha last night.

flip out			
flip out & flips out	flipping out	flipped out	flipped out

1. flip out *p.v.* [informal] When you **flip out**, you become very upset or very angry.

> Bob **flipped out** when the city doubled his property taxes.
> Keep your hands off Jim's computer — he'll **flip out** if you screw it up.

look out			
look out & looks out	looking out	looked out	looked out

1. look out (for) *p.v.* When you **look out** or **look out** for something, you remain alert for someone or something that is dangerous or important. When you tell people to **look out**, you are warning them of possible danger. **Look out** is the same as **watch out**.

> **Look out** for bears when you camp in the mountains.
> There's a lot of ice on the road, so **look out**.

lookout *n.* A **lookout** is someone who **looks out** for someone or something that is dangerous or important.

> The burglars had **lookouts** on every corner to warn them if the police came.

luck out			
luck out & lucks out	lucking out	lucked out	lucked out

1. luck out *p.v.* [informal] When you **luck out**, something good happens to you or you avoid something bad happening to you.

> Todd **lucked out** when he found that lottery ticket on the ground; it was a
> $1 million winner.
> I missed my flight, and the plane crashed. I guess I **lucked out**.

Infinitive

	present tense	-ing form	past tense	past participle
make out	make out & makes out	making out	made out	made out

1. make . . . out *p.v.* When you can **make** something **out**, you can see it or hear it even though it is difficult to do so.

> *The audio system is so bad in the bus station that I can never **make out** what the speakers are saying.*
> *I think that might be a mountain goat up there near the top of the mountain. I can just barely **make** it **out** with these binoculars.*

2. make . . . out *p.v.* [*always used with "to be"*] When you **make** people or things **out** to be a certain way or a certain thing, you describe or consider them to be this way or to be this thing.

> *Stop complaining — my food isn't as bad as you **make** it **out** to be.*
> *The critics **made** the film **out** to be a real bore, but I liked it.*

3. make . . . out (to) *p.v.* When you write the necessary information on the front of a check, you **make** the check **out**. When you write the name of a person, company, or other organization on the check, you **make** the check **out** to that person, company, or organization.

> *How should I **make** this check **out**?*
> *There must be a mistake; this check is **made out** to my brother, not to me.*
> *Nancy **made** a check **out** to the IRS for $17,000.*

made out *part.adj.* After the necessary information has been written on the front of a check, the check is **made out**.

> *Is the check **made out**, or is it blank?*

4. make out (on) *p.v.* When you **make out** or **make out** on something, you do something successfully or survive a situation even though it may be difficult.

> *Karen had a job interview yesterday. I wonder how she **made out**.*
> *Even though Jerry has lost his job, we'll **make out** somehow.*
> *How did you **make out** on the test yesterday?*

	run across & runs across	running across	ran across	run across
run across				

1. run across *p.v.* When people or things **run across** a place, room, or building, they move from one side to the other very quickly.

> *The receiver **ran across** the field and caught the ball.*
> *It's crazy to **run across** the street through the traffic instead of waiting for the light.*

2. run across *p.v.* When you **run across** people or things, you see or find them without planning or expecting to. **Come across** is similar to **run across**.

29

*I don't go to that supermarket anymore because I may **run across** my ex-husband.*
*Bob **ran across** one of his army buddies at the baseball game.*

EXERCISE 29a — Complete the sentences with phrasal verbs from this section. Be sure the phrasal verbs are in the correct tense.

1. Can you tell me what this says? I can't _____ it _____ without my glasses.

2. The store we're going to is on the right side of the street, so _____ _____ for it.

3. You didn't fix this very well; it's already _____ _____ again.

4. Okay, I'll give you the money. Who should I _____ the check _____ to?

5. I'm going to be in Dan's neighborhood tomorrow, so I might _____ _____

   on him for a quick visit.

6. Ann's going to _____ _____ when she sees this cigarette burn on her

   antique table.

7. Sally thinks she _____ _____ okay on her driving test.

8. I wasn't surprised when I _____ _____ Sam at the beach; he goes there a lot.

9. That's enough! If you don't stop bothering me, you're _____ _____ it.

10. A police officer stopped me for going forty miles over the limit, and all he did was give me

    a warning. I really _____ _____, didn't I?

11. Every night people call and _____ _____ money for one charity or another.

12. Leticia was right about that restaurant. It was just as good as she _____ it

    _____ to be.

EXERCISE 29b — Write answers to the questions using phrasal verbs and participle adjectives from this section. Be sure the phrasal verbs are in the correct tense.

1. You got very upset when I wrecked your car. What did you do?

2. Timmy might tell Santa Claus that he wants a new bicycle. What might Timmy do?

3. I unexpectedly met my college roommate at the airport this morning. What did I do at the

   airport this morning?

4. Tom wrote all the necessary information on the check. What did Tom do?

5. In Question 4, how would you describe the check after Tom wrote all the necessary information on it?

6. Betty isn't expecting me, but I might go to her house this evening to visit her. What might I do to Betty?

7. The pieces of this chair are becoming separated. What is the chair doing?

8. You didn't have your homework ready, but the teacher didn't find out because she forgot to ask you for it. What did you do?

9. I can't read what that sign says because it's so far away. What can't I do?

10. Susie's father told her to be careful about cars when she rides her bicycle in the street. What did Susie's father tell her to do?

EXERCISE 29c — **Write eight original sentences using phrasal verbs from this section.**

1. _____

2. _____

3. _____

4. _____

5. _____

6. _____

7. _____

8. _____

EXERCISE 29d, Review — **Complete the sentences with these nouns from previous sections. To check their meanings, review the section number given after each one.**

crackdown, 23	handover, 19	start-up, 26	warm-up, 19
cutoff, 11	holdout, 23	stickup, 14	
fixer-upper, 15	shutoff, 26	takeout, 11	

1. The company is accepting applications for the position until the _____ date, March 6th.

2. A _____ before exercise is a good idea.

3. We bought a _____, fixed a few things, added a bathroom, and sold it a year later for a nice profit.

4. Mom doesn't feel like cooking tonight, so we're getting _____ food.

5. Except for a few _____ hiding in the hills, all the rebels surrendered after the peace treaty.

6. The angry citizens demanded a _____ on crime in their neighborhood.

7. Most business _____ fail in less than three years.

8. If there's a problem with the machine, the _____ switch is right here.

9. The prime minister demanded the immediate _____ of the hostages.

10. The convenience store _____ was recorded on videotape.

> EXERCISE 29e, Review — **Complete the sentences with these phrasal verbs from previous sections. Be sure the phrasal verbs are in the correct tense. To check their meanings, review the section number given after each one.**

break up, 28	do with, 25	go up, 26	settle for, 25
call back, 28	dry off, 27	knock off, 27	stand up, 28
call up, 28	give away, 28	lighten up, 25	think up, 25
carry out, 28	go over, 26	mess up, 28	zip up, 21

1. The teacher was too strict with her students, and the principal suggested that she _____ _____.

2. Tom was expecting Nancy to come to his house for dinner, but she _____ him _____.

3. Letting Timmy use my computer was a mistake. He _____ it _____, and now it doesn't work.

4. They're asking $340,000 for their house, but they might _____ _____ $300,000.

5. I told the school principal that Hank might have something to _____ _____ the fish in the swimming pool.

6. Andrew Carnegie was a very rich man, but he _____ most of his money _____ before he died.

7. I gave Erik my telephone number, and he said he might _____ me _____ tonight.

8. Erik called while I was in the shower, so now I need to _____ him _____.

9. After the Soviet Union _____ _____ in 1991, several new nations came into existence.

10. The coach is worried that the rain-soaked football field might not _____ _____ in time for the game.

11. The company is planning to _____ _____ a major reorganization.

12. Don't put the candle there; the cat might _____ it _____ and start a fire.

13. The students didn't understand the lesson, so the teacher _____ _____ it again.

14. It's really cold out there — you might want to _____ your coat _____.

15. The Wilsons aren't sure where they will spend their vacation. They may _____ _____ to Alaska to visit their son.

16. Ned's a dreamer. He's always trying to _____ _____ a way to make money without working.

---

30. FOCUS ON: **participle adjectives formed from phrasal verbs, 2**

As we saw in Section 14, the past participles of many phrasal verbs can be used as participle adjectives. The adverb *all* is sometimes used to emphasize participle adjectives with the meaning of *very* or *completely*. But the sentence must be logical — *all* is used only to emphasize a participle adjective that describes a condition that can be partial, less than complete, and so on. Look at this example with *very* and two ordinary adjectives:

> makes sense: *He's very sick.*
> does not make sense: *He's very dead.*

> The first sentence above makes sense because it is possible to be very sick, but the second does not make sense because it is not possible to be very dead.

makes sense: *The man is* <u>*all*</u> ***spaced-out***.
does not make sense: *The man is* <u>*all*</u> ***locked in***.

The first sentence makes sense because it is possible to be slightly **spaced-out**, but it is not possible to be slightly **locked in** (a door is either locked or it isn't).
    When *all* is used with the meaning of *very* or *completely* in a sentence with a plural subject, it is identical in appearance to *all*'s more common meaning of *all the people, all the things,* and so on.

The men are <u>*all*</u> ***spaced-out***.

This sentence is ambiguous: it could be understood to mean that <u>every</u> man is **spaced-out** or that the men are *completely* **spaced-out**.

Infinitive

	present tense	-ing form	past tense	past participle
lock in	lock in & locks in	locking in	locked in	locked in

1. lock . . . in *p.v.* When you **lock** people **in**, you lock a door or gate so that they cannot leave a room, building, or other place.

*Seven people died because they were **locked in** the burning building.*
*It's dangerous to **lock** children **in** a car.*

locked in *part.adj.* When people cannot leave a room, building, or other place because the door or gate is locked, they are **locked in**.

*We're **locked in** — we'll have to break a window.*

2. lock . . . in *p.v.* When you **lock in** an interest rate, price, time slot, and so on, you make it definite so that it will not change in the future.

*I met with the loan officer at the bank and **locked in** a mortgage rate.*
*If you want to use the condo at the beach this weekend, you need to pay a deposit to **lock** it **in**.*

locked in *part.adj.* After you make an interest rate, price, time slot, and so on, definite so that it will not change in the future, it is **locked in**.

*The farmer isn't worried about what happens to the price of soybeans because the price of his crop is **locked in**.*

lock out	lock out & locks out	locking out	locked out	locked out

1. lock . . . out (of) *p.v.* When you **lock** people **out** or **lock** people **out** of a place, you lock a door or gate so that they cannot enter a room, building, or other place.

*The Youngs got home and found that their son had **locked** them **out** of their house.*
*I hide an extra key under the bumper of my car so that I won't get **locked out**.*

locked out *part.adj.* When people cannot enter a room, building, or other place because the door or gate is locked, they are **locked out**.

> We're **locked out**; we'll just have to wait outside until someone comes home.

2. lock ... out *p.v.* When a business **locks out** workers, the workers are prohibited from working by the business management.

> Management **locked** the workers **out** after they refused to sign the new contract.
> When the owners heard talk of a strike, they **locked** the employees **out**.

locked out *part.adj.* After a business **locks out** workers in order to prohibit them from working, the workers are **locked out**.

> We're **locked out**. How can we earn a living?

lockout *n.* When a business **locks out** workers in order to prohibit them from working, it is a **lockout**.

> The **lockout** lasted for three months.

Infinitive

	present tense	-ing form	past tense	past participle
punch in				
	punch in & punches in	punching in	punched in	punched in

1. punch ... in *p.v.* When you come to your workplace and put your time card in the time clock to record the time you have arrived, you **punch in**.

> Don't forget to **punch in** as soon as you get to work.
> Mark was late, so I **punched** him **in**.

punched in *part.adj.* When you are **punched in**, you are at your workplace, on duty, and being paid.

> If you're **punched in**, you shouldn't be sitting down smoking a cigarette.

punch out				
	punch out & punches out	punching out	punched out	punched out

1. punch ... out *p.v.* When you leave your workplace and put your time card in the time clock to record the time you have left, you **punch out**.

> Sally's not at work; she **punched out** at 5:08.
> Jim usually forgets, so his boss **punches** him **out**.

punched out *part.adj.* When you are **punched out**, you are not at your workplace, or if you are there, you are off duty and not being paid.

> The manager asked why I wasn't working, and I told him I was **punched out**.

put out				
	put out & puts out	putting out	put out	put out

1. put ... out *p.v.* When you extinguish a fire or something that is burning, you **put** it **out**.

Put that cigarette *out* immediately.

*It was two hours before the fire was **put out**.*

2. put . . . out *p.v.* When you take something from inside a building or storage place and leave it outside for someone to take, use, or deal with, you **put** it **out**.

*The garbage truck comes early tomorrow morning, so **put** the trash bags **out** tonight.*

*Judy **put** some clothes **out** for her daughter to wear the next day.*

3. put . . . out *p.v.* When you **put out** your hand, arm, foot, or leg, you extend it front of your body.

*Mike **put out** his leg and tripped me.*

*I **put** my hand **out**, but she refused to shake it.*

4. put . . . out *p.v.* When you **put** yourself **out**, you try very hard to help someone.

*Sofia really **put** herself **out** to make her new daughter-in-law feel welcome.*

*Don't **put** yourself **out**. I can make my own dinner.*

5. put . . . out *p.v.* When you **put** people **out**, you inconvenience them.

*Erik really **put** Bill **out** when he asked him for a ride to the airport at 3:00 in the morning.*

*You've done so much to help me. I'm sorry to have **put** you **out**.*

6. put out *p.v.* When you are **put out** by people, you are annoyed by something they have said or done.

*I was really **put out** by having to take a taxi to work because Mike hadn't returned my car.*

*Dan was **put out** by Sam's ungrateful attitude.*

put out *part.adj.* When you are annoyed by something that someone has said or done, you are **put out**.

*Maria's **put out**; the manager thanked everyone who worked on the project except her.*

7. put . . . out *p.v.* When a book, magazine, newspaper, or musical recording is published or issued, it is **put out**.

*The publisher is planning to **put** a new magazine **out** that will appeal to teenage girls.*

*Frank Sinatra **put out** several classic recordings in the 1950s.*

Infinitive

	present tense	-ing form	past tense	past participle
sort out				
	sort out & sorts out	sorting out	sorted out	sorted out

1. sort . . . out *p.v.* When you **sort** a group of things **out**, you separate them into smaller groups according to one or more characteristics.

*After you take the laundry out of the dryer, you have to **sort** it **out**.*
*The mail arrives at the post office all mixed together, and it has to be **sorted out***
before it can be delivered.

sorted out *part.adj.* After you separate things into smaller groups according to one or more characteristics, they are **sorted out**.

*The mail is **sorted out** and ready to be delivered.*

2. sort ... out *p.v.* When you do something to solve a problem or to correct a misunderstanding, you **sort** it **out**.

Janice was angry with me about what happened last night, but I called her and we
***sorted** everything **out**.*
*Everyone is confused about the new plan. We ought to talk to Mrs. Taylor and **sort***
*everything **out**.*

sorted out *part.adj.* After you do something to solve a problem or to correct a misunderstanding, it is **sorted out**.

*Mike and Tom had a big fight, but everything is **sorted out** now.*

Infinitive			
present tense	**-ing form**	**past tense**	**past participle**
space out			
space out & spaces out	spacing out	spaced out	spaced out

1. space ... out *p.v.* [*informal — used mostly by young people*] When you **space out** or when something **spaces** you **out**, something or someone confuses you and causes you to forget what you were saying or doing at that moment.

*This place is really weird — it's **spacing** me **out**.*
*Sorry, what did you say? I wasn't listening — I **spaced out**.*

spaced-out *part.adj.* When something or someone confuses you and causes you to forget what you were saying or doing at that moment, you are **spaced-out**.

*Half of what Jerry says doesn't make any sense; he's all **spaced-out**.*

wash up			
wash up & washes up	washing up	washed up	washed up

1. wash up *p.v.* When you **wash up**, you wash your hands thoroughly.

*Go and **wash up** — it's time for dinner.*
*The surgeon **washed up** before the operation.*

2. wash up *p.v.* When something in a lake, a river, or the sea **washes up**, it is carried by the water to the land and left there.

*The police were called when a dead body **washed up** on the beach.*
*Pieces of the sunken boat continued to **wash up** for weeks.*

30

EXERCISE 30a — Complete the sentences with phrasal verbs from this section. Be sure the phrasal verbs are in the correct tense.

1. I had to break a window when I _____ myself _____ of my car.

2. Judy was _____ _____ by her brother's criticism of the way she's raising her children.

3. The guard _____ the prisoner _____ her jail cell.

4. The Bakers organized a nice party for their daughter's birthday. They really _____ themselves _____.

5. My brown socks are mixed with my black socks. I have to _____ them _____.

6. Joe was late to work, so the manager _____ him _____.

7. The forest fire was _____ _____ by the rain.

8. The restaurant manager told the cook to_____ _____ before handling food.

9. The factory workers finished their shifts and _____ _____.

10. Thanks for helping me move my piano. I'm sorry to _____ you _____.

11. We got a fixed-rate mortgage so we could _____ _____ a low rate.

12. The workers were _____ _____ by management during a labor dispute.

13. I totally _____ _____ and forgot about the cake in the oven.

14. Sally and her brothers had a big argument, but they got everything _____ _____.

15. As I was falling, I _____ my arm _____ to protect my head.

16. Wreckage from the crashed airplane _____ _____ on the coast.

17. Jim _____ bowls of peanuts _____ for his guests.

18. The band hasn't _____ _____ a CD in three years.

EXERCISE 30b — Write three sentences using the objects in parentheses. Be sure to put the objects in the right place.

1. He *locked in.* (the crazy guy, him)

_____

_____

_____

2. Jim *locked out.* (his wife, her)

_____

_____

_____

3. Did you *punch in*? (Rosa, her)

_____

_____

_____

4. Would you *punch out*? (Linda and Erik, them)

_____

_____

_____

5. They couldn't *put out.* (the fire, it)

_____

_____

_____

6. The bright lights *spaced out.* (Janice, her)

_____

_____

_____

EXERCISE 30c — Complete the sentences with participle adjectives from this section.

1. Mark isn't working; he's taking a break. He must be _____ _____.

2. You can't leave the building because you're _____ _____.

3. The clothes were all mixed together, but now they're _____ _____.

4. I forgot my key, and I can't get in my office. I'm _____ _____.

5. We had a big misunderstanding, but it's all _____ _____ now.

6. Joe went to the store, but when he got there, he couldn't remember what he wanted.

   He was _____ _____.

7. Nancy invited her father-in-law for dinner, and after dinner he told Nancy that his other

   daughter-in-law was a better cook. Nancy was really _____ _____.

8. The manager asked, "If you're _____ _____, why aren't you working?"

> EXERCISE 30d — **Write answers to the questions using phrasal verbs and
> participle adjectives from this section. Be sure the phrasal verbs are in the
> correct tense.**

1. There was a fire in the wastebasket, so I got some water to extinguish it. What did I do?

2. I don't want the children in here while I'm working, so I'm going to push the button on the
   doorknob to lock the door. What am I going to do to the children?

3. In Question 2, how would you describe the children after I lock the door?

4. David forgot what he was going to say. What did David do?

5. In Question 4, how would you describe David when he forgot what he was going to say?

6. Sally told me to use soap and water to get my hands clean before I handle food. What did
   Sally tell me to do?

7. The newspaper is published only once a week. What is done to the newspaper only
   once a week?

8. Lydia put Jim's time card in the time clock when Jim was late for work. What did Lydia do
   for Jim?

9. In Question 8, how would you describe Jim after Lydia put his time card in the time clock?

10. Your books are all mixed together and you ought to separate them into different groups.
    What should you do to your books?

11. In Question 10, how would you describe your books after you separate them into
    different groups?

12. I made the thief stay until the police came by putting him in the closet and using a key to
    prevent him from leaving the closet. What did I do to the thief?

13. In Question 12, how would you describe the thief after I used the key to prevent him from leaving the closet?

14. It really annoyed Erik when Jane told him that he needed to lose weight. How was Erik affected by Jane's remark?

15. In Question 14, how would you describe Erik after Jane told him he needed to lose weight?

16. The employees can't put their time cards in the time clock and go home before 4:30. What can't the employees do?

17. In Question 16, after the employees put their time cards in the time clock, how would you describe them?

18. Jane didn't try very hard to make her brother and his family comfortable when they stayed with her. What didn't Jane do?

EXERCISE 30e, Review — **Complete the sentences with these participle adjectives from previous sections. To check their meanings, review the section number given after each one.**

beefed up, 28	lit up, 13	shut off, 26	worn off, 27
broken off, 27	made out, 29	torn off, 27	
closed off, 13	made-up, 23	washed off, 27	
dried off, 27	messed up, 28	wiped off, 27	

1. The children baked cookies this morning, and they left the kitchen all _____ _____.

2. The _____ _____ security force can handle any terrorist attack.

3. Charles didn't pay his bill, and now his electricity is _____ _____.

4. I can't read the sign because the paint is all _____ _____.

5. There aren't any tags on this mattress. They're all _____ _____.

6. Those apples aren't _____ _____, so don't eat them.

7. You can't drive down that street; it's _____ _____.

8. This check isn't blank; it's _____ _____.

9. The Christmas tree isn't _____ _____ now, but when it is it'll be beautiful.

10. I put the coffee cup with the _____ _____ handle downstairs. I'm going to fix it later.

11. The kitchen counter isn't_____ _____, so don't put those papers on it — they might get grease on them.

12. That was quite a rain we just had. I don't think I'll drive to work until the roads have _____ _____.

13. I didn't believe a word he said. It was just a lot of _____ nonsense.

EXERCISE 30f, Review — **Complete the sentences with these phrasal verbs from previous sections. Be sure the phrasal verbs are in the correct tense. To check their meanings, review the section number given after each one.**

ask for, 29	fill out, 14	make out, 29	wipe off, 27
butt in, 14	have on, 25	open up, 26	work out, 11
carry out, 28	head into, 17	stand up, 28	
drop in, 29	hurry up, 25	trade in, 24	
drop out, 23	knock over, 25	wash off, 27	

1. _____ _____ of school was the dumbest thing I ever did.

2. The loan application was rejected because it hadn't been _____ _____ properly.

3. I'm going to ask the car dealer how much I can _____ my car _____ for.

4. My feet are killing me. I've been _____ _____ all day.

5. Did you see what Sally was wearing yesterday? She _____ a green dress and purple shoes _____.

6. Mike _____ the bartender _____ a gin martini, but she made a vodka martini instead.

7. We'll have to _____ _____ if we're going to get to the theater before the movie starts.

8. Don't leave that glass there — the baby might _____ it _____.

9. Dad's hardware store went out of business after a huge discount store _____ _____ across the street.

10. You won't be able to _____ that paint _____ with water; you'll have to use turpentine.

11. It was raining, so I had to _____ the water _____ my glasses after I came inside.

12. Sergeant Jones has always _____ _____ his orders without fail.

13. If you're ever in my neighborhood, _____ _____; you're always welcome.

14. Things aren't _____ _____ at my new job, and I think I'm going to quit soon.

15. Judy left her home in the suburbs and _____ _____ the city.

16. When I met Jim I was surprised at how nice he was. Everyone always _____ him _____ to be a real jerk.

17. I would have been next, but then some jerk _____ _____ line.

---

31. FOCUS ON: **phrasal verbs and gerund subjects**

As we saw in Section 16, *gerunds* — verbs in the *-ing* form that function as nouns — can serve as the objects of many phrasal verbs. But gerunds can also serve as the subject of a sentence:

> <u>Eating</u> meat everyday was something we **did without**.
>
> *gerund*
>
> <u>Voting</u> was immediately **done away with** by the dictatorship.
>
> *gerund*

Infinitive

present tense	-ing form	past tense	past participle
care for			
care for & cares for	caring for	cared for	cared for

1. care for *p.v.* When you **care for** children or people who are old or sick, you provide them with the food or medicine they need or you do things to help them. When you **care for** machines or buildings, you keep them in good condition.

> *The nurses have to **care for** several very sick patients.*
> *John has been **caring for** his eighty-three-year-old mother since her stroke.*

2. care for *p.v.* When you **care for** people or things, you like them.

31

*Jane doesn't **care for** coffee; she prefers tea.*

*I asked Sally to go to the dance, but she said that dancing is not something
she **cares for**.*

Infinitive

cut out

present tense	-ing form	past tense	past participle
cut out & cuts out	cutting out	cut out	cut out

1. cut ... out (of) *p.v.* When you **cut** something **out** or **cut** something **out** of a piece of paper, cloth, or other material, you use scissors or a knife to remove part of it.

*The bank robber had a pillowcase over his head with two holes **cut out**.*

*I **cut** an interesting story **out** of the newspaper to show to my father.*

cutout *n.* Something that has been **cut out** of a piece of paper, cloth, or other material is a **cutout**.

*Timmy made some cardboard **cutouts** shaped like animals.*

2. cut ... out *p.v.* When you **cut out** part of a film, television program, book, magazine, and so on, you remove that part.

*The movie was too long, so the director **cut** a couple of scenes **out**.*

*Before the book was published, the parts that were critical of the king had to be **cut out** of Chapter 4.*

3. cut ... out *p.v.* When you **cut out** something that you consume, you stop using it. When you **cut out** doing something, you stop doing it. When you say "**Cut** it **out**" to people, you want them to stop doing or saying something.

*Smoking is the first thing you've got to **cut out** if you want to improve your health.*

*If you want to lose weight, you'll have to **cut** cookies and ice cream **out**.*

*It bothers me when you do that, so **cut** it **out**!*

4. cut out *p.v.* When a motor suddenly stops working, it **cuts out**.

*I was driving when the motor suddenly **cut out**.*

*This plane has only one engine, so if it **cuts out**, we're in big trouble.*

do away with

do away with & does away with	doing away with	did away with	done away with

1. do away with *p.v.* When you **do away with** something, you eliminate it or prohibit it.

***Doing away with** smoking is not something that will happen soon.*

*Some people think the electoral college is obsolete and should be **done away with**.*

2. do away with *p.v.* When you **do away with** people, you kill them.

*Marvin inherited a fortune after he **did away with** his older brother.*

*The woman was accused of **doing away with** her husband with arsenic.*

Infinitive

	present tense	-ing form	past tense	past participle
do without	do without & does without	doing without	did without	done without

1. do without *p.v.* When you **do without** something, you continue living or working without something that you want or need because it is not possible or available.

> *Washing your hair everyday is something you have to **do without** when you go camping.*
> ***Doing without** is something you get used to when you're poor.*

	present tense	-ing form	past tense	past participle
look into	look into & looks into	looking into	looked into	looked into

1. look into *p.v.* When you **look into** something or **look into** doing something, you investigate it or get more information about it.

> *After receiving many complaints about the company, the attorney general decided to **look into** the matter.*
> *Maybe leasing a car is something I should **look into**.*

	present tense	-ing form	past tense	past participle
plan on	plan on & plans on	planning on	planned on	planned on

1. plan on *p.v.* When you **plan on** something, you expect it.

> *They wanted a large family, but having thirteen children sure wasn't what they **planned on**.*
> *You should **plan on** at least two years to finish the master's degree program.*

2. plan on *p.v.* When you **plan on** doing something, you intend to do it.

> *What are you **planning on** doing tonight?*
> *I **plan on** fishing and taking a lot of pictures on my vacation.*

	present tense	-ing form	past tense	past participle
put off	put off & puts off	putting off	put off	put off

1. put . . . off *p.v.* When you **put off** something or **put off** doing something, you delay or postpone it. When you **put** people **off**, you delay doing something they want you to do.

> *Buying a new house will have to be **put off** until we can afford it.*
> *The students begged the teacher to **put** the test **off** until the next week.*
> *He pressured me for a decision, but I kept **putting** him **off**.*

2. put . . . off *p.v.* When people **put** you **off**, they do or say something that offends you.

> *Everyone was **put off** by his racist jokes.*
> *Todd went out to dinner with Nancy last night, and the way she treated the waiter really **put** him **off**.*

put off *part.adj.* After people do or say something that offends you, you are **put off**.

*What's wrong? You seem a little **put off**.*

Infinitive			
present tense	-ing form	past tense	past participle
rule out			
rule out & rules out	ruling out	ruled out	ruled out

1. rule . . . out *p.v.* When you **rule out** people or things, you eliminate them from a list. When you **rule out** doing something, you decide that it is something you will not do because you do not want to, because it is impossible, and so on.

> *The detective interviewed all the suspects and **ruled** everyone **out** except the victim's ex-wife.*
> *Ater the hurricane they **ruled out** moving to Florida.*
> *With all these medical bills to pay, maybe we should consider **ruling out** buying a new car.*

EXERCISE 31a — **Complete the sentences with phrasal verbs from this section. Be sure the phrasal verbs are in the correct tense.**

1. I suggested moving to Minnesota, but my wife _____ _____ moving anywhere cold.

2. My doctor says I should _____ _____ scuba diving until my ear gets better.

3. The health department wants to _____ _____ _____ smoking within twenty years.

4. I saw a funny cartoon in the paper, so I _____ it _____ and sent it to my brother.

5. Some countries have an excellent health care system. No one has to _____ _____ medical treatment.

6. I was a little _____ _____ by his unfriendliness.

7. Let's go to a different restaurant; I don't _____ _____ Chinese food.

8. I'm going to _____ _____ this situation to see what the problem is.

9. After the revolution, all members of the royal family were _____ _____ _____.

10. Several scenes of the film had to be _____ _____ before the censors would approve it.

11. Jim had to quit his job to _____ _____ his sick wife.

12. I had to take a taxi to work yesterday. My car's motor _____ _____ right in the middle of an intersection.

13. What a surprise! Being transferred to Hawaii is something I never _____ _____.

14. Getting that tooth fixed is not something you should _____ _____.

15. What are you _____ _____ doing with your time after you retire?

> EXERCISE 31b — **Write answers to the questions using phrasal verbs and participle adjectives from this section. Be sure the phrasal verbs are in the correct tense.**

1. You changed your vacation plans. You're not going next week; you're going to go later. What did you do to your vacation?

2. Everyone likes Jim more now that he has stopped acting like such a big shot. What did Jim do?

3. The President said that nothing has been eliminated from the list of things that might be done about the crisis. What did the President say about what might be done about the crisis?

4. Mike's parents don't like his new friend. How do Mike's parents feel about his new friend?

5. A law was passed that prohibits child labor. What does the law do to child labor?

6. There aren't any stores out here in the woods, so if you forgot something, you'll just have to continue without it. What will you have to do if you forgot something?

7. I'm so tired of this car's ugly color; I'm going to investigate having it painted. What am I going to do?

8. If you go to Chicago in January, you can expect to freeze to death. What can you do if you go to Chicago in January?

9. Betty was a little offended by Sam's behavior. How did Betty react to Sam's behavior?

10. In Question 9, how did Sam's behavior make Betty feel?

11. The police suspected that Mr. Mayfield had been killed by a coworker. What did the police suspect about Mr. Mayfield?

12. Dr. Smith removed the entire tumor with a knife. What did he do?

13. My father kept his car in good condition, and it lasted for forty years. What did my father do to his car?

EXERCISE 31c — **Write eight original sentences using phrasal verbs from this section. Try to use gerunds as the subjects of some of the sentences.**

1. _____

2. _____

3. _____

4. _____

5. _____

6. _____

7. _____

8. _____

EXERCISE 31d, Review — **Complete the sentences with these phrasal verbs from previous sections. Be sure the phrasal verbs are in the correct tense. To check their meanings, review the section number given after each one.**

ask for, 29	cut down, 23	get away, 23	luck out, 29
beef up, 28	drop in, 29	get back at, 17	make out, 29
come apart, 29	flip out, 29	get off, 18	make up, 23
crack down, 23	go about, 17	look out, 29	run across, 29

1. I'm thinking about investing in the stock market, but I'm not sure how to _____

_____ it.

2. The sound on the language lab tapes is so bad that I can't _____ _____

what they're saying.

3. The world is _____ _____ of many different countries.

4. We'll need to buy a new suitcase soon. This old one is _____ _____.

5. That was a terrible thing he did to me — I'll _____ _____ _____

him someday.

6. Hank fell from a fifth-floor window, but he landed in a swimming pool and wasn't hurt at all.

He sure _____ _____, didn't he?

7. The hockey coach said that the team's offense is good, but the defense needs to be

_____ _____.

8. My dentist said I should _____ _____ on sweets.

9. Frank really _____ _____ when he found that big snake under his bed.

10. Look at this interesting old book I _____ _____ at a used bookstore.

11. The police department is going to _____ _____ on crime.

12. You know what a bad temper Joe has. If you keep teasing him, you're _____ _____ trouble.

13. The accountant tried to embezzle $100,000, but he didn't _____ _____ with it.

14. Isn't that where Jane lives? Let's _____ _____ and say hello.

15. Jake was arrested and charged with bank robbery, but he _____ _____ because none of the witnesses could identify him.

16. There are a lot of big trucks on this road. You've really got to _____ _____ for them when you're driving.

---

32. FOCUS ON: **phrasal verbs with the particle *out***

The particle *out* is used in many phrasal verbs and has many meanings. Among the most frequent meanings of *out* are to say that something or someone literally moves from the inside to the outside of a place:

> He **fell out** of a tree.
> Melanie **came out** of the house.
> We always **go out** through the back door.
> Would you **take** the garbage **out**, please?

that something is done completely or thoroughly:

> I **cleaned out** the closet.
> The people quickly **cleared out**.
> She **emptied** her purse **out** on the table.
> Please **fill** this form **out**.

that an action or activity has ended:

> The fire **went out**.
> The light bulb **burned out**.
> Hank **dropped out** of school.
> Jane **chickened out** of asking her boss for a raise.

that something or someone is chosen, organized, shared, or distributed:

> *The manager **handed out** our paychecks.*
> *Tom **picked** a new shirt **out**.*
> *The mailroom clerk **sorted out** the mail.*

that something is produced by or released from a source:

> *His last book **came out** two years ago.*
> *Don't **let** the dog **out**.*
> *That group hasn't **put out** a new CD in a long time.*

that something is removed, eliminated, or excluded:

> *A page was accidentally **left out** of the book when it was printed.*
> *She **cut** a cartoon **out** of the paper.*
> *The negative test result **ruled out** cancer.*
> *His editor **took** several paragraphs **out** of the article.*

that something is perceived, sensed, found, or acquired:

> *I **figured out** the answer.*
> *Did you **find out** when the movie starts?*
> *That sign is too far away to **make out**.*
> *Mike **screwed me out** of a hundred bucks.*

that something increases in size, capacity, length, or area:

> *Paul started to **fill out** after he got married.*
> *After I gained twenty-five pounds I had to **let** my pants **out**.*
> *It's dangerous to **stick** your head **out** a car window.*

that something important or dangerous should be watched for:

> *Mike is supposed to meet us here, so **watch out** for him.*
> ***Look out**, this is a very busy intersection.*

or that something is done for a length of time:

> *The criminals **held out** for three hours before surrendering.*
> *College is hard work, but you've got to **stick** it **out**.*

Infinitive			
	present tense	-ing form	past tense	past participle
clean out			
	clean out & cleans out	cleaning out	cleaned out	cleaned out

1. clean . . . out *p.v.* When you **clean** something **out**, you clean the inside completely so that no dirt, dust, trash, and so on, remains inside.

> *Mark was fired and told to **clean** his desk **out** and leave.*
> *We **clean out** our garage every spring.*

cleaned out *part.adj.* After you clean the inside of something completely so that no dirt, dust, or trash, and so on, remains inside, it is **cleaned out**.

> Now that the garage is **cleaned out**, there's room for my car.

2. clean ... out (of) *p.v.* [informal] When people **clean** you **out** or **clean** you **out** of your money, they deceive you or pressure you into giving them all your money or spending all your money for their benefit. When an expense **cleans** you **out**, it requires you to spend all your money.

> A con artist **cleaned** my grandmother **out** of $50,000.
> Having three kids in college at the same time really **cleaned** me **out**.

3. clean ... out (of) *p.v.* [informal] If thieves **clean** a place **out** or **clean** a place **out** of something, they take everything that is valuable.

> I got home and found that my place had been **cleaned out**.
> The thieves **cleaned** the jewelry store **out** of all its diamonds and emeralds.

Infinitive

	present tense	-ing form	past tense	past participle
clear out	clear out & clears out	clearing out	cleared out	cleared out

1. clear ... out *p.v.* When people **clear out** or **clear out** of a place or they are **cleared out** of a place, they leave it.

> After the police threw tear gas, the crowd **cleared** right **out**.
> **Clear out!** This is private property.

2. clear ... out *p.v.* When you **clear out** a place, you remove things that are unwanted or in the way in order to make more room or to make the place cleaner.

> Look how much more room we have in the attic now that we've **cleared** all that junk **out**.
> The car dealer had a sale so that he could **clear out** some space for the new cars.

come out	come out & comes out	coming out	came out	come out

1. come out (of) *p.v.* When people or things leave a place, room, or house that you are not in, they **come out** of it.

> Susie's friend came to the door and asked her to **come out** and play.
> The police held their fire when they saw the gunman **coming out** of the house with his hands in the air.

2. come out (of) *p.v.* When something **comes out** of a certain place or area, it starts there.

> This speaker must not be connected; no sound is **coming out**.
> The most wonderful aroma **came out** of the kitchen.

3. come out (to) *p.v.* When people leave a city and **come out** to a place outside the city where you are, they travel to that place.

*Would you like to **come out** and visit our farm?*
*Ned loves it in the city; he hasn't **come out** to the suburbs in a long time.*

4. come out (of) *p.v.* When things or people go through an experience or treatment, the condition they are left in by that experience or treatment or the result of that experience or treatment is how they **come out**.

*It was a tough game, but our team **came out** on top.*
*How did the investigation **come out**?*
*I **came out** of that awful experience a wiser person.*

5. come out (with) *p.v.* When a book, magazine, musical recording, movie, or television show is finished and made available to the public, it **comes out**. When a book, magazine, musical recording, movie, or television show is finished and made available to the public, the company publishing it or the person who created it **comes out** with it.

*The band's new CD **came out** last month, and it's already number one on the charts.*
*Barron's is **coming out** with a new book on TOEFL soon.*

6. come out *p.v.* When information becomes known to the public, it **comes out**.

*Everyone was shocked when it **came out** that the butler had murdered the duke.*
What really happened when President Kennedy was assassinated may never
    ***come out**.*

7. come out (of) *p.v.* When dirt or a stain is removed by cleaning, it **comes out** or **comes out** of what it is in.

*Don't get grape juice on that white blouse — it'll never **come out**.*
*That paint might **come out** of the carpet if you try turpentine.*

8. come out *p.v.* When flowers or leaves start to grow, they **come out**.

*We had a very warm winter, and the flowers started **coming out** in February.*
*Oak tree leaves always **come out** later than the leaves of other trees.*

9. come out *p.v.* When clouds move and the sun becomes visible, it **comes out**.

*The rain stopped, the sun **came out**, and there was a beautiful rainbow.*
*Wait till the sun **comes out**; you'll get a better picture.*

10. come out (for/in favor of/against) *p.v.* When people with authority and influence **come out** for or **come out** in favor of people or things, they publicly announce support for them. When people with authority and influence **come out** against people or things, they publicly announce opposition to them.

*We were surprised when the mayor **came out** for legalizing gambling.*
*The senator from North Carolina **came out** against the tobacco legislation.*

Infinitive

	present tense	-ing form	past tense	past participle
empty out	empty out & empties out	emptying out	emptied out	emptied out

1. empty ... out *p.v.* When you completely remove the contents of a space or container, you **empty** it **out**.

*The police officer told me to **empty out** my pockets.*
*After we **empty** this room **out**, we can start painting.*

emptied out *part.adj.* After the contents of a container have been completely removed, the container is **emptied out**.

*Now that the room is **emptied out**, we can start laying the carpet.*

2. empty out *p.v.* When all the people in a place leave it, the place **empties out**.

*After the concert is over, it'll be twenty minutes before the auditorium **empties out**.*
*There was trash everywhere after the stadium **emptied out**.*

fall out				
	fall out & falls out	falling out	fell out	fallen out

1. fall out (of) *p.v.* When you fall from or through something that is above ground level to the ground below, you **fall out** or **fall out** of it.

*Did he **fall out** or was he pushed?*
*I found a baby bird that had **fallen out** of its nest.*

2. fall out (with/over) *p.v.* When you **fall out** with people, you become upset or angry with them. When two people **fall out** over something, they become upset or angry with each other because of a disagreement about that thing.

*Alfonso **fell out** with his sister when he criticized her husband.*
*Melanie and Sarah started a company, but they **fell out** over who would be president*
and who would be vice-president.

falling-out *n.* When people have a **falling-out**, they become upset or angry with each other and no longer have friendly relations.

*The manager of the baseball team quit after he had a **falling-out** with the owner.*

go out				
	go out & goes out	going out	went out	gone out

1. go out (of) *p.v.* When people or things leave a place, room, or house that you are in, they **go out** or **go out** of it. **Come in** is the opposite of **go out**.

*I'm trying to study — **go out** and play in the backyard.*
*Nancy was so sick that she didn't **go out** of the house for a week.*

2. go out (to) *p.v.* When people leave a city where you are and **go out** to a place outside the city, they travel to that place.

*Last weekend we **went out** to Jim's cabin on the lake.*
*This Thanksgiving I'm going to **go out** to my brother's house.*

3. go out *p.v.* When something that is burning **goes out**, it stops burning because it has no more fuel or because something, such as water or lack of oxygen, has caused it to stop burning.

*The campfire **went out** during the night.*
*The forest fire didn't **go out** until it started to rain.*

4. go out *p.v.* When an electrical light **goes out**, it stops producing light because it is no longer receiving power.

*The lights in the barracks **go out** every night at 10:00.*
*When the old tree fell on the power lines, every light in town **went out**.*

5. go out (with) *p.v.* When two people with a romantic interest in each other **go out**, they go together to a place of entertainment in order to have fun and spend time together.

*Mike's nervous — he's **going out** with Heather tonight.*
*Sally and Jim **went out** for three years before they got married.*

Infinitive

	present tense	-ing form	past tense	past participle
leave out				
	leave out & leaves out	leaving out	left out	left out

1. leave ... out *p.v.* When you **leave** people or things **out**, you accidentally or deliberately do not include them in a group.

*The director **left out** several parts of the book when she made the film.*
*Tell me the entire story from beginning to end. Don't **leave** anything **out**.*

left out *part.adj.* When you feel **left out**, you feel ignored and unappreciated by others in a group.

*No one talked to Jerry at the party. He just sat in the corner feeling **left out**.*

stick out				
	stick out & sticks out	sticking out	stuck out	stuck out

1. stick out *p.v.* When something **sticks out**, it extends from what it is attached to.

*Be careful walking in the woods, there are a lot of branches **sticking out**.*
*I cut myself on a nail that was **sticking out** of the wall.*

2. stick ... out *p.v.* When you **stick** something **out**, you extend it outward.

*Timmy **stuck** his tongue **out** when his mother gave him spinach.*
*We all **stuck** our heads **out** the window to get a better look.*

3. stick ... out *p.v.* When you **stick out** an unpleasant or difficult experience, you continue with it until it is over, rather than quit.

*I hate this job, but I need the money, so I'll just have to **stick** it **out** until I find a better one.*

*College isn't easy, but if you **stick** it **out**, you'll be glad you did.*

4. stick out *p.v.* When a characteristic or feature of something **sticks out**, that feature is very noticeable.

*Alan's nearly seven feet tall and has red hair, so he really **sticks out** in a crowd.*

*One thing that really **stuck out** about him was the strange way he laughed.*

EXERCISE 32a — **Complete the sentences with phrasal verbs from this section. Be sure the phrasal verbs are in the correct tense.**

1. Susie _____ _____ of her tree house and broke her arm.

2. The sun finally _____ _____ in the afternoon.

3. I heard some strange voices _____ _____ of the next room.

4. A sharp piece of wood was _____ _____, and I got a splinter from it.

5. When the truth finally _____ _____, you'll all be very surprised.

6. It was a good thing we had those candles when the lights _____ _____.

7. This temporary job will last only two weeks, so even though I'm bored, I guess I can

   _____ it _____.

8. That crook _____ me _____ of everything I owned.

9. David's story didn't make any sense because he _____ _____ the part about

   the missionaries and the cannibals.

10. Mike, it's starting to rain. _____ _____ and close the car windows, please.

11. Take these wastebaskets out to the Dumpster and _____ them _____.

12. It's a sure sign of spring when the tulips start to _____ _____.

13. This wood is green. Even if you can get it to burn, it'll _____ _____

   right away.

14. The Bakers said they would love to _____ _____ to visit us here at our ranch

   some weekend.

15. The soldiers were ordered to _____ the protesters _____ of the plaza.

16. Mike and Bob _____ _____ over who would pay for the window they broke

   playing baseball.

17. The reporter said that he expected the governor to _____ _____ against the proposed legislation.

18. Jim's going to be storing some of his stuff in the attic, so let's go up and _____ _____ some space for it.

19. Scott _____ _____ of the trial with his reputation badly damaged.

20. After the bomb threat was announced, the theater _____ _____ in about two minutes.

21. Betty has been _____ _____ with Erik since high school.

22. It's not very smart to _____ your arm _____ the window of a moving car.

23. I like it here in the city. When I _____ _____ to David's house in the country I get bored.

24. The talk show host asked the author about his new book which is _____ _____ soon.

25. The burglars _____ the coin shop _____ of its most valuable coins.

26. It's been an hour. Are you ever going to _____ _____ of the bathroom?

27. Don't even bother washing this blouse — the ink will never _____ _____.

28. Mike wants to sell his car, so he's going to _____ it _____ and wash it before anyone looks at it.

29. I don't remember much about Ned, but one thing _____ _____ — he always wore black.

EXERCISE 32b — **Complete the sentences with the correct second particles.**

1. The crooked lawyer *cleaned* them *out* _____ a small fortune.

2. Jake *came out* _____ the bank and surrendered.

3. Would you like to *come out* _____ my place in the country?

4. Several publishers are *coming out* _____ books on the subject.

5. The prime minister liked the idea, so we weren't surprised when he *came out* _____ the plan.

6. As expected, the leader of the opposition *came out* _____ the plan.

7. Mike *fell out* _____ his brother _____ who would pay their father's

medical bills.

8. Timmy's father told him not to *go out* _____ the house.

9. We're *going out* _____ the suburbs next weekend.

10. Heather's *going out* _____ Tom tonight.

11. Hank *fell out* _____ a hot air balloon.

EXERCISE 32c — **Write three sentences using the objects in parentheses. Be sure to put the objects in the right place.**

1. My son *cleaned out*. (the basement, it)

_____

_____

_____

2. I need to *clear out*. (the storeroom, it)

_____

_____

_____

3. Sarah *emptied out*. (the boxes, them)

_____

_____

_____

4. The factory *left out*. (an important part, it)

_____

_____

_____

5. Don't *stick out*. (your neck, it)

_____

_____

_____

EXERCISE 32d — **Write answers to the questions using phrasal verbs, participle adjectives, and nouns from this section. Be sure the phrasal verbs are in the correct tense.**

1. Some important information is being revealed to the public. What is happening to the information?

2. All the people in the plaza left. What did the people do?

3. All the people in the plaza left. What happened to the plaza?

4. I'm going to take my girlfriend to a nightclub. What am I going to do with her?

5. The soldier was killed in the battle. What didn't the soldier do?

6. We didn't ask Mark to join our club. What did we do to Mark?

7. In Question 6, how does Mark feel because we didn't ask him to join our club?

8. The IRS took all your money. What did they do to you?

9. The music company released a new CD last week. What did the music company do?

10. Everyone notices Harry because he has very long hair and a long beard. What does Harry do?

11. The *Chicago Tribune* announced in an editorial that they were for the Republican candidate. What did the *Chicago Tribune* do?

12. Bill's angry with Jim, and they're not speaking to each other. What did Bill do with Jim?

13. In Question 12, what did Bill and Jim have?

EXERCISE 32e, Review — **Complete the sentences with these phrasal verbs from previous sections. Be sure the phrasal verbs are in the correct tense. To check their meanings, review the section number given after each one.**

care for, 31	hold out, 23	punch out, 30	sort out, 30
cut out, 31	lock in, 30	put off, 31	space out, 30
do away with, 31	look into, 31	put out, 30	wash up, 30
do without, 31	punch in, 30	rule out, 31	watch out, 23

1. Susie, I told you to stop hitting your sister, so _____ it _____!

2. After I lost my job, I learned to _____ _____ a lot of things I used to think were necessities.

3. Watson made a real mess out of the project, so the boss asked me to _____ it _____.

4. I totally _____ _____ and drove twenty miles past where I was going.

5. Hey, that's really dangerous, you'd better _____ _____.

6. I'm going to get to work late tomorrow. Can you _____ me _____?

7. I'm really sick of this city. I'm going to fly to San Francisco and _____ _____ the job situation there.

8. Most of the players have signed their contracts, but a few are _____ _____.

9. Water won't _____ _____ an electrical fire.

10. The manager reminded me to _____ _____ before going home.

11. During Prohibition, the government tried to _____ _____ _____ drinking alcohol.

12. The chances that his horse will win the race are very small, but I wouldn't _____ it _____ completely.

13. Look how dirty your hands are! Go _____ _____ before you eat dinner.

14. I want to _____ _____ a low interest rate before rates go up again.

15. Thanks for inviting me to the concert, but I don't _____ _____ rap music.

16. Millions of people _____ _____ doing their taxes until the last minute.

33. FOCUS ON: **phrasal verbs and midsentence adverbs**

As we saw in Section 17, adverbs are words that modify verbs. Some adverbs are called *midsentence* adverbs because they are commonly placed in the middle of a sentence. Midsentence adverbs are usually placed before main verbs:

> *He X **goofs around**.*
> *She X **helped** him **out**.*

after any form of *be*:

> *He is X **goofing around**.*
> *She wasn't X **helping** him **out**.*

and between an auxiliary (helping) verb and the main verb:

> *He will X **goof around**.*
> *She can't X **help** him **out**.*

In questions, a midsentence adverb is usually placed between the subject and the main verb:

> *Does he X **goof around**?*
> *Is he X **goofing around**?*
> *Has she X **helped** him **out**?*

The following are common midsentence adverbs.

Adverbs of frequency

ever	*typically*	*normally*	*hardly ever*
always	*ordinarily*	*occasionally*	*almost never*
constantly	*often*	*sometimes*	*never*
almost always	*frequently*	*seldom*	*not ever*
usually	*generally*	*rarely*	

Other midsentence adverbs

already	*merely*	*ultimately*	*probably*
just	*finally*	*eventually*	*most likely*

Infinitive

	present tense	-ing form	past tense	past participle
blow up				
	blow up & blows up	blowing up	blew up	blown up

1. blow ... up *p.v.* When something **blows up** or when someone **blows** something **up**, it explodes.

> *Seven people were killed when the building **blew up**.*
> *The hijackers ultimately **blew** the plane **up**.*

2. blow ... up *p.v.* When something **blows up** or when someone **blows** something **up**, it becomes much larger because air or something else is being forced into it.

> *It always takes me an hour or more to **blow up** the balloons for a party.*
> *Hank **blew up** a beach ball and threw it in the pool.*

3. blow ... up *p.v.* When you make a picture or photograph larger, you **blow** it **up**.

> *I **blew** the photograph **up** and framed it.*
> *When you **blow** this photo of the car **up**, you can make out the license plate number.*

blowup *n.* A **blowup** is a picture or photograph that has been made larger.

> *I made a **blowup** of the photo and framed it.*

4. blow up (at/over) *p.v. [informal]* When you **blow up** or **blow up** at someone, you suddenly become very angry. When you **blow up** over something, you suddenly become very angry because of it.

> *Heather **blew up** when she saw her boyfriend dancing with Linda.*
> *Heather **blew up** at her boyfriend when she saw him dancing with Linda.*
> *Dad **blew up** over the increase in our property taxes.*

catch on

catch on & catches on	catching on	caught on	caught on

1. catch on *p.v.* When a fashion or habit becomes popular and is adopted by many people, it **catches on**. When a product or service becomes popular and is used or bought by many people, it **catches on**.

> *Beta VCRs never **caught on**.*
> *If his striped business suits **catch on**, the designer will become famous.*

2. catch on *p.v.* When you eventually begin to understand something or begin to learn a skill after practicing and studying, you **catch on**.

> *When Sally studies something, she usually **catches on** right away.*
> *Learning to dance the cumbia wasn't easy, but I eventually **caught on**.*

3. catch on (to) *p.v.* When you **catch on** or **catch on** to people, you realize that they are trying to trick or cheat you.

*If you keep lying to everyone, they'll eventually **catch on**.*
*It took me a while, but I finally **caught on** to him.*

Infinitive

	present tense	-ing form	past tense	past participle
come about				
	come about & coming about	come about	came about	come about

1. come about *p.v.* When something **comes about**, it happens, usually as a result of a series of events and actions.

*He was the richest man in town, and now he's bankrupt. How did that **come about**?*
*Several major medical advances have **come about** in the last fifty years.*

fall behind				
	fall behind & falls behind	falling behind	fell behind	fallen behind

1. fall behind *p.v.* When you are in a group that is walking, running, driving, and so on, and they move ahead of you because you are moving more slowly than the others, you **fall behind**. **Keep up** is the opposite of **fall behind**.

*Alfonso and Tom are walking so fast that I've **fallen behind**.*
*I was supposed to be following Linda to the party, but I **fell behind** and got lost.*

2. fall behind (in) *p.v.* When you are in a group that is studying, working, and so on, and they learn faster or get more work done because you are learning or working more slowly than the others, you **fall behind** or **fall behind** in your work, studies, and so on. When you do not complete work as fast as it was originally planned and expected, you **fall behind** schedule. **Get behind** is similar to **fall behind**. **Keep up** is the opposite of **fall behind**.

*Timmy was sick last semester, and he **fell behind** in his studies.*
*The sales manager wanted to know why I had **fallen behind** the rest of the department.*
*The building project will **fall behind** schedule if the construction workers go on strike.*

3. fall behind (in) *p.v.* When you do not make the regular payments you are required to make, you **fall behind** or **fall behind** in your payments.

*When I lost my job, I **fell behind** in my mortgage payments.*
*Don't **fall behind** in your payments, or your car will be repossessed.*

goof around				
	goof around & goofs around	goofing around	goofed around	goofed around

1. goof around *p.v.* [informal] When you waste time playing or doing silly or unimportant things, you **goof around**. **Fool around** is the same as **goof around**.

*My brother drives his teachers crazy. He constantly **goofs around** and creates problems.*
*Stop **goofing around** and get to work.*

Infinitive

	present tense	-ing form	past tense	past participle
help out				
	help out & helps out	helping out	helped out	helped out

1. help . . . out (with) *p.v.* When you **help out** or **help** people **out**, you assist them in doing some work or you lend or give them money or something else that they need.

*Can you **help** me **out**? I need a hundred bucks until payday.*
*We had a lot of work to do, so Maria **helped out**.*

know about				
	know about & knows about	knowing about	knew about	known about

1. know about *p.v.* When you **know about** a situation, plan, or other information, you are aware of it.

*Jim isn't here. Maybe he doesn't **know about** the schedule change.*
*Thanks for telling me, but I already **know** all **about** it.*

2. know about *p.v.* When you have studied something and learned it, you **know about** it.

*I don't **know** much **about** history. I was a business major.*
***Knowing about** art and being an artist are two different things.*

pull off				
	pull off & pulls off	pulling off	pulled off	pulled off

1. pull . . . off *p.v.* When you **pull** something **off**, you succeed in doing something difficult and possibly sneaky or illegal even though the chances of success are not high.

*Mike tried to juggle three butcher knives and two bowling balls at the same time, but he couldn't **pull** it **off**.*
*When Jake said he was going to try to rob a Las Vegas casino, no one believed he could **pull** it **off**.*

2. pull off *p.v.* When you are driving and you **pull off** the road, you drive to the side of the road and stop.

*If I get sleepy while I'm driving, I always **pull off** the road and take a nap.*
*When I heard that strange noise, I **pulled off** to the side and checked the engine.*

EXERCISE 33a — **Complete the sentences with phrasal verbs from this section. Be sure the phrasal verbs are in the correct tense.**

1. I need to move some furniture, and it's too heavy for me. Could you _____ me

_____ tonight?

2. Television was invented in the 1920s, but it didn't start to _____ _____ until the 1950s.

3. Math is very difficult for Mike. If he takes the advanced class, he'll most likely _____ _____.

4. I didn't think Todd could manage going to school and working at the same time, but he _____ it _____.

5. When Jim shows his terrible report card to his mother, she'll _____ _____.

6. Nancy's a hard worker. She never _____ _____.

7. The terrorists tried to _____ _____ the embassy.

8. A lot of changes have _____ _____ in the last few years.

9. The truck driver was lost, so he _____ _____ to the side of the road and checked his map.

10. Sam and Dave are so much faster on their bikes than I am that I always _____ _____.

11. Don't ask Ann; she doesn't _____ anything _____ it.

12. I used to be able to trick my rich uncle into giving me money, but he's starting to _____ _____ to me.

13. _____ _____ the balloons now; the party's going to start soon.

14. Bob started taking dance lessons, and he _____ _____ right away.

15. If you _____ _____ in your credit card payments, you'll damage your credit rating.

16. I usually ask Bill what he thinks before I buy a stock. He _____ a lot _____ investing.

17. I asked the photo lab to _____ the photo _____ 300 percent.

EXERCISE 33b — **Complete the sentences with the correct second particles.**

1. Todd was fired after he *blew up* _____ his boss.

2. Todd is usually so easygoing. What did he *blow up* _____?

3. Karen thinks she's so clever, but I'm starting to *catch on* _____ her.

4. If you don't start working harder, you're going to *fall behind* _____ math.

5. Thanks for *helping* me *out* _____ my algebra homework.

EXERCISE 33c — **Write answers to the questions using phrasal verbs from this section. Be sure the phrasal verbs are in the correct tense.**

1. The company started to sell chocolate toothpaste, but it never became popular. What didn't chocolate toothpaste do?

2. Sam has a lot of work to do before 5:00, so Lydia is doing some of it for him so that he won't have to work late. What is Lydia doing for Sam?

3. Nobody in the criminal gang thought they could steal an airplane, but they did. What did the gang do?

4. Ali doesn't usually do any work. He usually watches TV and listens to music. What does Ali usually do?

5. They sometimes destroy old buildings by making them explode. What do they sometimes do to old buildings?

6. The teacher frequently gets very angry at his students. What does the teacher frequently do?

7. Janice is aware of the problem because someone told her about it. What can you say about Janice and the problem?

8. The company was supposed to finish the project by September 1, but they didn't finish until November 14. What happened?

9. The professor asked you to explain how this situation happened. What did the professor ask you?

EXERCISE 33d, Review — **Complete the sentences with these phrasal verbs from previous sections. Be sure the phrasal verbs are in the correct tense. To check their meanings, review the section number given after each one.**

come out, 32	fall out, 32	look into, 31	rule out, 31
cut out, 31	give away, 28	plan on, 31	sort out, 30
do without, 31	go around, 20	put off, 31	space out, 30
empty out, 32	go out, 32	put out, 30	stick out, 32

33

1. Jake was in jail when the crime was committed, so the police were able to _____ him _____ as a suspect.

2. My fiancée's father got sick suddenly, so we had to _____ _____ the wedding until later.

3. I was a little _____ _____ when Melanie disagreed with me.

4. Linda's going to _____ _____ getting her teeth bleached.

5. No one was surprised when the news _____ _____.

6. The family business had to be sold after the family members _____ _____ with each other.

7. I _____ _____ and forgot to put socks on this morning.

8. I felt like an idiot — I had to _____ _____ all day without socks on.

9. You can still eat this apple — just _____ _____ the bad part.

10. When we decided on the Bahamas for our honeymoon, we didn't _____ _____ a hurricane.

11. I was angry with my sister, but we talked and _____ everything _____.

12. Timmy told his mother that he hadn't eaten any cake, but the chocolate frosting on his face _____ him _____.

13. If you're studying a language, you can't _____ _____ a dictionary.

14. Jim's job is very dangerous, but if he _____ it _____ for another year, he can retire with a pension.

15. These trash cans are getting full. Could you _____ them _____, please?

16. Put some more wood on the fire — it's starting to _____ _____.

34. FOCUS ON: **pronunciation of two- and three-word phrasal verbs, 2**

As we saw in Sections 5 and 6, phrasal verbs are sometimes accented on the verb and sometimes accented on the particle. It might seem difficult to know whether to accent the verb or the particle since it depends on whether the phrasal verb is separable or nonseparable, transitive or intransitive, or a two- or three-word phrasal verb; however, it boils down to this: always accent the particle after the verb unless the phrasal verb is a nonseparable, transitive, two-word phrasal verb — then accent the verb. Remember that some verbs can be both transitive and intransitive:

Nonseparable, two-word, intransitive

> *stick AROUND*
> *float AROUND*

Nonseparable, two-word, transitive

> *STICK to*
> *STAND for*
> *STICK around*
> *FLOAT around*

Nonseparable, three-word, transitive

> *lead UP to*

Separable, two-word, transitive

> *take BACK*
> *do OVER*

Separable, three-word, transitive

> *put UP to*

Infinitive			
present tense	**-ing form**	**past tense**	**past participle**
do over			
do over & does over	doing over	did over	done over

1. do ... over *p.v.* When you **do** something **over**, you do it again in order to improve it or to correct mistakes.

> *This is all wrong — it'll have to be **done over**.*
> *I got a bad grade on my paper, but the teacher said I could **do** it **over**.*

Infinitive

	present tense	-ing form	past tense	past participle
float around				
	float around & floats around	floating around	floated around	floated around

1. float around *p.v.* *[usually continuous]* When something is **floating around** a place, it is there somewhere, though you are not sure exactly where.

> *I don't know where the stapler is, but it's **floating around** here somewhere.*
> *The new schedule was **floating around** the office yesterday.*

2. float around *p.v.* When a rumor or some information is **floating around**, it is being repeated and discussed among a group of people or within a place.

> *There's a rumor **floating around** that the factory's going to be closed.*
> *Something about a change of management has been **floating around** lately. Have you heard anything?*

lead up to				
	lead up to & leads up to	leading up to	led up to	led up to

1. lead up to *p.v.* When one or more actions, events, or situations **lead up to** a final action, event, or situation, they precede and cause or partially cause it.

> *Several minor battles **led up to** a full-scale war.*
> *The detective said, "Jake didn't shoot Hank for no reason — something **led up to** it."*

2. lead up to *p.v.* When you **lead up to** something when you are speaking or writing, you gradually move toward an important point by saying or writing information that will support that point.

> *In his speech, the President didn't immediately announce that he would run for a second term; he **led up to** it by recalling the accomplishments of his first term.*
> *I've been listening to you talk for thirty minutes. What's your point? What are you **leading up to**?*

put up to				
	put up to & puts up to	putting up to	put up to	put up to

1. put ... up to *p.v.* When you persuade or pressure people to do something that is illegal, dangerous, foolish, or unwise, you **put** them **up to** it.

> *I didn't think it was a good idea to demand a raise, but my wife **put** me **up to** it.*
> *When Jake was arrested for shooting Hank, he said Raquel had **put** him **up to** it by threatening to tell the police about his other crimes.*

stand for				
	stand for & stands for	standing for	stood for	stood for

1. stand for *p.v.* When abbreviations, acronyms, or symbols represent longer words or groups of words, they **stand for** them.

> *The "DC" in Washington, DC, **stands for** "District of Columbia."*
> *"Scuba" **stands for** "self-contained underwater breathing apparatus."*

2. stand for *p.v.* When people or objects support, represent, or are identified with ideas, values, or beliefs, they **stand for** them.

> This flag **stands for** freedom.
> He was a great man who **stood for** equal rights and opportunity for all people.

3. stand for *p.v.* When you will not **stand for** something that you think is illegal, improper, or unjust, you will not tolerate it or allow it to happen.

> Cruelty to animals is one thing I will never **stand for**.
> I told my son I wouldn't **stand for** that kind of language in this house.

Infinitive			
present tense	-ing form	past tense	past participle
stick around			
stick around & sticks around	sticking around	stuck around	stuck around

1. stick around *p.v.* [informal] When you **stick around**, you stay where you are.

> Can you **stick around**? We're going to have lunch in an hour.
> Don't go yet — **stick around** until Sarah gets here; she'd love to see you.

stick to			
stick to & sticks to	sticking to	stuck to	stuck to

1. stick to *p.v.* When one thing **sticks to** another, it remains attached to it.

> The magnet **sticks to** the chalkboard because there's metal underneath.
> I used the wrong glue, and the tiles didn't **stick to** the floor.

2. stick to *p.v.* When you are speaking or writing and you **stick to** a certain subject, you talk or write about that subject only.

> The teacher said, "Do this paper over and **stick to** the point — don't talk about 100 other things that aren't important."
> In his news conference, the President **stuck to** the new tax legislation, but the reporters kept asking about the latest scandal.

3. stick to *p.v.* When you **stick to** a certain belief, claim, policy, habit, plan, type of work, and so on, you continue as before, without change. **Stick with** is similar to **stick to**.

> Jake claimed he was innocent of Hank's murder. He **stuck to** his alibi that he had been at the racetrack when the murder occurred.
> After the audition, the director told me I was a terrible actor and that I should **stick to** singing.

4. stick ... to *p.v.* [informal] When you **stick** it **to** people, you deliberately try to tease, annoy, or embarrass them with an accusation, provocative statement, or difficult question.

> Sam thinks the new manager is an idiot, and he likes to **stick** it **to** him.
> One woman at the shareholders' meeting really **stuck** it **to** the president of the company. She asked why he deserved a $19 million bonus even though the company had lost money that year and 4,000 workers had been laid off.

Infinitive

	present tense	-ing form	past tense	past participle
take back				
	take back & takes back	taking back	took back	taken back

1. take . . . back (to) *p.v.* When you **take** something **back** or **take** something **back** to a place, you take it to where it was before.

> *If you're finished working on the car, don't leave your tools here;* ***take*** *them* ***back*** *to the garage.*
>
> *Do you usually* ***take*** *the shopping carts* ***back*** *after you've put your groceries in your car?*

2. take . . . back (to) *p.v.* When you take something that you have bought to the place where you bought it and ask to have it repaired, to exchange it for something else, or for the money you paid for it, you **take** it **back** or **take** it **back** to the place where you bought it.

> *I have to* ***take back*** *these pants that I bought yesterday because the zipper's already broken.*
>
> *That new TV that Nancy bought was a piece of junk; she* ***took*** *it* ***back*** *to the store and demanded her money back.*

3. take . . . back (from) *p.v.* When you **take** something **back** or **take** something **back** from someone else, you accept it from the person you gave, sold, or lent it to.

> *The guy at the store said he wouldn't* ***take*** *my answering machine* ***back*** *because I had bought it on sale.*
>
> *The lady I bought this Persian rug from said she would be happy to* ***take*** *it* ***back*** *from me if I changed my mind.*

4. take . . . back (to) *p.v.* When you **take back** something that you have borrowed or **take back** something that you have borrowed to the person or place that you borrowed it from, you return it.

> *Lydia borrowed this book from the library six months ago, and she still hasn't* ***taken*** *it* ***back***.
>
> *I need to* ***take*** *Jim's lawn mower* ***back to*** *him.*

5. take . . . back (to) *p.v.* When you **take** people **back** or **take** people **back** to a place where they were before, you go with them to that place.

> *Our son was home from college for the summer, and we're* ***taking*** *him* ***back*** *tomorrow.*
>
> *Mike got sick again, so we* ***took*** *him* ***back*** *to the hospital.*

6. take . . . back *p.v.* When you **take back** something that you have said, you admit that what you said was untrue, unfair, or rude.

> *That's not true! You* ***take*** *that* ***back*** *right now!*
>
> *I'm sorry, that was very rude of me. I* ***take*** *it* ***back***.

7. take ... back (to) *p.v.* When something reminds you of a place where you were in the past or of something you experienced in the past, it **takes** you **back** or **takes** you **back** to a time in the past.

> Looking through my high school year book sure **takes** me **back**.
> My grandfather found his old uniform in the attic, and he said it **took** him **back** to when he was stationed in England during the war.

EXERCISE 34a — **Complete the sentences with phrasal verbs from this section. Be sure the phrasal verbs are in the correct tense.**

1. After being embarrassed last night, I'm going to _____ _____ a policy of minding my own business.

2. Have you seen the manual for this program? It's _____ _____ the office somewhere, but I can't find it.

3. It's too bad you can't _____ _____. I was just about to barbecue some chicken.

4. Look at these old pictures. They sure _____ me _____.

5. In my history class we studied the events that _____ _____ _____ World War II.

6. Rosa tried to return her engagement ring to her fiancé, but he wouldn't _____ it _____.

7. The lawyer told his client to _____ _____ the facts when she testifies.

8. The escaped prisoner was _____ _____ to prison.

9. It's not like Erik to do such a terrible thing. I think someone _____ him _____ _____ it.

10. I hate it when it's so humid that your clothes _____ _____ your skin.

11. "UAE" _____ _____ for United Arab Emirates.

12. I felt terrible about what I said, and I _____ it _____ immediately.

13. One of the guys at work is a real baseball nut from Chicago, so we love to _____ it _____ him about how bad the Cubs are.

14. I don't have Linda's electric drill anymore; I _____ it _____ yesterday.

15. When people see our company's logo, they know it _____ _____ quality at a fair price.

16. The tailor didn't do what I wanted him to do with this dress. I'm going to _____ it _____ to him.

17. The restaurant manager told the bartender that she would not _____ _____ drinking on the job.

18. Mark did such a bad job painting his house that he had to get a professional house painter to _____ it _____.

19. As soon as the company president mentioned the decrease in sales and the need to reduce labor costs, we knew what he was _____ _____ _____.

20. Don't leave these dirty dishes here; _____ them _____ to the kitchen.

21. Don't pay any attention to that rumor — it's been _____ _____ for three years.

EXERCISE 34b — **Review the explanation at the beginning of this section of how two- and three-word phrasal verbs are pronounced. Then, say each sentence in Exercise 34a aloud and circle the verb or particle that is accented.**

EXERCISE 34c — **Write answers to the questions using phrasal verbs from this section. Be sure the phrasal verbs are in the correct tense.**

1. Janice said I was a cheapskate, but she later admitted that it wasn't true. What did Janice do?

2. A number of situations and events helped to cause the Civil War. What did those situations and events do?

3. You've rewritten this story four times, and you're still not happy with it. What have you done to the story four times?

4. When I opened the box of cereal, it was full of bugs, so I returned it to the store. What did I do to the box of cereal?

5. Bill has a system for picking good stocks, and he always uses it. What does Bill do with his system?

6. Mr. Tucker's fifteen-year-old daughter wants to get a tattoo, but he absolutely will not allow it. What won't Mr. Tucker do?

7. Visiting his old high school brought back a lot of memories. What did visiting his old high school do to him?

8. Carlos came to my house and stayed for a while. What did Carlos do after he came to my house?

9. People in my office have been reading the latest issue of *Time* magazine and then giving it to someone else. What has the magazine been doing?

10. She asked me what "Ph.D." represents. What did she ask me?

11. I felt ridiculous dressing as a pink dinosaur for my nephew's birthday party, but my brother persuaded me to do it. What did my brother do?

EXERCISE 34d, Review — **Complete the sentences with these phrasal verbs from previous sections. Be sure the phrasal verbs are in the correct tense. To check their meanings, review the section number given after each one.**

bite off, 27	fall behind, 33	plan ahead, 25	shake up, 24
catch on, 33	get together, 26	print out, 24	stay out, 23
come about, 33	goof around, 33	pull off, 33	stop over, 24
come out, 32	let in on, 26	put together, 26	wear off, 27

1. I asked Sam how his job interview _____ _____, and he said it went great.

2. I asked my history teacher what led up to the American Revolution, and he said the war _____ _____ as a result of several factors.

3. After the tranquilizer _____ _____, the elephant will wake up.

4. The new owners of the company said they planned to _____ things _____.

5. When you're an adult, you can't just think about today; you have to _____ _____.

6. Tonight I'm going to _____ _____ with some friends and watch the game.

7. Mark has a rich father, so Mark doesn't work; he just _____ _____ most of time.

8. The finance minister _____ _____ a plan to revive the nation's economy.

9. That's a pretty big project. Are you sure you haven't _____ _____ more than you can chew?

10. The new system at the warehouse was a disaster, and we _____ _____ in filling orders.

11. I didn't sleep at all last night — I _____ _____ dancing until dawn, and I'm really beat.

12. People have been talking about picture phones for years, but they've never _____

_____.

13. The boss _____ me _____ _____ the new strategy.

14. If you're not busy, would you like to _____ _____ for a while? We could

watch TV or play cards.

15. The crooks tried to steal a 747 by pretending to be pilots, but they couldn't _____ it

_____.

16. I finished my letter, but I can't _____ it _____ because I'm out of toner.

---

35. FOCUS ON: **gerund phrasal verbs**

In Section 10 we looked at gerunds as the objects of phrasal verbs. Now we will look at phrasal verbs as gerunds themselves. Like ordinary verbs, gerund phrasal verbs can be the subject of a sentence:

> ***Narrowing down*** *the list will be difficult.*
> subject

the object of a sentence:

> *We discussed* ***narrowing down*** *the list.*
> object

or the object of a preposition:

> *We talked about* ***narrowing down*** *the list.*
> object of preposition

How and when phrasal verbs can be separated is unaffected by their use as gerunds:

> ***Narrowing*** *it* ***down*** *will be difficult.*
> *We discussed* ***narrowing*** *it* ***down***.
> *We talked about* ***narrowing*** *it* ***down***.

Infinitive

	present tense	-ing form	past tense	past participle
fool around				
	fool around & fools around	fooling around	fooled around	fooled around

1. fool around *p.v.* When you waste time playing or doing silly or unimportant things, you **fool around**. **Goof around** is the same as **fool around**.

> *My son is lazy. He spends his time **fooling around** instead of looking for a job.*
> *My boss said, "I'm not paying you to **fool around** — get to work!"*

2. fool around (with) *p.v.* When you **fool around** with something, you do something that may be dangerous or foolish.

> ***Fooling around** with drugs is pretty stupid.*
> *You shouldn't **fool around** with the insides of your computer unless you know what you're doing.*

3. fool around (with) *p.v.* [informal] When two people **fool around** or **fool around** with each other, they have sexual relations, even though one or both of them may be married to someone else or even though their families or society may not approve.

> *Sally's father caught her and Jim **fooling around** in the basement.*
> *Her husband's been **fooling around** with his secretary, and everyone in town knows it.*

go by				
	go by & goes by	going by	went by	gone by

1. go by *p.v.* When people **go by** a place or thing, they pass near that place or thing. When a thing **goes by** or **goes by** you, it passes near you.

> *We watched the parade **go by**.*
> *I **went by** Jim's house to see if his car was in the driveway.*

2. go by *p.v.* When you **go by** a place, you go there so that you can do something or get something.

> *Let's **go by** Raul's house to get his tools before we work on your car.*
> *You can forget about **going by** the dry cleaner to pick up your stuff — it's closed.*

3. go by *p.v.* When a period of time **goes by**, it passes.

> *I can't believe that thirty years have **gone by** since I got out of high school.*
> *As time **went by**, Betty moved up in the company until she was the head of the finance department.*

4. go by *p.v.* When you **go by** a policy or standard, you use it as a reference or a guide in making decisions and determining your behavior. When you **go by** the book, you follow rules, policies, or laws exactly.

> ***Going by** the book has always been my policy.*
> *Jim told me to do one thing, and Tom told me to do another, but since Tom is the boss, I'm going to **go by** what he says.*

5. go by *p.v.* When you **go by** a clock, you use it to tell the time.

> Don't **go by** the clock on the wall; it's fast. **Go by** the clock on the desk.
> No wonder I'm always late for work — the clock I've been **going by** is ten minutes slow.

Infinitive

present tense	-ing form	past tense	past participle
hold against			
hold against & holds against	holding against	held against	held against

1. hold ... against *p.v.* When you **hold** things **against** people, you continue to blame them for something and continue to be upset about it.

> Ten years ago I got a promotion that Ned thought he deserved, and he's **held** it **against** me ever since.
> Jane lost her job because of a mistake Bob made, but she doesn't **hold** it **against** him.

leave behind			
leave behind & leaves behind	leaving behind	left behind	left behind

1. leave ... behind *p.v.* When you **leave** someone or something **behind**, you go to a different place.

> The explorers **left** the mountains **behind** and entered the jungle.
> The enemy soldiers retreated and **left behind** a city in ruins.

2. leave ... behind *p.v.* When you **leave** something or someone **behind**, you do not take them with you because you forgot or because you cannot or do not want to take them.

> We packed too much luggage for our trip, so we had to **leave** some things **behind**.
> **Leaving** our children **behind** at a gas station was pretty dumb.

3. leave ... behind *p.v.* When you move, learn, or work faster than others in your group, you **leave** them **behind**.

> My husband walks so fast that he always **leaves** me **behind**.
> If you don't start working harder, you're going to be **left behind**.
> Mark was so good at calculus that he soon **left** the rest of the class **behind**.

live with			
live with & lives with	living with	lived with	lived with

1. live with *p.v.* When you **live with** someone, you live at the same address. When you say that one person **lives with** a person of the opposite sex, you mean that they live in the same place but are not married.

> **Living with** my in-laws is driving me crazy.
> Mike's been **living with** his girlfriend for five years. Are they ever going to get married?

2. live with *p.v.* When you **live with** a disease or other problem, you endure or put up with it.

Living with this disease is not easy.
I can't change the situation, so I'll just have to learn to live with it.

3. live with *p.v.* When you **live with** shame, guilt, or a painful memory, you continue with your life in spite of the shame, guilt, or painful memory.

Jake committed suicide rather than live with the shame of what he had done.
He said he couldn't go on living with the knowledge that he had caused the death of 14 innocent people.

Infinitive			
present tense	-ing form	past tense	past participle
make of			
make of & makes of	making of	made of	made of

1. make of *p.v.* What you **make of** something is your understanding or opinion of it.

So what did you make of the prime minister's speech?
What he said was so strange that I didn't know what to make of it.

narrow down			
narrow down & narrows down	narrowing down	narrowed down	narrowed down

1. narrow . . . down *p.v.* When you **narrow down** things or people in a list or group, you remove some of them so that the number of things or people is reduced.

All the candidates for the job have excellent qualifications. Narrowing the list down won't be easy.
The detective narrowed the suspects down to the butler, the cook, and the maid.

trick into			
trick into & tricks into	tricking into	tricked into	tricked into

1. trick . . . into *p.v.* When you **trick** people **into** doing something, you persuade them to do something by fooling or deceiving them. **Con into** is similar to **trick into**.

The con artist tricked them into giving him their life savings.
I was an idiot to let Hank trick me into selling him my car for so little money.

EXERCISE 35a — **Complete the sentences with phrasal verbs from this section. Be sure the phrasal verbs are in the correct tense.**

1. The man who was killed in the accident _____ a wife and three children

   _____.

2. The prosecutor _____ Jake _____ admitting his guilt.

3. I took a job in Japan, and six years _____ _____ before I returned to the

   United States.

4. Paul's been _____ _____ his parents since his house burned down.

5. There were fifty contestants at the beginning of the contest, but the judges _____ it _____ to five finalists.

6. Look at this strange letter I received. Read it and tell me what you _____ _____ it.

7. I was my parents' favorite, and my brother still _____ it _____ me.

8. Frank's wife filed for divorce after she learned that he was _____ _____ with her best friend.

9. The train always blows its whistle when it _____ _____.

10. _____ _____ diabetes means carefully monitoring your blood sugar.

11. _____ your friends and family _____ when you emigrate to a new country is very difficult.

12. Todd failed the test because he _____ _____ all evening instead of studying.

13. Sergeant Jones was very strict when he was in the Army. He always _____ _____ the book.

14. Don't let your kids _____ _____ with cigarette lighters; they might start a fire.

15. How can you _____ _____ yourself after the terrible thing you did?

16. Melanie has my biology book, so on the way to school I need to _____ _____ her house to get it.

17. Mike wasn't ready for the advanced algebra class, and he was quickly _____ _____ by the rest of the class.

18. I _____ _____ my wristwatch — not the wall clock — because it's more accurate.

EXERCISE 35b — **Write answers to the questions using phrasal verbs from this section. Be sure the phrasal verbs are in the correct tense.**

1. Her disease is incurable, so unfortunately she'll just have to learn to endure it. What will she have to do?

2. Jim and I worked on a project together, but Jim told everyone that he did all the work, and I'm still angry about it. How do I feel about what Jim did?

3. Sally and her sister's husband go to a motel sometimes during their lunch hour. What are they doing?

4. My father has a lot of horrible memories from the war. What does he have to do with them?

5. Bill made a list of cities that he might move to, and then he eliminated those that are too cold or have high crime rates. What did Bill do to his list of cities?

6. When the boss isn't in the office, you just play computer games and make personal phone calls. What do you do when the boss isn't in the office?

7. Hank told his sister that he needed money for his wife's doctor bills, but he really wanted money to buy drugs. What did Hank do to his sister?

8. The scientist asked her colleague his opinion of the test results. What did the scientist ask her colleague about the test results?

9. A police car passed me while I was driving. What did the police car do?

10. Susie's parents are going to take a vacation without her. What are Susie's parents going to do to her?

11. The last year passed quickly. What did the last year do?

EXERCISE 35c — **Write eight original sentences using phrasal verbs from this section. Try to make all the phrasal verbs gerunds and to use them as subjects, objects, or objects of prepositions.**

1. _____

2. _____

3. _____

4. _____

5. _____

6. _____

7. _____

8. _____

35

EXERCISE 35d, Review — **Complete the sentences with these phrasal verbs from previous sections. Be sure the phrasal verbs are in the correct tense. To check their meanings, review the section number given after each one.**

break up, 28	flip out, 29	lie around, 20	stand for, 34
come apart, 29	float around, 34	luck out, 29	stay up, 20
do over, 34	hang around, 20	mess up, 28	stick around, 34
end up, 20	lead up to, 34	run across, 29	take back, 34

1. The robber was only three feet away when he fired the gun at me, but the gun jammed and didn't fire. I really _____ _____.

2. Nancy said being sick wasn't so bad. She _____ _____ in bed all day watching TV and eating ice cream.

3. I'll _____ _____ if you drop my new camera in the swimming pool.

4. Dan's daughter was very sick last night, so Dan _____ _____ all night with her.

5. This is outrageous! I will not _____ _____ dishonesty in my company.

6. I told Mark that I would never speak to him again if he didn't _____ _____ the nasty things he said.

7. If you're looking for Hank, go to the bar on the corner. That's where he _____ _____.

8. A number of minor events will _____ _____ _____ the main event.

9. I had a very busy day planned, but I got a flat tire and that _____ _____ everything.

10. My boss is a jerk! I worked for three days on this, and just because he found one mistake he made me _____ it _____.

11. Sam has been very depressed since he _____ _____ with his girlfriend.

12. Have you seen the dictionary? It's _____ _____ the office somewhere, but I can't find it.

13. Don't stand on that chair — it's _____ _____.

14. Do you really have to leave now? Why don't you _____ _____ for a while.

15. Bill was talking about moving to Florida or Hawaii, but I'm not sure where he finally

   _____ _____.

16. Someone told me that Sarah is in town, but I haven't _____ _____ her yet.

36. FOCUS ON: **phrasal verbs with the particle *down***

The particle *down* is used in many phrasal verbs and has many meanings. *Down* can be used to say that something literally moves from a higher position to a lower position or from north to south:

> Bob **went down** the ladder.
> His friends **came down** from Canada.
> **Sit down;** dinner is ready.

that something decreases in size, intensity, quantity, or quality:

> Her fever has **gone down** to 100 degrees.
> The doctor gave her a sedative to **calm** her **down**.
> We've **narrowed** the list **down** to three choices.

that something or someone is fought, defeated, or overpowered:

> Hank **backed down** when he saw my shotgun.
> The police **cracked down** on street crime.

that something falls to the ground:

> The boy was running and **fell down**.
> The warehouse **burned down**.
> Open the door or I'll **break** it **down**!

or that a process or activity is ending or has ended:

> My car **broke down** on the highway.
> The FBI **tracked down** the spy.
> The campaign is **winding down**.

Infinitive			
present tense	-ing form	past tense	past participle
back down			
back down & backs down	backing down	backed down	backed down

1. back down *p.v.* When one side in a disagreement stops making threats and lets the other have what it wants or do what it wants, the side that stops making threats **backs down**.

*The dictator didn't **back down** after the United Nations Security Council voted in favor of sending in troops.*

*The police officer tried to force me to pay him a bribe, but when I said I would report him to the chief of police, he **backed down**.*

Infinitive

present tense	-ing form	past tense	past participle
calm down			
calm down & calms down	calming down	calmed down	calmed down

1. calm ... down *p.v.* When you **calm down**, you become less active, nervous, or upset. When you **calm** other people **down**, you do something to make them less active, nervous, or upset. **Settle down** is similar to **calm down**.

*I was very nervous about the test, but I **calmed down** when I saw how easy it was.*

*Mike tried to **calm** his sister **down** after she had a fight with her husband.*

2. calm ... down *p.v.* When a confused or violent situation becomes less confused or violent, it **calms down**. When you **calm** a confused or violent situation **down**, you make it less confused or violent and more calm. **Settle down** is similar to **calm down**.

*The neighborhood where the riot occurred **calmed down** after the army started patrolling the streets.*

*A conference between the two sides was organized to try to **calm** the situation **down**.*

fall down			
fall down & falls down	falling down	fell down	fallen down

1. fall down *p.v.* When people or things fall to the ground from a higher position, they **fall down**.

*I slipped on some ice on the sidewalk and **fell down**.*

*All the dishes on that shelf will **fall down** if there's another earthquake.*

go down			
go down & goes down	going down	went down	gone down

1. go down (to) *p.v.* When you move to a lower level or position or from north to south, you **go down** or **go down** to that place. **Go up** is the opposite of **go down**.

*Toronto is too cold, so we usually **go down** to Mexico in the winter.*

***Going down** the mountain was a lot easier than going up.*

2. go down (to) *p.v.* When the cost, rate, quality, quantity, or level of something decreases, it **goes down**. **Go up** is the opposite of **go down**.

*The temperature **went down** to zero last night.*

*The crime rate in New York City has **gone down**.*

3. go down (to) *p.v.* When something extends to a certain point that is farther south or at a lower elevation, it **goes down** to that point. **Go up** is the opposite of **go down**.

*How far south does this road **go down**?*

*Does this road **go down** to the south side of town?*

*After dinner we **went down** to the basement and played ping pong.*

4. go down *p.v.* When something **goes down** in a certain way, people react to or perceive it in this way.

> The new no smoking policy didn't **go down** very well with the smokers in the office.
> The judge's decision **went down** well with the prosecutor.

5. go down *p.v.* When a computer or computer network stops working because of a problem or because it has been disconnected, it **goes down**.

> I couldn't withdraw any money at the bank because its computers had **gone down**.
> If your computer terminal **goes down**, you can use the one in the next office.

6. go down *p.v.* When the sun goes below the horizon, it **goes down**.

> After the sun **goes down**, it'll get a little cooler.
> The sun **went down** at 8:34 last night.

Infinitive			
present tense	-ing form	past tense	past participle
lay down			
lay down & lays down	laying down	laid down	laid down

1. lay ... down (on) *p.v.* When you **lay** something **down**, you put it on a horizontal surface. **Put down** is similar to **lay down**.

> Marsha **laid** the tray **down**.
> The police ordered Jake to **lay down** his gun and surrender.

2. lay down *p.v.* When you **lay down** a new law, policy, rule, and so on, you create and announce it.

> The IRS **laid down** several new tax regulations.
> Congress decided against **laying down** any new campaign financing laws.

put down			
put down & puts down	putting down	put down	put down

1. put ... down *p.v.* When you **put** something **down**, you put something in your hand or something that you are carrying on a horizontal surface.

> The suitcase was so heavy that I had to **put** it **down** and rest for a minute.
> Susie, **put** that knife **down**. It's dangerous!

2. put ... down *p.v.* When you **put** people **down**, you criticize them.

> Jim hates his stepfather and **puts** him **down** constantly.
> I'm not inviting Sam to any more parties. I hate the way he **puts** everyone **down**.

put-down *n.* A **put-down** is an insult or critical remark.

> At the party Sam asked Nancy if she had made her dress from an old curtain.
>   What a **put-down**!

3. put ... down (on) *p.v.* When you **put** money **down** or **put** money **down** on something, you pay a portion of the cost of something you want to buy to be sure that it will still be available to you when you are able to pay the rest of the cost.

*The real estate agent asked me how much money I want to **put down** on the house.*
*I told her that I could **put** as much as $15,000 **down**.*

4. put ... down (on/for) *p.v.* When you add something to a list or other written material, you **put** it **down** or **put** it **down** on the list. When you add people to a list in order to assign something to them, you **put** them **down** or **put** them **down** for that assignment.

*Melanie's collecting money for charity, so I told her to **put** me **down** for $50.*
*I'm making a list of volunteers to help reelect Senator Dolittle. Can I **put** your name **down** on the list?*

5. put ... down (on) *p.v.* When an airplane **puts down** or a pilot **puts** an airplane **down**, the airplane lands.

*After the engine quit, the pilot looked for a place to **put down**.*
*Fortunately, the pilot was able to **put** the plane **down** on a frozen lake.*

Infinitive

	present tense	-ing form	past tense	past participle
run down				
	run down & runs down	running down	ran down	run down

1. run down (to) *p.v.* When you move quickly to a lower level or place, you **run down** or **run down** to that place.

*Mike was **running down** the stairs when he fell and broke his leg.*
*I saw someone trying to steal my car, and I **ran down** to the street to try to stop him.*

2. run ... down *p.v.* When vehicles or people driving vehicles hit and injure or kill someone, they **run** that person **down**.

*The man was **run down** and killed by a speeding taxi.*
*Ali was arrested after he **ran** three people **down**.*

3. run down *p.v.* When you discuss or review items on a list from the first to the last, you **run down** the list.

*Let's **run down** the Christmas list and decide what to give everyone.*
*The teacher **ran down** the list of students and marked the ones who are failing.*

rundown *n.* A **rundown** is a discussion or review of items on a list.

*The consultant gave the manager a **rundown** of the problems she had found.*

4. run down *p.v.* When batteries or machines **run down** or are **run down** by someone, they gradually lose power or energy.

*Don't leave the car lights on for too long when the car isn't running or the battery will **run down**.*
*What time is it? My watch **ran down** last night.*

rundown *part.adj.* A person or thing that is **rundown** is exhausted, without power or energy.

> *Maybe I need to go to the doctor; I feel so **rundown** all the time.*

rundown *part.adj.* A **rundown** building or neighborhood is in poor condition because it has not been maintained.

> *I went back to my old neighborhood, and I was shocked to see how **rundown** it had become.*

Infinitive

	present tense	-ing form	past tense	past participle
sit down	sit down & sits down	sitting down	sat down	sat down

1. sit down *p.v.* When you **sit down**, you change from a standing position to a sitting position.

> *The teacher told his students to **sit down** and open their books.*
> *I'm exhausted; I haven't **sat down** all day.*

2. sit ... down *p.v.* When you **sit** people **down**, you order them to sit, usually so that you can have a serious discussion.

> *When I found marijuana in my daughter's purse, I **sat** her **down** and had a serious talk with her.*
> *The detective **sat** Hank **down** and began to interrogate him.*

EXERCISE 36a — **Complete the sentences with phrasal verbs from this section. Be sure the phrasal verbs are in the correct tense.**

1. Heather thinks she's so high-class. She _____ _____ other people all the time.

2. The situation _____ _____ after the cease-fire was declared.

3. The sun comes up around 6:00, and it _____ _____ around 8:00.

4. Here's the list of candidates for the promotion. Let's _____ _____ the list

   and decide.

5. The old water tower _____ _____ during the storm.

6. You must be exhausted. Why don't you _____ _____ and take it easy?

7. I saw a tow truck looking for illegally parked cars, so I _____ _____ to my car

   and moved it.

8. My office is on the ninetieth floor, so sometimes it takes me fifteen minutes to _____

   _____ to the lobby.

9. It's hard to write sympathy notes. I never know what to _____ _____.

10. The company tried to reduce benefits, but they _____ _____ when the union threatened to go on strike.

11. The Appalachian Trail starts in Maine and _____ all the way _____ to Georgia.

12. Don't _____ the baby _____ there — she might fall.

13. I was furious about what Dan said, and I _____ him _____ and told him exactly what I thought about it.

14. If you _____ $100,000 _____ on that house, you won't need a very large mortgage.

15. What are you so worried about? Just _____ _____ — everything's going to be all right.

16. The union's proposal to reduce the workweek to four days didn't _____ _____ well with the company.

17. The Food and Drug Administration is expected to _____ _____ a new set of regulations regarding seafood inspection.

18. The price of computers has _____ _____ dramatically in the last few years.

19. Those boxes are too heavy for you. _____ them _____ and let me carry them for you.

20. A pedestrian was _____ _____ by a truck on Lincoln Avenue.

21. The stock exchange had to stop trading when its computers _____ _____.

22. _____ a jet _____ on an aircraft carrier at night is very difficult.

23. Someone left this flashlight on all night, and the batteries have _____ _____.

EXERCISE 36b — **Write three sentences using the objects in parentheses. Be sure to put the objects in the right place.**

1. The jockey *calmed down*. (the horse, it)

_____

_____

_____

2. The mechanic *laid down.* (her tools, them)

_____

_____

_____

3. I *put down.* (my books, them)

_____

_____

_____

4. The taxi *ran down.* (the traffic cop, him)

_____

_____

_____

EXERCISE 36c — **Write answers to the questions using phrasal verbs, participle adjectives, and nouns from this section. Be sure the phrasal verbs are in the correct tense.**

1. The car dealer reviewed the list of the car's options with me. What did the car dealer do?

2. In Question 1, what did the car dealer give me?

3. The king visited the area where the two tribes were fighting, and the fighting stopped. What did the king do to the area?

4. The houses in this part of town are in very bad condition. How can you describe this part of town?

5. Management's plan got a good reaction from the workers. What impression did the plan make on the workers?

6. Frank told Nancy that she was low-class. What did Frank do to Nancy?

7. In Question 6, what was Frank's comment?

8. Sam sat in a chair. What did Sam do?

9. The company's management stopped threatening to fire the workers and agreed to raise their wages. What did the company do?

10. The dentist's secretary wrote my name in her appointment book. What did the secretary do?

11. The soldiers stopped fighting and put their rifles on the ground. What did the soldiers do with their rifles?

12. You slipped and landed on the ground. What did you do?

EXERCISE 36d, Review — **Complete the sentences with these participle adjectives from previous sections. To check their meanings, review the section number given after each one.**

burned up, 22	locked in, 30	punched in, 30	spaced-out, 30
cleaned out, 32	locked out, 30	punched out, 30	sorted out, 30
emptied out, 32	paid up, 22	put out, 30	torn off, 27
left out, 32	plugged up, 22	shaken up, 24	

1. David's totally _____ today. He has even forgotten his girlfriend's name.

2. I like this coat, but I don't know what size it is because the tag's_____ _____.

3. I don't know why that guy from the collection agency called me — all my bills are _____ _____.

4. Nicole hasn't _____ _____ yet. Either she's late for work or she forgot.

5. Mark borrowed Bob's car and had an accident, and Mark's really _____ _____ about it.

6. The manager wondered why I wasn't working, but after I told her I was _____ _____, she said it was okay.

7. Take this medicine. It's great for _____ _____ noses.

8. Do you have a key? I'm _____ _____ and can't get out.

9. Do you have a key? I'm _____ _____ and can't get in.

10. Jane's really _____ _____. She just found out that her brother was murdered.

11. Jim's socks are mixed with his brother's socks. They're not _____ _____.

12. No one wants to sit with me in the school lunchroom, and it makes me feel _____ _____ .

13. My mother was really _____ _____ when Aunt Kathy said our house wasn't very clean.

14. Why isn't the basement _____ _____ yet? I told you I'm tired of looking at this junk!

15. There's nothing in the room. It's all _____ _____ .

EXERCISE 36e, Review — **Complete the sentences with these phrasal verbs from previous sections. Be sure the phrasal verbs are in the correct tense. To check their meanings, review the section number given after each one.**

blow up, 33	come about, 33	make of, 35	pull off, 33
care for, 31	do without, 31	make out, 29	put off, 31
catch on, 33	go out, 32	narrow down, 35	stick to, 34
clean out, 32	lock out, 30	plan on, 31	wash up, 30

1. Several bodies from the crashed plane _____ _____ the day after the crash.

2. After mother had a stroke, we had to hire nurses to _____ _____ her.

3. My father was seventy-two years old when he got his first computer, but he _____ _____ right away, and now he uses it all the time.

4. The President had a lot of big plans when he took office, but few of them ever _____ _____ .

5. Mark wasn't successful as a singer. He should have _____ _____ songwriting — that's what he does best.

6. How did you _____ _____ on your final exam?

7. I had to crawl in through the window after my daughter closed the door and _____ me _____ of the house.

8. This situation is very strange. I don't know what to _____ _____ it.

9. I have to finish my project tonight, and I haven't even started it. I _____ it _____ until the last minute.

10. No one thought Frank could run a mile in less than four minutes, but he _____ it _____ .

11. I really depend on my laptop computer when I travel on business. I don't know how I ever

_____ _____ it.

12. George and Linda _____ _____ for three years before they got married.

13. Several people were killed when the bomb _____ _____.

14. Bob and Marsha aren't _____ _____ spending more than $250,000 for their

new house.

15. My divorce settlement cost me a lot of money. It almost _____ me _____.

16. The FBI started with a list of six suspects, but they _____ it _____ to two.

37. FOCUS ON: **phrasal verbs used as nouns, 3**

When phrasal verbs are used as nouns, the verb is usually in the infinitive form; however, a small number use a different form of the verb.

For example, **left over** and **grow up** use the past participle:

> *We ate **leftovers** the day after Thanksgiving.*
> *The **grown-ups** sat at one table, and the children sat at another.*

talk to and go over use the -ing form:

> *Mr. Young gave his son a good **talking-to**.*
> *Before I buy this car, I'm going to give it a good **going-over**.*

and **grown-up** uses the past participle:

> *Only **grown-ups** are allowed to drive.*

Infinitive

present tense	-ing form	past tense	past participle
brush off			
brush off & brushes off	brushing off	brushed off	brushed off

1. brush ... off *p.v.* When you **brush** people **off**, you ignore them or refuse to listen to them because you are not interested in or do not like what they are saying.

> *My boss just **brushes** me **off** when I try to tell her how to increase our profits.*
> *The reporters tried to ask him some questions, but he **brushed** them **off**.*

brush-off *n.* When you give people the **brush-off**, you ignore them or refuse to listen to them because you are not interested in or do not like what they are saying.

> *The boss just gave me the **brush-off** when I tried to give him some advice.*

2. brush ... off *p.v.* When you **brush off** a critical remark or problem, you ignore it and continue as before without letting it affect you.

*I told Dr. Smith that he had made a mistake, but he **brushed** it **off**.*
*My father's cholesterol is very high, but he just **brushes** it **off**.*

Infinitive

	present tense	-ing form	past tense	past participle
come on	come on & comes on	coming on	came on	come on

1. come on *p.v.* When an electrical device or machine **comes on**, it begins to operate, usually automatically. **Go off** is the opposite of **come on**.

*It was so cold that the heat **came on** last night.*
*When you open the refrigerator door, the light **comes on** automatically.*

2. come on *p.v.* When a television or radio program **comes on**, it begins.

*Do you know when the news will **come on**?*
*The late movie **comes on** at 1:00 A.M.*

3. come on *p.v.* When you want to encourage people to do something or when you want them to do something quickly, you say "**Come on!**"

*Believe me, you're going to love this garlic ice cream. **Come on**, try it!*
***Come on**! I can't wait all day.*

4. come on *p.v.* [informal] When you think that people have done or said something improper or unreasonable, you say "**Come on**."

*Tom didn't study for one minute, and you're telling me he got 100 on the test? Oh, **come on**.*
*Hey, **come on**! I told you not to do that again.*

5. come on *p.v.* [always continuous] When you begin to feel a headache or an illness developing, you feel the headache or illness **coming on**.

*I might be sick tomorrow; I feel something **coming on**.*
*I feel a headache **coming on**. Do you have any aspirin?*

6. come on *p.v.* When you **come on** a certain way, you speak or deal with people in that way.

*Paul needs to learn to be more of a gentleman. He **comes on** too strong, and women don't like that.*
*Bob **comes on** kind of arrogant, but he's actually a nice guy.*

7. come on (to) *p.v.* [informal] When you **come on** to people, you approach them and try to interest them in romance or sex.

*Todd **came on** to Judy at the party, and she told him to get lost.*
*I can't stand that guy Ned. He's always **coming on** to me.*

come-on *n.* [informal] A provocative comment or action intended to interest a person in romance or sex is a **come-on**.

37

*Todd uses the same **come-on** with all the girls, and it never works.*

come-on *n.* A discount or special offer designed to get people to buy something is a **come-on**.

*The bank is offering a free VCR as a **come-on** if you open an account with them.*

Infinitive

present tense	-ing form	past tense	past participle
cover up			
cover up & covers up	covering up	covered up	covered up

1. cover . . . up *p.v.* When you cover something completely, you **cover** it **up**.

*I **covered** the cake **up** so no bugs would land on it.*
***Cover** this stuff **up** — I don't want anyone to see it.*

covered up *part.adj.* After something has been completely covered, it is **covered up**.

*Is the meat **covered up**? I don't want flies to land on it.*

2. cover . . . up *p.v.* When you **cover up** a crime, you do something to try to prevent other people from learning of it.

*There's no point in trying to **cover up** the crime. Too many people already know about it.*
*The mayor was accused of **covering up** his ties to organized crime.*

cover-up *n.* Something you do in order to prevent a crime from becoming known is a **cover-up**.

*The mayor denied being part of a **cover-up** and claimed he was innocent.*

hang out			
hang out & hangs out	hanging out	hung out	hung out

1. hang out *p.v.* [informal] When you **hang out** at a place, you spend time there without any important purpose. **Hang around** is similar to **hang out**.

*Doesn't Nancy have a job? It seems as if she **hangs out** at the beach every day.*
*I don't have any place to go. Do you mind if I **hang out** here for a while?*

hangout *n.* [informal] A **hangout** is a place where you spend time without any important purpose.

*The police closed the bar, saying it was a **hangout** for crooks and gang members.*

leave over			
			left over

1. leave over *p.v.* [always passive] When something is **left over**, it remains after people have used or taken as much of it as they need or want.

*I guess I made too much food; look how much is **left over**.*
*I paid all my bills and had only $17 **left over**.*

leftover *part.adj.* Something that is **left over** remains after people have used or taken as much of it as they need or want.

> *You can have this **leftover** pasta for lunch tomorrow.*

leftovers *n. [always plural]* Food items that remain uneaten after people have finished eating are **leftovers**.

> ***Leftovers** again? When are we going to have something different for dinner?*

Infinitive

present tense	-ing form	past tense	past participle
let down			
let down & lets down	**letting down**	**let down**	**let down**

1. let . . . down *p.v.* When you promise people you will do something and then fail to do it, you **let** them **down**.

> *My son promised to stop using drugs, but he **let** me **down**.*
> *I really need you to help me move tomorrow. Please don't **let** me **down**.*

let down *part.adj.* When people promise you they will do something and then fail to do it, you feel **let down**. When you are disappointed because you cannot have something you want to have, because you cannot do something you want to do, or because something is less exciting than you expected it to be, you feel **let down**.

> *You broke your promise to me that you would quit smoking. I feel very **let down**.*

letdown *n.* When you say that something is a **letdown**, you are disappointed because you cannot have or cannot do something you want to or because something is less exciting than you expected it to be.

> *I had tickets for the fifth game of the World Series, but my team lost in four games.*
>   *What a **letdown**.*
> *After the way everyone talked about how great the movie was, I thought it was some-*
>   *thing of a **letdown**.*

pay off

pay off & pays off	paying off	paid off	paid off

1. pay . . . off *p.v.* When you **pay off** money that you owe or **pay off** the person you owe the money to, you pay all the money that you owe.

> *I wasn't happy with the people we hired to paint our house. I **paid** them **off** and told*
>   *them not to return.*
> *It took ten years, but I finally **paid off** my school loan.*

paid off *part.adj.* After you pay all the money that you owe to someone or to a lending institution, the debt or loan is **paid off**.

> *I made my last payment yesterday, and now my car loan is **paid off**.*

2. pay . . . off *p.v.* When you pay people money so that they will do something illegal or allow you to do something illegal, you **pay** them **off**.

37

*The politician tried to cover up the crime by **paying off** the witnesses.*
Don't expect the police in this city to do anything about gambling — they're
*being **paid off**.*

payoff *n.* A **payoff** is money paid to someone to do something illegal or to allow you
to do something illegal.

*The chief of police was videotaped accepting a **payoff**.*

3. pay off *p.v.* When something you do **pays off**, it is successful and is worth the
effort you made.

*Medical school is a lot of hard work, but it'll **pay off** someday.*
*The restaurant changed its menu, and it really **paid off**. Business increased by*
30 percent.

payoff *n.* A benefit you gain because of an effort you make is a **payoff**.

*Linda doesn't get paid for the volunteer work she does. The **payoff** is knowing that*
she has helped other people.

Infinitive

	present tense	-ing form	past tense	past participle
talk to				
	talk to & talks to	talking to	talked to	talked to

1. talk to *p.v.* When you **talk to** people, you have a conversation with them.

*Are you **talking to** me?*
*I don't like Bob. He **talks to** me like I'm some kind of idiot.*

talking-to *n.* A **talking-to** is a serious discussion in which you scold or lecture
someone.

*Dan's behavior is outrageous. Someone should give him a good **talking-to**.*

EXERCISE 37a — **Complete the sentences with phrasal verbs from this section.**
Be sure the phrasal verbs are in the correct tense.

1. I forgot to _____ the chicken _____ after we finished dinner, and the cat ate it.

2. A patient died after Dr. Smith gave her the wrong medicine, and the hospital tried to

   _____ it _____.

3. I don't care what Nancy thinks of me. If she criticizes me, I'll just _____ her

   _____.

4. I worked for nine years to get my Ph.D., and now I can't find a job in my field. All that work sure

   didn't _____ _____.

5. I set the thermostat so that the air conditioner _____ _____ if it gets over

eighty degrees.

6. You can trust Erik to keep his promises. He won't _____ you _____.

7. I didn't like that car salesman we talked to last night. He _____ _____ too

strong.

8. I called Heather last night, but I didn't _____ _____ her; she was in the shower.

9. _____ _____ in bars isn't my idea of fun.

10. I tried to apologize to Jane, but she just _____ me _____ and continued walking.

11. I want to _____ my mortgage _____ early, so I'm making two payments

every month.

12. Look at *TV Guide* to see when the show _____ _____.

13. Karen sure isn't shy. Did you see how she was _____ _____ to my brother at

the party?

14. After Thanksgiving so much turkey will be _____ _____ that we'll be eating

it for two weeks.

15. I hope I'm not getting sick. I feel a cold _____ _____.

16. The contractor was accused of _____ _____ city officials in exchange

for contracts.

EXERCISE 37b — **Complete the sentences with nouns from this section.**

1. You need to finish school. The _____ won't come for years, but it's worth it.

2. I didn't have time to make anything for dinner, so we're having _____ tonight.

3. This place isn't as beautiful as it looked in the pictures. What a _____.

4. Judy isn't interested in anything I say; she always gives me the _____.

5. The senator was convicted of taking a _____.

6. The low interest rate the credit card company offers if you switch to their card is just a

_____. After six months they increase it to 18 percent.

7. The politician was accused of being part of a _____.

8. You can usually find Joe at the nightclub across the street. That's his favorite _____.

9. Timmy's not causing any problems today. Maybe someone gave him a _____.

EXERCISE 37c — **Write answers to the questions using phrasal verbs, participle adjectives, and nouns from this section. Be sure the phrasal verbs are in the correct tense.**

1. Ned spends a lot of time at Joe's Diner relaxing and talking to his friends. What does Ned do at Joe's Diner?

2. In Question 1, what is Joe's Diner to Ned?

3. Mark said something that I thought was ridiculous, and I told him to be serious and reasonable. What did I say to Mark?

4. You had $400, but after you went shopping, you had $100 remaining. What did you have?

5. My favorite TV show begins at 9:00. What does my favorite show do at 9:00?

6. Dan promised his daughter that he would take her to the circus, but he couldn't get off work that day. What did Dan do to his daughter?

7. Maria is going to pay her last car loan payment. What is she going to do to her car loan?

8. In Question 7, how would you describe Maria's car loan after she makes the last payment?

9. Nicole spoke with her brother about his drinking problem. What did she do to her brother?

10. In Question 9, what did Nicole give to her brother?

11. The heat in our house starts to operate when the temperature gets below sixty degrees. What does the heat in our house do?

12. For lunch you ate the spaghetti that your family didn't eat the night before. What did you eat for lunch?

13. The restaurant owner gave the health inspector $200 to ignore the rats in the kitchen. What did the restaurant owner do to the health inspector?

14. In Question 13, what was the $200 that the restaurant owner gave the health inspector?

THE ULTIMATE PHRASAL VERB BOOK

phrasal verbs used as nouns, 3

15. The head of the health department tried to keep the payoffs in his department a secret. What did the head of the health department do to the payoffs?

16. In Question 15, what would you call the head of the health department's attempt to keep the payoffs in his department a secret?

17. Linda complained to the city about the garbage in the streets, but the woman she talked to wasn't interested and told her to write to the mayor. What did the woman Linda talked to do?

18. In Question 17, what did the woman that Linda talked to give her?

19. Timmy's friend wanted him to walk faster, and he told Timmy to hurry. What did Timmy's friend say to Timmy?

20. Joe told me again and again how good his favorite restaurant is, but when I went there, I didn't think it was that good. What was my visit to the restaurant?

21. In Question 20, how did I feel after my visit to Joe's favorite restaurant?

EXERCISE 37d, Review — **Complete the sentences with these nouns from previous sections. To check their meanings, review the section number given after each one.**

blowup, 33	get-together, 26	grown-up, 10	put-down, 36
breakup, 28	giveaway, 28	lockout, 30	rundown, 36
cutout, 31	going-over, 26	lookout, 29	

1. The movie critic told the director that watching his new movie was worse than going to the dentist. That was quite a _____.

2. The _____ of the huge company created several smaller companies.

3. We're having a little _____ tonight. Would you like to come?

4. Only _____ are allowed to drink alcohol.

5. The _____ ended after the workers agreed to a 10 percent pay increase.

6. I heard a big _____ in Nancy's office. I wonder what the problem was.

7. The drug dealers had a _____ on every corner.

8. Timmy told his mother that he hadn't eaten any cookies, but he had chocolate all over his face, so she knew he was lying. The chocolate on his face was the _____.

9. Before you spend $13,000 on a used car, I suggest that you give it a thorough _____.

10. Carlos made paper _____ shaped like dinosaurs.

11. The police chief gave the mayor a _____ of the previous month's crime statistics.

EXERCISE 37e, Review — **Complete the sentences with these phrasal verbs from previous sections. Be sure the phrasal verbs are in the correct tense. To check their meanings, review the section number given after each one.**

calm down, 36	fall down, 36	hold against, 35	narrow down, 35
catch on, 33	fool around, 35	leave behind, 35	pull off, 33
do away with, 31	go by, 35	live with, 35	put down, 36
empty out, 32	go down, 36	make of, 35	sit down, 36

1. My best friend, Heather, really likes Mike, but Mike asked me to go to the dance with him. I hope Heather doesn't _____ it _____ me.

2. The real estate agent has shown us several houses, but we've _____ it _____ to three that we really like.

3. Mike took the wastebaskets outside and _____ them _____.

4. Before we go to the beach, let's _____ _____ Tom's house and see if he wants to come with us.

5. Maria's a fast learner. She had never played chess before, but she _____ _____ right away.

6. No one thought I could get 100 on the test, but I _____ it _____.

7. Nothing like that ever happened before. I didn't know what to _____ _____ it.

8. You can really screw up your computer with that program, so don't _____ _____ with it unless you know what you're doing.

9. Pets aren't allowed where we're moving, so we're going to have to _____ our dog _____.

10. Polio has been almost completely _____ _____ _____.

11. _____ _____ that jerk for fifteen years was horrible.

12. Joe was so upset after the accident that it was twenty minutes before he _____

    _____ enough to tell the police officer what happened.

13. Be careful on that icy sidewalk — you don't want to _____ _____ and break

    your neck.

14. In the summer the sun doesn't _____ _____ until 9:00 in the evening.

15. I'm going to _____ $4,000 _____ on my new car and finance the rest.

16. I've been standing all day. I need to _____ _____.

---

38. FOCUS ON: **the verb *keep* and adverbs and adverbials showing degrees of variability**

Phrasal verbs with *keep*

Several phrasal verbs are based on the verb *keep*, and it is important to understand that the essential meaning of *keep* in these phrasal verbs is *no change*. As you study these verbs, remember than in each meaning of each verb something is not changing, something is continuing in the same direction or in the same manner, or something is staying in the same place or in the same condition.

Adverbs and adverbials showing degrees of variability

A variety of adverbs and adverbial groups of words that together function as adverbs are used to modify phrasal verbs that relate to something variable, such as distance, time, cost, speed, temperature, amount, or quantity.

Adverbs and adverbials allow the speaker to be more precise about what is being measured — to say whether it was *a little* or *a lot* or to be precise about exactly *how much*. But the verb must be something that is variable. In cannot be something either/or, such as *shut off*, for example (a TV is either on or off — it cannot be in between). Adverbs and adverbials are used to strengthen the meaning of the verb:

> *He fell asleep on the train and **went** <u>well</u> **beyond** his stop.*
> *She **fell** <u>way</u> **behind** in her work when she was sick.*
> ***Keep** <u>far</u> **away** from the fire.*

to weaken the meaning of the verb:

> *I **went** <u>a bit</u> **over** my budget.*
> ***Keep** <u>slightly</u> **to** the right on that road.*
> *He **fell** <u>a little</u> **behind**.*
> *The meeting may **run** <u>somewhat</u> **over**.*

or to be exact:

> We **planned** <u>two</u> <u>weeks</u> **ahead**.
> **Go** <u>three</u> <u>floors</u> **up**.

Sometimes, in informal English, *way* is repeated for extra emphasis:

> What Jim said **went** <u>way, way, way</u> **beyond** impolite — it was outrageous.

Infinitive

present tense	-ing form	past tense	past participle
keep at			
keep at & keeps at	keeping at	kept at	kept at

1. keep at *p.v.* When you **keep at** it, you continue with an activity even though it may be difficult. When you say "**Keep at** it" to people, you encourage them to finish with an activity that is difficult.

> *I know this work is difficult, but you have to **keep at** it.*
> ***Keep at** it; you're almost finished.*

keep away			
keep away & keeps away	keeping away	kept away	kept away

1. keep away (from) *p.v.* When you **keep away** or **keep away** from people, you do not come close to them or associate with them. When you **keep away** or **keep away** from things, you do not touch them, come close to them, or use them. When you **keep away** or **keep away** from places, you do not come close to them or go to them.

> *Mark was very sick yesterday, so everyone **kept away** from him.*
> *We're going to eat dinner in a few minutes, so **keep away** from those cookies.*
> *That's a bad neighborhood, so **keep away** from it.*

2. keep ... away (from) *p.v.* When you **keep** people or things **away** or **keep** them **away** from something or someone else, you do not allow them to come close to or associate with someone or come close to or touch something.

> *That dog is dangerous, so **keep** it **away**.*
> *Paul has an alcohol problem, so **keep** him **away** from the bar at the party tomorrow.*

keep down			
keep down & keeps down	keeping down	kept down	kept down

1. keep ... down *p.v.* When you **keep** the cost, quantity, or amount of something **down**, you keep it a low level.

> *The company tried to **keep** its prices **down**.*
> *They wanted a small wedding, but they have such large families that it was hard to **keep** the number of guests **down**.*

2. keep ... down *p.v.* When you **keep** the volume of noise, music, or conversation **down**, you keep it at a low level. When people are being noisy and you want them to be quieter, you tell them to **keep** it **down**.

*Will you please **keep** it **down**; I'm trying to study.*
*You kids can watch TV, but **keep** the volume **down** — your mother is taking a nap.*

Infinitive

present tense	-ing form	past tense	past participle
keep from			
keep from & keeps from	keeping from	kept from	kept from

1. keep from *p.v.* When you **keep from** doing something, you do not do it even though it is hard not to.

*I was so angry that I don't know how I **kept from** punching that guy in the nose.*
*The movie was so sad that I couldn't **keep from** crying.*

2. keep . . . from *p.v.* When you **keep** people **from** doing something, you stop them from doing it.

*Jim's girlfriend's parents don't like him, and they try to **keep** him **from** seeing her.*
*When I was young, my poor health **kept** me **from** doing a lot of things the other kids did .*

keep off			
keep off & keeps off	keeping off	kept off	kept off

1. keep . . . off *p.v.* When you **keep off** something, you do not walk or stand on it. When you **keep** other people or things **off** something, you do not allow them to walk or stand on it.

*The sign says "**Keep off** the grass."*
*You should **keep** your kids **off** the streets and in school.*

2. keep . . . off *p.v.* When you **keep off** drugs, cigarettes, or other addictive substances, you do not use them. When you **keep** people **off** drugs, cigarettes, or other addictive substances, you prevent them from using them.

*Since getting out of jail, Hank has been able to **keep off** drugs.*
*Ned is a nice guy as long as you can **keep** him **off** booze.*

keep on			
keep on & keeps on	keeping on	kept on	kept on

1. keep on *p.v.* When you **keep on** doing something, you continue doing it.

*I told her to be quiet, but she just **kept** right **on** talking.*
*Don't stop — **keep on** going.*

2. keep . . . on *p.v.* When you **keep** people **on** at their place of employment, you continue to employ them.

*The company decided against laying all the workers off and will instead **keep** a few **on** to maintain equipment until business improves.*
*Everyone on the hotel staff was fired after the hotel went out of business, except for two guys who were **kept on** to clean and paint the building.*

Infinitive

present tense	-ing form	past tense	past participle
keep to			
keep to & keeps to	keeping to	kept to	kept to

1. keep ... to *p.v.* When you **keep** information **to** yourself, you do not tell anyone.

> This is a secret, so **keep** it **to** yourself.
> I wish she would **keep** her racist comments **to** herself; I don't want to hear them.

2. keep ... to *p.v.* When you **keep** something **to** a certain cost, quantity, or amount, you do not let the cost, quantity, or amount go higher than that level.

> Here's my credit card, but **keep** your spending **to** a minimum — don't go crazy with it.
> The room doesn't hold a great many people, so we have to **keep** the number of guests **to** 200.

3. keep to *p.v.* When you **keep to** the right or left, you continue moving to the right or left.

> When you pass a big red barn on the highway, **keep to** the right; the exit is right after the barn.
> Faster cars are supposed to **keep to** the left.

keep up			
keep up & keeps up	keeping up	kept up	kept up

1. keep ... up *p.v.* When you **keep** an activity **up**, you continue doing it.

> Leopards can run extremely fast, but they can't **keep** it **up** longer than a minute or two.
> I told you to stop doing that. If you **keep** it **up**, I'm going to get angry.

2. keep up (with) *p.v.* When you are in a group that is studying, working, and so on, and you are able to learn or work at the same rate as the others, you **keep up** or **keep up** with the group. **Fall behind** is the opposite of **keep up**.

> Lydia missed several days of school last month, and now she's having a hard time **keeping up** with the rest of the class.
> The assembly line was going so fast that no one could **keep up**.

3. keep up (with) *p.v.* When you **keep up** or **keep up** with people or things that are moving, you are able to move at the same rate. **Fall behind** is the opposite of **keep up**.

> Bob walks so fast that it's hard to **keep up** with him.
> The wounded soldiers couldn't **keep up** with the rest of the army.

4. keep up (with) *p.v.* When you can understand and respond to a situation that is changing, you are able to **keep up** with the situation.

> Computer technology is changing so fast. How can anyone **keep up** with it?
> Jane always has some new idea. I can't **keep up** with her.

5. keep ... up *p.v.* When people or things **keep** you **up**, they prevent you from going to bed, or if you are in bed, they prevent you from falling asleep.

> *Ned just would not leave last night; he **kept** me **up** until 2:00 in the morning.*
> *That noisy party across the alley **kept** me **up** all night.*

EXERCISE 38a — **Complete the sentences with phrasal verbs from this section. Be sure the phrasal verbs are in the correct tense.**

1. The student's excuse for not doing his homework was so ridiculous that his teacher couldn't

   _____ _____ laughing.

2. What I'm going to tell you is highly confidential, so _____ it _____ yourself.

3. The baby's crying _____ Judy _____ half the night.

4. Don't quit now — you're almost finished _____ _____ it

5. The company increased its profits by _____ costs _____.

6. I've tried to quit smoking a hundred times, but I just can't _____ _____

   cigarettes longer than a day.

7. Slower traffic should _____ _____ the right.

8. Now that I live in New York, I can't _____ _____ with local news in my hometown.

9. Sally is really angry at your brother, so it would be a good idea to _____ him

   _____ from her.

10. My algebra class is too difficult for me. I can't _____ _____.

11. You're going to have to walk faster than that if you want to _____ _____

    with us.

12. Please _____ your dog _____ our lawn.

13. If you don't _____ _____ your exercise program, you're going to gain all the

    weight back.

14. Could you _____ the music _____? Your mother's trying to sleep.

15. Parents try to _____ their children _____ making mistakes, but

    sometimes it isn't easy.

16. If you _____ _____ eating so much butter and so many eggs, you're going

    to have a heart attack.

17. The new owner said the company was losing too much money to _____ all the

    workers _____ and that some would have to be laid off.

18. Look at the prices on this menu! Let's try to _____ it _____ a hundred bucks,

    okay?

19. I don't want to talk to you ever again, so _____ _____ from me!

> EXERCISE 38b — **Write answers to the questions using phrasal verbs from
> this section. Be sure the phrasal verbs are in the correct tense.**

1. My father asked me to speak more quietly. What did my father ask me to do?

2. I told the travel agent that we have only $4,000 to spend on our vacation, so she has to make

   sure the cost doesn't go over that. What did I ask the travel agent to do?

3. My geometry class is so boring that I can't stop myself from falling asleep. What can't I do in

   my geometry class?

4. My teacher told me that calculus is difficult but that I have to continue trying to understand it.

   What did my teacher tell me?

5. The political situation in Washington changes every day, and it's hard to understand what is

   happening. What is it hard to do?

6. Sarah and I were running. I quit after three miles, but she continued running. What did

   Sarah do?

7. You've got to remain at a great distance from this area because it is radioactive. What have you

   got to do about the radioactive area?

8. Heather thinks Mike isn't telling her everything. What does Heather think about Mike?

9. Janice got excellent grades in her first year of college. I hope she can continue to do well.

   What do I hope Janice can do?

10. I asked my husband not to let the children near my computer. What did I ask my husband?

11. The economist said it's important not to let inflation go higher. What did the economist say?

12. Bill hasn't used drugs for five years. What has Bill done?

13. My son is eighteen, so I can't stop him if he wants to join the Army. What can't I do to my son?

14. Sarah's having a little trouble in school. It's hard for her to stay at the same level as the other students. What is hard for Sarah?

EXERCISE 38c — **Write eight original sentences using phrasal verbs from this section.**

1. _____

2. _____

3. _____

4. _____

5. _____

6. _____

7. _____

8. _____

EXERCISE 38d, Review — **Complete the sentences with these phrasal verbs from previous sections. Be sure the phrasal verbs are in the correct tense. To check their meanings, review the section number given after each one.**

back down, 36	come on, 37	goof around, 33	leave over, 37
brush off, 37	fall behind, 33	hang out, 37	run down, 36
calm down, 36	fall down, 36	know about, 33	sit down, 36
come about, 33	go down, 36	lay down, 36	talk to, 37

1. Raul is constantly criticizing me, but I usually just _____ him _____.

2. I can barely hear this radio. The batteries must be _____ _____.

3. When the electricians went on strike, the entire construction project _____ _____ schedule.

4. Jake's claim that he accidentally shot Tony six times didn't _____ _____ well with the jury.

5. The dictator _____ _____ after three aircraft carriers started sailing toward his country.

6. I need to check the furnace. The temperature got below sixty degrees last night, but the heat didn't _____ _____.

7. A big, old tree _____ _____ last night and smashed a hole in our roof.

8. _____ _____ — there's nothing to get upset about.

9. Several major changes in society _____ _____ as a result of the industrial revolution.

10. Are you going to do any work at all today or will you just _____ _____?

11. Don't waste your time asking Erik; he doesn't _____ anything _____ it.

12. Timmy's mother _____ him _____ and talked to him about his bad grades.

13. How much money was _____ _____ after you finished paying for everything?

14. You can _____ those papers _____ over there.

15. I don't have anything to do today. I'm just going to _____ _____ here and relax.

16. I'm so mad at her. I'll never _____ _____ her again!

---

39. FOCUS ON: **passive phrasal verbs, 3**

As we saw in Section 13, the passive is formed with _be_ and the past participle of the verb. A number of modal auxiliary verbs and similar constructions are commonly used with _be_:

> The meat <u>will</u> <u>be</u> **chopped up** by the cook.
> Mark <u>would</u> never <u>be</u> **picked up** at the airport by a limo.
> This mess <u>can</u> <u>be</u> **straightened out** only by me.
> Such a huge country <u>couldn't</u> <u>be</u> **taken over** easily.
> Her name <u>should</u> <u>be</u> **crossed off** the list.
> The gas tank <u>ought</u> <u>to</u> <u>be</u> **filled up** before you return the car.
> The concert <u>might</u> <u>be</u> **sold out**.
> Your paychecks <u>may</u> <u>not</u> <u>be</u> **picked up** until after 5:00.
> The enemy <u>must</u> <u>be</u> **wiped out**.
> I <u>have</u> <u>to</u> <u>be</u> **picked up** on time.
> The fruit <u>has</u> <u>to</u> <u>be</u> **chopped up** with a clean knife.
> This screwup <u>had</u> <u>better</u> <u>be</u> **straightened out** soon or you will be fired!
> This stuff <u>was</u> <u>supposed</u> <u>to</u> <u>be</u> **taken over** to Nancy's house yesterday.

Recall from Section 28 that phrasal verbs in the passive cannot be separated by an object because in a passive sentence there is no object.

Infinitive

	present tense	-ing form	past tense	past participle
chop up	chop up & chops up	chopping up	chopped up	chopped up

1. chop ... up *p.v.* When you **chop** something **up**, you cut it into small pieces with a knife or other sharp instrument.

> *Does this meat have to be **chopped up**?*
> ***Chop** it **up** into pieces about half an inch in size.*

chopped up *part.adj.* After something has been cut into small pieces with a knife or other sharp instrument, it is **chopped up**.

> *Mix the **chopped-up** onions and celery with the mayonnaise.*

	present tense	-ing form	past tense	past participle
cross off	cross off & crosses off	crossing off	crossed off	crossed off

1. cross ... off *p.v.* When you **cross** something **off** a list, you draw a line through it to remove it from the list.

> *Why was my name **crossed off** the invitation list?*
> ***Crossing** it **off** was a mistake.*

crossed off *part.adj.* After a line has been drawn through something on a list to remove it from the list, it is **crossed off**.

> *Here's the grocery list, but don't get this **crossed-off** stuff — I already got it.*

	present tense	-ing form	past tense	past participle
fill up	fill up & fills up	filling up	filled up	filled up

1. fill ... up *p.v.* When you **fill** something **up**, you fill it completely.

> *My radiator must be leaking; it has to be **filled up** with water every day.*
> *We always **fill** the tank **up** when we're in Indiana because gas is cheaper there.*

filled up *part.adj.* After something has been completely **filled up**, it is **filled up**.

> *These water containers don't weigh very much. Are you sure they're completely **filled up**?*

2. fill ... up (on) *p.v.* When you **fill up** or **fill up** on something, you eat so much that you are no longer hungry and cannot eat any more.

> *Don't **fill up** on salad — you won't have any room for dinner.*
> *I **filled up** on candy and was really sick about an hour later.*

3. fill up *p.v.* When a room or other area **fills up**, people enter it until it is full.

*The dance floor **filled up** quickly when the band began to play.*
*The hotels in Rio de Janeiro always **fill up** at carnival time.*

Infinitive

	present tense	-ing form	past tense	past participle
pick up				
	pick up & picks up	picking up	picked up	picked up

1. pick ... up *p.v.* When you **pick** something **up**, you lift it with your hand.

*All this trash has to be **picked up**.*
*Sam **picked up** his briefcase and left his office.*

2. pick ... up *p.v.* When you go to a place to get something that was created, prepared, or left for you and is now ready, you **pick** it **up**.

*The garbage is supposed to be **picked up** before 9:00 A.M.*
*The travel agent said I could **pick** the tickets **up** tomorrow.*

pickup *n.* Something that is to be **picked up** or the process of **picking** it **up** is a **pickup**.

*The restaurant uses the back door for **pickups** and deliveries.*

3. pick ... up *p.v.* When you **pick** people **up**, you stop your vehicle and give them a ride away from that place.

*You'll be **picked up** at the airport by the hotel van.*
***Picking up** hitchhikers is dangerous.*

pickup *n.* Someone who is to be **picked up** or the process of **picking** someone **up** is a **pickup**.

*The taxi driver went to 2122 N. Clark Street for a **pickup**.*

4. pick ... up *p.v.* When you **pick** something **up** in a store, you quickly go into a store to buy something you need.

*I need to **pick up** some milk on the way home.*
*Could you **pick** a loaf of bread **up** on your way over?*

5. pick ... up *p.v.* When you **pick up** a skill, you learn it easily. When you **pick up** a habit, you acquire the habit.

*Children can **pick up** a new language very quickly.*
*My son is **picking** some bad habits **up** from his friends.*

6. pick ... up *p.v.* When you resume doing something at the point where you stopped doing it earlier, you **pick up** at that point.

*The teacher started the class by **picking up** where she had left off the previous week.*
*When you return to work after a long vacation, it's hard to know where to **pick up**.*

7. pick ... up *p.v.* When you **pick up** a radio or television station or a certain frequency on a receiver, you are able to tune it to that station or frequency.

*When the weather is right, you can **pick** radio stations **up** that are hundreds of miles away.*

*General Johnston's radio transmission was **picked up** by the enemy.*

8. pick . . . up *p.v.* When the police or other authorities arrest people, they **pick** them **up**.

*The border patrol **picks up** several people every day trying to bring drugs into the country.*

*Charles was **picked up** for driving under the influence of alcohol.*

9. pick . . . up *p.v.* When you get something by chance without looking for it, you **pick** it **up**.

*I **picked up** a few stock tips from a guy I met on the plane.*

*Marsha **picked up** some interesting books at a used bookstore.*

10. pick . . . up *p.v.* When you **pick up** the check or the tab (a *tab* is a list of money that someone owes) in a restaurant or other place, you pay it.

*Tom's a real cheapskate; he never **picks up** the check.*

*Heather's father **picked up** the tab for the entire wedding.*

11. pick up *p.v.* When the speed, level, or condition of something increases or improves, it **picks up**.

*Business is slow this time of year, but it should **pick up** in December.*

*The song starts out slowly, but then it **picks up**.*

pickup *n.* An improvement in the speed, level, or condition of something is a **pickup**. If a motor vehicle is able to accelerate quickly, it has **pickup**.

*The company's profits increased after a **pickup** in sales.*

*I need to take my truck to the mechanic. It doesn't have any **pickup**.*

12. pick . . . up *p.v.* When you **pick up** a place that is messy, you organize or tidy it.

*Timmy's mother told him he couldn't play outside until he **picked up** his room.*

*Let's **pick** this place **up** — it's a mess.*

13. pick . . . up *p.v.* [informal] When you **pick up** members of the opposite sex, you approach and successfully interest them in a sexual or romantic encounter.

*Hank tried to **pick up** Frank's sister at the party last night, but she wasn't interested.*

*Pat **picked up** someone, and they went to a cheap motel.*

Infinitive			
present tense	-ing form	past tense	past participle
sell out			
sell out & sells out	selling out	sold out	sold out

1. sell out (of) [often passive] *p.v.* When a store **sells out** of something or is **sold out** of something, it sells all of it.

*The toy store **sold out** of antigravity boots in two days.*

*I wanted to buy that new computer game, but every store I went to was **sold out** of it.*

sold out *part.adj.* After all of something for sale in a store has been sold, the item is **sold out**.

*I saw the most beautiful shoes at the mall, but my size was all **sold out**.*

sold out *part.adj.* After all the tickets to a concert, play, or other public performance have been sold, the event is **sold out**.

*You'll never get a ticket for the Superbowl — it's been **sold out** for weeks.*

Infinitive

present tense	-ing form	past tense	past participle
straighten out			
straighten out & straightens out	straightening out	straightened out	straightened out

1. straighten . . . out *p.v.* When something is bent, crooked, or curved and you make it straight, you **straighten** it **out**.

*My elbow is so swollen that I can't **straighten** my arm **out**.*

*As the city grew, many of the winding streets were **straightened out**.*

2. straighten . . . out *p.v.* When you **straighten out** a confused situation or misunderstanding, you take steps to make it understandable and satisfactory to everyone involved. **Sort out** is similar to **straighten out**.

*My hotel had me booked for the wrong days in the wrong room, but the manager **straightened** everything **out**.*

*Save your questions for the meeting. Everything will be **straightened out** then.*

straightened out *part.adj.* After a confused situation or misunderstanding has been made understandable and satisfactory to everyone involved, it is **straightened out**. **Sorted out** is similar to **straightened out**.

*Erik was upset with Dan, but they had a talk and now everything is **straightened out**.*

3. straighten . . . out *p.v.* When you **straighten out** people who are acting foolishly, you do or say something that causes them to act more responsibly. When you **straighten out** people who are confused, you help them to understand.

*I told my son that if he gets in trouble one more time, I'm going to send him to military school. That really **straightened** him **out**.*

*I'm totally confused about what I'm supposed to do. Can you **straighten** me **out**?*

take over			
take over & takes over	taking over	took over	taken over

1. take . . . over (to) *p.v.* When you take something from one place to another, you **take** it **over** or **take** it **over** to a person or place.

*Jane's at home sick, so I'm going to **take** some chicken soup **over**.*

*After I finished my report, I **took** it **over** to the finance department.*

2. take ... over *p.v.* When people, groups, or countries take control of a place by force, they **take** it **over**.

>*After the government troops fled, the country was **taken over** by the rebels.*
>*The hijackers **took over** the plane and ordered the pilot to fly to Havana.*

takeover *n.* A **takeover** is an action to take control of a country, city, building, or other place by force.

>*If the situation doesn't stabilize soon, there's a real chance of a military **takeover**.*

3. take over (from/as) *p.v.* When people are elected, appointed, or hired to take control of a country, state, city, business, school, building, and so on, and to replace the people in control, they **take over**, **take over** as something, or **take over** from someone.

>*Carlos Ortega will be **taking over** as sales manager next year.*
>*Ortega **took over** from Margaret Cummings, who had been the sales manager for 14 years.*

takeover *n.* When people who are elected, appointed, or hired take control of a country, state, city, business, school, building, and so on, and replace the people in control, a **takeover** occurs.

>*After the **takeover**, the new president made a lot of changes.*

4. take over (for) *p.v.* When you start to do a job or some work that other people are doing in order to allow them to take a break or because the previous shift has ended and a new shift has begun, you **take over**. When you assume an obligation or accept responsibility from someone, you **take** it **over**.

>*We work from 4:00 P.M. to midnight, and then the graveyard shift **takes over**.*
>*When Linda was sick she couldn't care for her children, so her sister **took over** for her until she was well again.*

| Infinitive | | | |
present tense	-ing form	past tense	past participle
wipe out			
wipe out & wipes out	wiping out	wiped out	wiped out

1. wipe ... out *p.v.* When you remove dirt or liquid from the inside of a container with a cloth, sponge, or paper towel, you **wipe** it **out**.

>***Wipe** the microwave **out** — it's got spaghetti sauce inside it.*
>*I **wiped out** the inside of the glasses so they wouldn't dry with spots.*

2. wipe ... out *p.v.* When you are trying to kill people, weeds, insects, and so on, and you kill all of them, you **wipe** them **out**.

>*An entire regiment was **wiped out** in the battle.*
>*The general said he would **wipe out** the rebels.*

wipeout *n.* A situation in which all people, weeds, insects, and so on, are killed is a **wipeout**.

>*The battle was a complete **wipeout**. Not a single soldier survived.*

39

EXERCISE 39a — Complete the sentences with phrasal verbs from this section. Be sure the phrasal verbs are in the correct tense.

1. Your pictures are ready and can be _____ _____ between 10:00 A.M. and 6:00 P.M.

2. I didn't get the book I wanted because the store was _____ _____ of them.

3. There's a lot of confusion about the new policy. We need to have a meeting to _____ everything _____.

4. The vice-president _____ _____ after the president died.

5. Susie, your room is very messy. Come in here and _____ it _____ right now!

6. Mr. Nelson asked me to _____ _____ for Lydia while she's on vacation.

7. Sales of air conditioners always _____ _____ in the spring.

8. If we get a bigger antenna, we might be able to _____ a lot more stations _____.

9. It took me an hour to _____ _____ everything for the beef stew.

10. The soldiers were ordered to _____ _____ the rebels.

11. Sally called and asked me to _____ _____ a few things on the way home.

12. A country this small could be _____ _____ in a few days.

13. I wish I hadn't _____ _____ on bread. Now I can't finish my dinner.

14. I'm going to play golf with Charles next week. He's really good, so maybe I can _____ _____ a few ways to improve my game.

15. The theater _____ _____ ten minutes before the start of the opera.

16. My car's frame was so badly damaged in the accident that there was no way it could be _____ _____.

17. You don't need to take any money to the restaurant. Karen said she would _____ _____ the check.

18. Don't just clean the outsides of the desks — _____ the insides _____, too.

19. I'll be arriving at 3:40 A.M. Would _____ me _____ that early be a problem?

20. Hank's giving orders like he's the president of the company. Someone needs to _____ him _____.

21. Smoking is a bad habit that I _____ _____ in the Navy.

22. Let's _____ _____ these canteens before we begin our hike.

23. This couch is really heavy. Can you help me _____ it _____?

24. After you get your paycheck, you can _____ it _____ to the cashier to cash it.

25. Can you believe what Hank did? He tried to _____ _____ the boss's daugh-

    ter at the company picnic.

26. I finished page 47 yesterday, so I'll _____ _____ on page 48 today.

27. You can _____ my name _____ the list; I've changed my mind.

> EXERCISE 39b — **Write three sentences using the objects in parentheses. Be sure to put the objects in the right place.**

1. Have you *chopped up*? (the onions, them)

_____

_____

_____

2. You can *cross off*. (Linda's name, her)

_____

_____

_____

3. *Fill up* with water. (the aquarium, it)

_____

_____

_____

4. I need to *pick up* at the train station. (my parents, them)

_____

_____

_____

5. Can you *straighten out*? (this mess, it)

_____

_____

_____

6. The rebels *took over*. (the royal palace, it)

_____

_____

_____

7. They *wiped out*. (the palace guard, them)

_____

_____

_____

EXERCISE 39c — **Write answers to the questions using phrasal verbs, participle adjectives, and nouns from this section. Be sure the phrasal verbs are in the correct tense.**

1. The construction business always improves in the spring. What does the construction business always do?

2. Pirates might take control of the ship. What might happen to the ship?

3. In Question 2, if pirates took control of the ship, what would this action be called?

4. There was a misunderstanding at work, but Nicole explained everything to the people involved, and now they understand. What did she do?

5. In Question 4, how would you describe the misunderstanding now?

6. Frank was supposed to go to the factory so he could give Ned a ride home. What was supposed to happen to Ned?

7. All the people in the town will be killed when the enemy captures it. What will happen to all the people in the town?

8. Someone ought to draw a line through Karen's name on the list. What ought to be done to Karen's name?

9. In Question 8, how would you describe Karen's name after someone draws a line through it?

10. Sarah went to the store to buy a CD, but they had all been sold. What did the store do?

11. In Question 10, how would you describe the CDs?

12. Tom tried to buy a ticket for the concert, but all the tickets had been sold. Why couldn't Tom buy a ticket for the concert?

13. You cut some bacon into very small pieces before you put it on your salad. What was done to the bacon?

14. The laundry closes at 6:00, so Jane has to go there before 6:00 to get her dress. What has to be done to the dress?

15. The copilot flew the plane so that the pilot could eat dinner. What did the copilot do?

16. Todd often asks me to stop at the store and buy a newspaper. What does Todd often ask me to do?

17. I'll tell Susie not to make the water in the bathtub rise all the way to the top. What will I tell Susie?

18. I stopped writing my book at page 94 and later started writing again on page 95. What did I do?

EXERCISE 39d, Review — **Complete the sentences with these phrasal verbs from previous sections. Be sure the phrasal verbs are in the correct tense. To check their meanings, review the section number given after each one.**

bite off, 27	come out, 32	leave out, 32	pull over, 19
blow up, 33	cut down, 23	look over, 21	settle down, 21
break off, 27	hand over, 19	make up, 23	slow down, 24
bring back, 19	knock off, 27	pick on, 21	wear down, 17

1. David's mother told him she'd like some grandchildren, but he's having too much fun as a bachelor and isn't interested in _____ _____.

2. I didn't finish my work because I was training a new employee, and explaining everything really

_____ me _____.

3. Bob's doctor told him he was doing too much weight lifting and that he should _____

_____.

4. The movie wasn't the same as the novel. Several characters were _____ _____.

5. When I caught my sixteen-year-old daughter smoking cigarettes, I really _____

_____.

6. I didn't say you could use my car. _____ _____ those keys right now!

7. There must be something wrong with my camera — none of the pictures I took _____

_____.

8. Can I borrow your food processor? I promise I'll _____ it _____ tomorrow.

9. We've been working since 7:00 A.M. Let's _____ _____ and finish tomorrow.

10. Everything on the menu looks delicious. I just can't _____ _____ my mind.

11. If you don't stop _____ _____ me, I'm going to tell Mommy.

12. I told Mark not to pet the lion, but he didn't listen, and his hand was _____

_____.

13. He realized he was lost, so he _____ his car _____ and looked at a map.

14. My son asked me for a motorcycle for his birthday, but I told him no, so he's trying to

_____ me _____ by asking me again and again and again.

15. I gave my job application to the human resources director, and he said he'd _____ it

_____ and give me a call.

16. Do you have any glue? One of the arms has _____ _____ this ceramic doll.

40. FOCUS ON: gerund phrasal verbs vs. phrasal verbs followed by the *-ing* form

We have seen in previous sections that phrasal verbs are sometimes followed by the *-ing* form. We have also seen that transitive phrasal verbs sometimes take gerund objects. At a glance, there seems to be no difference between these two constructions:

> Jim **went away** <u>singing</u>.
>> -ing form
>
> Jim **stuck with** <u>singing</u>.
>> gerund

But because a gerund is a verb functioning as a noun, it can be replaced with an ordinary nongerund noun. However, this is not true of the *-ing* form:

> ~~Jim **went away** it.~~
> Jim **stuck with** <u>it</u>.

Infinitive			
present tense	-ing form	past tense	past participle
blow off			
blow off & blows off	blowing off	blew off	blown off

1. blow . . . off *p.v. [informal]* When you do not do something that you are supposed to do because you do not want to or because you do not think it is important, you **blow** it **off**.

> *I was supposed to report for jury duty Monday morning, but I **blew** it **off**.*
> *Bob had a hangover, so he **blew off** helping Marsha fix her car.*

bring up			
bring up & brings up	bringing up	brought up	brought up

1. bring . . . up (to) *p.v.* When people bring something from a higher level or position or from south to north to where you are, they **bring** it **up** or **bring** it **up** to where you are.

> *Would you please go downstairs and **bring up** the package that was just delivered?*
> *The rescue workers **brought** morphine **up** to the injured mountain climber.*

2. bring . . . up *p.v.* When you introduce a new topic into a conversation, you **bring** it **up**.

> *Last night during dinner, Dad **brought up** the idea of saving money by staying home instead of taking a vacation this year.*
> *You and your big mouth! We were having a great time until you **brought** that **up**.*

3. bring . . . up (to) *p.v.* When you **bring up** children, you care for them as they grow to adulthood. When you **bring up** children to believe something or to behave in a certain way, you try to teach this belief or behavior to them.

*Tom was born in Canada, but he was **brought up** in the United States.*
***Bringing** quadruplets **up** is a lot of work.*
*I was **brought up** to believe in honesty and compassion.*

Infinitive			
present tense	**-ing form**	**past tense**	**past participle**
burst out			
burst out & bursts out	bursting out	burst out	burst out

1. burst out *p.v.* When you **burst out** laughing or crying, you begin laughing or crying loudly and suddenly.

> *Heather **burst out** laughing when I fell into the swimming pool.*
> *When Sam heard the news, he **burst out** crying.*

come back			
come back & comes back	coming back	came back	come back

1. come back (to/from) *p.v.* When people return to a place where you are, they **come back** or **come back** to that place or **come back** from the place where they were before.

> *Todd went to Florida thinking it would be hot and sunny, but he **came back** talking about how cold and rainy it was.*
> *I'm never **coming back** to this awful place again.*

2. come back *p.v.* When people, organizations, companies, or athletes overcome difficulties and become successful again, they **come back**.

> *My home team **came back** from last place and won the championship.*
> *Senator Dolittle lost in 1988, but he **came back** to win in 1994.*

comeback *n.* When people, organizations, companies, or sports teams overcome difficulties and become successful again, they make a **comeback**.

> *The Bulls were down by 34 points but won the game with an 18-point lead — what a **comeback**!*

3. come back *p.v.* When a condition, problem, situation, or activity returns or greatly increases, it **comes back**.

> *I need to see the doctor. The pain in my shoulder has **come back**.*
> *There isn't much chance that double-digit inflation will **come back** any time soon.*

comeback *n.* When a condition, problem, situation, or activity returns or greatly increases, it makes a **comeback**.

> *Health officials are concerned that tuberculosis is making a **comeback**.*

4. come back *p.v.* When a fashion or fad **comes back**, it becomes popular again.

> *Miniskirts are **coming back** this year.*
> *Western movies and TV shows go out of style and then **come back** every few years.*

comeback *n.* When a fashion or fad becomes popular again, it makes a **comeback**.

*I saved all my wide neckties because I knew they'd make a **comeback** someday.*

Infinitive

	present tense	-ing form	past tense	past participle
get off on				
	get off on & gets off on	getting off on	got off on	gotten off on

1. get off on *p.v.* *[informal]* When you **get off on** something or **get off on** doing something, you find it enjoyable and exciting.

*Sally loves winter sports, and she especially **gets off on** snowboarding.*
*Mountain climbing is what I **get off on**.*

go away				
	go away & goes away	going away	went away	gone away

1. go away *p.v.* When you leave a place or leave a person, you **go away**.

***Go away!** I'm trying to study.*
*Mark **went away** not realizing he had left his briefcase behind.*

2. go away (for) *p.v.* When you travel for a period of time, you **go away** for this time.

*We always **go away** for a few weeks in the winter.*
*Lydia is going to **go away** for a while.*

3. go away (to) *p.v.* When you leave your home and live temporarily at another place, such as a school, you **go away** to that place.

*Jane didn't **go away** to school; she went to a school near her home.*
*Some young people are nervous about **going away** to school, but others look forward to it.*

4. go away *p.v.* When a condition, problem, situation, or activity disappears or greatly decreases, it **goes away**.

*I have a pain in my back that never **goes away**.*
*If the rain doesn't **go away**, we'll have to call off the game.*

run around				
	run around & runs around	running around	ran around	run around

1. run around *p.v.* When you **run around** a place, you run to various parts of it.

*The cat **ran around** the room chasing the mouse.*
*The children were **running around** the museum, and the guard told them to stop.*

2. run around *p.v.* When you **run around** doing something, you go to various places trying urgently to accomplish something that is important to you.

*The woman was **running around** the store looking for her lost child.*
*We **ran around** the house trying to rescue whatever we could from the rising floodwater.*

runaround *n.* When people are not honest with you or helpful to you, they give you the **runaround**.

> *Why didn't you just tell me the truth instead of giving me the **runaround**?*

Infinitive			
present tense	-ing form	past tense	past participle

stick with

stick with & sticks with	sticking with	stuck with	stuck with

1. stick with *p.v.* When you **stick with** a habit, plan, or type of work, you continue as before, without change. **Stick to** is similar to **stick with**.

> *I don't like computers. I'll **stick with** writing letters by hand.*
> *Todd thought about a career change but decided to **stick with** teaching.*

2. stick with *p.v.* When you **stick with** something that you use, you continue to use it.

> *My wife wants me to switch to decaffeinated coffee, but I'm going to **stick with** regular.*
> *My mother has **stuck with** Ivory soap for forty years.*

3. stick with *p.v.* When you **stick with** people, you remain with them or remain loyal to them.

> *It'll be very crowded at the festival, so **stick with** me so you don't get lost.*
> *That other guy running for senator has some good ideas, but I'm going to **stick with** Senator Dolittle.*

4. stick . . . with *p.v.* When you **stick** people **with** something, you force them to take something or deal with something undesirable or unpleasant.

> *I'm sorry to **stick** you **with** all this work, but you're the only one who can do it.*
> *The shoes I bought don't fit, but the store where I bought them doesn't accept returns, so I guess I'm **stuck with** them.*

EXERCISE 40a — **Complete the sentences with phrasal verbs from this section. Be sure the phrasal verbs are in the correct tense.**

1. I didn't know anyone at the party except Leticia, so I _____ _____ her.

2. All Timmy's friends are _____ _____ for the summer, so he won't have anyone to

   play with.

3. I have a job interview at 8:30 Monday morning, but that's too early for me, so maybe I'll just

   _____ it _____.

4. Miguel was surprised how much he enjoyed watching figure skating. He really _____

   _____ _____ it.

5. Linda _____ _____ from the party talking about what a good time she had.

6. Susie's birthday party exhausted me. The kids were _____ _____ yelling and

   screaming for hours.

7. I gave my grandfather a computer, but he said he'd rather _____ _____ his

   old typewriter.

8. My grandmother was _____ _____ on a farm, but she moved to the city when she

   got married.

9. Dan _____ _____ buying a motorboat, but his wife said it was a crazy idea.

10. I know running is great exercise, but I'm going to _____ _____ swimming.

11. I hope high-heel shoes never _____ _____; they're so uncomfortable.

12. The strange noise in my engine has _____ _____, so I'm going to take the

    car to a mechanic again.

13. I asked the mechanic why the sound keeps _____ _____ and coming back.

14. Bob's joke was pretty funny. Everyone _____ _____ laughing.

15. Betty smelled smoke, and she _____ _____ the house frantically looking for

    the source.

16. Why does the boss _____ me _____ making coffee every morning? Why

    can't someone else do it?

17. I saved my father a lot of money by not _____ _____ to school.

18. After his defeat, the former champion said he would _____ _____.

19. Frank came to my door with flowers and an apology, but I told him to _____ _____.

20. Whenever my brother in Florida visits me here in Minnesota, he _____ some oranges

    _____.

> EXERCISE 40b — **Write answers to the questions using phrasal verbs and**
> **nouns from this section. Be sure the phrasal verbs are in the correct tense.**

1. They're not following the original plan. What aren't they doing?

2. I took some aspirin, and my headache was gone for a while, but now I have a headache again.

   What did my headache do?

3. You started to cry suddenly and loudly. What did you do?

4. Hank was supposed to meet with his parole officer in the morning, but he didn't go because he wanted to sleep late. What did Hank do to his meeting with his parole officer?

5. The hotel desk clerk didn't tell me he had canceled my reservation by mistake. Instead he invented a lot of crazy excuses that he knew weren't true. What did the hotel desk clerk do?

6. Todd's sister was very upset, and he asked what the problem was, but she told him to leave her alone. What did Todd's sister ask him to do?

7. Skiing is what Heather likes more than anything. How does Heather feel about skiing?

8. Everyone in the factory was busy, so when the delivery truck came, David was forced to unload it by himself. What happened to David?

9. Nancy began talking about joining the Peace Corps. What did Nancy do?

10. The number of people with malaria decreased, but now the number is increasing every year. What is malaria doing?

11. Poverty is a problem that never decreases or disappears. What doesn't poverty do?

12. You went on a business trip three weeks ago, and you haven't returned yet. What haven't you done yet?

13. Ned had to call his broker immediately, so he ran to various places looking for a telephone. What did Ned do?

14. It would be nice to leave this city for a week or two. What would be nice?

15. When I was young, my parents taught me to believe in the golden rule. What did my parents do?

EXERCISE 40c — **Write eight original sentences using phrasal verbs from this section. Try to use either gerunds or the -ing form.**

1. _____

2. _____

3. _____

4. _____

5. _____

6. _____

7. _____

8. _____

EXERCISE 40d, Review — **Complete the sentences with these phrasal verbs from previous sections. Be sure the phrasal verbs are in the correct tense. To check their meanings, review the section number given after each one.**

back down, 36	go down, 36	lead up to, 34	stick around, 34
do over, 34	go out, 32	make of, 35	stick to, 34
fool around, 35	hold against, 35	put up to, 34	take back, 34
go by, 35	lay down, 36	run down, 36	trick into, 35

1. At school, Luis got into a lot of trouble for something I did, and now he _____ it

   _____ me.

2. If I could _____ it _____ again, I'd do it differently.

3. The price of gas is expected to _____ _____ to $1 a gallon within a month.

4. The light suddenly _____ _____, and I couldn't see a thing.

5. Do you have to go already? Can't you _____ _____ for a few minutes?

6. We don't want to forget anything, so let's _____ _____ the list one more

   time to be sure.

7. The announcement was a real surprise. I'm not sure what to _____ _____ it.

8. This book I bought is missing some pages. Can you _____ it _____ to the

   bookstore for me tomorrow?

9. Crime was getting out of control, so a new sheriff was elected who promised to _____

   _____ the law.

10. That gun is loaded, so I wouldn't _____ _____ with it if I were you.

11. After I threatened to go to the police and tell them everything, he _____

    _____ and stopped making threats.

12. My brother always thought I would be a failure, so now that I'm rich, I love to _____ It

    _____ him by complaining about how hard it is to keep a thirty-room house clean.

13. My son is a good boy. If he was shoplifting, I'm sure someone _____ him

_____ . _____ it.

14. In my history class we studied the various things that _____ _____

_____ the current situation.

15. The month we spent in Italy was a lot of fun, but it seemed to _____ _____

so quickly.

16. My brother-in-law is so sneaky. He tried to _____ me _____ telling him the

combination to my safe.

41. FOCUS ON: two-word phrasal verbs with the particle *in* that require *into* when used with an object

We have seen in Sections 9 and 23 that some two-word phrasal verbs require a second particle when they are transitive, which makes them three-word phrasal verbs. Many phrasal verbs with the particle *in* have a meaning that relates to *entering* or *penetrating*. When what is being entered or penetrated is named, these verbs become transitive; however, this is not done by adding a second particle but by changing *in* to *into*. Another way to look at it is to consider *into* two particles, *in* and *to*, written as one word:

> The thief **broke in**.
> The thieves **broke into** the jewelry store.

But this is true only for meanings of the phrasal verb that relate to entering or penetrating, not for all meanings. Some meanings with *in* have no *into* version (and are included in this section), and some meanings with *into* have no *in* version (and are not included in this section). Moreover, sometimes *into* is optional, and the verb can be used transitively with either *in* or *into*.

We see also in this section that there is often a phrasal verb with an opposite meaning with *in* and *into* corresponding to *out* and *out of*:

> I **sneaked in**.
> I **sneaked out**.

> I **sneaked into** the house.
> I **sneaked out of** the house.

Infinitive

present tense	-ing form	past tense	past participle
break in & breaks in	**breaking in**	**broke in**	**broken in**

break in

1. break in/into *p.v.* When you **break in** or **break into** a place, you enter illegally using force or deception.

> A thief **broke in** and stole my TV.
> When I saw the smashed glass in the street, I knew my car had been **broken into**.

break-in *n.* A **break-in** is an illegal entry into a place using force or deception.

> The police investigated a **break-in** at the liquor store.

2. break ... in *p.v.* When you **break in** a new mechanical device or a car, you use it slowly and carefully until you are sure it ready for heavier use. When you **break in** a pair of shoes, you wear them only occasionally and for a short time until they are comfortable. When you **break in** people at a new job, you train and supervise them and give them less than the normal amount of work until they are ready for something more difficult.

> I don't want to wear these boots on the expedition. I haven't **broken** them **in** yet.
> We're **breaking in** a new secretary, so things have been a bit confused at our
>   office lately.

broken in *part.adj.* After you **break in** a new mechanical device or a car, a pair of shoes, or people at a new job, they are **broken in**.

> I don't want to wear those shoes to the dance. They're not **broken in** yet.

check in

check in & checks in	checking in	checked in	checked in

1. check in/into *p.v.* When you arrive at a hotel and arrange for a room, you **check in** or **check into** the hotel.

> After I arrive in Denver, I'll go straight to my hotel and **check in**.
> Jim **checked into** the hotel while I called home to check on the kids.

2. check ... in *p.v.* When you arrive at an airport and give your ticket to an agent and receive a boarding pass, you **check in**.

> You should **check in** at least two hours before your flight.
> You can wait over there in the lobby while I **check** you **in**.

check-in *n.* The counter at an airport where you give your ticket to an agent and receive a boarding pass is the **check-in** or the **check-in** counter. The process of **checking in** is check-in.

> Before your flight you have to go to the **check-in** counter.

3. check ... in *p.v.* When you give your luggage to an airline agent so that it will be carried in the baggage compartment rather than the passenger compartment, you **check** it **in**.

41

*That bag is too big for carry-on — you'll have to **check** it **in**.*

checked in *part.adj.* Luggage that has been **checked in** or passengers that have **checked in** are **checked in**.

*Now that we're **checked in**, we can wait in the boarding lounge.*

4. check in (with) *p.v.* When you visit or call people briefly and regularly because you want to get or receive important information from them or to make sure that a situation you are both interested in is satisfactory, you **check in** or **check in** with them.

> *After surgery, you'll need to **check in** once in a while to make sure the bone is healing properly.*
> *If Hank doesn't **check in** with his parole officer every week, the police will arrest him.*

Infinitive

	present tense	-ing form	past tense	past participle
check out	check out & checks out	checking out	checked out	checked out

1. check out (of) *p.v.* When you pay your bill, return your key, and leave a hotel, you **check out** or **check out** of the hotel.

> *There's always a long line of people waiting to **check out** at that time of the morning.*
> *Mrs. Garcia **checked out** of her hotel and took a taxi to the airport.*

checked out *part.adj.* After you have paid your bill, returned your key, and left a hotel, you are **checked out**.

> *Okay, we're **checked out**; now let's get a taxi and go to the airport.*

checkout *n.* The time before which you must **check out** of a hotel in order to avoid paying for another day is the **checkout** time.

> *We can sleep late tomorrow; **checkout** time isn't until 1:00 P.M.*

2. check ... out *p.v.* When you **check** a place or thing **out**, you inspect it carefully or learn more about it.

> *That new Mexican restaurant is great — you should **check** it **out**.*
> *Hey George, **check out** that car Todd is driving. When did he buy it?*

3. check ... out *p.v.* When you **check** people **out**, you investigate them in order to learn more about them. If you say that people **check out**, you mean that the information they have given you about themselves, such as their education and work experience, has been investigated and found to be accurate.

> *Applicants for child care jobs should be thoroughly **checked out**.*
> *Before you give that guy money to invest, you should **check** him **out**.*
> *Frank didn't get the job he wanted with the CIA. Some things on his résumé didn't **check out**.*

4. check out *p.v.* When you **check out** at a store, you bring the items you want to buy to the cashier and pay for them.

*The store's closing in a few minutes. We'd better **check out**.*
*Look at this line. It's going to take forever to **check out**.*

checkout *n.* The **checkout** or the **checkout** counter is where you pay for items in a store.

> *You get the bathroom stuff, I'll get the groceries, and we'll meet at the **checkout** counter.*

Infinitive

	present tense	-ing form	past tense	past participle
go in				
	go in & goes in	going in	went in	gone in

1. go in/into *p.v.* When you **go in** or **go into** a place, building, room, and so on, you enter it.

> *It's getting too dark to play tennis. Let's **go in**.*
> *Frank **went into** the kitchen to get a cup of coffee.*

2. go in *p.v.* When something **goes in** or **goes into** a place, container, enclosure, and so on, it belongs there, fits there, or can be put there.

> *That dish **goes in** the cabinet next to the stove.*
> *All those clothes will never **go in** this small suitcase.*

3. go in *p.v.* When soldiers enter combat or an area where combat is likely, they **go in**. **Pull out** is the opposite of **go in**.

> *The National Guard was ordered to **go in** and stop the riot.*
> *The marine shouted, "We're **going in**!" as he jumped from the landing craft.*

let in				
	let in & lets in	letting in	let in	let in

1. let ... in/into *p.v.* When you **let** people or things **in** or **let** people or things **into** a place, building, room, and so on, you allow them to enter by giving them permission to enter or by opening a door, gate, and so on.

> *When the guests arrived, the butler opened the door to **let** them **in**.*
> *The guard wouldn't **let** me **into** the stadium because I had forgotten my ticket.*

2. let ... in/into *p.v.* When an opening, such as a window, door, hole, crack, and so on, allows something to enter, it **lets** it **in**.

> *That small window doesn't **let in** enough light to read by.*
> *The hole in the screen is **letting** the mosquitoes **into** the house.*

plug in				
	plug in & plugs in	plugging in	plugged in	plugged in

1. plug ... in/into *p.v.* When you connect an electrical device to an electrical outlet, you **plug** it **in** or **plug** it **into** the outlet. When you connect any cord or cable to a socket designed to receive it, you **plug** it **in** or **plug** it **into** the socket.

*I **plugged** my 110-volt TV **into** a 220-volt outlet and ruined it.*
*This phone isn't broken; you just forgot to **plug** the phone cord **in**.*

plugged in *part.adj.* When an electrical device is connected to an electrical outlet, it is **plugged in**.

*Be careful with that iron — it's **plugged in**.*

Infinitive			
present tense	-ing form	past tense	past participle
sneak in			
sneak in & sneaks in	sneaking in	sneaked in	sneaked in

1. sneak in/into *p.v.* When you enter a place without anyone seeing or hearing you, you **sneak in** or **sneak into** the place.

*When I was a kid I used to **sneak into** the movie theater through the emergency exit.*
*If you don't have a ticket for the game, you'll have to **sneak in**.*

sneak out			
sneak out & sneaks out	sneaking out	sneaked out	sneaked out

1. sneak out (of) *p.v.* When you leave a place without anyone seeing or hearing you, you **sneak out** or **sneak out** of the place.

*Susie's father told her to stay upstairs in her room, but she **sneaked out** through the window.*
*The principal caught me **sneaking out** of my chemistry class.*

EXERCISE 41a — **Complete the sentences with phrasal verbs from this section. Be sure the phrasal verbs are in the correct tense.**

1. Close the door! You're _____ the bugs _____.

2. One of the students _____ _____ and stole the answers for the final exam.

3. My grandfather always _____ _____ a new car by not driving it over 50 miles per hour until it had gone 1,000 miles.

4. Mark told me he bought a large-screen TV. Let's go to his house and _____ it _____.

5. My laptop computer is in this bag, so I think it would be better to keep it with me on the flight than to _____ it _____.

6. These speakers _____ _____ sockets in the back of the stereo.

7. Are you sure this is the right key for this lock? It won't _____ _____.

8. When I'm away on a business trip, I always _____ _____ with my office every morning.

41

9. I was late for class, so I waited until the teacher wasn't looking and _____ _____.

10. The soldiers were ordered to _____ _____ and capture the enemy position.

11. I don't trust that guy my daughter wants to marry. I'm going to _____ him _____.

12. Dinner is being served. Let's _____ _____ the dining room.

13. There's a crack in the basement wall that's _____ _____ water.

14. At the supermarket you can _____ _____ in the express line only if you have fewer than 15 items.

15. We'll _____ _____ the Grand Hotel on Wednesday.

16. After a week at the hotel, we'll _____ _____ and go home.

17. Any burglar who tries to _____ _____ my house is going to get a big surprise — I've got three big dogs that aren't very friendly.

18. I _____ _____ only 15 minutes before my flight time, and I almost missed the plane.

EXERCISE 41b — **Write answers to the questions using phrasal verbs, participle adjectives, and nouns from this section. Be sure the phrasal verbs are in the correct tense.**

1. Janice entered the house quietly so that no one would hear her. What did Janice do?

2. Lydia unlocked the door so that her brother could enter the house. What did Lydia do?

3. Ms. Cummings paid her hotel bill and left. What did Ms. Cummings do?

4. In Question 3, Ms. Cummings had to leave the hotel before noon so that she would not have to pay for another day. What is noon at the hotel?

5. The window of Nancy's house was broken, and her jewelry, TV, and computer were gone. What happened to Nancy's house?

6. In Question 5, what happened at Nancy's house?

7. When I arrive at the airport, I'll give my ticket to the agent, and she'll give me a boarding pass. What will I do at the airport?

8. In Question 7, where will I go in the airport?

9. The room is full of cigarette smoke, and Karen doesn't want to enter it. What doesn't Karen want to do?

10. I saw an interesting house with a "for sale" sign on Pine Street as I was driving home. Tomorrow I'll stop and learn more about it. What will I do to the house tomorrow?

11. When Erik flies to Colorado to go skiing, he always gives his skis to the airline agent so that they will be put in the baggage compartment. What does Erik always do with his skis?

12. In Question 11, how would you describe Erik's skis after he gives them to the airline agent?

13. You opened the window quietly, when no one was looking, and left your house. What did you do?

14. Mr. Baker hasn't arrived at his hotel and arranged for a room yet. What hasn't Mr. Baker done yet?

15. Hank bought a new CD player and connected the plug to the outlet. What did Hank do?

16. In Question 15, how would you describe Hank's new CD player?

17. Before Ned was hired for his job in a nursing home, the human resources manager at the nursing home called his previous employer and asked questions about Ned. What was done to Ned?

18. My feet are killing me. It wasn't very smart to wear new hiking boots that aren't soft and comfortable. Why are my feet killing me?

EXERCISE 41c — **Write seven original sentences using phrasal verbs from this section.**

1. _____

2. _____

3. _____

4. _____

5. _____

6. _____

7. _____

EXERCISE 41d, Review — **Complete the sentences with these phrasal verbs from previous sections. Be sure the phrasal verbs are in the correct tense. To check their meanings, review the section number given after each one.**

blow off, 40	help out, 33	start out, 20
come on, 37	leave over, 37	straighten out, 39
fill up, 39	let down, 37	take over, 39
get off on, 40	live with, 35	talk to, 37
go away, 40	narrow down, 35	
hang out, 37	put down, 36	

1. I hope you like spaghetti, because so much was _____ _____ after the party that we're going to be eating it for a week.

2. My son has promised me a hundred times that he'll stay out of trouble and work harder in school, but he always _____ me _____.

3. I want to watch the news. It's going to _____ _____ as soon as this game is over.

4. Even though you don't like your brother, you shouldn't _____ him _____ in front of his children.

5. Today _____ _____ cold and rainy, but now the sun is out, and it's a lot warmer.

6. I can't drive because of my broken leg, but Carmen said she'd _____ me _____ if I need anything.

7. I've got an appointment to get my teeth cleaned tomorrow at 4:00, but if you want to go to the beach, I can _____ my appointment _____.

8. The company was considering eight cities for the new factory, but they've _____ it _____ to three.

9. A lot of the employees are confused about the new contract. We should ask management to have a meeting so that we can _____ everything _____.

10. Lydia is going to _____ _____ for Judy during her maternity leave.

11. Her husband said he wasn't going to stop smoking and that she would just have to learn to _____ _____ it.

12. The commercial on TV said that if you _____ your car's gas tank _____ with their gas, you'd get better mileage and a cleaner engine.

13. We're planning to _____ _____ for a few weeks. Would you mind watering our plants until we return?

14. David put a pool table and a pinball machine in his basement. It's a great place to _____ _____ and relax.

15. Can you believe how rude that guy was to me? Nobody has ever _____ _____ me like that before.

16. Bob is very kind and generous. He _____ _____ _____ helping other people.

42. FOCUS ON: **phrasal verbs with *get*, 1**

Many phrasal verbs are based on the verb *get*, and it is important to understand that the meaning of *get* in these verbs is not the same as the nonphrasal form of *get,* meaning *receive.* Instead, *get* has a meaning similar to *become* or *change to*:

> I ***got up*** at 6:00. (I was not up before, and then I became up — I changed from not being up to being up.)

Many phrasal verbs with *get* that relate to a change in physical location might seem identical in meaning to a variety of phrasal verbs using *come, go,* and other verbs that describe physical movement, such as *walk, run, move,* and so on, and often they can be used with little difference in meaning:

> I ***came back*** last night.
> I ***got back*** last night.

But there is a difference: *get* emphasizes the change in location; *come, go,* and so on, emphasize the movement from one location to another.

It is very common to use the adverbs *right* and *back* with *get* phrasal verbs. To review the adverb *right*, see Sections 19 and 22. To review the adverb *back*, review Section 26 (and do not confuse the adverb *back* with the particle *back*).

Note that two forms of the past participle of *get* are shown: *gotten* and *got*. *Gotten* is more common in American English, but *got* is occasionally used. Both are correct.

Infinitive

	present tense	-ing form	past tense	past participle
get back	get back & gets back	getting back	got back	gotten/got back

1. get back (to) *p.v.* When you return to a level or place where you were before, you **get back** or **get back** to that place.

*We left three weeks ago, and we didn't **get back** until yesterday.*

*Where are you going? **Get** right **back** here!*

*Mark lost a lot of weight when he was sick, and it took him a long time to **get back** to his old weight.*

2. get ... back (to) *p.v.* When you **get** something **back** or **get** something **back** to a person or place, you return it to that person or place.

*Jim uses his mother's car in the morning, but she needs it to go to work at 4:30, so he has to **get** it **back** before then.*

*I have to **get** these books **back** to the library — they're overdue.*

3. get ... back (from) *p.v.* When you **get** something **back** or **get** something **back** from someone or someplace, you have something that you had before.

*I couldn't believe I **got** my stolen car **back**.*

*Jim borrowed a book from me three years ago, and I still haven't **gotten** it **back** from him.*

4. get back (from) *p.v.* When you **get back** or **get back** from something that is very hot or dangerous or that you should not be near, you move away from it so that there is more distance between you and it.

***Get back** from the edge of the cliff! You might fall.*

*As the President came closer, the police told the crowd to **get back.***

Infinitive

	present tense	-ing form	past tense	past participle
get behind				
	get behind & gets behind	getting behind	got behind	gotten/got behind

1. get behind (in) *p.v.* When you are in a group that is studying or working, and so on, and they learn faster or get more work done because you are learning or working more slowly than the others, you **get behind** or **get behind** in your studies or work. When you do not complete work as fast as originally planned and expected, you **get behind** schedule. **Keep up** is the opposite of **get behind**. **Fall behind** is similar to **get behind**.

*Linda had some problems last semester, and she **got behind** in her studies.*

*With all the bad weather we've been having, the construction project has **gotten** way **behind** schedule.*

get by				
	get by & gets by	getting by	got by	gotten/got by

1. get by *p.v.* When you **get by** or **get by** something, you pass something or someone while you are walking or driving even though it may be difficult because there is not enough room.

*Can you move all that junk in the hallway please? It's hard for people to **get by**.*

*There was an accident on the highway, and no one could **get by**.*

2. get by (on) *p.v.* When you **get by** or **get by** on a certain amount of money, you continue with your work or continue with your life even though it may be difficult.

*Don't worry about me; I'll **get by** somehow.*
*It's not easy **getting by** on $250 a week.*

3. get by *p.v.* When something, such as a mistake or a problem, **gets by** you, you do not notice it.

*I've got a great editor; no mistakes **get by** her.*
*I checked this report twice. How did all these misspellings **get by** me?*

Infinitive

present tense	-ing form	past tense	past participle
get down			
get down & gets down	getting down	got down	gotten/got down

1. get down (to) *p.v.* When you move to a lower level or place or from north to south, you **get down** or **get down** to that level or place. **Get up** is the opposite of **get down**. **Go down** is similar to **get down**.

*You're going to fall out of that tree and break your neck. **Get down** right now!*
*The first thing I did after I **got down** to Miami was go to the beach.*

2. get ... down (from) *p.v.* When you **get** things or people **down**, you move them from a higher level or place to a lower one.

*Why do you always put the dishes on the top shelf? I can't **get** them **down**.*
*The firefighters **got** the people **down** from the roof of the burning building.*

3. get down *p.v.* When you bend your body and lower your head to avoid danger or to prevent people from seeing you, you **get down**.

*When the enemy soldiers started shooting, the sergeant ordered his men to **get down**.*
***Get down**! If the police catch us here we'll be in a lot of trouble.*

4. get ... down *p.v.* When things or people **get** you **down**, they make you sad or depressed.

*Don't let your troubles **get** you **down**. Everything will be all right.*
*Jim's marriage problems are really **getting** him **down**.*

get in

get in & gets in	getting in	got in	gotten/got in

1. get in/into *p.v.* When you **get in** or **get into** a place, building, room, car, boat, and so on, you enter it.

***Get in** the car! We're going now.*
*We'd better **get into** the school — the bell's going to ring soon.*

2. get ... in/into *p.v.* When you **get in** or **get into** a place, building, club, restaurant, meeting, and so on, you obtain permission to enter. When you **get** other people **in** or **get** other people **into** a building, club, restaurant, meeting, and so on, you arrange for them to enter.

*We'll never **get into** that club; we don't know the right people.*
*I didn't have an invitation to the party, but Nancy **got** me **in**.*

3. get . . . in/into *p.v.* When you **get** something **in** or **get** something **into** a place, building, room, container, enclosure, and so on, you get the object inside even though it is difficult.

> *The shoes are too small — I can't **get** my feet **in**.*
> *How did they **get** that elephant **into** its cage?*

4. get . . . in/into *p.v.* When you **get in** trouble or **get into** a difficult situation or a mess (a *mess* is a confused or difficult situation), you become involved in it. When you **get** people **in** trouble or **get** them **into** a difficult situation or a mess, you cause them to become involved in it.

> *Susie **got in** a lot of trouble at school today.*
> *I don't see any solution to this problem. How did I ever **get into** this mess?*

5. get in/into *p.v.* When you **get in** or **get into** a place, you arrive. When the vehicle you are in **gets in** or **gets into** a place, it arrives. **Come in** is similar to **get in**.

> *I'm exhausted. I **got in** really late last night.*
> *I'll be waiting for you at the station when your train **gets into** the station.*

6. get . . . in *p.v.* When a store **gets** something **in**, it receives a delivery of something that it will offer for sale.

> *Karen asked the sales clerk when the store was going to **get** some summer dresses **in**.*
> *I wanted to buy that new book, but the bookstore hasn't **gotten** it **in** yet.*

7. get . . . in *p.v.* When you **get** an activity **in**, you find the time for it or make the time for it.

> *Dinner isn't until 7:30, so we've got time to **get** a tennis game **in**.*
> *Whenever I go to San Francisco on business, I try to **get** a baseball game **in**.*

Infinitive			
present tense	-ing form	past tense	past participle
get out			
get out & gets out	getting out	got out	gotten/got out

1. get out (of) *p.v.* When you **get out** or **get out** of a place, building, room, car, boat, and so on, you leave or escape from it.

> *When Bob heard his car's engine making a strange noise, he **got out** and looked under the hood.*
> *We smelled gas and **got out** of the building just seconds before it exploded.*

2. get out (to) *p.v.* When you go to a place that is west of where you are or to a place outside a large city, you **get out** or **get out** to that place.

> *I love it here in the city. I almost never **get out** to the suburbs anymore.*
> *I told my friend in New York, "If you ever **get out** to California, please visit me."*

3. get . . . out (of) *p.v.* When you **get** people **out** or **get** them **out** of a place, you take them out or you arrange for them to leave.

*The soldiers were surrounded, so they called for a helicopter to **get** them **out**.*
*After Hank was arrested, his lawyer **got** him **out** of jail.*

4. get ... out (of) *p.v.* When you **get out** or **get out** of a dangerous, awkward, or difficult situation, you avoid it. When you **get** people **out** of a dangerous, awkward, or difficult situation, you help them to avoid it.

*Erik made a date with two girls for the same night. How is he going to **get out of** this mess?*
*You got me into this mess — you **get** me **out**!*

5. get ... out (of) *p.v.* When you **get** something **out** or **get** something **out** of a container or place, you remove it.

*Mother's coming for dinner tonight, so let's **get** the good china **out**.*
*The videotape is jammed; I can't **get** it **out** of the VCR.*

6. get ... out (of) *p.v.* When you **get** dirt or a stain **out** or **get** dirt or a stain **out** of a material, you remove it by cleaning.

*This detergent's ad claims it'll **get** dirt **out** even in cold water.*
*Do you think bleach will **get** this wine stain **out** of my white blouse?*

7. get out *p.v.* When information **gets out**, it becomes known to people who are not supposed to know it.

*Be careful — we'll be in a lot of trouble if this information **gets out**.*
*There was a huge scandal after the news **got out**.*

8. get out (of) *p.v.* When you leave your house and do things that are relaxing and fun, you **get out** or **get out** of the house.

*You work too hard; you should **get out** more.*
*Ned doesn't **get out** of the house much; he prefers to stay home and play computer games.*

Infinitive			
	present tense	-ing form	past tense	past participle
get over			
	get over & gets over	getting over	got over	gotten/got over

1. get over (to) *p.v.* When you **get over** to a place, you go there. When you tell people to **get over** here, you want them to come where you are.

*Francisco called and he said he needs you to help him with something, so **get over** to his house right away.*
*Susie, **get over** here and clean up this mess immediately!*

2. get over *p.v.* When you **get over** a problem, illness, or emotionally painful experience, you stop letting it affect you and continue with your life.

*I've got a bad cold. I've been sick for a week, and I still haven't **gotten over** it.*
*You can't feel sorry for yourself forever — you've got to **get over** it and get on with your life.*

3. get over *p.v.* When something happens that surprises you or makes you angry, and you cannot stop thinking about it, you cannot **get over** it.

    *I can't **get over** seeing my ex-wife with her new husband.*
    *The coach couldn't **get over** losing the state championship 47 to 0.*

Infinitive

present tense	-ing form	past tense	past participle
get up			
get up & gets up	getting up	got up	gotten/got up

1. get up (to) *p.v.* When you move to a higher level or place, or from south to north, you **get up** or **get up** to that level or place. **Get down** is the opposite of **get up**. **Go up** is similar to **get up**.

    *Tom, your brother is in the basement. Please go tell him to **get** right **up** here and start*
        doing his homework.
    *I haven't **gotten up** to my brother's house in Canada for a long time.*

2. get ... up *p.v.* When you **get up** or someone **gets** you **up**, you rise from your bed. When you **get** people **up**, you cause them to rise from their beds.

    *I don't usually **get up** until 11:00 on weekends.*
    *I make breakfast; **getting** the children **up** and ready for school in the morning is*
        Bill's job.

3. get up *p.v.* When you change from a sitting or lying position to a standing position, you **get up**. **Stand up** is similar to **get up**.

    *The teacher told the sleeping students to **get up**.*
    *After he hit me, I **got** right **up** and hit him back.*

EXERCISE 42a — **Complete the sentences with phrasal verbs from this section. Be sure the phrasal verbs are in the correct tense.**

1. That bomb might explode. Maybe we should _____ _____ a little.

2. As soon as the car stopped, I _____ right _____ and went inside the house.

3. I'll lose my job if this information _____ _____, so don't tell anyone.

4. _____ _____ Jim's death took me a long time.

5. Now the police are outside. Look at all the trouble you've _____ me _____!

6. I thought these pants were ruined after I got ink on them, but this detergent _____

    the ink right _____.

7. I was working in my office on the third floor, and my boss called from his office on the sixth

    floor and told me to _____ _____ there immediately.

8. Work, work, work — that's all you do. You need to _____ _____ more often.

9. It's 4:10. If we hurry, we might _____ a round of golf _____ before it gets dark.

10. I was trying to leave work a little early, but my boss said, "You can't go home until 5:00. _____ back _____ here!"

11. Would you like to go shopping at Wal-Mart tomorrow? They just _____ some new stuff _____.

12. The game is sold out, but I know someone who might be able to _____ us _____.

13. What time did your plane _____ _____ last night?

14. Hank is in a lot of trouble. If he _____ _____ of it, it'll be a miracle.

15. Nicole does her work very carefully and never makes mistakes. Nothing _____ _____ her.

16. Your sister's upstairs sleeping. Go tell her to _____ right _____ here and eat breakfast.

17. Look, there's a bear! _____ _____ — it might see us.

18. My husband spent his whole paycheck on beer and lottery tickets. I don't know how we're going to _____ _____ this month.

19. I wish I hadn't _____ _____ late. I missed the bus, and now I have to walk to school.

20. This is a very difficult class. If you don't study hard, you'll _____ _____.

21. The teacher said, "Your midterm score wasn't very good, but I'm sure if you study hard, you'll do a lot better on the final. Don't let it _____ _____ you."

22. Excuse me, could you move? I can't _____ _____.

23. Mike usually leaves around 8:00 in the morning and _____ _____ around 5:30.

24. My cat has been in that tree for three days. Can you help me _____ her _____?

25. It's amazing. I can't _____ _____ how great Tom looks. I'll bet he's lost forty pounds.

26. If you lose your receipt, _____ your money _____ for something you bought is usually impossible.

27. Timmy's mother said, "Who said you could leave the table? _____ back

    _____ here and finish your vegetables!"

28. Our neighbor called and said, "Your dog is in my garden. _____ it _____!"

29. The situation in that country is very dangerous, so Washington is making plans to

    _____ its embassy staff _____.

30. David was so sick he couldn't even _____ _____ of bed.

31. It isn't easy to _____ this big car _____ that small garage.

> EXERCISE 42b — **Write answers to the questions using phrasal verbs from this section. Be sure the phrasal verbs are in the correct tense.**

1. My father came into my bedroom, shook my shoulder, and told me that breakfast was almost ready. What did my father do?

2. I live in New Orleans, and it's difficult to find the time to travel to Minnesota to visit my sister. What is difficult?

3. After you were arrested for drunken driving, you were in a lot of trouble. What did you do?

4. You need to return to your home very quickly. What do you need to do?

5. After Judy pays her bills, she just barely has enough money to survive until the end of the month. What can Judy just barely do?

6. If Heather doesn't work harder in her math class, she will not be able to stay at the same level as the other students. What will happen to Heather if she doesn't work harder?

7. It's been five years, but Frank is still sad about his brother's death. What hasn't Frank done yet?

8. I was trapped in my car after an accident, but a rescue worker removed me from my car. What did the rescue worker do?

9. Alex is removing his toy train from the closet. What is Alex doing to his toy train?

10. Carlos is standing on a table so that he can get the toy airplane that he threw on top of the refrigerator. What is Carlos doing?

11. The sofa was too big, and the movers couldn't bring it inside our new house. What couldn't the movers do?

12. There is a huge truck in front of us, and we can't pass it. What can't we do?

13. Lydia left the building when she heard the fire alarm. What did Lydia do?

14. After getting out of her car, Janice entered it again. What did Janice do?

15. Erik's bicycle was stolen, but now he has it again. What did Erik do?

16. The pilot had mechanical problems with her airplane, but the controllers on the ground helped her land. What did the controllers do to the pilot?

17. Bill called and asked me to come to his house very quickly. What did Bill ask me to do?

EXERCISE 42c, Review — **Complete the sentences with these phrasal verbs from previous sections. Be sure the phrasal verbs are in the correct tense. To check their meanings, review the section number given after each one.**

brush off, 37	float around, 34	punch in, 30	sneak out, 41
call back, 28	go in/into, 41	punch out, 30	start up, 26
call up, 28	leave behind, 35	run around, 40	
clear out, 32	pick up, 39	sell out, 39	
cross off, 39	plug in/into, 41	sneak in/into, 41	

1. There's nothing to eat for dinner tonight. Can you _____ some takeout food _____ when you come home from work tonight?

2. My brother wants to store some of his stuff in my attic, so tonight I'm going to _____ some of the junk up there _____ to make more room.

3. If you want to get a ticket for the Superbowl, you'll need to hurry — they're _____ _____ fast.

4. When I go on vacation, I want to relax at the beach and _____ my worries _____.

5. Ned is worried. There's a rumor _____ _____ that someone is going to get fired.

6. I can't find the toy my daughter wants for her birthday anywhere. I've been _____ _____ all day looking for it.

7. I'm going to be late for work. Would you mind _____ me _____?

8. Dan must still be here in the office somewhere. He hasn't _____ _____ yet.

9. I haven't talked to Nancy in a long time. I think I'll _____ her _____ tonight.

10. Nancy was in the shower when I called, but her brother said she'd _____ me right

_____ .

11. Are you sure this is the right key? It won't _____ _____ the lock.

12. Margaret Cummings decided to leave her job with a big company and _____

_____ her own company.

13. _____ _____ the theater was easy. One of our friends went inside and

opened the fire exit for the rest of us.

14. My father won't let me go to the dance, so I'm going to _____ _____ after he

goes to bed.

15. None of the bad things people say about Charles bother him. He just _____ it

_____ .

16. I made a list of people to invite to my wedding, but after I heard all those nasty things Sarah

said about my fiancé, I _____ her name _____ the list.

17. Well, I think I've fixed the vacuum cleaner. Let's _____ it _____ and see if it

works now.

43. FOCUS ON: **modals and present perfect phrasal verbs**

Remember that the present perfect is formed with *have* or the contraction *'ve* and the past participle. The only difference is that *has* is not used for the third person singular:

> He <u>has</u> **run up** a big bill.
> He <u>would</u> <u>have</u> **run up** a big bill.

The meanings of the modal and semimodal auxiliaries are unchanged in the present perfect, except for *may* and *might*.

Past speculation and you <u>do</u> <u>not</u> <u>know</u> what happened: *might have* or *may have*

When discussing something that was possible in the past and you <u>do</u> <u>not</u> <u>know</u> what happened, either *might have* or *may have* can be used:

*I wonder where Jim is. He <u>might</u> <u>have</u> **stopped off at** the bar.*
*I wonder where Jim is. He <u>may</u> <u>have</u> **stopped off at** the bar.*

Because you do not know whether Jim stopped off at the bar, either *might have* or *may have* can be used.

Past speculation and you <u>know</u> what happened: only *might have*

When discussing something that was possible in the past and you <u>know</u> what happened, only *might have* can be used:

*Climbing that tree was stupid. You <u>might</u> <u>have</u> **fallen out**.*
Climbing that tree was stupid. ~~You may have fallen out.~~

Because I know that the person I am talking to did not fall out of the tree, only *might have* can be used.

Infinitive

present tense	-ing form	past tense	past participle
blow out			
blow out & blows out	**blowing out**	**blew out**	**blown out**

1. blow . . . out *p.v.* When a flame **blows out** or is **blown out** by a strong wind, it stops burning. When you **blow out** a flame, you use your breath to make the flame stop burning.

*Don't open the window — the candles will **blow out**.*
*I couldn't light my cigarette; the wind kept **blowing** the match **out**.*
*The stove isn't working. Maybe the pilot light has **blown out**.*

2. blow . . . out (of) *p.v.* When something is moved outward away from where it was by an explosion or a very strong wind, it is **blown out** or **blown out** of where it was before.

*The force of the explosion **blew** all the windows **out**.*
*Look, there's a dead bird. The wind might have **blown** it **out** of its nest.*

blowout n. When a tire bursts and suddenly loses its air while you are driving, you have a **blowout**.

*Maria had a **blowout** while she was driving, lost control of her car, and hit a tree.*

3. blow . . . out *p.v.* When a piece of electrical equipment or a fuse **blows out**, it fails because too much electricity is passing through it.

*Don't be surprised if the fuse **blows out** — you have seven lights, your computer, and your TV all plugged into one outlet.*
*When lightning hit our house, it **blew** all the telephones **out**.*

Infinitive

	present tense	-ing form	past tense	past participle
give out	give out & gives out	giving out	gave out	given out

1. give ... out (to) *p.v.* When you distribute something to other people, you **give** it **out** or **give** it **out** to them. **Hand out** is similar to **give out**.

> They **gave out** free hats to the first 5,000 fans to enter the stadium.
> The aid workers would have **given** more food **out** to the famine victims, but they
>   didn't have enough.

2. give out (on) *p.v.* When a mechanical or electrical device stops working, it **gives out** or **gives out** on you. When a supply of something is completely used, it **gives out** or **gives out** on you.

> The explorers lost their way in the desert and died after their water **gave out**.
> I bought a Chevrolet in 1964 and drove it more than 300,000 miles before it finally
>   **gave out** on me.

gross out	gross out & grosses out	grossing out	grossed out	grossed out

1. gross ... out *p.v.* [informal] When something **grosses** you **out**, it upsets you or makes you sick because you think it is disgusting.

> You had to dissect a cadaver in your biology class? Yuk, that would've really **grossed**
>   me **out**.
> Alex hates changing his little brother's diapers — it **grosses** him **out**.

grossed out *part.adj.* When something upsets you or makes you sick because you think it is disgusting, you are **grossed out**.

> I was eating an apple, and I found half a worm in it. I was so **grossed out** that I
>   almost threw up.

head toward	head toward & heads toward	heading toward	headed toward	headed toward

1. head toward *p.v.* When you **head toward** a certain location, you move toward it. When you say that you are **headed toward** or are **heading toward** a certain location, you mean that you are planning to go there or that you are going there but have interrupted your journey and will resume it. **Head for** is the same as **head toward**.

> The escaped convicts must have **headed toward** Mexico.
> I'm **heading toward** Portland. Where are you going?

run up	run up & runs up	running up	ran up	run up

1. run up (to) *p.v.* When you run to a higher level or place, you **run up** or **run up** to that place.

> **Run up** and answer the phone if it rings, okay?
> If I'd heard the baby crying, I would have **run up** to his bedroom.

2. run . . . up *p.v.* When you accumulate a number of debts, resulting in a total debt of a certain amount, you **run up** a bill for that amount.

> *Giving my son a credit card was a mistake — he **ran up** a $2,500 bill in only one month.*
> *Calling your family every week from Australia must have **run** a big phone bill **up**.*

run-up *n.* A large, sudden increase in the price, value, or cost of something is a **run-up**.

> *Bill was lucky to buy 500 shares of the stock just before the big **run-up**.*

3. run up (to) *p.v.* When you run toward people, you **run up** or **run up** to them.

> *The prince didn't have any bodyguards. Anyone could have **run up** and attacked him.*
> *After the explosion, a man covered with blood **ran up** to me and asked for help.*

Infinitive

present tense	-ing form	past tense	past participle
shut up			
shut up & shuts up	shutting up	shut up	shut up

1. shut up (about) *p.v. [informal]* When people stop talking, they **shut up** or **shut up** about something they are talking about. When you are angry and want people to stop talking, you tell them to **shut up**.

> *Marvin talks and talks and talks — he never **shuts up**.*
> *I said I was sorry about crashing your car. Now will you please **shut up** about it!*

2. shut . . . up *p.v. [informal]* When people or things cause you to stop talking, they **shut** you **up**.

> *Todd was making jokes about his wife at the party until she gave him a look that **shut** him right **up**.*
> *I can't hear the TV — can you **shut** those kids **up**?*

stop off			
stop off & stops off	stopping off	stopped off	stopped off

1. stop off (at/in) *p.v.* When you **stop off** at a place or **stop off** in an area on the way to another place, you stop there briefly before continuing your journey.

> *I would have **stopped off** at Sally's house this morning, but I was late for work.*
> ***Stopping off** in Cairo on our way to India would be fun.*

try on			
try on & tries on	trying on	tried on	tried on

1. try . . . on *p.v.* When you **try on** an item of clothing before deciding whether you will buy it or borrow it from someone in order to see if it fits or to see if you like it, you **try** it **on**.

> *She must have **tried on** twenty pairs of shoes before making up her mind.*
> *Would you like to borrow this dress for the dance tonight? Here, **try** it **on**.*

EXERCISE 43a — Complete the sentences with phrasal verbs from this section. Be sure the phrasal verbs are in the correct tense.

1. I got into Atlanta last night, and tomorrow I'm going to _____ _____ Miami.

2. I should've _____ this sweater _____ before I bought it. It's too small, and now I have to return it.

3. Nicole figured out why all the lights were off: a fuse _____ _____.

4. Sam couldn't have finished the marathon; his strength completely _____ _____.

5. It's a good thing Linda has health insurance; she has _____ _____ a huge bill at the hospital.

6. When the gas exploded, all the doors and windows _____ _____.

7. Marsha's always bragging about how smart she is and teasing me about my bad grades, but when I got 100 on the algebra test and she got 52, it really _____ her _____.

8. We're not flying directly to Japan; we're going to _____ _____ in Hawaii for a few days.

9. Hank's bad breath _____ everyone _____.

10. _____ _____! I'm tired of listening to your constant criticism.

11. I was so excited to see Karen after so many years that I _____ _____ to her and gave her a big hug.

12. This gas stove isn't working. I think the pilot light may have _____ _____ when you opened the window.

13. Job applications were _____ _____ to everyone standing in line.

14. When I saw smoke coming from the third floor window, I _____ _____ to look for the fire.

EXERCISE 43b — Complete the sentences with the correct second particles.

1. The flight attendant was *blown out* _____ the hole in the airplane's fuselage.

2. Free samples will be *given out* _____ every customer who walks through the door.

3. His diseased heart finally *gave out* _____ him.

4. I was so angry that when I saw him I *ran up* _____ him and hit him.

5. George and Tom might have *stopped off* _____ New York.

6. Maybe they *stopped off* _____ Jim's house in the suburbs.

EXERCISE 43c **Write three sentences using the objects in parentheses. Be sure to put the objects in the right place.**

1. The wind *blew out*. (the candle, it)

_____

_____

_____

2. They *gave out*. (information, it)

_____

_____

_____

3. She *ran up*. (a $4,000 bill, it)

_____

_____

_____

4. Can I *try on*? (these pants, these)

_____

_____

_____

5. The smell *grossed out*. (everyone, them)

_____

_____

_____

EXERCISE 43d — **Write answers to the questions using phrasal verbs, participle adjectives, and nouns from this section. Be sure the phrasal verbs are in the correct tense.**

1. Rosa bought a coat, but it's too small. What should Rosa have done?

2. Your car's transmission finally stopped working after several days of problems. What did your car's transmission do?

3. The price of gold increased a lot very quickly. What would you call this increase in the price of gold?

4. Todd didn't know that the taco he ate at Miguel's house was made with cow brains. When Miguel told Todd what he had eaten, what must that have done to Todd?

5. In Question 4, how must Todd have been?

6. The children ran toward Betty very quickly. What did the children do?

7. The truck driver wouldn't have traveled toward Detroit. What wouldn't the truck driver have done?

8. Janice used her breath to stop the kerosene lamp from burning. What did Janice do?

9. Stopping Marvin from talking is nearly impossible. What is impossible?

10. Sally asked her brother how he could have accumulated such a large credit card bill. What did Sally ask her brother?

11. David stayed for a couple of nights in Denver before continuing to Las Vegas. What did David do?

12. My tire burst while I was driving. What did I have?

EXERCISE 43e, Review — **Complete the sentences with these participle adjectives from previous sections. To check their meanings, review the section number given after each one.**

broken in, 41	crossed off, 39	plugged in, 41
checked in, 41	filled up, 39	put off, 31
checked out, 41	leftover, 37	rundown, 36
chopped up, 39	let down, 37	sold out, 39
covered up, 37	paid off, 37	straightened out, 39

1. If you're hungry, there's some _____ pizza in the refrigerator.

2. This meat isn't _____ _____ enough; the pieces are too big.

3. That food isn't _____ _____; flies are going to land on it.

4. Someday John wants to move from this _____ neighborhood to a better one.

5. My feet really hurt because these shoes aren't _____ _____ yet.

6. My car loan is _____ _____; I made my final payment last month.

7. After forty-five years with the company, I thought they would give me more than this cheap pen at my retirement party. I feel _____ _____.

8. There aren't eight names on the list; there are only five — three are _____ _____.

9. We're _____ _____ now; we can take our luggage up to our hotel room.

10. We can get a taxi for the airport now; we're _____ _____.

11. The game isn't _____ _____; there are plenty of tickets left.

12. No wonder this radio doesn't work — it's not _____ _____.

13. The tank isn't _____ _____ yet; there's room for another gallon or two.

14. Is everything _____ _____, or do I need to explain it again?

15. Why are you so _____ _____? Did I say something that offended you?

EXERCISE 43f, Review — **Complete the sentences with these phrasal verbs from previous sections. Be sure the phrasal verbs are in the correct tense. To check their meanings, review the section number given after each one.**

burst out, 40	go in/into, 41	keep from, 38	keep up, 38
come back, 40	keep at, 38	keep off, 38	sneak in/into, 41
get back, 42	keep away, 38	keep on, 38	sneak out of, 41
get behind, 42	keep down, 38	keep to, 38	wipe out, 39

1. Susie _____ _____ the kitchen and took a cookie when her mother wasn't looking.

2. When I was a teenager, I used to _____ _____ of the house and meet my friends after my parents went to bed.

3. I just shampooed the carpet in the living room, so _____ _____ it.

4. I need to see my physical therapist. That pain I used to have in my knee is _____ _____.

5. Do you have a bigger envelope? This letter won't _____ _____ this small one.

6. Betty asked the bus driver to stop, but he didn't hear her and _____ right _____ going.

7. Maria leaves for work at 7:00 in the morning, and she doesn't usually _____ _____ to her house until after 8:00 in the evening.

8. Jim has _____ way _____ in his studies because he's been in the hospital for several weeks.

9. Marvin was acting like such an idiot when he was angry that I couldn't _____ _____ laughing.

10. Don't give up now — _____ _____ it!

11. It was hard to _____ my magazine article _____ only 2,000 words — there was so much I wanted to say.

12. Mike _____ _____ crying when his wife told him she wanted a divorce.

13. I try to take notes in my history class, but the teacher talks so fast that I can't _____ _____.

14. The enemy soldiers were almost completely _____ _____ in the attack.

15. That dog of yours is dangerous, so please _____ it _____ from my children.

16. The candy company has _____ the cost of its products _____ despite the rise in the cost of sugar.

44. FOCUS ON: **participle adjectives and passive phrasal verbs with the verb *get***

It is important to understand two different but related uses of *get* in forming the passive voice.

get + adjectives: *get = become*

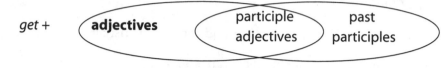

It is very common in English to use *get* followed by an adjective. This is not the passive. In this case *get* is similar to *become*:

> She <u>got</u> sick yesterday.
> She <u>became</u> sick yesterday.

get + past participles: a form of the passive

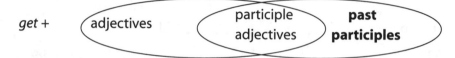

It is also very common to use *get* in place of *be* to form the passive voice. The construction is the same; *get* is followed by the past participle:

> Judy <u>got</u> **kicked out** of school.
> Judy <u>was</u> **kicked out** of school.

There is a difference, however, between the passive formed with *be* and the passive formed with *get*: When the passive is formed with *get*, there is often (but not always) a suggestion that the subject of the sentence was somehow responsible or partially responsible for what happened:

> Judy <u>got</u> **kicked out** of school.

A person hearing the sentence above might think that perhaps Judy did something wrong that resulted in her getting **kicked out** of school. Sometimes, to leave no doubt that the subject is responsible for what happened, a reflexive pronoun is used:

> Judy got <u>herself</u> **kicked out** of school.

get + participle adjectives: adjective or passive?

As we have seen, in English the past participles of many verbs are used as adjectives. When *get* is followed by a past participle, it is not always clear whether the sentence is passive or whether the past participle is functioning as an adjective:

*I <u>got</u> **mixed up** last week.*
*I <u>became</u> **mixed up** last week.*

In the examples above, we can see that the past participle is clearly functioning as an adjective since *get* can be replaced with *become*, but notice that the sentence can also pass the *by* test (discussed in Section 13), which indicates that it is passive:

*I <u>got</u> **mixed up** <u>by</u> <u>all</u> <u>the</u> <u>confusing</u> <u>road</u> <u>signs</u> last week.*

Again, we see how closely related adjectives and past participles are in English and how it is not always easy to distinguish between the two. Fortunately, it is not usually very important. What is important is to be comfortable using past participles as adjectives, and the key to doing so is *not* to understand the difference between true adjectives derived from past participles and past participles with an adjective function but instead to understand that there often is no difference.

Infinitive

	present tense	-ing form	past tense	past participle
beat up	beat up & beats up	beating up	beat up	beaten up

1. beat . . . up *p.v.* *[informal]* When you **beat** people **up**, you hit them or kick them repeatedly.

*The muggers stole my money and then **beat** me **up**.*
*Timmy got **beaten up** at school today.*

beat-up *part.adj.* When something is in bad condition because of heavy use, it is **beat-up**.

*My car is an old, **beat-up** piece of junk.*

carry away				carried away

1. carry away (with) *p.v.* *[always passive]* When you get **carried away** or **carried away** with something, you do more than is necessary or proper because you enjoy it or because you think it is important.

*I was going to make a dozen cupcakes for desert tonight, but I got **carried away** and ended up making forty.*
*You should always start a new exercise program slowly. If you get **carried away** with it, you might hurt yourself.*

kick out	kick out & kicks out	kicked out	kicking out	kicking out

1. kick . . . out (of) *p.v.* When you **kick** people **out** or **kick** people **out** of a group, place, building, room, and so on, you order them to leave. **Throw out** is similar to **kick out**.

*David drank too much and got himself **kicked out** of the bar.*
Bob's in our car pool, but he's always arguing with the other guys about something,
    *so we're going to **kick** him **out**.*

Infinitive

present tense	-ing form	past tense	past participle
lock up			
lock up & locks up	locking up	locked up	locked up

1. lock ... up *p.v.* When you lock all the doors and windows of a building, you **lock** it **up**.

> *The manager always **locks up** before he goes home.*
> *We **locked** our house **up** before we went on vacation.*

locked up *part.adj.* After all the doors and windows of a building have been locked, it is **locked up**.

> *You can't get in the house — it's **locked up**.*

2. lock ... up *p.v.* When you **lock** people **up**, you put them in prison.

> *The police **locked** Hank **up** after they caught him shoplifting.*
> *Whoever committed that terrible crime ought to be **locked up** forever.*

locked up *part.adj.* Someone who has been put in prison is **locked up**.

> *Being **locked up** in jail was a terrible experience.*

lockup *n.* A prison or other place where people are **locked up** is a **lockup**.

> *Omar was put in the **lockup** after he was arrested for drunken driving.*

mix up			
mix up & mixes up	mixing up	mixed up	mixed up

1. mix ... up *p.v.* When you **mix** something **up** that has two or more ingredients, you stir it so that the ingredients will be thoroughly combined.

> *Put in the eggs, butter, sugar, flour, and water and then **mix** it **up** well.*
> *An electric mixer will **mix up** the ingredients better than a hand mixer.*

2. mix ... up *p.v.* When you **mix** two things **up**, you confuse them with each other.

> *Jerry and his twin brother look exactly the same, and everyone **mixes** them **up**.*
> *Newborn babies sometimes get **mixed up** in the hospital.*

mixed up *part.adj.* When you are confused about something that you want to understand, or when you have emotional or behavioral problems, you are **mixed up**.

> *Can you help me with my calculus homework? I'm really **mixed up**.*
> *Jimmy is a **mixed-up** kid who gets in trouble with the police a lot.*

mix-up *n.* A mistake, misunderstanding, or confused situation is a **mix-up**.

> *Waiter, I think there's been a **mix-up**. I asked you for a chicken salad sandwich, but*
>   *you brought me a tuna salad sandwich.*

Infinitive

present tense	-ing form	past tense	past participle
piss off			
piss off & pisses off	pissing off	pissed off	pissed off

1. piss . . . off *p.v.* [informal and offensive to some people] When you make people angry, you **piss** them **off**.

*You'd better stop that! You're **pissing** me **off**.*
*Don't make a lot of noise when Mark is trying to study; it **pisses** him **off**.*

pissed off *part.adj.* When you are angry, you are **pissed off**.

*Melanie got really **pissed off** at Heather for borrowing her necklace without asking and then losing it.*

rip off			
rip off & rips off	ripping off	ripped off	ripped off

1. rip . . . off *p.v.* [informal] When you **rip** people **off**, you steal something from them, cheat them, or charge them more money for something than it is worth.

*Don't do business with Marvin; he **rips** everyone **off**.*
*Hank got **ripped off** by the drug dealer.*

rip-off *n.* When someone steals something from you, cheats you, or charges too much for something, this is a **rip-off**.

*I paid nine dollars to see that awful movie? What a **rip-off**!*

stress out			
stress out & stresses out	stressing out	stressed out	stressed out

1. stress . . . out *p.v.* [informal] When people or things **stress** you **out**, they make you worried, nervous, or tense.

*Having that new manager around watching me all the time is **stressing** me **out**.*
*Sally's sister has to take care of quadruplets all day without any help. That must **stress** her **out**.*

stressed-out *part.adj.* When you are worried, nervous, or tense, you are **stressed-out**.

*I had to make a speech at work today, and I was so **stressed-out** afterward that I took the rest of the day off.*

EXERCISE 44a — **Complete the sentences with phrasal verbs from this section. Be sure the phrasal verbs are in the correct tense.**

1. The prison guard put Jake in a cell and _____ him _____.

2. Tom asked the barber to just cut his hair a little bit, but when he looked in the mirror, he could

   see that the barber was getting _____ _____ and cutting his hair too short.

3. Erik promised me that he would come to my house to help me move some stuff this morning, but he still hasn't shown up. He's always doing things like that, and it really _____ me _____.

4. If Janice doesn't pass her chemistry test tomorrow, she won't graduate with the rest of her class, and worrying about it so much is really _____ her _____.

5. I got _____ _____ of school after I got caught cheating on the test.

6. The robbers _____ _____ the shop owner so badly that she had to be hospitalized.

7. Add a cup of water and four eggs to the cake mix and _____ it _____ well.

8. The night manager forgot to _____ _____ when she left the restaurant.

9. The jewelry store _____ me _____; I paid $5,000 for a diamond ring made of glass.

10. The teacher has two students with the same name, and she always _____ them _____.

EXERCISE 44b — **Write three sentences using the objects in parentheses. Be sure to put the objects in the right place.**

1. The thugs *beat up*. (the woman, her)

_____

_____

_____

2. The hotel manager *kicked out*. (the rock group, them)

_____

_____

_____

3. The cops are going to *lock up*. (the crook, her)

_____

_____

_____

4. *Mixing up* is easy. (the twins, them)

_____

_____

_____

5. Getting a tattoo must have *pissed off*. (your father, him)

_____

_____

_____

6. The contractor was accused of *ripping off*. (homeowners, them)

_____

_____

_____

7. All these problems are *stressing out*. (the staff, them)

_____

_____

_____

EXERCISE 44c — **Write answers to the questions using phrasal verbs, participle adjectives, and nouns from this section. Be sure the phrasal verbs are in the correct tense.**

1. Tom paid a mechanic to replace his car's generator with a new one, but the mechanic put a used generator in and still charged Tom for a new one. What did the mechanic do to Tom?

2. In Question 1, what would you call what the mechanic did to Tom?

3. If they don't stop making so much noise, the manager is going to tell them to leave. What is the manager going to do?

4. You locked all the doors and windows in your house. What did you do?

5. In Question 4, how would you describe your house after you locked all the doors and windows?

6. Many cars look the same these days, and it's hard to tell them apart. If it is hard to tell them apart, what is it easy to do?

7. Scratching my brother's new car really made him angry. What did scratching my brother's new car do to my brother?

8. In Question 7, how would you describe my brother?

9. Linda is very confused about how to use her computer. How would you describe Linda?

10. Driving in all this traffic is making you nervous and tense. What is driving in all this traffic doing to you?

11. In Question 10, how would you describe yourself?

12. I let Charles use my skis, and when he returned them, they were in very bad condition. How were my skis when Charles returned them?

13. Sam's father was sent to prison for bank robbery. What happened to Sam's father?

14. In Question 13, how would you describe Sam's father?

15. Karen went to the store planning to buy a pair of shoes, but she ended up buying five pairs of shoes, three dresses, four blouses, and a new winter coat. What happened to Karen?

16. When the angry people caught the thief, they hit and kicked him again and again. What did the angry crowd do?

17. When you put all the ingredients in, you have to stir them so they will be combined. What do you have to do?

EXERCISE 44d, Review — **Complete the sentences with these phrasal verbs from previous sections. Be sure the phrasal verbs are in the correct tense. To check their meanings, review the section number given after each one.**

break in/into, 41	keep at, 38	keep off, 38	pay off, 37
bring up, 40	keep away, 38	keep on, 38	put up to, 34
cover up, 37	keep down, 38	keep to, 38	stick with, 40
help out, 33	keep from, 38	keep up, 38	take over, 39

1. The newspaper story claimed that the governor had taken a bribe and had then tried to

    _____ it _____.

2. That stock I bought really _____ _____. It went up nearly 100 percent in

only three months.

3. After the new manager _____ _____ next month, you can expect a lot of changes.

4. Will you kids _____ it _____, please? I'm on the phone.

5. I told you to stop. If you _____ _____ doing that, I'm going to get pissed off.

6. The police think the burglars may have _____ _____ through the back door.

7. If you kids go outside to play, _____ _____ from that pile of junk — it's full of broken glass.

8. I need to talk to Jerry about his bad breath, but I'm nervous about _____ it _____.

9. Dan is so sad about what happened that he can't _____ _____ crying.

10. When I went to the car rental office, they had already rented all the good cars, and they _____ me _____ a beat-up piece of junk.

11. The legislature passed a tough new law designed to _____ drunken drivers _____ the streets.

12. When you're depressed you should talk to people about what's troubling you, not _____ it _____ yourself.

13. I'm broke — do you think you could _____ me _____ till payday?

14. Nothing the inventor tried worked, but he _____ _____ it until he solved the problem.

15. I can't believe that my daughter would steal money from me. That awful boyfriend of hers must have _____ her _____ _____ it.

16. Jane did very well in her first semester of college. I hope she can _____ it _____ for the next four years.

45

45. FOCUS ON: **phrasal verbs with the verb** *turn*

Many phrasal verbs are based on the verb *turn*. In most cases, phrasal verbs with *turn* involve two options and a change from one option to the other or, when it is possible, a move closer to one option and farther away from the other. In other words, choosing either A or B or, when it is possible to be somewhere between A and B, moving closer to A and farther away from B, or vice versa.

Infinitive			
present tense	-ing form	past tense	past participle
turn down			
turn down & turns down	turning down	turned down	turned down

1. turn ... down *p.v.* When you **turn down** an electrical or mechanical device, you change the controls to decrease the level of what it is producing or doing. **Turn up** is the opposite of **turn down**.

> Could you **turn** the radio **down**? I'm trying to sleep.
> If it gets too cold, I'll **turn down** the air conditioner.

2. turn ... down *p.v.* When you deny a request, you **turn down** the request or **turn down** the person who has made the request.

> I asked Nancy to go to the dance with me, but she **turned** me **down**.
> My request for a pay raise was **turned down**.
> Getting **turned down** every time I apply for a job is getting me down.

turn in			
turn in & turns in	turning in	turned in	turned in

1. turn ... in (to) *p.v.* When you inform the police that certain people have committed crimes or tell the police where they are, you **turn** them **in** or **turn** them **in** to the police.

> The escaped prisoner got tired of running and **turned** himself **in**.
> When Jake told me that he had murdered Luis, I knew I had to **turn** him **in** to the police.

2. turn ... in (to) *p.v.* When you return something that was given to you by a person in authority, you **turn** that thing **in** or **turn** it **in** to a person in authority. **Hand in** is similar to **turn in**.

> The police officer was ordered to **turn in** her badge after she was caught taking a bribe.
> The delivery truck drivers have to **turn** their keys **in** to the dispatcher before they go home.

3. turn ... in (to) *p.v.* When you complete a test, report, or project and you give it to the person who assigned the work to you, you **turn** it **in** or **turn** it **in** to the person who assigned the work. **Hand in** is similar to **turn in**.

*Melanie asked her teacher if she could **turn** her project **in** late.*
*I have to finish this report and **turn** it **in** to the sales manager by tomorrow.*

4. turn in *p.v.* When you go to bed, you **turn in**.

*I'm really tired; I'm going to **turn in** early.*
*It's getting late; I'm **turning in**.*

Infinitive

	present tense	-ing form	past tense	past participle
turn into				
	turn into & turns into	**turning into**	**turned into**	**turned into**

1. turn into *p.v.* When something **turns into** something else, it becomes that thing.

*It was cold and rainy this morning, but it **turned into** a nice day.*
*It's amazing that this small seed can **turn into** a huge tree.*

2. turn . . . into *p.v.* When you **turn** something **into** something else, you change it into that thing.

*The Youngs are thinking of **turning** their house in the country **into** a hotel.*
*The children **turned** the big box **into** a playhouse.*

turn off				
	turn off & turns off	**turning off**	**turned off**	**turned off**

1. turn . . . off *p.v.* When you **turn off** an electrical or mechanical device, you change the controls to stop it from producing or doing something. **Turn on** is the opposite of **turn off**. **Switch off** and **shut off** are similar to **turn off**.

*Would you **turn** the light **off**? I want to go to bed.*
*When I'm driving and have to wait for a long freight train to pass, I always **turn** my car **off**.*

turned off *part.adj.* After you have changed the controls of an electrical or mechanical device to stop it from producing or doing something, it is **turned off**. **Turned on** is the opposite of **turned off**. **Switched off** and **shut off** are similar to **turned off**.

*I can't see anything — the lights are **turned off**.*

2. turn . . . off *p.v.* [informal] Something that **turns** you **off** offends you and causes you to lose interest in something or someone. Something about a person of the opposite sex that **turns** you **off** causes you to lose sexual or romantic interest in that person. **Turn on** is the opposite of **turn off**.

*When I met Dan I thought he was a nice guy, but his racist comments **turned** me **off**.*
*I got **turned off** when she lit a cigarette.*

turned off *part.adj.* When something about a person of the opposite sex causes you to lose sexual or romantic interest in that person, you are **turned off**. **Turned on** is the opposite of **turned off**.

*What's wrong with Nicole? She was having a good time with Frank a little while ago, but now she seems kind of **turned off**.*

turnoff *n.* Something that offends you and causes you to lose interest in something or someone is a **turnoff**. Something about a person of the opposite sex that causes you to lose sexual or romantic interest in that person is a **turnoff**. A **turn-on** is the opposite of a **turnoff**.

> *I don't like tattoos. To me they're a real **turnoff**.*

3. turn off *p.v.* When you **turn off** a road or path that you are traveling on, you leave it and start to travel on another road or path. When a road or path leaves another road or path and travels in a different direction, it **turns off**.

> *Be careful you don't **turn off** the main road — you'll get lost.*
> *The path to the cabin **turns off** just after the big tree stump.*

turnoff *n.* A road or path that leaves another road or path and travels in a different direction is a **turnoff**.

> *We're lost — I think we should have taken that **turnoff** we passed a few miles back.*

Infinitive

	present tense	-ing form	past tense	past participle
turn on				
	turn on & turns on	turning on	turned on	turned on

1. turn . . . on *p.v.* When you **turn on** an electrical or mechanical device, you change the controls to make it start producing or doing something. **Turn off** is the opposite of **turn on**. **Switch on** is the same as **turn on**.

> *Can you **turn** the light **on** please? It's dark in here.*
> *This October has been so warm that I haven't **turned** the heat **on** once yet.*

turned on *part.adj.* After you have changed the controls of an electrical or mechanical device to make it start producing or doing something, it is **turned on**. **Turned off** is the opposite of **turned on**. **Switched on** is similar to **turned on**.

> *Be careful of the stove — it's **turned on**.*

2. turn . . . on *p.v.* [informal] Something that **turns** you **on** pleases you and causes you to gain interest in something or someone. Something about a person of the opposite sex that **turns** you **on** causes you to become sexually or romantically interested in that person. **Turn off** is the opposite of **turn on**.

> *When I saw this house from the outside, I didn't think I would buy it, but the beautiful woodwork inside really **turned** me **on**.*
> *Erik's blue eyes **turn on** his wife.*

turned on *part.adj.* When something about a person of the opposite sex causes you to become sexually or romantically interested in that person, you are **turned on**. **Turned off** is the opposite of **turned on**.

> *Paul was really **turned on** after seeing all the beautiful women in the Victoria's Secret catalog.*

turn-on *n.* Something that pleases you and causes you to gain interest in something or someone is a **turn-on**. Something about a person of the opposite sex that causes you to become sexually or romantically interested in that person is a **turn-on**. A **turnoff** is the opposite of a **turn-on**.

> *I bought my wife an ankle bracelet for Valentines Day; I think they're a **turn-on**.*

3. turn on *p.v.* When people or animals that you had good relations with **turn on** you, they stop being friendly and try to hurt you.

> *Lydia used to be my friend, but now she's telling people terrible things about me. I wonder why she **turned on** me like that?*
> *Wild animals don't make good pets. They can be friendly one minute and **turn on** you the next.*

4. turn ... on (to) *p.v.* [*informal*] When you **turn** people **on** to something, you tell them about something you think they will like or something that will help them.

> *Maria **turned** me **on** to a great Colombian restaurant.*
> *This was a good book. Thanks for **turning** me **on** to it.*

Infinitive

present tense	-ing form	past tense	past participle
turn out			
turn out & turns out	turning out	turned out	turned out

1. turn out *p.v.* [*usually followed by "to be" plus an adjective, an infinitive verb plus a noun, or a complete sentence*] When things or people **turn out** to be a certain way, it is discovered or considered that they are that way. When things or people **turn out** to be something, it is discovered or considered that they are that thing. When you say that it **turns out** (that) or **turned out** (that) and then make a statement of fact, you mean that this information, which is contrary to what you believed or expected, was discovered to be true.

> *I didn't think I would like my brother's new wife, but she **turned out** to be very nice.*
> *Before I met Rusty's son, Danny, I assumed he had red hair like his father, but Danny **turned out** to have black hair.*
> *I thought Sam bought a Mercedes-Benz, but it **turns out** that he bought a BMW.*
> *I thought Sam bought a Mercedes-Benz, but it **turned out** that he bought a BMW.*

2. turn out *p.v.* When something **turns out**, it becomes what you want it to become. When something **turns out** a certain way, it becomes that way.

> *Did the pictures you took at the wedding **turn out**?*
> *The pictures **turned out** perfectly.*
> *Your plan was excellent, but it didn't **turn out** well.*

3. turn ... out *p.v.* When people, companies, factories, workshops, and so on, **turn out** something, they manufacture it or produce it.

> *This new factory will **turn out** 50,000 units per year.*
> *High schools in America are **turning out** people who can barely read.*

4. turn out (for) *p.v.* When people **turn out** or **turn out** for an event, they attend or participate in the event. When people **turn out** to do something, they go to a place to do it.

> *Are you nuts? How many people do you think would **turn out** for an outdoor concert in the middle of winter?*
> *Thousands of people **turned out** to see the Pope when he visited.*

turnout *n.* The number of people who attend or participate in an event is the **turnout**.

> *Voter **turnout** for the election was only around 30 percent.*

Infinitive

	present tense	-ing form	past tense	past participle
turn over	turn over & turns over	turning over	turned over	turned over

1. turn ... over *p.v.* When you **turn** something **over**, you move it so that the side that was on the bottom is on the top, and vice versa. When something **turns over**, it moves so that the side that was on the bottom is on the top, and vice versa.

> *When one side of the steak is cooked, **turn** it **over** and cook the other side.*
> *The driver was killed when his car **turned over**.*

2. turn ... over (to) *p.v.* When you give something to someone because that person demands or requires it or because you are not its rightful owner, you **turn** it **over** or **turn** it **over** to that person. **Hand over** is similar to **turn over**.

> *The detective always **turns** the evidence from the crime scene **over** to the lab for analysis.*
> *After the thieves are captured, the stolen items will be **turned over** to the rightful owners.*

3. turn ... over (to) *p.v.* When the police or other authorities are looking for people and you take these people or transfer control of them to the police or authorities, you **turn** them **over** or **turn** them **over** to the police or authorities.

> *I caught a burglar in my basement, and I **turned** him **over** to the police.*
> *The local police chief was relieved to **turn** the terrorist **over** to the FBI.*

4. turn over *p.v.* When employees of a company leave their jobs and are replaced by new employees, they **turn over**.

> *Conditions at the factory were so bad that employees **turned over** at a high rate.*
> *We have a very stable work force in our plant. Employees **turn over** very slowly.*

turnover *n.* The rate at which employees of a company leave and are replaced by new employees is the **turnover**.

> *The new personnel manager said her top priority would be reducing the high turnover.*

5. turn over *p.v.* When a business **turns over** something that it sells, it continually sells it and replaces it with new merchandise.

> We're **turning over** forty cases of bananas a week in this supermarket.
> Snowmobiles and skis **turn over** very slowly in the summer.

turnover *n.* How much money a business has made in a certain time period is its **turnover**.

> The company's annual **turnover** increased by 36 percent compared to the
>   previous year.

Infinitive

present tense	-ing form	past tense	past participle
turn up			
turn up & turns up	turning up	turned up	turned up

1. turn ... up *p.v.* When you **turn up** an electrical or mechanical device, you change the controls to increase the level of what it is producing or doing. **Turn down** is the opposite of **turn up**.

> Will you **turn up** the TV? I can't hear it.
> It was freezing in here last night, so I **turned up** the heat.

2. turn ... up *p.v.* When you **turn up** something, you find it or learn of it as a result of an investigation or search. When something **turns up**, it is found or is learned of as a result of an investigation or search.

> The police **turned up** enough evidence to convict Jake of murder.
> Despite a thorough search, the murder weapon still hasn't **turned up**.

3. turn up *p.v.* When people or things **turn up** at a place, they appear there. **Show up** is similar to **turn up**.

> It's hard to plan a picnic when I don't know how many people will **turn up**.
> Every few years my worthless brother **turns up** at my door asking for money.

EXERCISE 45a — **Complete the sentences with phrasal verbs from this section. Be sure the phrasal verbs are in the correct tense.**

1. I thought going camping would be a lot of fun, but it sure didn't _____

   _____ that way.

2. It's 2:30 in the morning — don't you think you ought to _____ _____ soon?

3. Heather was sort of interested in Tom, but his childish behavior _____ her _____.

4. The store manager said that she usually _____ _____ only twenty or twenty-five units

   per month.

5. Jake thought Hank was his best friend, but Hank _____ _____ Jake and now they're enemies.

6. All the medical students must _____ their lab equipment _____ before leaving the lab.

7. Any spies caught behind enemy lines will be _____ _____ to the military for questioning.

8. The investigation _____ _____ evidence of corruption in City Hall.

9. This old house looks pretty bad now, but with enough time and money, you could _____ it _____ something really nice.

10. I want to watch TV; please _____ it _____.

11. The volume is too low; please _____ it _____.

12. Now the volume is too high; please _____ it _____.

13. There's nothing good on TV; please _____ it _____.

14. The first thing I noticed when I met my wife for the first time was her beautiful smile; it really _____ me _____.

15. Employees _____ _____ at a very high rate in this industry.

16. Not many people are likely to _____ _____ for the parade in this miserable weather.

17. The boy was given a reward for _____ _____ the bag of money that he found in the street.

18. To get to Uncle John's house, you have to _____ _____ the main road after you cross the bridge and drive north for three miles.

19. Mark knows a lot about wine. He's _____ me _____ to some excellent wines from California.

20. My supervisor _____ _____ my request to be transferred to San Diego.

21. The first few chapters of this novel were a little boring, but now that I'm near the end, it's _____ _____ to be a pretty good book.

22. Please _____ the carpet _____. I want to read the label on the back.

23. A huge crowd is expected to _____ _____ at the airport to welcome the

    returning Stanley Cup champions.

24. This company has been _____ _____ first-rate merchandise for a hundred

    years.

25. I told the teacher that I'd been in the hospital and wouldn't be able to _____

    _____ my project on time.

26. We've had one problem after another — this is _____ _____ to be a

    bad day.

27. When Jake told his mother that he had murdered someone, she told him he had to

    _____ himself _____.

EXERCISE 45b — **Write answers to the questions using phrasal verbs, participle adjectives, and nouns from this section. Be sure the phrasal verbs are in the correct tense.**

1. Caterpillars become butterflies. What do caterpillars do?

2. Dan appeared at his uncle's funeral. What did Dan do?

3. Frank was thinking of asking Jane for a date, but when he saw her smoking one cigarette after another, he changed his mind. What did Jane's smoking do to Frank?

4. In Question 3, what does Frank think smoking is?

5. In Question 3, how did Frank feel when he saw Jane smoking?

6. Whenever my wife wears my favorite perfume, I feel romantic. What does the perfume do to me?

7. In Question 6, what do I think the perfume is?

8. In Question 6, how do I feel whenever my wife wears my favorite perfume?

9. You're changing the controls of the heater to make it warmer. What are you doing?

10. The rate at which old employees are replaced with new employees in my company is very low. What is very low at my company?

11. This factory manufactures 25,000 cars every year. What does the factory do?

12. Nicole didn't change the controls of her radio to make it louder. What didn't Nicole do?

13. The detective asked every bank employee a lot of questions about the missing money, but she hasn't discovered anything. What hasn't the detective done?

14. After the gas station went out of business, it was bought and changed into a Chinese restaurant. What happened to the gas station?

15. Sally wanted to dye her hair red, but it became orange. What did Sally's hair do?

16. Karen's father asked her if he could borrow enough money to pay his property taxes, and Karen couldn't say no to him. What couldn't Karen do?

17. Todd's company will probably make $4 million this year. What will Todd's company probably do this year?

18. Ned hasn't given his paper to his teacher. What hasn't Ned done?

19. Lydia knows that her brother robbed a bank, but she's not going to tell the police. What isn't Lydia going to do to her brother?

20. So many people attended the political rally that there wasn't enough room in the auditorium. Why wasn't there enough room at the political rally?

21. In Question 20, the number of people who attended the rally was large. What was large?

22. David was too lazy to wash the rug, so he put the dirty side on the bottom and the clean side on the top. What did David do to the rug?

EXERCISE 45c — **Write eight original sentences using phrasal verbs from this section.**

1. _____

2. _____

3. _____

4. _____

5. _____

6. _____

7. _____

8. _____

EXERCISE 45d, Review — **Complete the sentences with these phrasal verbs from previous sections. Be sure the phrasal verbs are in the correct tense. To check their meanings, review the section number given after each one.**

beat up, 44	get by, 42	get over, 42	lock up, 44
carry away, 44	get down, 42	get up, 42	run up, 43
get back, 42	get in/into, 42	gross out, 43	stop off, 43
get behind, 42	get out, 42	head toward, 43	try on, 43

1. I lost a very expensive gold watch, and I'll be very surprised if I ever _____ it _____.

2. I had dinner with some friends, and we _____ _____ a $500 tab.

3. Have you _____ _____ to see your parents in Alaska lately?

4. I should have _____ these pants _____ before buying them — they're too small.

5. Carlos was hitting his brother Alex, so Alex said to Carlos, "_____ _____ of here!"

6. I called my brother in Miami and told him that I was leaving Boston at 8:40 in the morning and that I should _____ _____ there around 1:00 in the afternoon.

7. I wish you'd chew with your mouth closed — you're _____ me _____.

8. Our flight won't _____ _____ Santa Fe until after midnight.

9. After I leave Texas, I'm going to _____ _____ Mississippi.

10. Karen's expecting me for dinner tonight at her house way out in the suburbs, but my car is in the shop. I don't know how I'm going to _____ _____ there.

11. The night manager has to leave early tonight, so I'm going to _____ _____ for him.

12. Hank had a fight with a guy in a bar and got _____ _____ pretty badly.

13. I had a bad day at work, so I _____ _____ at a bar for a drink before going home.

14. Sofia is having a lot of trouble in her history class and is _____ further and further _____.

15. After her husband died, she had a hard time _____ _____ it.

16. You can use my credit card to buy a few things, but don't get _____ _____.

46. FOCUS ON: pronunciation of phrasal verbs with the particle *into*

As we saw in Section 6, three-word phrasal verbs are normally accented on the second, or middle, particle whether they are separable or nonseparable. This also applies to phrasal verbs that convert *in* to *into* when they are used with an object. Although these verbs are not made up of three words, recall that *into* is actually a combination of the particles *in* and *to* — two words written as one. For this reason, it is the first syllable of *into* that is accented:

> *The speakers are **built INto** the wall.*

This is also true of phrasal verbs using *into* that do not have an *in* version:

> *I **bumped INto** an old friend.*

Infinitive

	present tense	-ing form	past tense	past participle
build in	build in & builds in	building in	built in	built in

1. build ... in/into *p.v.* When you **build** something **in** or **build** something **into** something else, you put it in the item you are making during its construction or assembly rather than adding it later.

> *I told the builder that I wanted him to **build** some shelves **in**.*
> *In the past, FM radios weren't **built into** cars — you had to add one later if you wanted one.*

built-in *part.adj.* When something has been put into something else during its construction or assembly, rather than being added later, it is **built-in**.

> *The sound from the stereo goes to **built-in** speakers in every room of the house.*

bump into				
	bump into & bumps into	bumping into	bumped into	bumped into

1. bump into *p.v.* When you **bump into** things or people, you accidentally hit them with your body.

> *I couldn't see where I was going in the dark, and I **bumped into** the door.*
> *Would you please move these boxes — I keep **bumping into** them.*

2. bump into *p.v.* When you meet people unexpectedly or unintentionally, you **bump into** them. **Run into** is the same as **bump into**.

> *We **bumped into** Sarah at the mall today.*
> ***Bumping into** one of my neighbors while I was in Rome sure was a surprise.*

Infinitive

	present tense	-ing form	past tense	past participle
con into	con into & cons into	conning into	conned into	conned into

1. con . . . into *p.v.* [informal] When you **con** people **into** something or **con** people **into** doing something, you persuade them to do it by fooling or deceiving them. **Trick into** is similar to **con into**.

> They weren't sure that it was a good idea to give all their money to Marvin, but he **conned** them **into** it.
> That crooked mechanic tried to **con** me **into** paying for a lot of repairs my car didn't need.

con out of	con out of & cons out of	conning out of	conned out of	conned out of

1. con . . . out of *p.v.* [informal] When you **con** people **out of** something, you persuade them to give it to you by fooling or deceiving them.

> Marvin **conned** them **out of** their life savings.
> That crooked mechanic tried to **con** me **out of** $547.

freak out	freak out & freaks out	freaking out	freaked out	freaked out

1. freak . . . out *p.v.* [informal] When you **freak out**, you become very upset or very angry. When you **freak** other people **out**, you cause them to become very upset or very angry.

> Melanie **freaked out** when she learned that her husband had been arrested for murder.
> I wish you would take that Halloween mask off — you're **freaking** me **out**.

make for	make for & makes for	making for	made for	made for

1. make for *p.v.* When something causes another thing, situation, or event to have a certain quality or characteristic, it **makes for** the other thing, situation, or event.

> Beer, pizza, football, and the kids staying with their grandparents **make for** a perfect Sunday afternoon.
> Alcohol and teenage drivers **make for** trouble.

2. make for *p.v.* [informal] When you **make for** a place, you go there in a hurry.

> After the robbery, the bank robbers **made for** the border.
> The enemy soldiers are getting closer — let's **make for** the hills.

talk into	talk into & talks into	talking into	talked into	talked into

1. talk . . . into *p.v.* When you **talk** people **into** something or **talk** people **into** doing something, you persuade them to do it.

46

*My father didn't want to let me use his car Friday night, but I **talked** him **into** it.*

*This museum is really boring. I wish I hadn't let you **talk** me **into** coming here with you.*

talk out of

talk out of & talks out of	talking out of	talked out of	talked out of

1. talk ... out of *p.v.* When you **talk** people **out of** something or **talk** people **out of** doing something, you persuade them not to do it.

*That man was going to jump off the building, but the police officer **talked** him **out of** it.*

*Erik's parents **talked** him **out of** changing his major from business to philosophy.*

EXERCISE 46a — **Complete the sentences with phrasal verbs from this section. Be sure the phrasal verbs are in the correct tense.**

1. My daughter is trying to _____ me _____ getting her a pony, but I keep telling her we can't afford one.

2. When I ordered my computer, I had them _____ _____ some extra memory.

3. It was a nice surprise to _____ _____ Aunt Kathy today. I hadn't seen her in years.

4. Don't tell your mother you're going to shave your head — she'll _____ _____.

5. Joe says he's going to quit school, and we can't _____ him _____ _____ it.

6. Their sleazy son-in-law _____ them _____ lending him $14,000.

7. It was so dark last night that I _____ _____ a tree and broke my nose.

8. Nancy and Tom don't have anything in common — that doesn't _____ _____ a happy marriage.

9. Don't trust Marvin — he'll _____ you _____ _____ your last penny.

10. When the enemy soldiers attacked, we _____ _____ the woods.

EXERCISE 46b — **Write answers to the questions using phrasal verbs and participle adjectives from this section. Be sure the phrasal verbs are in the correct tense.**

1. Karen is trying to persuade me to help her paint her house. What is Karen trying to do?

2. Francisco unexpectedly met Raul downtown a couple of days ago. What did Francisco do?

3. That lawyer is lying to you and trying to persuade you to give him everything you own. What is the lawyer trying to do?

4. Having both of my ex-wives at the party will make the evening very uncomfortable. What will having both of my ex-wives at the party do?

5. That dishonest guy deceived my Aunt Kathy to get her to sell her house for a lot less than it's worth. What did the dishonest guy do to my Aunt Kathy?

6. Carmen is upset and very nervous because she can't find her children at the shopping center. What is Carmen doing?

7. When my house was constructed, a shelf for a TV was made in the wall. What was done to the wall?

8. In Question 7, how would you describe the shelf?

9. Bob has decided to quit his job, and no one can persuade him not to. What can no one do to Bob?

EXERCISE 46c — **Write eight original sentences using phrasal verbs from this section.**

1. _____

2. _____

3. _____

4. _____

5. _____

6. _____

7. _____

8. _____

EXERCISE 46d, Review — **Complete the sentences with these nouns from previous sections. To check their meanings, review the section number given after each one.**

blowout, 43	checkout, 41	mix-up, 44	takeover, 39
break-in, 41	comeback, 40	pickup, 39	wipeout, 39
check-in, 41	lockup, 44	run-up, 43	

1. The guy that got arrested didn't have enough money for bail, so he was put in the

   _____.

2. The baseball player had a few bad years, but last year he made an amazing

   _____ and had his best year ever.

3. Not one person was left alive after the battle — it was a complete _____.

4. _____ is two hours before the flight.

5. The hotel's _____ time is 11:00 A.M.

6. There was a tragic _____ at the hospital — a patient's healthy left kidney was

   removed instead of his diseased right kidney.

7. The detective asked the store owner for a complete list of items stolen during the

   _____.

8. Is this a _____ or a delivery?

9. After the military _____, hundreds of people were executed.

10. Unfortunately, I sold my house before the big _____ in real estate prices.

11. The truck driver was killed in an accident after she had a _____ on the highway.

EXERCISE 46e, Review — **Complete the sentences with these phrasal verbs from previous sections. Be sure the phrasal verbs are in the correct tense. To check their meanings, review the section number given after each one.**

blow off, 40	give out, 43	lock up, 44	stick with, 40
bring up, 40	go away, 40	piss off, 44	stress out, 44
burst out, 40	kick out, 44	shut up, 43	turn in, 45
get by, 42	let in/into, 41	stand for, 34	turn into, 45

1. Sooner or later he'll get tired of running from the police, and he'll _____ himself

   _____.

2. I _____ my children _____ to be honest.

3. When we leave our summer home to go back to the city, we always _____ it _____ securely.

4. I took three aspirin, but this headache still hasn't _____ _____.

5. Do you know what "Ph.D." _____ _____?

6. I usually check my work pretty carefully. I don't know how this mistake _____ _____ me.

7. Worrying about how I'm going to find the money to pay my taxes is really _____ me _____.

8. I'm tired of listening to my brother talk about winning four million dollars in the lottery. I wish he would just _____ _____.

9. Those new computers are really fast, but I'm going to _____ _____ the one I have; it's fine for writing letters.

10. The tennis player had to retire when his elbow _____ _____.

11. I'm going to talk to my husband about _____ the garage _____ an apartment for my mother.

12. Joe promised that he'd help me fix my car yesterday, but he never came; he just _____ me _____.

13. Joe does that sort of thing all the time, and it's very rude. He really _____ me _____.

14. The door was locked, so I knocked on it again and again until someone _____ me _____.

15. What did Nancy do to get herself _____ _____ of school?

16. When I heard about the crazy thing that Nancy had done at school, I _____ _____ laughing.

47. FOCUS ON: particles used without verbs

The particles of many phrasal verbs, especially phrasal verbs that relate to physical movement, are frequently used alone with a form of *be*. This is very common in conversation when the verb has already been stated at least once and does not need to be repeated:

> Customer: *Have you **run out** of coffee?*
> Store clerk: *We're **out** of regular coffee, but we're not **out** of instant.*

> Marsha: *When do you have to **move out** of your apartment?*
> Nancy: *I have to be **out** by next Wednesday.*

> Jim: *Did you **turn** the air conditioner **on**?*
> Bob: *No, it was **on** when I came in.*

> Mother: *Has your sister **woken up** yet?*
> Susie: *No, she's still not **up**.*

Using the particle without a verb is also common when a phrasal verb can be understood from the context. Sometimes, only one verb is obvious:

> Raul: *Are you **through**?*
> Todd: *No, I won't be **through** until after 4:00.*

If this conversation occurred at a place of employment, the phrasal verb could only be **get through**. But often, in a particular situation, more than one verb might be understood, but to the speakers it is not important or necessary to be specific about which one:

> Carlos: *Is Karen **in**?*
> Paul: *No. she isn't.*

If this conversation occurred in an office building, several verbs might be understood: **come in**, **go in**, **get in**, (be) **let in**.

Infinitive

	present tense	-ing form	past tense	past participle
brush up				
	brush up & brushes up	brushing up	brushed up	brushed up

1. brush up (on) *p.v.* When you **brush up** or **brush up** on something, you study or practice a skill or subject you used to know but have forgotten or partly forgotten.

> *It's been a long time since I studied algebra, but I'm going to need it if I go back to school to study for my master's degree, so I'd better **brush up**.*
> *Frank's going to Peru next month, so he's been **brushing up** on his Spanish.*

Infinitive

	present tense	-ing form	past tense	past participle
come in	come in & comes in	coming in	came in	come in

1. come in/into *p.v.* When people or things enter a place, room, house, and so on that you are in, they **come in** or **come into** it. **Go out** is the opposite of **come in**.

> *Welcome to my house. Please **come in**.*
> *The burglar **came into** the house through the back door.*

2. come in *p.v.* When a train, bus, airplane, or ship **comes in**, it arrives. **Get in** is similar to **come in**.

> *Do you know when the train from Kankakee **comes in**?*
> *David's plane hasn't **come in** yet.*

3. come in *p.v.* When people arrive at the place where they work, they **come in**. **Get in** is similar to **come in**.

> *The manager is angry with Linda because she **comes in** late every day.*
> *I called to tell the boss that I was sick and wouldn't be **coming in**.*

4. come in *p.v.* When something that a store will sell **comes in**, it is delivered to the store.

> *Let's go shopping at Macy's tomorrow; the summer clothes have **come in**.*
> *I couldn't buy that new book I wanted; it hasn't **come in** yet.*

5. come in *p.v.* When a thing or skill **comes in** handy, it is something useful that you like to have available when you need it.

> *When I travel, I always take a small sewing kit with me; it really **comes in** handy if*
>   *a button falls off.*
> *I don't know how to speak Japanese, but knowing how to say the numbers and*
>   *"please" and "thank you" when I was in Japan sure **came in** handy.*

cut back				
	cut back & cuts back	cutting back	cut back	cut back

1. cut back (on) *p.v.* When you **cut back**, or **cut back** on the amount of money you spend, you spend less.

> *The President said he was against **cutting back** on spending for education.*
> *My father said that we're spending too much and have to **cut back**.*

cutback *n.* A **cutback** is a reduction in the amount of money you spend on something.

> *The people who work on the air force base are worried that they'll lose*
>   *their jobs because of military spending **cutbacks**.*

2. cut back (on) *p.v.* When you **cut back** or **cut back** on something that you consume, you use it less. When you **cut back** or **cut back** on something that you do, you do it less. **Cut down** is similar to **cut back**.

*Mark hasn't been able to quit smoking, but he has **cut back** a bit.*
*You're getting a little overweight; maybe you should **cut back** on sweets.*

Infinitive

	present tense	-ing form	past tense	past participle
move in	move in & moves in	moving in	moved in	moved in

1. move in/into *p.v.* When you **move in** or **move into** a place, you bring your furniture and other personal possessions into a place where you will live. **Move out** is the opposite of **move in/into**.

*The landlord said we could **move** right **in** if we want to.*
*Erik's **moving into** a bigger apartment next week.*

2. move ... in/into *p.v.* When you **move** people **in** or **move** them **into** a place, you bring their furniture and other personal possessions into a place where they will live. When you **move** things **in** or **move** them **into** a place, you take them in. **Move out** is the opposite of **move in/into**.

*The movers **moved** me **in** in less than two hours.*
***Moving** all this furniture **into** a fifth-floor apartment isn't going to be easy.*

3. move in (with) *p.v.* When you **move in** or **move in** with people, you bring your furniture and other personal possessions into a place where you will live.

*Bill moved out of his house for a while when he separated from his wife, but yesterday he **moved** back **in**.*
*My Aunt Kathy might **move in** with her son and his family.*

move out	move out & moves out	moving out	moved out	moved out

1. move out (of) *p.v.* When you **move out** or **move out** of a place, you take your furniture and other personal possessions out of a place where you lived. **Move in/into** is the opposite of **move out**.

*Could you help me **move out**? I have to be out by the end of the month.*
*Mr. and Mrs. Baker **moved out** of their big house and into a smaller place after their children grew up.*

2. move ... out (of) *p.v.* When you **move** people **out** or **move** them **out** of a place, you take their furniture and other personal possessions out of a place where they lived. When you **move** things **out** or **move** them **out** of a place, you take them out. **Move in/into** is the opposite of **move out**.

*One of our roommates wasn't paying his rent, so we **moved** his stuff **out** while he was at work.*
*The company had a sale to try to **move** some merchandise **out** of the warehouse.*

Infinitive

	present tense	-ing form	past tense	past participle
pull out	pull out & pulls out	pulling out	pulled out	pulled out

1. pull out (of) *p.v.* When a car, truck, or other vehicle **pulls out** or **pulls out** of a parking space, it leaves the place where it was parked and starts driving in the street. When the drivers of cars, trucks, or other vehicles **pull out** or **pull out** of a parking space, they leave the place where they were parked and start driving in the street.

*The accident happened when the Ford **pulled out** in front of the Chevy.*
*You should fasten your seat belt before you **pull out** of the parking space.*

2. pull out (of) *p.v.* When you **pull out** or **pull out** of an agreement or arrangement, you leave it because you decide that you do not want to participate any longer.

The French company reconsidered its agreement to build a plant in Canada
*and decided to **pull out**.*
*I wish I hadn't **pulled out** of that business deal. Now everyone who stayed in*
is making a lot of money.

3. pull . . . out (of) *p.v.* When soldiers leave a combat zone or an area where combat is likely, they **pull out** or are **pulled out**. **Go in** is the opposite of **pull out**.

When Sergeant Jones saw the enemy soldiers getting closer, he ordered his men
*to **pull out**.*
*General Johnston **pulled** all the troops **out** of the occupied territory.*

pullout *n.* When soldiers leave a combat zone or an area where combat is likely, a **pullout** takes place.

*General Johnston ordered an immediate **pullout** of all troops in the occupied territory.*

put in	put in & puts in	putting in	put in	put in

1. put . . . in/into *p.v.* When you **put** something **in** or **put** something **into** a container, storage place, or building, you place it inside. **Take out** is the opposite of **put in/into**.

*Please **put** your clothes **in** the closet.*
*The clerk **put** the bottle **into** the bag and gave me a receipt.*

2. put . . . in/into *p.v.* When you **put** money **in** or **put** money **into** a bank or an account at a bank, you deposit the money. **Put in/into** is the opposite of **take out**.

*I'm going to the bank today. How much money do you think I should **put in**?*
*We **put** $10,000 **into** our savings account.*

3. put . . . in/into *p.v.* When you **put** people **in** or **put** them **into** a prison, hospital, school, or other institution, you take them there or require them to go there.

*Jake got **put in** jail for twenty years.*
*Marvin should be **put into** a mental institution.*

4. put ... in/into *p.v.* When you **put** time or effort **in** or **put** time or effort **into** something, you spend time and work hard to accomplish it.

> At the Christmas party, the manager thanked his employees for all the work they had **put in**.
>
> I **put** a lot of time **into** becoming a doctor.

5. put ... in/into *p.v.* When you **put** money **in** or **put** money **into** something, you contribute money to help pay for something or as an investment you hope will return a profit.

> When the check came for dinner, we each **put** $25 **in**.
>
> I've already **put** $100,000 **into** this business. I hope it starts making money soon.

6. put ... in *p.v.* When you construct or install something in a building, you **put** it **in**.

> We're having new carpeting **put in** next week.
>
> Erik and Nancy are thinking about **putting in** central air conditioning.

7. put ... in *p.v.* When you cause people to be in a situation, position, or condition, you **put** them **in** that situation, position, or condition.

> You've **put** Jim **in** a very awkward situation.
>
> Margaret Cummings was **put in** charge of the sales department.

Infinitive

	present tense	-ing form	past tense	past participle
run out				
	run out & runs out	running out	ran out	run out

1. run out (of) *p.v.* When people or things **run out** or **run out** of a place, room, building, and so on, they leave it very quickly. **Run in/into** is the opposite of **run out**.

> There's Sofia across the street — **run out** and ask her to come over here.
>
> When I opened the door, the dog **ran out** of the house.

2. run out (of) *p.v.* When you do not have any more of something because you have used, consumed, or sold all of it, you **run out** or **run out** of it.

> I'm sorry I can't give you sugar for your coffee — I've **run out**.
>
> Sam was late to work this morning because he **ran out** of gas.

3. run out *p.v.* When something is completely used, consumed, or sold, it **runs out**.

> I played poker last night, and for a while I was ahead by $3,000. But then my luck **ran out**, and I ended up losing it all.
>
> My brother is too lazy to look for a job. He asks me for money, and when the money **runs out** he comes back for more.

EXERCISE 47a — **Complete the sentences with phrasal verbs from this section. Be sure the phrasal verbs are in the correct tense.**

1. We have a lot of shopping to do, but the store closes in twenty minutes, so let's try to finish before we _____ _____ of time.

2. Michael _____ a lot of time _____ getting his pilot's license.

3. The government threatened to _____ _____ of the cease-fire agreement

    after the latest terrorist bombing.

4. This little flashlight on my key chain _____ _____ handy when it's

    dark outside.

5. I haven't stopped drinking completely, but I have _____ way _____.

6. When Timmy's mother saw him outside throwing rocks at cars, she _____

    _____ and stopped him.

7. We bought a house in Milwaukee, and we're _____ _____ it next month.

8. Instead of spending all your money, maybe you should _____ some of it

    _____ the bank.

9. I'm starting a new job as a secretary next week, so I need to _____ _____ on my typing.

10. After my mother died, I asked my father to _____ _____ with me.

11. I'll be waiting for you at the station when your train _____ _____.

12. All these problems are _____ me _____ a bad mood.

13. How much money are you going to _____ _____ this investment fund?

14. We're very busy at work, so my boss asked me to _____ _____ early tomorrow.

15. I need to find a new place to live soon. I have to _____ _____ of the place

    I'm in now by the end of the month.

16. These computers are being sold at 15 percent off the regular price for three days only, so hurry

    before time _____ _____.

17. Linda hired a carpenter to _____ some shelves _____ her son's room.

18. We lost the key for the front door, so everyone's been _____ _____ through

    the back door all day.

19. Since Jim lost his job, we've had to _____ _____ a lot on our

    spending.

20. The troops were _____ _____ of Vietnam and sent back to

    the United States.

47

21. I bought a new bed for Susie, so I'm going to _____ her old bed _____ of her room and into her brother's room.

22. After my surgery, I was _____ _____ the intensive care unit.

23. The store clerk says the new computer I want is supposed to _____ _____ tomorrow.

24. My couch is huge — there's no way I can _____ it _____ my new place without help.

25. Erik _____ too much salt _____ the soup, and now it tastes terrible.

26. Safe drivers always look both ways before they _____ _____ and drive away.

EXERCISE 47b — Write answers to the questions using phrasal verbs and nouns from this section. Be sure the phrasal verbs are in the correct tense.

1. Tom is going to live with his Uncle John. What is Tom going to do?

2. The government is spending less on the military. What is the government doing?

3. In Question 2, what would you call this reduction in military spending?

4. I can't figure out where the mosquitoes are entering my house. What can't I figure out?

5. My plane didn't arrive on time. What didn't my plane do?

6. Bob's taking all his furniture out of his old apartment. What is Bob doing?

7. You spent all your money, and now you're broke. What did you do?

8. Nancy's truck was parked, but now she's driving it into the street. What is Nancy doing?

9. Sarah shouldn't have built a pool in such a small backyard. What shouldn't Sarah have done?

10. Daniela hasn't studied Italian since high school, but she's been studying it again lately because she's going to Italy soon. What is Daniela doing?

11. Charles might change his mind and decide not to participate in a business deal. What might Charles do?

12. Your dentist told you that you should eat less candy. What did your dentist tell you?

13. Ned is going to arrive at work late tomorrow. What is Ned going to do?

14. Jane is working very hard to learn Chinese. What is Jane doing?

15. The basketball game ended before Jim's team could score enough points to win it. Why didn't Jim's team win the game?

16. Joe hasn't placed his clothes in the washing machine. What hasn't Joe done?

17. Tom asked Sally when she was taking her furniture into her new apartment. What did Tom ask Sally?

18. Bill deposits $1,000 every month in his checking account. What does Bill do every month?

EXERCISE 47c, Review — **Complete the sentences with these phrasal verbs from previous sections. Be sure the phrasal verbs are in the correct tense. To check their meanings, review the section number given after each one.**

bump into, 46	get down, 42	kick out, 43	stop off, 43
con into, 46	get in/into, 42	make for, 46	talk into, 46
con out of, 46	get out, 42	rip off, 44	talk out of, 46
freak out, 46	get up, 42	shut up, 43	try on, 43

1. Alfonso must have _____ _____ thirty pairs of pants before picking one out.

2. Bob got _____ _____ of the bar after he started a fight.

3. You can't trust Marvin at all. He _____ _____ everyone he does business with.

4. I can't reach those books on the top shelf. Would you _____ them _____ for me, please?

5. That sneaky real estate agent _____ me _____ selling her my house for a lot less than it was worth.

6. My parents live between my job and my home, so sometimes on the way home from work I _____ _____ for a visit.

7. Sam's wife didn't want to go camping with him, but he finally _____ her _____ it.

8. My father-in-law was _____ _____ _____ $800 by a house painter who took the money but never came back to start painting the house.

9. When I was a child, my mother was on drugs and my father was in jail. That situation didn't _____ _____ a very happy childhood.

10. Carlos _____ _____ the table, and a glass of wine fell on the floor.

11. All you ever do is talk, talk, talk. Will you please _____ _____?

12. It sure was hot yesterday. It must have _____ _____ to 100 degrees.

13. Our daughter has decided to get her nose pierced, and there's no way we can _____ her _____ _____ it.

14. I found my old army uniform in the attic, and I can still _____ _____ it even though it's twenty-five years old.

15. My teacher caught me cheating on the test today, and he said he's going to call my parents tomorrow to tell them. How am I going to _____ _____ of this mess?

16. I saw a guy today who looked exactly like my dead brother. It really _____ me _____.

---

48. FOCUS ON: **modals and present perfect passive phrasal verbs**

In Section 43, we discussed the use of several modal and semimodal auxiliaries in the present perfect. These same modals and semimodals are commonly used in passive sentences. The modal or semimodal is followed by *have* or the contraction *'ve, been,* and the past participle:

> ***could*** + *have* + *been* + past participle
> ***would*** + *have* + *been* + past participle
> ***should*** + *have* + *been* + past participle
> ***have to*** + *have* + *been* + past participle
> ***must*** + *have* + *been* + past participle
> ***might*** + *have* + *been* + past participle
> ***may*** + *have* + *been* + past participle

Let's compare a present perfect active sentence containing a modal with a present perfect passive sentence containing a modal:

active: *Jane <u>might</u> <u>have</u> **switched on** the light.*
passive: *The light <u>might</u> <u>have</u> <u>been</u> **switched on**.*

As we have seen, the object of the active sentence becomes the subject of the passive sentence. Also, there is no object in the passive sentence, so the passive phrasal verb cannot be separated. The object of the active sentence can be used in a *by* phrase:

active: *Jane <u>might</u> <u>have</u> **switched on** the light.*
passive: *The light <u>might</u> <u>have</u> <u>been</u> **switched on** (by Jane).*

And once again we see that it is not always easy to distinguish between a past participle:

> *The burglar alarm <u>must</u> <u>have</u> <u>been</u> **switched off** (by the night manager because he's the only one with a key).*

and a participle adjective:

> *The burglar alarm <u>must</u> <u>have</u> <u>been</u> **switched off** (because if it had been on, everyone in the neighborhood would have heard it when the burglars smashed the window of the jewelry store).*

Infinitive

present tense	-ing form	past tense	past participle
close down			
close down & closes down	closing down	closed down	closed down

1. close . . . down *p.v.* When you **close down** a business or a business is **closed down**, it closes permanently or for a long time.

> *The restaurant was **closed down** by the health department.*
> *The ski resort will **close down** for the summer on May 1.*

knock out			
knock out & knocks out	knocking out	knocked out	knocked out

1. knock . . . out *p.v.* When you **knock** people **out**, you hit them hard enough to cause them to lose consciousness. When people are **knocked out**, they are hit by someone or something hard enough to cause them to lose consciousness.

> *The boxer **knocked** his opponent **out** with a blow to the head.*
> *David fell and hit his head on the sidewalk so hard that it **knocked** him **out**.*

knockout *n.* A hit hard enough to cause someone to lose consciousness is a **knockout**.

> *At the count of ten the referee declared a **knockout**.*

2. knock . . . out *p.v.* If something **knocks** you **out**, it impresses or surprises you a lot.

*Tom's new house is fabulous! It really **knocked** me **out**.*
The Youngs' daughter is only twelve and she's already in college? That just
    ***knocks** me **out**.*

knockout *n.* A **knockout** is something that impresses or surprises you a lot.

> *Have you seen Erik's new girlfriend? She's a real **knockout**.*

3. knock . . . out *p.v.* When you try very hard to please other people, you **knock**
yourself **out** or **knock** yourself **out** to do something.

> *Marsha's Thanksgiving dinner was fabulous. She really **knocked** herself **out**.*
> *Thanks for inviting me to spend the weekend with you, but don't **knock** yourself*
>   ***out** — I don't mind sleeping on the couch.*

4. knock . . . out *p.v.* When soldiers **knock out** a piece of the enemy's equipment,
they destroy it or damage it enough so that it no longer operates.

> *The enemy radar installation was **knocked out** by a 500-pound bomb.*
> *I can't contact headquarters. I think our communications system might have*
>   *been **knocked out** during the attack.*

Infinitive

present tense	-ing form	past tense	past participle
look down on			
look down on & looks down on	looking down on	looked down on	looked down on

1. look down on *p.v.* When you **look down on** people, you consider them to
be less intelligent, less educated, or from a lower level of society than you.

> *Some people **look down on** Hank because his father was in prison.*
> ***Looking down on** people because of things they have no control over is stupid.*

look up to			
look up to & looks up to	looking up to	looked up to	looked up to

1. look up to *p.v.* When you **look up to** people, you admire and respect them.

> *I've always **looked up to** my father because of his honesty and concern for others.*
> *You should **look up to** people who have overcome difficulties to become successful.*

put back			
put back & puts back	putting back	put back	put back

1. put . . . back *p.v.* When you **put** something **back**, you return it to where
it was before.

> *After you finish listening to my CDs, please **put** them **back**.*
> *Susie, I told you we're eating dinner in ten minutes, so **put** that cookie right **back**!*

2. put . . . back *p.v.* When something slows the development or progress of project,
it **puts** the project **back** or it **puts** the people involved in the project **back**.

> *The hurricane **put** the hotel construction project **back** by at least three months.*
> *I had planned to finish college last year, but being hospitalized for several months*
>   ***put** me **back**.*

3. put . . . back *p.v.* When you **put back** the date that you plan to do or complete something by, you postpone it.

> The closing on the house I'm selling might have to be **put back** if the buyers
>   can't get their loan approved in time.
> The graduation date will have to be **put back** if the teachers strike doesn't end soon.

4. put . . . back *p.v.* [informal] When you **put back** alcoholic beverages, you drink a lot of them.

> Did you see how much David was drinking last night? He sure can **put** it **back**.
> I'm not surprised he has a hangover — he must have **put back** half a bottle of tequila.

Infinitive

	present tense	-ing form	past tense	past participle
switch off				
	switch off & switches off	switching off	switched off	switched off

1. switch . . . off *p.v.* When you **switch off** an electrical or mechanical device, you change the controls to stop it from producing or doing something. **Turn off** is similar to **switch off**. **Switch on** is the opposite of **switch off**.

> Try to remember to **switch off** the lights when you leave the room.
> I **switched** the engine **off** and got out of the car.

switched off *part.adj.* After you have changed the controls of an electrical or mechanical device to stop it from producing or doing something, it is **switched off**. **Switched on** is the opposite of **switched off**. **Turned off** is similar to **switched off**.

> Last night the light in the hallway was **switched off**, and I fell down the stairs.

switch on				
	switch on & switches on	switching on	switched on	switched on

1. switch . . . on *p.v.* When you **switch on** an electrical or mechanical device, you change the controls to make it start producing or doing something. **Turn on** is similar to **switch on**. **Switch off** is the opposite of **switch on**.

> Push this button to **switch** the computer **on**.
> The sign should have been **switched on** by the manager in the morning.

switched on *part.adj.* After you have changed the controls of an electrical or mechanical device to make it start producing or doing something, it is **switched on**. **Switched off** is the opposite of **switched on**. **Turned on** is similar to **switched on**.

> When I drove by the restaurant, I noticed that the sign wasn't **switched on**.

throw out				
	throw out & throws out	throwing out	threw out	thrown out

1. throw . . . out *p.v.* When you **throw** something **out**, you dispose of it by putting it in the wastebasket, trash, and so on. **Throw away** is the same as **throw out**.

> I can't find some important papers, and I think they might've been
>   accidentally **thrown out**.
> Don't **throw** that newspaper **out** — I haven't read it yet.

2. throw ... out (of) *p.v.* When you **throw** people **out** or **throw** people **out** of a group, place, building, or room, you order them to leave. **Kick out** is similar to **throw out**.

> Frank started a fight and got ***thrown out*** of the bar.
> I haven't paid the rent in six months, and I'm worried that the sheriff will come and ***throw*** us ***out***.

EXERCISE 48a — **Complete the sentences with phrasal verbs from this section. Be sure the phrasal verbs are in the correct tense.**

1. We might _____ our wedding _____ until September so that Rosa's parents can attend.

2. Please _____ the lights _____ — I'm trying to sleep.

3. Bob was _____ _____ when the baseball hit him in the head.

4. When I was a little girl, I _____ _____ _____ my grandfather and wanted to be like him.

5. Sam must have _____ _____ three gin and tonics in about a half an hour last night.

6. It's cold in here — the air conditioner shouldn't have been _____ _____.

7. Mrs. Flores was so angry with her husband that she _____ him right _____ of the house.

8. My wife thinks I forgot our anniversary again, so she's going to be _____ _____ when I give her this gold bracelet.

9. The blizzard has _____ _____ our efforts to find the crashed plane, but we'll keep looking until we find it.

10. I'm tired of looking at all this junk — why don't you _____ it _____?

11. Citizens of the neighborhood have demanded that the noisy bar be _____ _____.

12. Charles _____ _____ _____ anyone who comes from the poor side of town.

13. If you're finished with these tools, _____ them _____.

14. The soldier used a bazooka to _____ _____ an enemy tank.

15. Timmy's mother planned a really nice birthday party for Timmy and all his friends. She really

_____ herself _____.

EXERCISE 48b — **Write three sentences using the objects in parentheses. Be sure to put the objects in the right place.**

1. The health department should *close down*. (the restaurant, it)

_____

_____

_____

2. Ali's left hook *knocked out*. (Joe, him)

_____

_____

_____

3. General Johnston had to *put back*. (the attack, it)

_____

_____

_____

4. Have you *switched on*? (the TV, it)

_____

_____

_____

5. Are you going to *switch off*? (the lights, them)

_____

_____

_____

6. *Throwing out* is going to be a big job. (all this junk, it)

_____

_____

_____

48

EXERCISE 48c — **Write answers to the questions using phrasal verbs, participle adjectives, and nouns from this section. Be sure the phrasal verbs are in the correct tense.**

1. The judge's decision has slowed our fight for justice. What has the judge's decision done to us?

2. Jim respects his uncle and wants to be like him. What does Jim do to his uncle?

3. Todd was really amazed at how good Erik's new book is. What did Erik's book do to Todd?

4. In Question 3, what would Todd call Erik's book?

5. You pushed the button on the remote, and now the TV is on. What did you do to the TV?

6. In Question 5, how would you describe the TV after I pushed the button on the remote?

7. The lights were on, but they're not on anymore. What must have been done to the lights?

8. In Question 7, how would you describe the lights now?

9. The bar owner will be ordered to close his bar permanently. What will be done to the bar?

10. Charles thinks people from that part of town are low-class. What does Charles do to people from that part of town?

11. Joe would have been ordered to leave his house if he hadn't paid his late mortgage payments. What would have happened to Joe if he hadn't paid his late mortgage payments?

EXERCISE 48d, Review — **Complete the sentences with these nouns from previous sections. To check their meanings, review the section number given after each one.**

carryout, 28	lookout, 29	turnoff, 45	turnover, 45
cutback, 47	make-up, 23	turn-on, 45	rip-off, 44
falling-out, 32	pullout, 47	turnout, 45	runaround, 40

1. Heather kind of liked Ann's brother until she saw him smoking. To her that's a big

   _____.

2. The Senate voted against a _____ in spending for AIDS research.

3. Lydia doesn't want anyone to take pictures of her without her _____ on.

4. Bill thinks that Nicole's short skirt is a _____.

5. The soldiers were ordered to prepare for a _____.

6. I hate cooking, so we eat _____ food almost every night.

7. I've gone to every office in City Hall about my problem, but no will help me. They just

give me the _____.

8. The company's high _____ rate is one reason why it lost money last year.

9. Can you believe the frames for these glasses cost $300? What a _____.

10. One thief broke into the store while the other stayed outside as a _____.

11. The _____ for the parade would have been a lot bigger if it hadn't been raining.

12. George had a _____ with his brother and hasn't spoken with him for

fifteen years.

EXERCISE 48e, Review — **Complete the sentences with these phrasal verbs from previous sections. Be sure the phrasal verbs are in the correct tense. To check their meanings, review the section number given after each one.**

blow out, 43	con into, 46	pull out, 47	talk into, 46
brush up, 47	con out of, 46	put in/into, 47	talk out of, 46
bump into, 46	move in/into, 47	stick out, 32	turn over, 45
carry away, 44	move out, 47	stress out, 44	turn up, 45

1. Your work isn't very good. You ought to _____ more effort _____ it.

2. I was so mad at my boss that I almost quit my job. Fortunately, my wife _____ me

_____ _____ it.

3. Did you see Mike's house? He said he was going to put a few Christmas tree lights on the roof,

but there must be 5,000. I guess he got _____ _____.

4. Don't let that crooked contractor _____ you _____ _____ any

money for unnecessary home repairs.

5. France was a member of NATO until it _____ _____ in 1966.

6. Don't quit now, we're almost finished. You've just got to _____ it _____ for

a little while longer.

7. What a surprise! I _____ _____ Bob at the train station yesterday. I hadn't

seen him in years.

49

8. The police acted on a tip that the suspect would be at the bus station on Saturday morning,

    but he didn't _____ _____.

9. If you're not careful that crook will _____ you _____ selling him your land

    for a lot less than it's worth.

10. Mike used to speak Arabic pretty well, but he ought to _____ _____ before

    he goes to Egypt.

11. How could I have been _____ _____ doing something stupid?

12. The apartment has been cleaned and painted. You can _____ right _____

    any time you want.

13. _____ it _____. I want to see what's on the other side.

14. Living with Sam is driving me crazy — I have to _____ _____.

15. After you make a wish you can _____ _____ the candles.

16. Living in a house with seven dogs is really _____ my cat _____.

49. FOCUS ON: **combinations of *get*, *right*, *back*, and *to***

The focus of this section is an expanded definition of the two-word phrasal verb **get to** and the three-word phrasal verb **get back to**. The purpose is to try to make some sense out of a seemingly limitless number of idiomatic combinations of *get*, *to*, and various particles and adverbs, in particular *right* and *back*, and to demonstrate that many phrasal verbs comprised of *get* and a particle are actually variations of **get to** that can be modified with *right* and/or *back*.

Remember that *back* is sometimes part of a phrasal verb and sometimes an adverb used to modify a phrasal verb (review Section 26), although we will see that there is often no difference in meaning between the phrasal verb **get back** (to), discussed in Section 42, and the phrasal verb **get to** modified by back (**get** back **to**).

The numbers in the chart correspond with the meanings in the definitions.

get to

1. Although the phrasal verb **get to** is defined here as meaning arrive, it can be understood as the basis for some of the phrasal verbs that were discussed in Section 42:

> Bill **got to** Peoria. (Bill arrived in Peoria.)
> Bill **got back** to Peoria. (Bill returned to Peoria.)
> Bill **got up** to Peoria. (Bill arrived in Peoria from the south.)
> Bill **got down** to Peoria. (Bill arrived in Peoria from the north.)

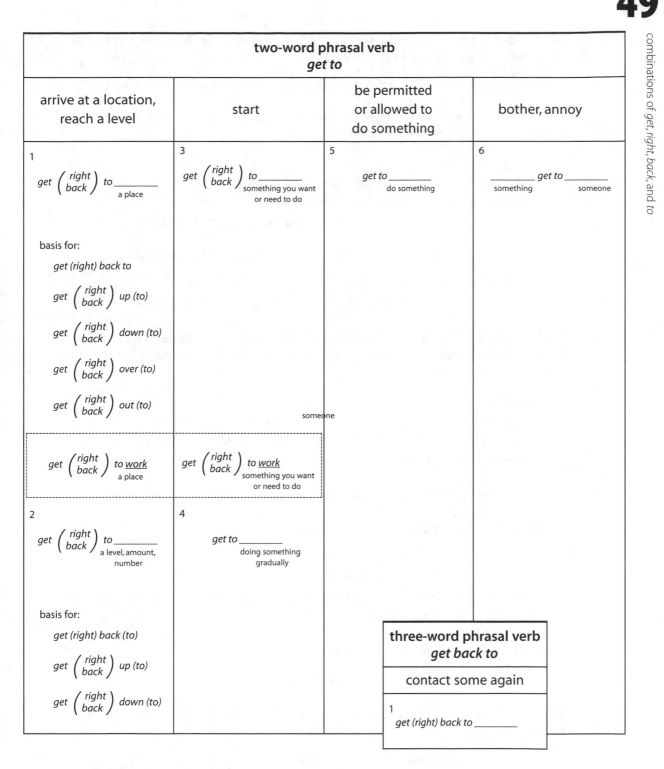

two-word phrasal verb *get to*			
arrive at a location, reach a level	**start**	**be permitted or allowed to do something**	**bother, annoy**
1 get $\left(\begin{array}{c}right\\back\end{array}\right)$ to _____ a place	3 get $\left(\begin{array}{c}right\\back\end{array}\right)$ to _____ something you want or need to do	5 get to _____ do something	6 _____ get to _____ something someone
basis for: get (right) back to get $\left(\begin{array}{c}right\\back\end{array}\right)$ up (to) get $\left(\begin{array}{c}right\\back\end{array}\right)$ down (to) get $\left(\begin{array}{c}right\\back\end{array}\right)$ over (to) get $\left(\begin{array}{c}right\\back\end{array}\right)$ out (to)			
	someone		
get $\left(\begin{array}{c}right\\back\end{array}\right)$ to <u>work</u> a place	get $\left(\begin{array}{c}right\\back\end{array}\right)$ to <u>work</u> something you want or need to do		
2 get $\left(\begin{array}{c}right\\back\end{array}\right)$ to _____ a level, amount, number	4 get to _____ doing something gradually		
basis for: get (right) back (to) get $\left(\begin{array}{c}right\\back\end{array}\right)$ up (to) get $\left(\begin{array}{c}right\\back\end{array}\right)$ down (to)			

three-word phrasal verb *get back to*
contact some again
1 get (right) back to _____

*Bill **got over** to Peoria.* (Bill arrived in Peoria from the east or west.)
*Bill **got out** to Peoria.* (Bill arrived in Peoria from the east or from
    a larger city.)

We see that ***get back*** *(to)*, ***get up*** *(to)*, ***get down*** *(to)*, ***get over*** *(to)*, and ***get out*** *(to)*
are variations of ***get to*** but with additional information. These verbs
can be modified with *right*, meaning *immediately*, *quickly*, or *directly* (see Section
10):

*Bill **got** <u>right</u> **back** to Peoria.* (Bill returned to Peoria quickly.)

Get to work has two meanings, similar but not the same. ***Get to*** work can refer to *an arrival at a place where someone works*:

> *Ann **got to** work.* (Ann arrived at the place where she works.)

But ***get to*** work (see meaning 3) can also mean *start working*, without any reference to a change of location:

> *Joe **got to** work.* (Joe started working.)
> *Joe **got** <u>back</u> **to** work.* (Joe started working again.)
> *Joe **got** <u>right</u> **to** work.* (Joe started working immediately.)
> *Joe **got** <u>right back</u> **to** work.* (Joe started working again immediately.)

The difference in these two meanings is illustrated by the following sentence:

> *I **<u>got to</u>** <u>work</u> at 9:00, but I didn't **<u>get to</u>** <u>work</u> until 10:00, which can paraphrased as I <u>arrived at my office</u> at 9:00, but I didn't <u>start working</u> until 10:00.*

2. Although the phrasal verb ***get to*** is defined here as meaning *reach a certain level, number, or amount*, it can be understood as the basis for some of the phrasal verbs discussed in Section 42:

> *Jane **got to** 120 pounds.*
> *Jane **got back** to 120 pounds.* (Jane weighs 120 pounds again.)
> *Jane **got up** to 120 pounds.* (Jane used to weigh less that 120 pounds.)
> *Jane **got down** to 120 pounds.* Jane used to weigh more that 120 pounds.)

We see that ***get back*** *(to),* ***get up*** *(to),* and ***get down*** *(to)* are variations of ***get to*** but with additional information.
  Get up *(to)* and ***get down*** *(to)* can be modified by *back*:

> *Jane **got** <u>back</u> **up** to 120 pounds.* (Jane used to weigh 120 pounds, lost weight, and then gained it back.)
> *Jane **got** <u>back</u> **down** to 120 pounds.* (Jane used to weigh 120 pounds, gained weight, and then lost it.)

3. If you start to do something, you ***get to*** it:

> *I'll try to **get to** my homework after dinner.*

If you start to do something, stop doing it, and then later start to do it again, you ***get*** <u>back</u> **to** it:

> *I'll try to **get** <u>back</u> **to** my homework after dinner.*

If you start to do something, stop doing it, and then later quickly start to do it again, you ***get*** right back **to** it:

> *I'll try to **get** <u>right</u> <u>back</u> **to** my homework after dinner.*

Remember that when both *right* and *back* are used, *right* always comes first:

> ~~*I'll try to **get** <u>back</u> <u>right</u> **to** my homework after dinner.*~~

get back to

1. ***Get back to*** is a three-word verb meaning *talk to someone again later.*
Get back to does not vary in form — neither *back* nor *to* is optional.

Infinitive	present tense	-ing form	past tense	past participle
clog up	clog up & clogs up	clogging up	clogged up	clogged up

1. clog ... up *p.v.* When people or things **clog up** a drain or something else that liquids must flow through, they put something in it that prevents water or other liquids from going through it or that prevents it from working properly.

*Don't pour that bacon grease in the sink — you'll **clog** the drain **up**.*
*Dr. Smith said my arteries were so **clogged up** by plaque deposits that it was
a miracle I was still alive.*

clogged up *part.adj.* When a drain or something else that liquids must flow through is **clogged up**, something is in it that prevents water or other liquids from going through it or that prevents it from working properly.

*The mechanic told me that the engine valves in my car were **clogged up**.*

get ahead	get ahead & gets ahead	getting ahead	got ahead	gotten/got ahead

1. get ahead *p.v.* When you **get ahead**, you become more successful and make progress in your job or your life.

*With your pessimistic attitude, you'll never **get ahead**.*
***Getting ahead** is pretty easy when your father owns the company.*

get back to	get back to & gets back to	getting back to	got back to	gotten/got back to

1. get back to *p.v.* When you **get back to** people, you talk to them later, usually because you do not have time to talk to them at the time or because you will have information for them later that you do not have now.

*I don't have time to talk now; I'm really busy. Can I **get back to** you?*
*That real estate agent still hasn't **gotten back to** me to let me know if our
offer was accepted.*

Infinitive	present tense	-ing form	past tense	past participle
get on	get on & gets on	getting on	got on	gotten/got on

1. get on *p.v.* When you move your body toward something and stand, sit, or lie on it, you **get on** it.

*The nurse asked me to take off my shirt and **get on** the examination table.*
*If you **get on** that chair you can reach the top shelf.*

2. get on *p.v.* When you mount an animal, bicycle, motorcycle, and so on, you **get on** it.

> ***Getting on*** *a camel isn't as easy as **getting on** a horse.*
> *The children **got** back **on** their bikes and went home.*

3. get on *p.v.* When you enter a bus, train, airplane, ship, and so on, you **get on** it.

> *The bus stopped so that I could **get on**.*
> *Only people who are going on the cruise can **get on** the ship.*

4. get ... on *p.v.* When you **get** an item of clothing **on**, you put it on your body.

> ***Get*** *your coat **on**. It's cold outside.*
> *These gloves are too small. I can't **get** them **on**.*

5. get on (with) *p.v.* When you continue doing something, you **get on**, **get on** with what you were doing, or **get on** with it.

> *It's getting late. If we're going to finish this work today we'd better **get on** with it.*
> *I didn't say you could stop! **Get on** with your work.*

get to

get to & gets to	getting to	got to	gotten/got to

1. get ... to *p.v.* When you **get to** a place, you arrive there. When you **get** people **to** a place, you help them to go there or take them there. When you **get to** work, you arrive at the place where you work.

> *Sarah left her house at 8:30 and **got to** the beach at 9:15.*
> *When I **get to** Tokyo, I'll call to let you know I arrived safely.*
> *Frank got fired because he kept **getting to** work late.*
> *I went to the restaurant across the street for lunch, and I didn't **get** back **to** work until 2:30.*

2. get to *p.v.* When things or people **get to** a certain level, number, or amount, they reach it.

> *It sure was hot yesterday. It must have **gotten to** 100 degrees.*
> *When I run, I always try to **get to** five miles before I quit.*

3. get to *p.v.* When you **get to** something that you want or need to do, you find the time to do it. When you **get to** work, you start working.

> *I didn't have time to do the ironing last night. I'll try to **get to** it tonight.*
> *Karen finally **got** back **to** her school project yesterday. She hadn't worked on it for weeks.*
> *You've wasted the entire morning. When are you going to **get to** work?*
> *My boss told me to get off the phone and **get** back **to** work.*

4. get to *p.v.* [informal] When you **get to** doing something, you begin to do it gradually.

> *Dad **got to** thinking that maybe we ought to move to Los Angeles and try to find work there.*

*After seeing all those strange lights in the sky, I **got to** wondering if maybe*
UFOs really exist after all.

5. get to *p.v.* When you **get to** do something, you are allowed to do it or are
able to do it.

*Timmy was excited because he **got to** ride a pony.*
*I hope I **get to** shake the President's hand after his speech.*

6. get to *p.v.* When something **gets to** you, it bothers or annoys you, either
psychologically or physically.

*Jim's constant complaining is really starting to **get to** his wife.*
*Let's sit down and rest — this heat is **getting to** me.*

Infinitive

	present tense	-ing form	past tense	past participle
hang on				
	hang on & hangs on	hanging on	hung on	hung on

1. hang on (to) *p.v.* When you **hang on** or **hang on** to something, you hold it tightly
so that you will not fall or be hurt. **Hold on** is similar to **hang on**.

*I fell off the horse because I wasn't **hanging on** tightly enough.*
*If she'd **hung on** to my hand, she wouldn't have fallen off the cliff.*

2. hang on *p.v.* [informal] When you **hang on**, you wait for a short time. **Hold on** is
the same as **hang on**.

***Hang on** for a minute — I'll be right back.*
*Judy's coming to the phone now — can you **hang on**?*

start off				
	start off & starts off	starting off	started off	started off

1. start off (with/by) *p.v.* When an activity or event **starts off**, it begins. When you
start an activity or event **off** with something, you begin with it. When you **start** an
activity or event **off** by doing something, you begin by doing it.

*The singer **started** the concert **off** with a song from her latest CD.*
*Many speakers like to **start off** a speech by telling a joke.*

2. start off *p.v.* When people or things **start off** a certain way, they are this way at
the beginning of a process that changes them. **Start out** is similar to **start off**.

*The day **started off** nice, but it got cold and cloudy.*
*I thought the movie was good, but it **started off** kind of boring.*

Infinitive

	present tense	-ing form	past tense	past participle
throw away				
	throw away & throws away	throwing away	threw away	thrown away

1. throw . . . away *p.v.* When you **throw** something **away**, you dispose of it by putting it in the wastebasket, trash, and so on. **Throw out** is the same as **throw away**.

> *If you're finished with these papers, **throw** them **away**.*
> *Nancy's outside looking in the trash for her wedding ring; it was*
> *accidentally **thrown away**.*

2. throw ... away *p.v.* When you **throw away** something important or valuable, you foolishly do something that causes you to lose it.

> *This is your last chance to save your marriage, so don't **throw** it **away**.*
> *When I got mad and quit my job, I **threw away** a chance to become vice-president*
> *of the company.*

EXERCISE 49a — **Complete the sentences with phrasal verbs from this section. Be sure the phrasal verbs are in the correct tense.**

1. We were lucky that the floodwater didn't _____ _____ the second floor.

2. These steps have ice on them, so _____ _____ to my arm.

3. I usually _____ _____ work at 8:40.

4. It's important to _____ your day _____ with a good breakfast.

5. I never used to care about Maria's bad attitude, but now it's starting to _____

   _____ me.

6. I'm a little busy now. Give me your phone number, and I'll _____ right _____

   _____ you.

7. Go _____ your shoes _____ — we're leaving in a minute.

8. Ann cut her hair in the bathroom, and she _____ the sink _____ with hair.

9. Don't let the baby _____ _____ the table — he might fall off.

10. If you hadn't _____ _____ the theater late, you wouldn't have missed

    the beginning of the movie.

11. _____ _____ all that junk in the garage made a lot more room.

12. As Jerry was _____ _____ the train, he realized that he had forgotten his ticket.

13. Whenever I _____ _____ feeling depressed, I call my mother.

14. If you want to _____ _____ in this world, you need a good education.

15. The trail to the top of the mountain _____ _____ level, but then it gets

    steeper and steeper.

16. Maybe you should _____ _____ with your work and stop wasting time.

17. _____ _____ for a couple of minutes — I'm almost ready.

18. This is a great opportunity. Don't be stupid and _____ it _____.

19. I know you're busy, but when do you think you might have time to _____ back _____ fixing that leak in the roof?

20. I waited outside Mr. Baker's office for two hours, but I never _____ _____ talk to him.

21. Madeleine fell off her bike, but she _____ right back _____ again.

22. _____ _____ work! This has to be finished in three hours, and you haven't even started.

EXERCISE 49b — **Write answers to the questions using phrasal verbs and participle adjectives from this section. Be sure the phrasal verbs are in the correct tense.**

1. Linda's three-year-old daughter can't put her shoes on. What can't Linda's three-year-old daughter do?

2. Luis started to feel a little depressed. What did Luis do?

3. Marvin had a nice family and a good job, but he lost them because of drugs. What did Marvin do to his family and job?

4. After I take a break, I'm going to continue working immediately. What am I going to do?

5. Betty doesn't have the information I want, so she's going to call me when she does. What is Betty going to do?

6. The sewer drain became blocked by dead leaves. What happened to the sewer drain?

7. In Question 6, how would you describe the sewer drain after it became blocked?

8. Ned has never arrived at his office after 9:30. What has Ned never done?

9. You continued with your work. What did you do?

10. When the temperature inside the turkey reaches 190 degrees, take it out of the oven. When should the turkey be taken out of the oven?

11. Bill said that he couldn't wait any longer. What did Bill say?

12. My taxes are due in three days, so I've got to do them tonight. What have I got to do?

13. Sam's birth certificate must have been accidentally put in the trash. What must have happened to Sam's birth certificate?

14. Dan showed me how to mount a horse. What did Dan show me?

15. Their marriage began well, but things got worse. What did their marriage do?

16. My brother told me that I shouldn't let it bother me. What did my brother tell me?

17. Alex was allowed to pet a baby tiger at the zoo. What happened to Alex?

18. The mountain climber held the rope tightly. What did the mountain climber do?

19. Mike went to the diving board and stood on it. What did Mike do?

20. The bus driver stepped out of the bus to check the tires, and then he entered the bus again immediately. What did the bus driver do after he checked the tires?

21. It's been only fifteen minutes since Heather left. She could not have arrived at the airport already. What couldn't Heather have done already?

22. The salesperson always begins his presentation by introducing himself. What does the salesperson always do?

23. Having an MBA should help you to progress in your career. What should an MBA do?

EXERCISE 49c — **Write five original sentences using *get to* and *get back to*. Try to use *right* and *back* in some of the sentences.**

1. _____

2. _____

3. _____

4. _____

5. _____

EXERCISE 49d, Review — **Complete the sentences with these phrasal verbs from previous sections. Be sure the phrasal verbs are in the correct tense. To check their meanings, review the section number given after each one.**

close down, 48	get over, 42	look down on, 48	switch on, 48
come in/into, 47	knock out, 48	look up to, 48	throw out, 48
cut back, 47	know about, 33	put back, 48	trick into, 35
get off on, 40	let in/into, 41	switch off, 48	turn down, 45

1. The company has decided to save money by _____ _____ on advertising.

2. Look at the arrival monitor to see if his plane has _____ _____ yet.

3. That sneaky car salesperson _____ me _____ paying for a lot of options I didn't want.

4. Those shoes are so ugly. Why don't you just _____ them _____?

5. Anyone who has done as much good for other people as he has deserves to be _____ _____ _____.

6. Charles used to _____ _____ _____ me because he went to college and I didn't.

7. What do you _____ _____ changing the meeting from Tuesday to Wednesday? No one has said anything to me about it.

8. The opening of the new factory had to be _____ _____ because some equipment hadn't been delivered.

9. Janice loves to cook, and she especially _____ _____ _____ baking fancy pastries.

10. The antigovernment newspaper was _____ _____ by the dictator.

11. Rio de Janeiro is so beautiful. It _____ me _____ when I saw it.

12. Jim asked Lydia to marry him, but she _____ him _____.

13. That chimney is _____ a lot of cold air _____.

14. Most people _____ _____ a cold in four or five days.

15. If it gets too cold in here, _____ _____ the air conditioner.

16. Could you _____ the lights _____ please, it's getting dark.

50. FOCUS ON: **Keep at it!**

I hope the time and effort you've **put into finding out** more about phrasal verbs has **paid off**. If you've **knocked** yourself **out**, **stuck with** it, and not **fallen behind** or gotten **mixed up** or **burned out**, a great improvement in your ability to under-stand and use English has **come about** — you've **ended up** being better able to **figure out** what you read and hear and better able to **come up with** the right word when you write or speak. But don't get **stressed out** and **give up** if you can't remember every meaning of every verb — improving your vocabulary takes time. It **comes down to** regularly **brushing up** on what you have learned and, when you **come across** a word you don't know, **looking** it **up** in a dictionary. **Keep at** it!

Infinitive

	present tense	-ing form	past tense	past participle
ask out				
	ask out & asks out	asking out	asked out	asked out

1. ask ... out *p.v.* When you **ask** people **out**, you ask them to go with you to a place of entertainment in order to have fun and spend time together.

> Being **asked out** by Tom was quite a surprise to Judy.
> The Bakers called and **asked** the Ortegas **out**.

come down to				
	come down to & comes down to	coming down to	came down to	come down to

1. come down to *p.v.* When the key to understanding a situation or problem is knowledge and consideration of a certain aspect of the situation or problem, this aspect of the situation or problem is what the situation or problem **comes down to**.

> Learning a language **comes down to** practice, practice, practice.
> Our marriage problems aren't really that complicated. What it **comes down to** is whether you're willing to deal with your drinking problem.

deal with				
	deal with & deals with	dealing with	dealt with	dealt with

1. deal with *p.v.* When you **deal with** a project or a problem, you do what you must do to complete the project or to solve the problem.

> There are many problems, but I can **deal with** only one at a time.
> After school the principal will **deal with** the boys who broke the window.

2. deal with *p.v.* When a book, film, article, speech, and so on, **deals with** a certain subject, that is what it is about.

> The governor's speech **dealt with** the growing crime rate.
> I read an interesting article **dealing with** the issue of legalizing marijuana.

Infinitive	present tense	-ing form	past tense	past participle
hold on	hold on & holds on	holding on	held on	held on

1. hold on (to) *p.v.* When you **hold on** or **hold on** to something, you hold it tightly so that you will not fall or be hurt. **Hang on** is similar to **hold on**.

> When the horse jumped over the fence, I **held on** as hard as I could.
> **Hold on** to the rail when you get out of the bathtub — it's slippery.

2. hold on (to) *p.v.* When you **hold on** or **hold on** to people, you hold them tightly to protect them or to prevent them from leaving. When you **hold on** or **hold on** to things, you hold them tightly to protect them or to prevent them from being taken.

> Sam grabbed the robber's legs and **held on** while the guard handcuffed her.
> We were **holding on** to each other as the tornado passed.

3. hold on *p.v.* [informal] When you **hold on**, you wait for a short time. **Hang on** is the same as **hold on**.

> Can you **hold on** just a little longer? I'll be right with you.
> I've been **holding on** for fifteen minutes. I can't wait any longer.

pay back	pay back & pays back	paying back	paid back	paid back

1. pay . . . back *p.v.* When you **pay** people **back**, you give them money that you borrowed from them.

> Would you lend me $200? I'll **pay** you **back** next Friday when I get paid.
> Mark has never been **paid back** for all his sister's medical bills.

2. pay . . . back (for) *p.v.* When you **pay** people **back** or **pay** people **back** for something bad they have done to you, you do something bad to them.

> I'll **pay** that guy **back** for the terrible things he's done to me if it takes the rest
>   of my life.
> Jake shot Hank to **pay** him **back** for turning him in to the police.

take up on	take up on & takes up on	taking up on	took up on	taken up on

1. take . . . up on *p.v.* When you **take** people **up on** an offer, you accept their offer.

> My brother has invited us many times to visit him in Hawaii, and last winter we **took**
>   him **up on** the offer.
> Nicole has never **taken** me **up on** my offer to lend her the money she needs for her
>   dental bills.

Infinitive	present tense	-ing form	past tense	past participle
turn around	turn around & turns around	turning around	turned around	turned around

1. turn ... around *p.v.* When you **turn around**, you move a vehicle or your body so that it faces the opposite direction. When you **turn** something **around**, you move it so that it faces the opposite direction.

*Someone called my name, and I **turned around** to see who it was.*
*You should **turn** this house plant **around** so that the other side can get some light.*

2. turn ... around *p.v.* When you **turn around** a bad situation, a failing business, a losing game, and so on, you improve it so that it is successful.

***Turning** this money-losing company **around** is going to take several years.*
*The quarterback completed four passes in the last five minutes of the football game and completely **turned** it **around**.*

turnaround *n.* A **turnaround** is a major improvement in a bad situation, a failing business, a losing game, and so on.

*We won the game in a last-minute **turnaround**.*
*This company was losing money, but there's been a major **turnaround** since the new manager took over.*

wear out

wear out & wears out	wearing out	wore out	worn out

1. wear ... out *p.v.* When something **wears out** or you **wear** it **out**, it becomes damaged or weak from use and age and is no longer usable.

*People who live in the city **wear out** their car brakes faster than people who live in the country.*
*The carpet in the hallway **wore out** and had to be replaced.*

worn-out *part. adj.* When something is **worn-out**, it has become damaged or weak from use and age and is no longer usable.

*I need new running shoes. These are totally **worn-out**.*

2. wear ... out *p.v.* When something **wears** you **out**, it makes you very tired.

*Playing with his grandchildren really **wore** Fred **out**.*
*Shoveling snow for three hours would **wear** anyone **out**.*

worn-out *part.adj.* When something has made you very tired, you are **worn-out**.

*I have to sit down and rest for a minute — I'm **worn-out**.*

EXERCISE 50a — **Complete the sentences with phrasal verbs from this section. Be sure the phrasal verbs are in the correct tense.**

1. I lent Sally $1,000 last year, but she still hasn't _____ me _____.

2. Children usually get too big for their clothes long before the clothes _____

_____.

3. The company's new CEO promised the shareholders that he would _____ the company _____.

4. Judy told me that she said all those terrible things about me at work to _____ me _____ for stealing her boyfriend.

5. Dr. Wood's new book _____ _____ with preventive medicine.

6. Carrying those boxes of books up to the attic _____ me _____.

7. Like so many things in life, this problem _____ _____ _____ money.

8. Jim drove right past Bob's house, so he had to _____ _____ and go back.

9. _____ _____ to my hand, Susie — it's very crowded here, and I don't want you to get lost.

10. I _____ _____ that problem yesterday, so you don't need to worry about it anymore.

11. Linda isn't sure who she'll go to the dance with, but she said she might _____ Todd _____.

12. It was so windy that I had to _____ _____ to a signpost to keep from falling over.

13. Mike has invited me to his house for dinner several times, but I've never _____ him _____ _____ the offer.

14. _____ _____ just a minute! Where do you think you're going?

EXERCISE 50b — **Write answers to the questions using phrasal verbs, participle adjectives, and nouns from this section. Be sure the phrasal verbs are in the correct tense.**

1. Tom's been waiting for ten minutes. What has Tom been doing?

2. My shoes have holes in the bottom, and now I can't wear them. What has happened to my shoes?

3. In Question 2, how would you describe my shoes?

4. The country's economy was bad, but now it's improving. What is the country's economy doing?

5. The main thing that Lydia will consider when she chooses a college is how good the MBA program is. What is important to Lydia in choosing a college?

6. You called Betty and asked her to go to a movie. What did you do?

7. Bill's baseball team was way behind, but they ended up winning the game. What would you call the game?

8. Mike lent Frank $20, and tomorrow Frank is going to give Mike $20. What is going to happen to Mike tomorrow?

9. Sarah asked me if I would like her to come to my house to help me with my homework, and I said yes. What did I do?

10. Ms. Cummings will do whatever she needs to do to solve the problem after dinner. What will Ms. Cummings do after dinner?

11. The purse snatcher couldn't take my mother's purse because she held it tightly in her hand. What did my mother do to her purse?

12. Shampooing the carpet was a lot of work, and it made Janice really tired. What did shampooing the carpet do to Janice?

13. In Question 12, how did Janice feel after shampooing the carpet?

EXERCISE 50c — **Write eight original sentences using phrasal verbs from this section.**

1. _____

2. _____

3. _____

4. _____

5. _____

6. _____

7. _____

8. _____

EXERCISE 50d, Review — **Complete the sentences with these participle adjectives from this section and previous sections. To check their meanings, review the section number given after each one.**

beat-up, 44	mixed up, 44	turned off, 45
built-in, 46	pissed off, 44	turned on, 45
clogged up, 49	stressed-out, 44	worn-out, 50
grossed out, 43	switched off, 48	
locked up, 44	switched on, 48	

1. Trying to take care of my family and work full-time has made me really _____.

2. You should get rid of those _____ shoes and buy some new ones.

3. I felt really _____ _____ after dancing the merengue with Maria.

4. Maria seemed a little _____ _____ when she saw my big belly hanging over my belt.

5. While I was driving on the interstate, about a billion bugs splattered all over the windshield. I was really _____ _____

6. My car looks pretty _____, but it runs all right.

7. This sink is all _____ _____. We'll have to call a plumber.

8. Could you help me with my calculus homework? I don't understand it at all, and I'm totally _____ _____.

9. You should keep guns_____ _____ if there are children in the house.

10. Mike's really _____ _____ about having to work on Sunday. He was planning to go to the football game, but now he can't.

11. Most computers today have a _____ CD-ROM drive.

12. I like to leave the radio _____ _____ when I'm not home so that burglars will think that someone is at home.

13. It sure is hot in here. Why is the air conditioner _____ _____?

EXERCISE 50e, Review — **Complete the sentences with these phrasal verbs from previous sections. Be sure the phrasal verbs are in the correct tense. To check their meanings, review the section number given after each one.**

build in/into, 46	get on, 49	throw away, 49	turn off, 45
clog up, 49	get to, 49	turn down, 45	turn on, 45
get ahead, 49	hang on, 49	turn in, 45	turn out, 45
get back to, 49	make for, 46	turn into, 45	turn up, 45

1. Jake was nice when he was a boy, but as he got older he _____ _____ a criminal.

2. Stop bothering me about washing the dishes — I'll _____ _____ it when I have time.

3. The teacher said, "After you _____ _____ your tests, you can leave."

4. These stereo speakers weren't added later; they were _____ right _____ the wall.

5. Business has been very good; in fact, this may _____ _____ to be our best year ever.

6. I'll have to _____ _____ _____ you — I don't have time to talk now.

7. If I had known you wanted those old clothes, I wouldn't have _____ them _____.

8. It was getting dark, so I _____ _____ the light.

9. I've gained so much weight that I can't _____ these pants _____.

10. Having a good education helped me to _____ _____.

11. _____ _____, I'm almost ready.

12. It's too hot in here; could you _____ the heat _____ a little?

13. My father said, "_____ the TV _____ and do your homework."

14. Who put all this stuff in the sink and _____ it _____?

15. The champagne, flowers, and gourmet dinner _____ _____ a very special evening.

16. It's hot in here; who keeps _____ _____ the heat?

EXERCISE 50f, Review — **Complete the sentences with these phrasal verbs from this section and previous sections. Be sure the phrasal verbs are in the correct tense. To check their meanings, review the section number given after each one.**

ask out, 50	get ahead, 49	hold on, 50	start off, 49
come down to, 50	get back to, 49	pay back, 50	take up on, 50
deal with, 50	get to, 49	put in/into, 47	turn around, 50
freak out, 46	give out, 43	run out, 47	wear out, 50

1. I like to go to the supermarket on Saturday because they _____ _____ free samples.

2. My teacher said that my project wasn't very good and that it was obvious I hadn't _____ much effort _____ it.

3. Don't lend money to Marvin; he'll never _____ you _____.

4. Thanks for inviting me to go sailing with you. I just might _____ you _____ _____ the offer someday.

5. Sergeant Jones _____ _____ the problem in his usual efficient manner.

6. We're _____ _____ of coffee. Can you make some more?

7. Jim likes Maria, but he's too shy to _____ her _____.

8. Nowadays, it's hard to _____ _____ in the business world if you don't know something about computers.

9. Janice was talking to her father on the other telephone line when I called, so she asked me to _____ _____ for just a minute while she said good-bye to him.

10. Ann used to have a lot of problems, but she has _____ her life _____, and now she is very happy and successful in her job.

11. I called the restaurant manager to complain about the bad food we were served yesterday, and she said she would investigate and _____ _____ _____ me.

12. Heather was very excited that she had _____ _____ go backstage after the concert and meet the band.

13. We had a hard time deciding which of the two houses to buy. We liked both of them, but it _____ _____ _____ which one was in a better school district.

14. I'm not as young as I used to be. That fifteen-mile hike _____ me _____.

15. I hate walking through cemeteries at night; it really _____ me _____.

16. The president of the company _____ the meeting _____ by welcoming everyone.

Answers

When questions require complete sentences as answers, several variations of the answer are often possible depending on whether contractions are used, whether separable phrasal verbs are separated, and whether the object of the phrasal verb is repeated in the answer, replaced by a pronoun, or elipted (not repeated because it is understood). The answers given below would be natural and likely in everyday American English — contractions are used more often than not and separable phrasal verbs are separated more often than not — but any grammatical and logical sentence with the correct verb in the correct tense is acceptable. Phrasal verbs separated by their objects (but not adverbs or adverbials) are indicated with three dots between the verb and particle. Remember that questions asked with *I* or *we* are answered with *you*, and questions asked with *you* are answered with *I* or *we*.

1a
1. took off
2. took off
3. put . . . on
4. run . . . into
5. shows up
6. showed up
7. came from
8. put . . . on
9. figure . . . out
10. take . . . off
11. coming from
12. put on
13. took off
14. looked for
15. gave back
16. run into
17. take . . . off
18. Take off
19. run into
20. Taking . . . off
21. putting . . . on
22. put . . . on
23. put on
24. took . . . off
25. ran into

1b
1.
I finally *figured out* the instructions.
I finally *figured* the instructions *out*.
I finally *figured* them *out*.
2.
Give back my tools when you are finished.
Give my tools *back* when you are finished.
Give them *back* when you are finished.
3.
She *put* on her slippers.
She *put* her slippers *on*.
She *put* them *on*.
4.
I *took off* my shoes.
I *took* my shoes *off*.
I *took* them *off*.
5.
The hurricane *took off* the roof.
The hurricane *took* the roof *off*.
The hurricane *took* it *off*.

1c
1. They didn't *show up*.
2. He *figured* it *out*.
3. It's *taking off*.
4. It was a *takeoff*.
5. He speaks Arabic because he *comes from* Egypt.

6. You *took off*.
7. You *ran into* him.
8. It *came from* the tenth floor.
9. I almost *ran into* a tree.
10. He *put* his name *on* it.
11. You have to *take* it *off*.
12. You *figured* it *out*.
13. You're *taking* them *off*.
14. They *took off*.
15. She's *looking for* it.
16. They don't *show up*.
17. He always forgets to *put* them *on* the table.
18. He *took* Friday *off*.
19. She *gave* it *back*.

2a
1. falling for
2. came off
3. dozed off
4. threw up
5. fell for
6. pulls through
7. stay off
8. came off
9. giving in
10. heard about
11. throwing up
12. come off

2b
1. Did the sick boy *throw up*?
2. Does Rosa *fall for* every boy she meets?
3. Do the tops *come off* easily?
4. Does the dog *stay off* the bed?
5. Did Erik *hear about* the new job?

2c
1. I don't always *give in* to her demands.
2. Mr. and Mrs. Taylor didn't *fall for* the salesman's promises.
3. These machines don't *throw up* sparks.
4. The patient didn't *pull through*.
5. The plot didn't *come off* as planned.

2d
1. She told you to *stay off* it.
2. He *fell for* it.

3. They're starting to *doze off*.
4. She *hears about* everything.
5. It didn't *come off* the way you planned it.
6. One of the wheels *came off* my car.
7. You're not *giving in*.
8. You *fell for* them.
9. She doesn't think Ted will *pull through*.
10. He was *throwing up*.

2e
1. take off
2. showed up
3. took off
4. looking for
5. came from
6. Give back
7. ran into
8. figure out

3a
1. go in for
2. put up with
3. go along with
4. looks down on
5. feel up to
6. screw . . . out of
7. looking forward to
8. get . . . over with
9. go along with

3b
1. He *talks down* to him.
2. She should get it *over with*.
3. He *screwed* them *out of* $5,000.
4. She's *looking forward to* it.
5. I have to *put up with* it.
6. He doesn't *feel up to* it.
7. You *went along with* it.

3c
1. fall for
2. threw up
3. come off
4. gave in
5. stay off
6. pull through
7. dozed off
8. heard about

4a
1. wrap . . . up
2. put . . . to
3. points to
4. pay for
5. cheated on
6. put . . . to
7. looking . . . up

8. went after
9. cheated on
10. plan for
11. pointing to
12. went after
13. pay for
14. looked up
15. wrapped . . . up
16. going after
17. look up
18. going after
19. put . . . to

4b
1.
I was *looking up* a word in the dictionary.
I was *looking* a word *up* in the dictionary.
I was *looking* it *up* in the dictionary.
2.
I was in Boston *looking up* some old army buddies.
I was in Boston *looking* some old army buddies *up*.
I was in Boston *looking* them *up*.
3.
Dad's in the bedroom *wrapping up* Mom's birthday present.
Dad's in the bedroom *wrapping* Mom's birthday present *up*.
Dad's in the bedroom *wrapping* it *up*.
4.
The committee is *wrapping up* their discussion.
The committee is *wrapping* their discussion *up*.
The committee is *wrapping* it *up*.

4c
1. He *pointed* it *out*.
2. You're *planning for* them.
3. It's *looking up*.
4. He *went after* him.
5. She's going to *go after* it.
6. You *put* him *to* a lot of trouble.
7. You're *paying for* it.
8. It's *paid for*.
9. They're *wrapping* it *up*.
10. She *looked* her *up*.
11. He *put* it *to* me.
12. She's *looking up* Erik's telephone number.

13. He *cheated on* her.

4d
1. fell for
2. came from
3. showed up
4. figure . . . out
5. pulled through
6. gave in
7. heard about
8. looking for

5a
1. broke down
2. set up
3. pile up
4. handed . . . back
5. find out
6. called in
7. looked at
8. breaks down
9. breaking . . . down
10. set . . . up
11. look at
12. break . . . down
13. look at
14. calling in
15. break down
16. burn down
17. setting up
18. broke down
19. piling up
20. looking at

5b
1. broke DOWN
2. set UP
3. pile UP
4. handed . . . BACK
5. find OUT
6. called IN
7. LOOKED at
8. breaks DOWN
9. breaking . . . DOWN
10. set . . . UP
11. LOOK at
12. break . . . DOWN
13. LOOK at
14. calling IN
15. break DOWN
16. burn DOWN
17. setting UP
18. broke DOWN
19. piling UP
20. LOOKING at

5c
1.
The firefighters *broke down* the door.
The firefighters *broke* the door *down*.
The firefighters *broke* it *down*.
2.
They *burned down* the old barn.
They *burned* the old barn *down*.

Answers

They *burned* it *down*.
3.
He *called in* Dr. Shapiro.
He *called* Dr. Shapiro *in*.
He *called* her *in*.
4.
Our teacher *handed back* the papers.
Our teacher *handed* the papers *back*.
Our teacher *handed* them *back*.
5.
I *set up* the ironing board.
I *set* the ironing board *up*.
I *set* it *up*.

5d
1. She *set* it *up*.
2. It was *set up*.
3. They're *piling up*.
4. They're *piled up*.
5. He *handed* it *back*.
6. It *broke down*.
7. It's *broken-down*.
8. He had a *break-down*.
9. They *burned* it *down*.
10. It *burned down*.
11. He *broke down*.
12. He had a *break-down*.
13. She was angry because I didn't *call in*.
14. She *set* it *up*.
15. It's *set up*.
16. He *broke in*.
17. You *found out* that Ali's excuse was a big lie.

5e
1. put up with
2. felt up to
3. Stay off
4. come off
5. looking forward to
6. go along with
7. threw up
8. goes in for
9. talked down to
10. get ... over with

6a
1. coming down with
2. went through with
3. come up with
4. get around to
5. got ... out of
6. get ... out of
7. boils down to
8. monkey around with
9. get out of
10. gone back on

6b
1. He *went through with* it.
2. You didn't *get around to* it.
3. You told him you'd

get around to it tomorrow.
4. She *gets* a lot of satisfaction *out of* it.
5. She *came up with* a way to manufacture her company's products more cheaply.
6. It *comes down to* location.
7. I feel like I'm *coming down with* a cold.
8. You'll *monkey around with* it.
9. You *got* it *out of* her.
10. She *went back on* her promise.

6c
1. wrap ... up
2. plan for
3. looked ... up
4. cheated on
5. look at
6. finds out
7. going after
8. pointed to
9. put ... to
10. pile up
11. handed ... back
12. burned down

6d
1. wrap ... UP
2. PLAN for
3. looked ... UP
4. CHEATED on
5. LOOK at
6. finds OUT
7. GOING after
8. POINTED to
9. put ... TO
10. pile UP
11. handed ... BACK
12. burned DOWN

7a
1. let out
2. holding ... up
3. ran over
4. let out
5. cut ... up
6. pointed out
7. let ... out
8. taken in
9. took ... in
10. taking ... apart
11. holding up
12. took in
13. hold up
14. seeing about
15. let out
16. held up
17. ran over
18. pointed ... out
19. ran over
20. take ... in
21. take ... in
22. held ... up
23. run over
24. see about
25. hold up

7b
1.
The cook *cut up* the meat.

The cook *cut* the meat *up*.
The cook *cut* it *up*.
2.
The snowstorm *held up* air travelers.
The snowstorm *held* air travelers *up*.
The snowstorm *held* them *up*.
3.
Don't *let out* the dog.
Don't *let* the dog *out*.
Don't *let* it *out*.
4.
The real estate agent *pointed out* the swimming pool.
The real estate agent *pointed* the swimming pool *out*.
The real estate agent *pointed* it *out*.
5.
The truck *ran over* the man.
The truck *ran* the man *over*.
The truck *ran* him *over*.
6.
I'm going to *take apart* the broken doorknob.
I'm going to *take* the broken doorknob *apart*.
I'm going to *take* it *apart*.
7.
The tailor *took in* the pants.
The tailor *took* the pants *in*.
The tailor *took* them *in*.

7c
1. You're going to *see about* changing to a different room.
2. They haven't *held up*.
3. She's going to *take* them *in*.
4. He was *taken in*.
5. I was *run over*.
6. He *pointed* them *out*.
7. It *held up* the game.
8. She's *cutting* a piece of paper *up*.
9. They're *holding* it *up*.
10. She *held* the bank *up*.
11. There was a *holdup*.
12. You *took* it *in*.
13. He *took* it *apart*.
14. It *ran over*.
15. They *took* you *in*.
16. He *let* it *out*.
17. You *ran over* and grabbed it.
18. She *let out* a scream.
19. It has *held up*.
20. He *let* them *out*.
21. He *took* it *in*.

22. It's *running over*.
23. You're *letting* them *out*.

7d
1. go through with
2. come off
3. got out of
4. get around to
5. monkeying around with
6. boil down to
7. figure out
8. put ... on
9. went after
10. gone back on
11. came up with
12. looking forward to
13. dozed off
14. came down with

8a
1. fallen over
2. burned out
3. fought back
4. ring ... up
5. work in
6. pick out
7. picked out
8. burn ... out
9. rung ... up
10. heard of
11. fell ... over
12. burned out
13. hear of
14. fight back
15. tear down

8b
1.
The sheriff *burned out* the escaped convicts.
The sheriff *burned* the escaped convicts *out*.
The sheriff *burned* them *out*.
2.
Bill has *picked out* a new car.
Bill has *picked* a new car *out*.
Bill has *picked* it *out*.
3.
The clerk hasn't *rung up* these CDs yet.
The clerk hasn't *rung* these CDs *up* yet.
The clerk hasn't *rung* them *up* yet.
4.
The new owners have *torn down* the garage.
The new owners have *torn* the garage *down*.
The new owners have *torn* it *down*.
5.
The mayor tried to *work in* a tour of the factory.
The mayor tried to *work* a tour of the factory *in*.

The mayor tried to *work* it *in*.

8c
1. He said he wouldn't *hear of* it.
2. It's *burned* itself *out*.
3. He's *rung* them *up*.
4. They've *picked* it *out*.
5. She couldn't *fight back* the tears.
6. It *burned out*.
7. It's *burned out*.
8. They *fell over*.
9. It was *burned out*.
10. It's *burned out*.
11. You didn't *fight back*.
12. You've *worked* it *in*.
13. She hasn't *rung* you *up*.
14. They *tore* it *down*.
15. He *fell* all *over* himself.
16. You asked him if he's ever *heard of* the new seafood restaurant in the mall.

8d
1. took ... apart
2. pull through
3. shown up
4. ran over
5. taken in
6. fall for
7. cut ... up
8. held up
9. pointed to
10. looked ... up
11. let ... out
12. gave in
13. get ... over with
14. see about
15. goes in for
16. put up with

9a
1. give up
2. broke out
3. getting along
4. work up
5. gave ... up
6. catch up
7. hang up
8. worked up
9. catch up
10. getting along
11. gave up
12. hang up
13. chickened out
14. hook up
15. catch up
16. broken out
17. hook up

9b
1. on
2. to
3. on
4. of
5. with
6. with
7. of
8. to

Answers

9. on

9c

1.
Tonight I'm going to try to *hook up* my fax machine.
Tonight I'm going to try to *hook* my fax machine *up*.
Tonight I'm going to try to *hook* it *up*.

2.
After my accident, I had to *give up* scuba diving.
After my accident, I had to *give* scuba diving *up*.
After my accident, I had to *give* it *up*.

3.
You can *hang up* your coat in the closet.
You can *hang* your coat *up* in the closet.
You can *hang* it *up* in the closet.

9d
1. You want to *catch up*.
2. She has to give *up driving*.
3. She needs to *catch up*.
4. I was *worked up*.
5. *Hooking up* a computer to a printer is easy.
6. It's *hooked up*.
7. They're going to try to *break out*.
8. It would be called a *breakout*.
9. They don't *get along*.
10. You *gave up* on it.
11. Fights *break out*.
12. He *worked up* the courage to ask his boss for a raise.
13. He didn't *chicken out*.
14. They told him to *give up*.
15. She's *working up* to it.
16. She *hung up* on him.

9e
1. heard of
2. piled up
3. put ... to

4. fallen over
5. looked at
6. pick ... out
7. ran into
8. pointed to
9. hand ... back
10. cheating on
11. work ... in
12. fight back
13. rang up
14. found out
15. torn down
16. burned out

10a
1. hand ... out
2. screw ... up
3. fallen off
4. gave up
5. screwed ... up
6. laid off
7. growing up
8. kick back
9. went ahead
10. fill ... in
11. go ahead
12. fall off
13. lay off
14. fill ... in
15. kick back
16. fill in
17. Grow up

10b
1. grown-ups
2. screwup
3. kickbacks
4. handouts
5. fill-in
6. handout
7. layoffs
8. falloff
9. go-ahead

10c
1.
You haven't *filled in* all the spaces.
You haven't *filled* all the spaces *in*.
You haven't *filled* them *in*.

2.
Is the teacher *handing out* the tests?
Is the teacher *handing* the tests *out*?
Is the teacher *handing* them *out*?

3.
The company is going to *lay off* my brother.
The company is going to *lay* my brother *off*.
The company is going to *lay* him *off*.

4.
I'm sorry I *screwed up* your plan.
I'm sorry I *screwed* your plan *up*.

I'm sorry I *screwed* it *up*.

10d
1. You *went ahead* with it.
2. She told you to *fill* it *in*.
3. It's *filled in*.
4. She's *screwing* it *up*.
5. It's *screwed up*.
6. I *kick back* $3,000 to the mayor.
7. It's a *kickback*.
8. She was *laid off*.
9. He *screwed* you *up*.
10. You *grew up* there.
11. It's for *grown-ups*.
12. It will *fall off*.
13. It would be called a *falloff*.
14. She told him to *lay off*.
15. He's *filling in* for Omar.
16. They'll be *handed out*.
17. She *filled* her *in*.

10e
1. takeoff
2. breakdown
3. hookup
4. breakout
5. holdup
6. setup
7. put-on

10f
1. work up
2. gave up
3. pick out
4. hook up
5. get along
6. talk down to
7. catch up
8. chickened out of

11a
1. cut ... off
2. back up
3. back up
4. work out
5. backing ... up
6. cut ... off
7. back ... up
8. follows up
9. drop ... off
10. backed ... up
11. wake up
12. work out
13. take out
14. back up
15. worked out
16. works out
17. drops off
18. cut off
19. taking ... out
20. back up
21. cut ... off
22. fell off

23. try ... out
24. woke ... up
25. worked out
26. try out
27. take out
28. worked out
29. cut off
30. took ... out
31. taken ... out

11b
1.
Did you *back up* your work?
Did you *back* your work *up*?
Did you *back* it *up*?

2.
They're *cutting off* the power.
They're *cutting* the power *off*.
They're *cutting* it *off*.

3.
I *dropped off* Frank at the airport.
I *dropped* Frank *off* at the airport.
I *dropped* him *off* at the airport.

4.
Mom asked me to *take out* the garbage.
Mom asked me to *take* the garbage *out*.
Mom asked me to *take* it *out*.

5.
Alex *tried out* his new bicycle.
Alex *tried* his new bicycle *out*.
Alex *tried* it *out*.

6.
Mike has *woken up* Ali.
Mike has *woken* Ali *up*.
Mike has *woken* him *up*.

11c
1. It's his *backup* camera.
2. It's the *cutoff* date.
3. She's his *back-up*.
4. I gave it a *tryout*.
5. She made a *follow-up* visit.
6. Your *workout* clothes got dirty.
7. You ate *takeout* food.
8. There was a *backup* on the interstate.
9. There has been a *falloff*.

10. She didn't make a *backup*.
11. There's a *dropoff*.
12. You gave it a *workout*.

11d
1. They *cut* it *off*.
2. You bought *takeout* food.
3. *Working out* is good for my health.
4. You're going to *try* it *out*.
5. They're letting me give their service a *tryout*.
6. It *cut* them *off*.
7. They were *cut off*.
8. I'm *backing* it *up*.
9. It's a *backup*.
10. She's *following up*.
11. My *workout* routine is difficult.
12. He *backed up* his accusation with photographs.
13. She wants to *try out*.
14. It *backs* it *up*.
15. It's a *backup*.
16. She *drops* her *off*.
17. It's a *follow-up* appointment.
18. It's not *working out* the way she expected.
19. He *took* Judy *out*.
20. It *works out* to $9,000.
21. You've never *woken up* at 3:30 in the morning.

11e
1. lay off
2. handed out
3. grew up
4. screwed up
5. go ahead
6. fell off
7. stay off
8. looking for
9. coming from
10. feel up to
11. screw ... out of
12. kick back
13. go along with
14. give ... back
15. fill in
16. heard of

12a
1. sign ... out
2. came up
3. put up
4. came across

5. signed out
6. fell through
7. puts up
8. back off
9. fallen through
10. come up
11. put up
12. screw ... on
13. sign in
14. put up
15. screwed ... on
16. put ... up
17. came up
18. come across
19. put up
20. comes across
21. came up
22. put ... up
23. coming up

12b
1. He'd *backed off*.
2. He had *signed in*.
3. She'd *fallen through*.
4. He had *put up* a fight.
5. It had *come across* well.
6. She had *put up* the money.
7. He'd said that it was *coming up*.
8. He'd *screwed* it *on*.
9. It was *screwed on*.
10. It had *put* them *up*.
11. Something had *come up*.
12. It had *fallen through*.
13. It had *come up*.
14. They'd *put up* a fence.
15. I had *come across* some old newspapers.
16. He'd *come up* to New York.
17. She had *signed out*.

12d
1. pay for
2. followed up
3. thrown up
4. fallen off
5. put to
6. work out
7. drop ... off
8. woke ... up
9. try ... out
10. back up
11. pointed to
12. wrap up
13. cut off
14. planned for
15. take out
16. go after

13a
1. let ... off
2. called off
3. hit on

Answers

4. light up
5. tracked ... down
6. lighting up
7. closed off
8. left off
9. hit on
10. handed in
11. drop ... off
12. left off
13. hand in
14. let ... off
15. hand in

13b

1.
The bride hasn't *called off* the wedding.
The bride hasn't *called* the wedding *off*.
The bride hasn't *called* it *off*.
2.
Are they *closing off* the gallery?
Are they *closing* the gallery *off*?
Are they *closing* it *off*?
3.
The accountant *handed in* her report.
The accountant *handed* her report *in*.
The accountant *handed* it *in*.
4.
Have you *left off* Carmen?
Have you *left* Carmen *off*?
Have you *left* her *off*?
5.
The judge *let off* the pickpocket.
The judge *let* the pickpocket *off*.
The judge *let* him *off*.
6.
I told him not to *light up* the cigarette.
I told him not to *light* the cigarette *up*.
I told him not to *light* it *up*.
7.
The EPA *tracked down* the polluters.
The EPA *tracked* the polluters *down*.
The EPA *tracked* them *down*.

13c

1. It was *tracked down*.
2. They were *handed in*.
3. They're always *let off*.
4. She was *hit on*.
5. It was *left off*.
6. It was *called off*.
7. It's being *closed off*.
8. It's *closed off*.
9. It was *lit up*.
10. It was *lit up*.

13d

1. burned down
2. taken off
3. talked down to
4. set up
5. screwed out of
6. let out
7. called in
8. pointed out
9. run into
10. piled up
11. given back
12. handed back
13. taken apart
14. planned for
15. run over
16. looked at

14a

1. wound up
2. fill ... out
3. put away
4. stick ... up
5. dress up
6. dries up
7. put ... away
8. winding up
9. stuck ... up
10. winding ... up
11. dressed up
12. dries up
13. wind ... up
14. stick up
15. filled out
16. put away
17. stuck up
18. put away
19. used ... up
20. butts in

14b

1. dried up
2. dressed up
3. filled out
4. stuck-up
5. used up
6. wound up
7. put away

14c

1.
Janice *dressed up* her son.
Janice *dressed* her son *up*.
Janice *dressed* him *up*.
2.
The sun quickly *dries up* the water.
The sun quickly *dries* the water *up*.
The sun quickly *dries* it *up*.
3.
Filling out the entire form isn't necessary.
Filling the entire form *out* isn't necessary.
Filling it *out* isn't necessary.
4.
Ed *put away* six beers in an hour.
Ed *put* six beers *away* in an hour.
Ed *put* them *away* in an hour.
5.
They *stuck up* notices.
They *stuck* notices *up*.
They *stuck* them *up*.
6.
I'm *winding up* my clock.
I'm *winding* my clock *up*.
I'm *winding* it *up*.

14d

1. He *wound up* in the hospital.
2. She kept *butting in*.
3. It *dried up*.
4. He *put* them *away*.
5. They're *put away*.
6. They're *dried up*.
7. You *wound* it *up*.
8. It was *wound up*.
9. She *dressed up*.
10. She was *dressed up*.
11. He *filled* it *out*.
12. It was *filled out*.

14e

1. hung up
2. paid for
3. hooked up
4. cut off
5. broken-down
6. set up
7. filled in
8. screwed up
9. caught up
10. worked up
11. grown-up
12. cut up
13. burned-out
14. backed up
15. wake-up
16. piled up

15a

1. blew ... away
2. set ... up
3. came through
4. fix ... up
5. tell ... on
6. comes through
7. heading/headed for
8. fix ... up
9. comes through
10. heading/headed for
11. go with
12. dried out
13. blow ... away
14. come through
15. set ... up
16. go with
17. came through
18. blown away
19. went with
20. came through
21. went with
22. head back
23. go with

15b

1. He's going to *fix you up* with a table next to the fireplace.
2. She's sure that her father will *come through*.
3. It's going to *blow* him *away*.
4. He'll *fix* it *up*.
5. It will be *fixed up*.
6. He won't *tell on* her.
7. It's going to *blow* them *away*.
8. They won't *come through* it.
9. She'll *fix* herself *up*.
10. She'll be *fixed up*.
11. I'm going to *head for* Tucson.
12. I'm going to *head back* to San Diego.
13. He won't *set* Mike up with his sister.
14. She isn't going to *go with* blue.
15. It's going to *blow away* the competition.
16. He's going to *come through* town.
17. It's going to *dry up*.
18. It'll be *dried up*.

15d

1. came up
2. fell through
3. light ... up
4. put up
5. track down
6. lit up
7. closed off
8. screw ... on
9. call ... off
10. back off
11. hand in
12. left ... off
13. sign in
14. signed out
15. let ... off
16. came across

16a

1. thinking about
2. carry ... on
3. counting on
4. go for
5. believe in
6. get through
7. count on
8. get through
9. held off
10. put ... past
11. carried on
12. held off
13. went for
14. going for
15. carry on
16. get ... through
17. believe in
18. carry on
19. believe in
20. get through
21. goes for
22. get through
23. count on

16b

1. She *goes for* it.
2. She didn't *get through* studying until 11:00 P.M.
3. They *carried* them on.
4. They kept *carry-on* bags with them.
5. She's *thinking about* spending the summer in Bolivia.
6. He doesn't *believe in* it.
7. He couldn't *carry on* his career as a dancer.
8. You *held off* having children.
9. I wouldn't *put* stealing *past* him.
10. She's going to try to *get through* to her.
11. I can't *count on* him.
12. He *carried on*.
13. You can't *count on* it.
14. They *believe in* monsters.

16d

1. stuck-up
2. fixed up
3. used up
4. put away
5. wound up
6. wrapped up
7. filled out
8. dried up
9. dressed up
10. screwed on
11. closed off
12. lit up

16e

1. wound up
2. goes in for
3. put up with
4. looking forward to
5. give up
6. feel up to
7. see ... about
8. get around to
9. get out of
10. get ... over with
11. left off
12. worked out
13. broke down
14. took ... in
15. put ... up
16. broke out
17. butt in

17a

1. came over
2. falling apart
3. rip ... up
4. heading/headed into
5. got back at
6. came over
7. worn down
8. go about
9. grow out of
10. falling apart
11. wear ... down
12. fell apart
13. come over
14. grows out of

17b
(any two of the possible sentences shown are acceptable)

1.
Frequently Ms. Taylor *comes over*.
Ms. Taylor frequently *comes over*.

Ms. Taylor *comes over*
   frequently.
2.
Sometimes these cheap
   toys *fall apart*.
These cheap toys *some-*
   times fall apart.
These cheap toys *fall*
   apart sometimes.
3.
Nervously he *went*
   about making the
   bomb.
He nervously *went*
   about making the
   bomb.
He went *about*
   making the bomb
   nervously.
4.
Eventually Sally
   will *grow out of* her
   childish behavior.
Sally will eventually
   grow out of her
   childish behavior.
Sally will *grow out of* her
   childish behavior
   eventually.
5.
Reluctantly Jim *headed*
   into the swamp.
Jim reluctantly *headed*
   into the swamp.
Jim *headed* reluctantly
   into the swamp.
Jim *headed into*
   the swamp reluc-
   tantly.
6.
Suddenly Pat *ripped up*
   Mike's letter.
Pat suddenly *ripped up*
   Mike's letter.
Pat *ripped up*
   Mike's letter
   suddenly.
7.
Soon Frank will *get back*
   at Todd.
Frank will soon *get back*
   at Todd.
Frank will *get back at*
   Todd soon.
8.
Gradually he *wore down*
   my resistance.
He gradually *wore down*
   my resistance.
He *wore down* my resis-
   tance gradually.
17c
1. It was *ripped up*.
2. It was *ripped up*.
3. It's *falling apart*.
4. They *came over*.
5. He doesn't know
   how to *go about*
   applying for a mort-
   gage.
6. We're going to *head*
   into the city.
7. She *grew out* of it.
8. They've *worn down*.
9. They're *worn down*.

10. He's *gotten back* at
   you.
11. They *came over*
   before Columbus.
12. She *came over*
   and looked at my
   paper.
13. He *fell apart*.
14. She'll *grow out of* it
   soon.
15. It's *falling apart*.
16. They're trying to
   wear her *down*.
17d
1. find out
2. get along
3. go through with
4. chickened out of
5. set up
6. work in
7. fight back
8. came down with
9. monkey around
   with
10. kicking back
11. heard of
12. boils down to
13. come up
14. fell over
15. Go ahead

18a
1. get off
2. break through
3. tell … apart
4. get off
5. line up
6. stood around
7. goes beyond
8. get … off
9. figured on
10. get off
11. lined up
12. get … off
13. broke through
14. Get off
15. lift up
16. get off
17. line up
18. Get off
18b
1. He said he'd *get* it
   off the table.
2. You can't *tell* them
   apart.
3. He can't *lift* it *up*.
4. He said he hadn't
   figured on snow in
   May.
5. She *lined up* a great
   band.
6. It's *lined up*.
7. He said it *goes*
   beyond that.
8. They *broke through*
   it.
9. He *gets off* at 5:00.
10. I *got off* with a
   warning.
11. He *lined up* the
   desks.
12. They're *lined up*.
13. She asked you to
   get off the phone.
14. You *stood around*

waiting for the
   bus.
15. He said you'd *get*
   Sundays *off*.
16. They have to be
   lined up.
17. He *got off* the train.
18. He told him to *get*
   off the grass.
18d
1. went for
2. thought about
3. held off
4. goes with
5. came through
6. counting on
7. told on
8. put … past
9. come over
10. goes along with
11. head for
12. head back
13. carried on
14. get off
15. grown out of
16. believe in
19a
1. heat … up
2. pulled over
3. bring … back
4. cool … off
5. go back
6. brought back
7. hand over
8. brought back
9. aiming at
10. bring … over
11. warm up
12. aim … at
13. handed … over
14. cooled off
15. aimed at
16. goes back
17. warm up
18. went back
19. cools off
20. pulled over
21. warm up
19b
1.
Could you *bring back*
   my tool kit.
Could you *bring*
   my tool kit *back*.
Could you *bring* it *back*.
2.
I'll *bring over* your tool
   kit.
I'll *bring* your tool kit
   over.
I'll *bring* it *over*.
3.
The air conditioner
   quickly *cooled off*
   my apartment.
The air conditioner
   quickly *cooled* my
   apartment *off*.
The air conditioner
   quickly *cooled* it *off*.
4.
Todd *handed over* his
   wallet.
Todd *handed* his wallet
   over.

Todd *handed* it *over*.
5.
The sheriff *pulled over*
   the suspects.
The sheriff *pulled* the
   suspects *over*.
The sheriff *pulled* them
   over.
6.
The drivers are *warming*
   up their trucks.
The drivers are *warming*
   their trucks *up*.
The drivers are *warming*
   them *up*.
19c
1. It *warmed* right *up*.
2. I'll *go* right *back* to
   work.
3. It *cooled* right *off*.
4. You would *pull* right
   over.
5. He *aimed* it right *at*
   him.
6. She told you to *give*
   her dictionary right
   back.
7. He told her to *hand*
   it right *over*.
8. She *brought* it right
   over.
19d
1. broke through
2. standing around
3. went beyond
4. track down
5. headed into
6. backed off
7. come up with
8. hit on
9. fell through
10. wind up
11. tell … apart
12. figure on
13. came across
14. lifted up
15. put up
16. let … off

20a
1. go off
2. went around
3. go on
4. go off
5. hang around
6. ended up
7. lies around
8. hangs around
9. start out
10. go around
11. stay up
12. ended up
13. lying around
14. went around
15. go on
16. goes off
17. going around
18. go off
19. stay up
20. goes around
21. hangs around
22. go around
23. went on
24. went around
25. Go ahead

26. go on
27. went on
28. went around
29. goes around
30. go on
20b
1. I'm going to
   lie around watching
   TV.
2. She *went around*
   making decorating
   plans.
3. It *ended up* in
   Australia.
4. It *goes off* at 2:00.
5. He asked, "What's
   going on?"
6. He *goes around*
   telling awful jokes.
7. She *stayed up* all
   night.
8. He *hangs around*
   the house.
9. It didn't *go off*.
10. He *went around*
   wearing a Hawaiian
   shirt.
11. They *go on* auto-
   matically.
12. They didn't get a
   hot dog because I
   didn't buy enough
   to *go around*.
13. You have to *go*
   around the pot-
   holes.
14. You *ended up* buy-
   ing the red car.
15. You couldn't *go on*.
16. She *started out*
   thinking it would
   take only a few
   weeks.
20d
1. screwed … out of
2. cooled off
3. ripped … up
4. blow … away
5. gave up
6. work up
7. paid for
8. heard of
9. came over
10. called off
11. see … about
12. go about
13. dry out
14. aimed at
15. broke out
16. bring … over
21a
1. take … out on
2. step on
3. picking on
4. looked around
5. settling down
6. looked over
7. settle … down
8. zip … up
9. settled down
10. look around
11. think ahead
12. step on
21b
1. He should *look* it

Answers

over.
2. I *looked around.*
3. They *settled down.*
4. I should *zip* it *up.*
5. It's *zipped up.*
6. She didn't *think ahead.*
7. He *picks on* him.
8. He *took* it *out on* his wife.
9. He *stepped on* it.

21c
1. Business in this restaurant *should/ought to fall off* in January.
2. They *should/ought to* be *winding up* the investigation.
3. These cheap shoes *shouldn't hold up* more than three months.
4. Jim flies from Florida to Boston every year in April, and it's April now. Jim *should/ought to come up* to Boston soon.
5. It almost always gets cooler in October, and it's October 1st today, so it *should/ought to cool off* soon.
6. Raul's disease is not serious, so he *should/ought to pull through.*
7. Francisco almost never works past 5:00, and it's 4:50 now. He *should/ought to get off* in a few minutes.
8. Lydia likes skiing a lot, so if you suggest that we go skiing next weekend, she *should/ought to go for* the idea.
9. The enemy soldiers have been trying to smash a hole in the wall of the fort for two hours, and they *should/ought to break through* soon.
10. Sally said she would come to my house at 5:30 and it's 5:40 now. She *should/ought to come over* soon.
11. This work normally takes four hours to finish, so if you start at 9:00 you *should/ought to get through* around 1:00.
12. The train almost always passes

through town at 3:25, and it's 3:20 now, so the train *should/ought to come through* town in five minutes.
13. I put a lot of wood on the fire, so it *shouldn't burn out* before morning.
14. The car heater is on maximum, so it *should/ought to warm up* soon.

21d
1. went around
2. Hand … over
3. goes off
4. pull over
5. line up
6. stayed up
7. falls apart
8. get back at
9. started out
10. hang around
11. end up
12. brought back
13. lie around
14. go on
15. rang up
16. go back

22a
1. eat up
2. plug … up
3. burns … up
4. clear … up
5. pay up
6. cleared up
7. count up
8. cleared up
9. burn up
10. wipe up
11. heat … up
12. burn up
13. ate up

22b
1.
They *burned up* the wood.
They *burned* the wood *up.*
They *burned* it *up.*
2.
He ought to *clear up* the misunderstanding.
He ought to *clear* the misunderstanding *up.*
He ought to *clear* it *up.*
3.
Would you *count up* the votes?
Would you *count* the votes *up?*
Would you *count* them *up?*
4.
Have they *eaten up* all the candy?
Have they *eaten* all the candy *up?*
Have they *eaten* it *up?*
5.
I can't *plug up* the hole.
I can't *plug* the hole *up.*

I can't *plug* it *up.*
6.
Wipe up that water right now!
Wipe that water *up* right now!
Wipe it *up* right now!

22c
1. I *plugged* it *up.*
2. It was *plugged up.*
3. You're *heating* it *up.*
4. It'll be *heated up.*
5. He hasn't *counted up* his money.
6. I'll *pay* it *up.*
7. I'll be *paid up.*
8. They *burned* them *up.*
9. They're *burned up.*
10. It *cleared* right *up.*
11. She's *wiping* it *up.*
12. He *eats* his food right *up.*

22d
1. count on
2. go with
3. Think ahead
4. signed in
5. signed out
6. put away
7. hand … in
8. go with
9. dress up
10. looked around
11. step on
12. dry up
13. Zip up
14. takes … out on
15. heading/headed for
16. head back

23a
1. make … up
2. Watch out
3. cut down
4. cut down
5. Stay out
6. hold out
7. made up
8. drop out
9. make up
10. crack down
11. got away
12. hold … out
13. gotten away
14. stay out
15. holding out
16. make up
17. gotten away
18. get away
19. stayed out
20. cuts down
21. hold out
22. made up
23. make up

23b
1. on
2. on
3. of
4. with
5. for
6. for
7. of

23c
1. They're *holding out*

for a 10 percent raise.
2. They're *holdouts.*
3. They *made up.*
4. He *dropped out.*
5. He's a *dropout.*
6. I *made up* my mind.
7. She told me to *cut down* on tennis.
8. They're *holding out.*
9. They're *holdouts.*
10. They *stayed out* until 3:00 A.M.
11. It has to *hold out.*
12. He *made up* a story.
13. It was *made-up.*
14. He has *gotten away* with it.
15. I have to *watch out* for big trucks.
16. They're going to *crack down* on crime.
17. It's a *crackdown.*

23d
1. grown out of
2. hold off
3. wipe up
4. think about
5. get through
6. tell … apart
7. break through
8. counted up
9. aimed at
10. falling apart
11. went for
12. put past
13. burned up
14. believes in
15. stand around
16. come over

24a
1. slow down
2. Shake up
3. come down
4. traded … in
5. come down
6. Stopping over
7. shaken up
8. showed … off
9. let up
10. come down
11. print … out
12. shook … up
13. stop … over

24b
1. shake-up
2. stopover
3. comedown
4. letup
5. trade-ins
6. slowdown
7. printout
8. show-off

24c
1.
The rain *slowed down* traffic.
The rain *slowed* traffic *down.*
The rain *slowed* it *down.*
2.
He *printed out* his letter.
He *printed* his letter *out.*

He *printed* it *out.*
3.
The bad news has *shaken up* Jim and Nancy.
The bad news has *shaken* Jim and Nancy *up.*
The bad news has *shaken* them *up.*
4.
I got $5,000 for *trading in* my old car.
I got $5,000 for *trading* my old car *in.*
I got $5,000 for *trading* it *in.*
5.
Chelsea's parents *showed off* her perfect report card.
Chelsea's parents *showed* her perfect report card *off.*
Chelsea's parents *showed* it *off.*

24d
1. You *printed* them *out.*
2. It's a *printout.*
3. He's going to *come down* to New Orleans.
4. He *shows off.*
5. He's a *show-off.*
6. You'll *trade* it *in.*
7. It's a *trade-in.*
8. He *shook* things *up.*
9. It was a *shake-up.*
10. She's *come down* in life.
11. It's a *comedown.*
12. It *let up.*
13. It was a *letup.*
14. It *slowed* it *down.*
15. It was a *slowdown.*
16. I *stopped over.*
17. It was a *stopover.*
18. It *shook* him *up.*
19. He was *shaken up.*

24e
1. follow-up
2. crackdown
3. dropout
4. lineup
5. tryout
6. workout
7. backup
8. drop-off

24f
1. stay out
2. lift … up
3. goes beyond
4. told on
5. watch out
6. figure on
7. cool … off
8. holding out
9. bringing over
10. look around
11. settle down
12. step on
13. counted up
14. wipe up

403

Answers

15. hung up
25a
1. hurry up
2. settle for
3. had ... on
4. lighten up
5. knocked ... over
6. do with
7. plan ahead
8. think up
9. hurry ... up
10. lighten ... up
11. have ... on
25b
1. He *had* a red shirt *on*.
2. He won't *settle for* less.
3. She's *planning ahead*.
4. He *knocked* him *over*.
5. He told him to *hurry up*.
6. It had to *do with* my income taxes.
7. He should *lighten up*.
8. She's *thinking up* a Halloween costume.
25d
1. zipped up
2. warmed up
3. cleared up
4. dried up
5. made-up
6. paid up
7. shaken up
8. ripped up
9. lined up
10. warmed up
11. plugged up
12. burned up
13. worn down
25e
1. come down
2. hook up
3. screw ... on
4. show off
5. called in
6. stops over
7. trade in
8. stuck ... up
9. cleared up
10. let up
11. warm up
12. slow down
13. hand out
14. print ... out
15. gone back
26a
1. get ... together
2. start ... up
3. go over
4. open ... up
5. went up
6. put ... together
7. shut off
8. go up
9. let ... in on
10. go over
11. goes up
12. go over
13. put ... together

14. opens up
15. goes ... up
16. go over
17. get ... together
18. gets together
19. went over
20. open ... up
21. Put ... together
22. goes up
23. start up
26b
1.
I wish they would *open up* a branch office near me.
I wish they would *open* a branch office *up* near me.
I wish they would *open* one *up* near me.
2.
Lydia *put together* the food processor.
Lydia *put* the food processor *together*.
Lydia *put* it *together*.
3.
Do you know how to *shut off* the photocopier?
Do you know how to *shut* the photocopier *off*?
Do you know how to *shut* it *off*?
4.
Push this button to *start up* the generator.
Push this button to *start* the generator *up*.
Push this button to *start* it *up*.
26c
1. He *went over* it.
2. He gave it a good *going-over*.
3. She *went up* to the king and gave him the petition.
4. He *let* you *in on* a secret.
5. They're going to *get together*.
6. It's called a *get-together*.
7. It *starts up* from the hard disk.
8. It's the *start-up* disk.
9. It *went over* well.
10. It *shuts off*.
11. It's called the *shutoff* point or the *shutoff* temperature.
12. I quit my job so that I could *start up* my own company.
13. I'd call it a *start-up* company.
14. I *put* it *together*.
15. It *goes up* to December 31.
16. It *opens up* at 7:00 A.M.

26d
1. settle for
2. lighten up
3. knocked ... over
4. ended up
5. hurry up
6. takes ... out on
7. looked ... over
8. Put ... on
9. hurry up
10. gone off
11. picked on
12. think up
13. do with
14. showing off
15. go on
16. have ... on
27a
1. tore ... off
2. wiped ... off
3. knock off
4. dries off
5. bite ... off
6. wear off
7. wash ... off
8. knocked off
9. broke off
10. Knock ... off
11. worn off
12. broke down
13. knock off
14. wore off
15. knock ... off

27b
1.
Alex has *bitten off* the head of the gingerbread man.
Alex has *bitten* the head of the gingerbread man *off*.
Alex has *bitten* it *off*.
2.
The movers *broke off* the cup handle.
The movers *broke* the cup handle right *off*.
The movers *broke* it right *off*.
3.
Please *dry off* the dishes.
Please *dry* the dishes *off*.
Please *dry* them *off*.
4.
Don't *knock off* the ashtray.
Don't *knock* the ashtray *off*.
Don't *knock* it *off*.
5.
Can I *tear off* these mattress tags?
Can I *tear* these mattress tags *off*?
Can I *tear* them *off*?
6.
The janitor *washed off* the blood.
The janitor *washed* the blood right *off*.

The janitor *washed* it right *off*.
7.
She didn't *wipe off* the milk.
She didn't *wipe* the milk *off*.
She didn't *wipe* it *off*.
27c
1. You *washed* it *off*.
2. He *broke* them *off*.
3. They're *broken off*.
4. It *bit* it right *off*.
5. It *wore off*.
6. It's *worn off*.
7. You *knocked* it *off*.
8. I *wiped* it *off*.
9. It's *wiped off*.
10. I have to *dry* it *off*.
11. It's *dried off*.
12. I *tore* it *off*.
13. It's *torn off*.

27d
1. cut off
2. pay up
3. let up
4. thought ahead
5. cleared ... up
6. go over
7. put ... together
8. came down
9. opened up
10. ate ... up
11. heats ... up
12. gone up
13. let ... in on
14. trade ... in
15. started up
16. plugged ... up
28a
1. break up
2. messed ... up
3. give ... away
4. beef up
5. call ... up
6. carried out
7. stand up
8. broke up
9. messed ... up
10. stood ... up
11. broke ... up
12. carry ... out
13. broke up
14. call ... back
15. given ... away
16. broke up
17. called ... back
18. give ... away
28b
1.
The White House *beefed up* security.
The White House *beefed* security *up*.
The White House *beefed* it *up*.
2.
The police are *breaking up* the protest.
The police are *breaking* the protest *up*.
The police are *breaking* it *up*.
3.

The janitor *washed* it right *off*.
7.
She didn't *wipe off* the milk.
She didn't *wipe* the milk *off*.
She didn't *wipe* it *off*.

A trained technician ought to *carry out* the experiment.
A trained technician ought to *carry* the experiment *out*.
A trained technician ought to *carry* it *out*.
4.
The foundation *gave away* the money.
The foundation *gave* the money *away*.
The foundation *gave* it *away*.
5.
Susie always *messes up* the bathroom.
Susie always *messes* the bathroom *up*.
Susie always *messes* it *up*.
6.
Todd *stood up* Heather.
Todd *stood* Heather *up*.
Todd *stood* her *up*.
28c
1. It will be *carried out* by Dr.Wood.
2. It was *broken up*.
3. It was *messed up*.
4. It was *messed up*.
5. He was *stood up*.
6. She wasn't *called back*.
7. It was *given away*.
8. It's being *beefed up*.
9. It's *beefed up*.
10. They'll be *called up*.
28d
1. backed up
2. torn down
3. used up
4. woken up
5. taken in
6. taken out
7. blown away
8. torn down
9. laid off
10. cut off
11. ripped up
12. held up
13. handed out
14. held up
15. dropped off
16. tracked down
29a
1. make ... out
2. look out
3. coming apart
4. make ... out
5. drop in
6. flip out
7. made out
8. ran across
9. asking for
10. lucked out
11. ask for
12. made ... out
29b
1. I *flipped out*.
2. He might *ask* Santa

Answers

Claus *for* a new
bicycle.
3. You *ran across* your
college roommate.
4. He *made* the check
out to Fred Baker.
5. It's *made out*.
6. You might *drop in*
on her.
7. It's *coming apart*.
8. I *lucked out*.
9. You can't *make* it
out.
10. He told her to *look
out* for cars.
29d
1. cutoff
2. warm-up
3. fixer-upper
4. takeout
5. holdouts
6. crackdown
7. start-ups
8. shutoff
9. handover
10. stickup
29e
1. lighten up
2. stood . . . up
3. messed . . . up
4. settle for
5. do with
6. gave . . . away
7. call . . . up
8. call . . . back
9. broke up
10. dry off
11. carry out
12. knock . . . off
13. went over
14. zip . . . up
15. go up
16. think up
30a
1. locked . . . out
2. put out
3. locked . . . in
4. put . . . out
5. sort . . . out
6. punched . . . in
7. put out
8. wash up
9. punched out
10. put . . . out
11. lock in
12. locked out
13. spaced out
14. sorted out
15. put . . . out
16. washed up
17. put . . . out
18. put out
30b
1.
He *locked in* the crazy
guy.
He *locked* the crazy
guy *in*.
He *locked* him *in*.
2.
Jim *locked out* his wife.
Jim *locked* his wife *out*.
Jim *locked* her *out*.
3.
Did you *punch in* Rosa?

Did you *punch* Rosa *in*?
Did you *punch* her *in*?
4.
Would you *punch out*
Linda and Erik?
Would you *punch* Linda
and Erik *out*?
Would you *punch*
them *out*?
5.
They couldn't *put out*
the fire.
They couldn't *put* the
fire *out*.
They couldn't *put* it *out*.
6.
The bright lights *spaced
out* Janice.
The bright lights *spaced*
Janice *out*.
The bright lights *spaced*
her *out*.
30c
1. punched out
2. locked in
3. sorted out
4. locked out
5. sorted out
6. spaced out
7. put out
8. punched in

30d
1. You *put* it *out*.
2. You're going to *lock*
them *out*.
3. They're *locked out*.
4. He *spaced out*.
5. He is *spaced-out*.
6. She told you to
wash up.
7. It's *put out*.
8. She *punched* him *in*.
9. He's *punched in*.
10. I should *sort* them
out.
11. They're *sorted out*.
12. You *locked* him *in*.
13. He's *locked in*.
14. He was *put out*.
15. He was *put out*.
16. They can't *punch
out* before 4:30.
17. They're *punched
out*.
18. She didn't *put*
herself *out*.
30e
1. messed up
2. beefed up
3. shut off
4. worn off
5. torn off
6. washed off
7. closed off
8. made out
9. lit up
10. broken off
11. wiped off
12. dried off
13. made-up
30f
1. Dropping out
2. filled out
3. trade . . . in

4. standing up
5. had . . . on
6. asked . . . for
7. hurry up
8. knock . . . over
9. opened up
10. wash . . . off
11. wipe . . . off
12. carried out
13. drop in
14. working out
15. headed into
16. made . . . out
17. butt in
31a
1. ruled out
2. cut out
3. do away with
4. cut . . . out
5. do without
6. put off
7. care for
8. look into
9. done away with
10. cut out
11. care for
12. cut out
13. planned on
14. put off
15. planning on
31b
1. I *put* it *off*.
2. He *cut out* acting
like such a big
shot.
3. He said that noth-
ing has been *ruled
out*.
4. They don't *care for*
him.
5. It *does away with*
child labor.
6. I'll have to *do
without* it.
7. You're going to *look
into* having it
painted.
8. You can *plan on*
freezing to death.
9. She was *put off*.
10. She was *put off*.
11. They suspected that
he had been *done
away with* by a
coworker.
12. He *cut* it *out*.
13. He *cared for* it.
31d
1. go about
2. make out
3. made up
4. coming apart
5. get back at
6. lucked out
7. beefed up
8. cut down
9. flipped out
10. ran across
11. crack down
12. asking for
13. get away
14. drop in
15. got off
16. look out
32a

1. fell out
2. came out
3. coming out
4. sticking out
5. comes out
6. went out
7. stick . . . out
8. cleaned . . . out
9. left out
10. Go out
11. empty . . . out
12. come out
13. go out
14. come out
15. clear . . . out
16. fell out
17. come out
18. clear out
19. came out
20. emptied out
21. going out
22. stick . . . out
23. go out
24. coming out
25. cleaned . . . out
26. come out
27. come out
28. clean . . . out
29. sticks out
32b
1. of
2. of
3. to
4. with
5. for/in favor of
6. against
7. with, over
8. of
9. to
10. with
11. of
32c
1.
My son *cleaned out* the
basement.
My son *cleaned* the
basement *out*.
My son *cleaned* it *out*.
2.
I need to *clear out* the
storeroom.
I need to *clear* the storeroom *out*.
I need to *clear* it *out*.
3.
Sarah *emptied out* the
boxes.
Sarah *emptied* the
boxes *out*.
Sarah *emptied* them *out*.
4.
The factory *left out* an
important part.
The factory *left* an
important part *out*.
The factory *left* it *out*.
5.
Don't *stick out* your
neck.
Don't *stick* your neck
out.
Don't *stick* it *out*.
32d
1. It's *coming out*.
2. They *cleared out*.

3. It *cleared out*.
4. You're going to *go
out* with her.
5. He didn't *come
out* of the battle
alive.
6. You *left* him *out*.
7. He feels *left out*.
8. They *cleaned* me
out.
9. They *came out* with
a new CD.
10. He *sticks out*.
11. They *came out* for/in
favor of the
Republican candi-
date.
12. He *fell out* with him.
13. They had a
falling-out.
32e
1. cut . . . out
2. do without
3. sort . . . out
4. spaced out
5. watch out
6. punch . . . in
7. look into
8. holding out
9. put out
10. punch out
11. do away with
12. rule . . . out
13. wash up
14. lock in
15. care for
16. put off
33a
1. help . . . out
2. catch on
3. fall behind
4. pulled . . . off
5. blow up
6. goofs around
7. blow up
8. come about
9. pulled over
10. fall behind
11. know about
12. catch on
13. Blow up
14. caught on
15. fall behind
16. knows about
17. blow . . . up
33b
1. at
2. over
3. to
4. in
5. with
33c
1. It didn't *catch on*.
2. She's *helping* him
out.
3. They *pulled* it *off*.
4. He *goofs around*.
5. They *blow* them *up*.
6. He *blows up*.
7. She *knows about* it.
8. They *fell behind*.
9. She asked me to
explain how the
situation *came
about*.

33d
1. rule ... out
2. put off
3. put out
4. look into
5. came out
6. fell out
7. spaced out
8. go around
9. cut out
10. plan on
11. sorted ... out
12. gave ... away
13. do without
14. sticks ... out
15. empty ... out
16. go out

34a
1. stick to
2. floating around
3. stick around
4. take ... back
5. led up to
6. take ... back
7. stick to
8. taken back
9. put ... up to
10. stick to
11. stands for
12. took ... back
13. stick ... to
14. took ... back
15. stands for
16. take ... back
17. stand for
18. do ... over
19. leading up to
20. take ... back
21. going around

34b
1. STICK to
2. FLOATING around
3. stick AROUND
4. take ... BACK
5. led UP to
6. take ... BACK
7. STICK to
8. taken BACK
9. put ... UP to
10. STICK to
11. STANDS for
12. took ... BACK
13. STICK ... to
14. took ... BACK
15. STANDS for
16. take ... BACK
17. STANDS for
18. do ... OVER
19. leading UP to
20. take ... BACK
21. going AROUND

34c
1. She *took* it *back.*
2. They *led up* to it.
3. I've *done* it *over.*
4. You *took* it *back.*
5. He *sticks* to it.
6. He won't *stand for* it.
7. It *took* him *back.*
8. He *stuck around.*
9. It's been *floating around.*
10. She asked you what "Ph.D." *stands for.*

34d
1. came out
2. came about
3. wears off
4. shake ... up
5. plan ahead
6. get together
7. goofs around
8. put together
9. bitten off
10. fell behind
11. stayed out
12. caught on
13. let ... in on
14. stop over
15. pull ... off
16. print ... out

35a
1. left ... behind
2. tricked ... into
3. went by
4. living with
5. narrowed ... down
6. make of
7. holds against
8. fooling around
9. goes by
10. Living with
11. Leaving ... behind
12. fooled around
13. went by
14. fool around
15. live with
16. go by
17. left behind
18. go by

35b
1. She'll have to learn to *live with* it.
2. You *hold* it *against* him.
3. They're *fooling around.*
4. He has to *live with* them.
5. He *narrowed* it *down.*
6. I *fool around.*
7. He *tricked* her *into* giving him money.
8. She asked him what he *made of* the test results.
9. It *went by* you.
10. They're going to *leave* her *behind.*
11. It *went by* quickly.

35d
1. lucked out
2. lay around
3. flip out
4. stayed up
5. stand for
6. take back
7. hangs out
8. lead up to
9. messed up
10. do ... over
11. broke up
12. floating around
13. coming apart
14. stick around
15. ended up
16. run across

36a
1. puts down
2. calmed down
3. goes down
4. run down
5. fell down
6. sit down
7. ran over
8. go down
9. put down
10. backed down
11. goes down
12. lay ... down
13. sat ... down
14. put ... down
15. calm down
16. go down
17. lay down
18. gone down
19. Put ... down
20. run down
21. went down
22. Putting ... down
23. run down

36b
1.
The jockey *calmed down* the horse.
The jockey *calmed* the horse *down.*
The jockey *calmed* it *down.*
2.
The mechanic *laid down* her tools.
The mechanic *laid* her tools *down.*
The mechanic *laid* them *down.*
3.
I *put down* my books.
I *put* my books *down.*
I *put* them *down.*
4.
The taxi *ran down* the traffic cop.
The taxi *ran* the traffic cop *down.*
The taxi *ran* him *down.*

36c
1. He *ran down* the list.
2. He gave me a *run-down* of the car's options.
3. He *calmed* it *down.*
4. It's *rundown.*
5. It *went down* well.
6. He *put* her *down.*
7. It was a *put-down.*
8. He *sat down.*
9. It *backed down.*
10. She *put* my name *down.*
11. They *laid* them *down.*
12. I *fell down.*

36d
1. spaced-out
2. torn off
3. paid up
4. punched in
5. burned up
6. punched out

36e
1. washed up
2. care for
3. caught on
4. came about
5. stuck with
6. make out
7. locked ... out
8. make of
9. put ... off
10. pulled ... off
11. did without
12. went out
13. blew up
14. planning on
15. cleaned ... out
16. narrowed ... down

37a
1. cover ... up
2. cover ... up
3. brush ... off
4. pay off
5. comes on
6. let ... down
7. came on
8. talk to
9. Hanging out
10. brushed ... off
11. pay ... off
12. comes on
13. coming on
14. left over
15. coming on
16. paying off

37b
1. payoff
2. leftovers
3. letdown
4. brush-off
5. payoff
6. come-on
7. cover-up
8. hangout
9. talking-to

37c
1. He *hangs out* there.
2. It's a *hangout.*
3. You told him to *come off* it.
4. I had $100 *left over.*
5. It *comes on.*
6. He *let* her *down.*
7. She's going to *pay* it *off.*
8. It's *paid off.*
9. She *talked to* him.
10. She gave him a *talking-to.*
11. It *comes on.*
12. I ate *leftovers.*
13. He *paid* him *off.*
14. It was a *payoff.*
15. He tried to *cover* them *up.*
16. It was a *cover-up.*

36e (continued)
7. plugged up
8. locked in
9. locked out
10. shaken up
11. sorted out
12. left out
13. put out
14. cleaned out
15. emptied out

17. He *brushed* her *off.*
18. He gave her the *brush-off.*
19. He said, "*Come on.*"
20. It was a *letdown.*
21. You were *let down.*

37d
1. put-down
2. breakup
3. get-together
4. grown-ups
5. lockout
6. blowup
7. lookout
8. giveaway
9. going-over
10. cutouts
11. rundown

37e
1. hold ... against
2. narrowed ... down
3. emptied ... out
4. go by
5. caught on
6. pulled ... off
7. make of
8. fool around
9. leave ... behind
10. done away with
11. Living with
12. calmed down
13. fall down
14. go down
15. put ... down
16. sit down

38a
1. keep from
2. keep ... to
3. kept ... up
4. Keep at
5. keeping ... down
6. keep off
7. keep to
8. keep up
9. keep ... away
10. keep up
11. keep up
12. keep ... off
13. keep up
14. keep ... down
15. keep ... from
16. keep on
17. keep ... on
18. keep ... to
19. keep away

38b
1. He asked you to *keep* it *down.*
2. You asked her to *keep* it *to* $4,000.
3. You can't *keep from* falling asleep.
4. You have to *keep at* it.
5. It's hard to *keep up* with the political situation in Washington.
6. She *kept on* running.
7. I've got to *keep away.*
8. She thinks he's

Answers

keeping something *from* her.
9. You hope she can *keep* it *up.*
10. You asked him to *keep* the children *away* from your computer.
11. He said it's important to *keep* inflation *down.*
12. He's *kept off* drugs for five years.
13. You can't *keep* him *from* joining the Army.
14. It's hard for her to *keep up* with the other students.

38d
1. brush ... off
2. running down
3. fell behind
4. go down
5. backed down
6. come on
7. fell down
8. Calm down
9. came about
10. goof around
11. know ... about
12. sat ... down
13. left over
14. lay ... down
15. hang out
16. talk to

39a
1. picked up
2. sold out
3. straighten ... out
4. took over
5. clean ... up
6. take over
7. pick up
8. pick ... up
9. chop up
10. wipe out
11. pick up
12. taken over
13. filled up
14. pick up
15. filled up
16. straightened out
17. pick up
18. wipe ... out
19. picking ... up
20. straighten ... out
21. picked up
22. fill up
23. pick ... up
24. take ... over
25. pick up
26. pick up
27. cross ... off

39b
1.
Have you *chopped up* the onions?
Have you *chopped* the onions *up?*
Have you *chopped* them *up?*
2.

You can *cross off* Linda's name.
You can *cross* Linda's name *off.*
You can *cross* her *off.*
3.
Fill up the aquarium with water.
Fill the aquarium *up* with water.
Fill it *up* with water.
4.
I need to *pick up* my parents at the train station.
I need to *pick* my parents *up* at the train station.
I need to *pick* them *up* at the train station.
5.
Can you *straighten out* this mess?
Can you *straighten* this mess *out?*
Can you *straighten* it *out?*
6.
The rebels *took over* the royal palace.
The rebels *took* the royal palace *over.*
The rebels *took* it *over.*
7.
They *wiped out* the palace guard.
They *wiped* the palace guard *out.*
They *wiped* them *out.*

39c
1. It always *picks up* in the spring.
2. It might be *taken over* by pirates.
3. It would be a *takeover.*
4. She *straightened* everything *out.*
5. It's *straightened out.*
6. He was supposed to be *picked up.*
7. They'll be *wiped out.*
8. It ought to be *crossed off.*
9. It'll be *crossed off.*
10. It *sold out* of the CDs.
11. They were *sold out.*
12. It had *sold out.*
13. It was *chopped up.*
14. It has to be *picked up* before 6:00.
15. He *took over* for the pilot.
16. He often asks you to *pick up* a newspaper.
17. You'll tell her not to let the water *run over.*
18. You *picked up* on page 95.

39d
1. settling down

2. slowed ... down
3. cut down
4. left out
5. blew up
6. Hand ... over
7. came out
8. bring ... back
9. knock off
10. make up
11. picking on
12. bitten off
13. pulled ... over
14. wear ... down
15. look ... over
16. broken off

40a
1. stuck with
2. going away
3. blow ... off
4. got off on
5. came back
6. running around
7. stick with
8. brought up
9. brought up
10. stick with
11. come back
12. come back
13. going away
14. burst out
15. ran around
16. stick ... with
17. going away
18. come back
19. go away
20. brings up

40b
1. They're not *sticking with* the original plan.
2. It *came back.*
3. I *burst out* crying.
4. He *blew* it *off.*
5. He gave me the *runaround.*
6. She asked him to *go away.*
7. She *gets off on* it.
8. He *got stuck* with unloading the truck.
9. She *brought up* joining the Peace Corps.
10. It's *coming back.*
11. It never *goes away.*
12. I haven't *come back.*
13. He *ran around* looking for a telephone.
14. It would be nice to *get away.*
15. They *brought* me *up* to believe in the golden rule.

40d
1. holds ... against
2. do ... over
3. go down
4. went out
5. stick around
6. run down
7. make of
8. take ... back
9. lay down
10. fool around

11. backed down
12. stick ... to
13. put ... up to
14. led up to
15. go by
16. trick ... into

41a
1. letting in
2. sneaked in
3. broke in
4. check ... out
5. check ... in
6. plug into
7. go in
8. check in
9. sneaked in
10. go in
11. check ... out
12. go into
13. letting in
14. check out
15. check into
16. check out
17. break into
18. checked in

41b
1. She *sneaked in.*
2. She *let* him *in.*
3. She *checked out.*
4. It's the *checkout* time.
5. It was *broken into.*
6. There was a *break-in.*
7. You'll *check in.*
8. You'll go to *check-in.*/You'll go to the *check-in* counter.
9. She doesn't want to *go in.*
10. You'll *check* it *out.*
11. He *checks* them *in.*
12. They're *checked in.*
13. I *sneaked out.*
14. He hasn't *checked in.*
15. He *plugged* it *in.*
16. It's *plugged in.*
17. He was *checked out.*
18. You didn't *break in* your boots.

41d
1. left over
2. lets ... down
3. come on
4. put ... down
5. started out
6. help ... out
7. blow ... off
8. narrowed ... down
9. straighten ... out
10. take over
11. live with
12. filled up
13. go away
14. hang out
15. talked to
16. gets off on

42a
1. get back
2. got out
3. gets out
4. Getting over
5. gotten into
6. got ... out

7. get up
8. get out
9. get ... in
10. Get in
11. got ... in
12. get ... in
13. get in
14. gets out
15. gets by
16. get down
17. Get down
18. get by
19. gotten up
20. get behind
21. get to
22. get by
23. gets back
24. get ... down
25. get over
26. getting ... back
27. get over
28. Get ... out
29. get ... out
30. get out
31. get into

42b
1. He *got you up.*
2. It's difficult to *get up* to Minnesota.
3. I *got into* a lot of trouble.
4. I need to *get* right *back* home.
5. She can barely *get by.*
6. She'll *get behind.*
7. He hasn't *gotten over* it.
8. She *got* me *out* of it.
9. He's *getting* it *out.*
10. He's *getting* it *down.*
11. They couldn't *get* it *in.*
12. You can't *get by.*
13. She *got out.*
14. She *got* back *in.*
15. He *got* it *back.*
16. They *got* her *down.*
17. He asked you to *get* right *over* to his house.

42c
1. pick ... up
2. clear ... out
3. selling out
4. leave ... behind
5. floating around
6. running around
7. punching ... in
8. punched out
9. call ... up
10. call ... back
11. go in
12. start up
13. Sneaking into
14. sneak out
15. brushes ... off
16. crossed ... off
17. plug ... in

43a
1. head toward
2. tried ... on
3. blew out
4. gave out
5. run up

407

6. blew out
7. shut ... up
8. stop off
9. grosses ... out
10. Shut up
11. ran up
12. blown out
13. given out
14. ran up

43b
1. of
2. to
3. on
4. to
5. in
6. at

43c
1.
The wind *blew out* the candle.
The wind *blew* the candle *out*.
The wind *blew* it *out*.
2.
They *gave out* information.
They *gave* information *out*.
They *gave* it *out*.
3.
She *ran up* a $4,000 bill.
She *ran* a $4,000 bill *up*.
She *ran* it *up*.
4.
Can I *try on* these pants?
Can I *try* these pants *on*?
Can I *try* them *on*?
5.
The smell *grossed out* everyone.
The smell *grossed* everyone *out*.
The smell *grossed* them *out*.

43d
1. She should have *tried* it *on*.
2. It *gave out*.
3. It was a *run-up*.
4. It must have *grossed* him *out*.
5. He must have been *grossed out*.
6. They *ran up* to her.
7. She wouldn't have *headed toward* Detroit.
8. She *blew* it *out*.
9. *Shutting* him *up* is nearly impossible.
10. She asked him how he could have *run up* such a large credit card bill.
11. He *stopped off* in Denver.
12. You had a *blowout*.

43e
1. leftover
2. chopped up
3. covered up
4. rundown
5. broken in
6. paid off

7. let down
8. crossed off
9. checked in
10. checked out
11. sold out
12. plugged in
13. filled up
14. straightened out
15. put off

43f
1. sneaked into
2. sneak out
3. keep off
4. coming back
5. go into
6. kept ... on
7. get back
8. gotten ... behind
9. keep from
10. keep at
11. keep ... to
12. burst out
13. keep up
14. wiped out
15. keep ... away
16. kept ... down

44a
1. locked ... up
2. carried away
3. pisses ... off
4. stressing ... out
5. kicked out
6. beat up
7. mix ... up
8. lock up
9. ripped ... off
10. mixes ... up

44b
1.
The thugs *beat up* the woman.
The thugs *beat* the woman *up*.
The thugs *beat* her *up*.
2.
The hotel manager *kicked out* the rock group.
The hotel manager *kicked* the rock group *out*.
The hotel manager *kicked* them *out*.
3.
The cops are going to *lock up* the crook.
The cops are going to *lock* the crook *up*.
The cops are going to *lock* her *up*.
4.
Mixing up the twins is easy.
Mixing the twins *up* is easy.
Mixing them *up* is easy.
5.
Getting a tattoo must have *pissed off* your father.
Getting a tattoo must have *pissed* your father *off*.
Getting a tattoo must have *pissed* him *off*.

6.
The contractor was accused of *ripping off* homeowners.
The contractor was accused of *ripping* homeowners *off*.
The contractor was accused of *ripping* them *off*.
7.
All these problems are *stressing out* the staff.
All these problems are *stressing* the staff *out*.
All these problems are *stressing* them *out*.

44c
1. He *ripped* him *off*.
2. It was a *rip-off*.
3. She's going to *kick* them *out*.
4. I *locked up*.
5. It's *locked up*.
6. It's easy to *mix* them *up*.
7. It *pissed* him *off*.
8. He was *pissed off*.
9. She's *mixed up*.
10. It's *stressing* me *out*.
11. I'm *stressed out*.
12. They were *beat up*.
13. He was *locked up*.
14. He was *locked up*.
15. She got *carried away*.
16. They *beat* him *up*.
17. I have to *mix* them *up*.

44d
1. cover ... up
2. paid off
3. takes over
4. keep ... down
5. keep on
6. broken in
7. keep away
8. bringing ... up
9. keep from
10. stuck ... with
11. keep ... off
12. keep ... to
13. help ... out
14. kept at
15. put ... up to
16. keep ... up

45a
1. turn out
2. turn in
3. turned ... off
4. turns over
5. turned on
6. turn ... in
7. turned in
8. turned up
9. turn ... into
10. turn ... on
11. turn ... up
12. turn ... down
13. turn ... off
14. turned ... on
15. turn over
16. turn up

17. turning in
18. turn off
19. turned ... on
20. turned down
21. turning out
22. turn ... over
23. turn out
24. turning out
25. turn in
26. turning out
27. turn ... in

45b
1. They *turn into* butterflies.
2. He *turned up*.
3. It *turned* him *off*.
4. He thinks it's a *turnoff*.
5. He was *turned off*.
6. It *turns you on*.
7. You think it's a *turn-on*.
8. You feel *turned on*.
9. I'm *turning* it *up*.
10. *Turnover* is very low.
11. It *turns out* 25,000 cars every year.
12. She didn't *turn* it *up*.
13. She hasn't *turned up* anything.
14. It was *turned into* a Chinese restaurant.
15. It *turned out* orange.
16. She couldn't *turn* him *down*.
17. It will probably *turn over* $4 million.
18. He hasn't *turned* his paper *in*.
19. She's not going to *turn* him *in*.
20. There wasn't enough room because so many people *turned out*.
21. The *turnout* was large.
22. He *turned* it *over*.

45d
1. get ... back
2. ran up
3. gotten up
4. tried ... on
5. Get out
6. get there
7. grossing ... out
8. get into
9. head toward
10. get out
11. lock up
12. beaten up
13. stopped off
14. getting behind
15. getting over
16. carried away

46a
1. talk ... into
2. build in
3. bump into
4. freak out
5. talk ... out of
6. conned ... into
7. bumped into
8. make for

9. con ... out of
10. made for

46b
1. She's trying to *talk* you *into* helping her paint her house.
2. He *bumped into* Raul.
3. He's trying to *con* me *out of* everything I own.
4. It will *make for* an uncomfortable evening.
5. He *conned* her *into* selling him her house for a lot less than it's worth.
6. She's *freaking out*.
7. A shelf was *built into* it.
8. It's *built-in*.
9. No one can *talk* him *out of* quitting his job.

46d
1. lockup
2. comeback
3. wipeout
4. check-in
5. checkout
6. mix-up
7. break-in
8. pickup
9. takeover
10. run-up
11. blowout

46e
1. turn ... in
2. brought ... up
3. lock ... up
4. gone away
5. stands for
6. got by
7. stressing ... out
8. shut up
9. stick with
10. gave out
11. turning ... into
12. blew ... off
13. pisses ... off
14. let ... in
15. kicked out
16. burst out

47a
1. run out
2. put ... into
3. pull out
4. comes in
5. cut back
6. ran out
7. moving into
8. put ... in
9. brush up
10. move in
11. comes in
12. putting ... in
13. put in
14. come in
15. move out
16. runs out
17. put ... in
18. coming in
19. cut back
20. pulled out

21. move ... out
22. put in
23. come in
24. move ... into
25. put ... in
26. pull out

47b
1. He's going to *move in* with his Uncle John.
2. It's *cutting back.*
3. It's a *cutback.*
4. You can't figure out where they're *coming in.*
5. It didn't *come* in on time.
6. He's *moving out.*
7. I *ran out* of money.
8. She's *pulling out.*
9. She shouldn't have *put* a pool *in* such a small backyard.
10. She's *brushing up* on Italian.
11. He might *pull out.*
12. She told me to *cut back* on candy.
13. He's going to *come in* late.
14. She's *putt ing* a lot of effort *into* learning Chinese.
15. They *ran out* of time.
16. He hasn't *put* them *in.*
17. He asked her when she was *moving in.*
18. He *puts* $1,000 *into* his checking account.

47c
1. trled on
2. kicked out
3. rips off
4. get ... down
5. conned ... into
6. stop off
7. talked ... into
8. conned out of
9. make for
10. bumped into
11. shut up
12. gotten up
13. talk ... out of
14. get into
15. get out
16. freaked ... out

48a
1. put ... back
2. switch ... off
3. knocked out
4. looked up to
5. put back
6. switched on
7. kicked ... out

8. knocked out
9. put back
10. throw ... out
11. closed down
12. looks down on
13. put ... back
14. knock out
15. knocked ... out

48b
1.
The health department should *close down* the restaurant.
The health department should *close* the restaurant *down.*
The health department should *close* it *down.*
2.
Ali's left hook *knocked out* Joe.
Ali's left hook *knocked* Joe *out.*
Ali's left hook *knocked* him *out.*
3.
General Chambers had to *put back* the attack.
General Chambers had to *put* the attack *back.*
General Chambers had to *put* it *back.*
4.
Have you *switched on* the TV?
Have you *switched* the TV *on?*
Have you *switched* it *on?*
5.
Are you going to *switch off* the lights?
Are you going to *switch* the lights *off?*
Are you going to *switch* them *off?*
6.
Throwing out all this junk is going to be a big job.
Throwing all this junk *out* is going to be a big job.
Throwing it *out* is going to be a big job.

48c
1. It has *put back* your fight for justice.
2. He *looks up* to him.
3. It *knocked* him *out.*
4. It's a *knockout.*
5. I *switched* it *on.*
6. It's *switched on.*
7. They must have been *switched off.*
8. They're *switched off.*

9. It will be *closed down.*
10. He *looks down on* them.
11. He would have been *kicked out.*

48d
1. turnoff
2. cutback
3. make-up
4. turn-on
5. pullout
6. carryout
7. runaround
8. turnover
9. rip-off
10. lookout
11. turnout
12. falling-out

48e
1. put ... into
2. talked ... out of
3. carried away
4. con ... out of
5. pulled out
6. stick ... out
7. bumped into
8. turn up
9. con ... into
10. brush up
11. talked into
12. move in
13. Turn ... over
14. move out
15. blow out
16. stressing ... out

49a
1. get to
2. hang on
3. get to
4. start ... off
5. get to
6. get back to
7. get ... on
8. clogged ... up
9. get on
10. gotten to
11. Throwing away
12. getting on
13. get to
14. get ahead
15. starts off
16. get on
17. Hang on
18. throw away
19. get to
20. got to
21. got on
22. Get to

49b
1. She can't *get* her shoes *on.*
2. He *got to* feeling depressed.
3. He *threw* them *away.*
4. You're going to *get back to* work.
5. She's going to *get back to* me.
6. It got *clogged up.*

7. It was *clogged up.*
8. He has never *gotten to* work after 9:30.
9. I *got on* with work.
10. It should be taken out when the temperature *gets to* 190 degrees.
11. He said he couldn't *hang on* any longer.
12. You've got to *get to* them.
13. It must have been *thrown away.*
14. He showed you how to *get on* a horse.
15. It *started off* well, but things got worse.
16. He told you that you shouldn't let it *get to* you.
17. He *got to* pet a baby tiger.
18. He *hung on* to the ropes.
19. He *got on* the diving board.
20. He *got* right back *on.*
21. She couldn't have *gotten to* the airport already.
22. He always *starts off* by introducing himself.
23. It should help you to *get ahead.*

49d
1. cutting back
2. come in
3. conned ... into
4. throw ... out
5. looked up to
6. look down on
7. know about
8. put back
9. gets off on
10. closed down
11. knocked ... out
12. turned ... down
13. letting ... in
14. get over
15. turn down
16. switch ... on

50a
1. paid ... back
2. wear out
3. turn ... around
4. pay ... back
5. deals with
6. wore ... out
7. comes down to
8. turn around
9. Hold on
10. dealt with
11. ask out
12. hold on
13. taken ... up on
14. Hold on

50b
1. He's been *holding on* for ten minutes.
2. They *wore out.*
3. They're *worn-out.*
4. It's *turning around.*
5. It *comes down to* the MBA program.
6. I *asked* her *out.*
7. It was a *turnaround.*
8. He's going to be *paid back.*
9. You *took* her *up on* the offer.
10. She'll *deal with* the problem.
11. She *held on* to it.
12. It *wore* her *out.*
13. She felt *worn-out.*

50d
1. stressed-out
2. worn-out
3. turned on
4. turned off
5. grossed out
6. beat-up
7. clogged up
8. mixed up
9. locked up
10. pissed off
11. built-in
12. turned on
13. turned off

50e
1. turned into
2. get to
3. turn in
4. built into
5. turn out
6. get back to
7. thrown ... away
8. turned on
9. get ... on
10. get ahead
11. Hang on
12. turn ... down
13. Turn ... off
14. clogged ... up
15. made for
16. turning up

50f
1. give out
2. put ... into
3. pay ... back
4. take ... up on
5. dealt with
6. running out
7. ask ... out
8. get ahead
9. hold on
10. turned ... around
11. get back to
12. gotten to
13. came down to
14. wore ... out
15. freaks ... out
16. started ... off

Index of Phrasal Verbs by Section

The number after each phrasal verb is the section in which that phrasal verb is described.